Educational Research
Selected Readings

Edited by

WILLIAM J. GEPHART
Director of Research Services
Phi Delta Kappa

ROBERT B. INGLE
University of Wisconsin-Milwaukee

CHARLES E. MERRILL PUBLISHING CO.
COLUMBUS, OHIO

A Bell & Howell Company

MERRILL'S INTERNATIONAL SERIES IN EDUCATION

Under the Editorship of the late

KIMBALL WILES

Dean of the College of Education
University of Florida

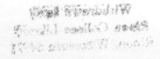

Standard Book Number: 675-09521-2

Library of Congress Catalog Card No.: 69-15049

1 2 3 4 5 6 7 8 9 10–75 74 73 72 71 70 69

PRINTED IN THE UNITED STATES OF AMERICA

This volume is dedicated to our students whose perceptive questions drove us into this array of literature, to our teachers who left us with answers still to be found, to our wives, Mary and Maria, who encouraged us in the search, and to our future students—may it help you see clearly those still unanswered questions.

The Editors

William J. Gephart is Director of Research Services for Phi Delta Kappa and Lecturer in Education at Indiana University. He has been a consultant to numerous research and development projects and has served as a proposal evaluator and principle investigator for the U. S. Office of Education. Dr. Gephart has also published and edited a number of reports, articles, and books about educational and behavioral research.

Robert B. Ingle is Associate Professor of Educational Psychology at the University of Wisconsin-Milwaukee. He is the author of a number of articles in professional journals. For the past three years, Dr. Ingle has directed a federally funded program for the preparation of research specialists for the public schools.

Preface

Most of the texts on the research process do an adequate job of outlining the elements of that process. Most of their authors and practically all of their users recognize that one text has strengths in some areas and weaknesses in others. It is generally accepted that no single text is adequate for engendering in the student the subtle nuances in decisions made in conducting research.

As the editors of this publication worked with students, a variety of articles from the periodical literature seemed to augment the available texts. In some cases the articles provide basic conceptual material not contained in standard texts. Others provide the clarity of discussion of subtle aspects of research techniques which would seem to create an imbalance in a standard text. In one case, Chamberlin's, "The Method of the Multiple Working Hypothesis," a classic statement is made which perhaps is more applicable now than it was when it was written.

We believe that this anthology can serve as a basic book in a research course or as a supplement to any one of the standard texts. It should also serve as a reference for the researcher when he encounters the need for deeper meaning of some of the knotty problems inherent in the process.

In a book of readings the work of many persons is merged. Naturally, the editors are indebted to the contributing authors for their initial effort and to the editors of the publications in which these materials were initially presented. Special appreciation is due to Mrs. Marcia Conlin for her sterling editorial assistance with the materials written by the editors. Finally, thanks go to Mrs. Susan Rymer, Mrs. Patti Brennan, and Mrs. LuAnn Day who played a part in grinding out the manuscript.

Table of Contents

chapter 1

Educational Research:
Its Nature and Logical Basis

The motivation for the compilation of this book and the major focus of this chapter is the belief that knowledge about the process of research is the ingredient most crucial to the improvement of the practice and product of education.

Educating the young of society is accepted, both by those involved in the process and those external to it, as one part science and many parts art. This mixture is a source of two problems as educators and policy makers wrestle with the continual task of improving the quality of the product—the education attained by the young.

An art typically advances at an evolutionary rather than a revolutionary rate, while the sciences make comparatively rapid strides. As this art-science entity advances, both evolutionary and revolutionary changes occur. The slowness of the rate of evolutionary changes conflicts with the rapidity of the revolutionary changes. As education's scientific element creates a new technique and proves its effectiveness, the phasing problem is encountered. The new technique is never a complete system. It must be merged with ongoing elements of the school. The imperfection of the fit is a continuing difficulty.

Certainly society cannot continue to allow the educational community the luxury of the 20- to 50-year time lag in incorporating new techniques that has been documented by Mort[1] and Miles.[2] Hopefully

---

[1] Paul R. Mort, *Principles of School Administration* (New York: McGraw-Hill Book Company, 1946), pp. 199-200.

[2] Matthew B. Miles, "Educational Innovation: The Nature of the Problem," in *Innovation in Education*, Matthew B. Miles, Editor (New York: Bureau of Publications, Teachers College, Columbia University, 1964).

1

the study of the process of change[3] will enable the development of procedures by which an educational innovation proved sound today can be adopted by most schools within the academic lifetime of today's first graders.

Researches into the change process should also investigate the phasing problem, for there appears to be concensus that education can and must be improved at a rate not normally achieved by an art. In the turn to greater scientism, educators need to develop clear understanding about the manner in which knowledge is accumulated.

Examination of the progress of man in many fields discloses four activities that have aided him in gaining knowledge: experience, philosophizing, revelation, and empirical research. This book and in particular this chapter focus on the latter toward the end that educators may better comprehend the nature of research and its contribution to knowledge.

The omission of the first three activities is not intended as a negation of their importance to knowledge accumulation. Each makes vital contributions. At the same time each has inherent weaknesses that tend to bias the knowledge gained. For example, when a new teaching procedure is experienced by two persons, one an optimist and the other a pessimist, the optimist sees that all but three children in the class are actively engaged in learning and concludes that the new procedure is a good one. The pessimist sees the three children not engaged and concludes that the new procedure is faulty. Thus on the surface the knowledge gained via this experiencing seems contradictory. What must be learned is that the conclusions one man reaches as a result of an experience or a series of experiences are biased by his previous experiences. This same type of learning must be developed for each of the sources of knowledge.

Although empirical research on educational topics has a history predating the twentieth century, that history's importance as a factor in shaping the practice of educators is minimal with two-thirds of the century passed. Among the many reasons for the lack of scientism in schooling are two problems that have importance for this discussion. First, the expenditure of time and funds in educational research has been insufficient, typically less than one-half of 1 per cent of our annual education budget. Second, educators in general do not understand

---

[3] Indiana University has recently established a National Institute for the Study of Educational Change directed by Egon G. Guba. The principal focus of NISEC is the study of the educational change process. See also Virgil Blanke, "Strategies for Educational Change," a Cooperative Research Project in process at The Ohio State University.

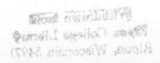

the research process nor the nature of its contribution to knowledge. The first of these problems seems on its way toward resolution. Through actions of the Congress of the United States, major philanthropic agencies, and state and local funding agencies, more educational research funds are available now than researchers dreamed possible in their wildest fantasies of two decades ago.

The second problem is also the object of much attention. The Elementary and Secondary Education Act of 1965 (PL 89-10) set aside funds for research training. With these funds intensive training in research is available to more persons than ever before. Although the future holds the promise that the number of educators with thorough knowledge of the research process will be significantly increased, clear and concise statements about the research process must be made available to the many educators who have completed their formal training. Through such statements, practicing educators can better their understanding of the research process and of the contribution of empirical research activities to the body of knowledge on which they base their professional behavior.

The readings contained in this chapter are of two types, articles on the nature of research in education and articles on the logical argument inherent in any research project. In the first category, Ausubel presents a generalized discussion of the nature of educational research. Cornell's discussion of research methodologies gives applicability to the concepts introduced by Ausubel. The nature of research and its similarity to the work of the practicing educator is discussed by Barns and Corey. Barns focuses on the relationship between research and the teaching-learning process, while Corey discusses the applicability of research in decision making in education.

The final three articles by Masson, Raths, and Platt focus upon the reasoning processes by which empirical observations contribute to acceptance or rejection of hypothesized facts. Masson's statement is a generalized discussion of scientific reasoning. Raths presents a modified syllogistic argument that is inherent in reasoning from all educational experimentation to fact in our growing body of knowledge. In discussing the manner in which scientific knowledge is made cumulative, Platt rounds out the logical framework of research.

David P. Ausubel*

The Nature of
Educational Research

Educational research should be uniquely applicable to education, but unfortunately it does not always seem to be. Conducting research in schools is, for
a variety of reasons, frequently difficult. The types of research that are conducted in schools are often not even illuminating of the processes under consideration. In this opening article, Ausubel briefly considers some of the problems that face educational researchers and some of the varieties of research
that advance scientific knowledge. He makes a plea for a particular type of
research that seems uniquely relevant for education. Although Ausubel does
not delineate the specific steps necessary to carry on the type of research that
he feels will be most productive, he does provide a clear framework for what
must be done if education is to progress through research.

David P. Ausubel. "The Nature of Educational Research," *Educational Theory*, 3:314-20,
October, 1953. Reprinted with permission.

Few persons would take issue with the proposition that education is
an applied or engineering science. It is an applied[1] science because it
is concerned with the realization of certain practical ends which have
social value. The precise nature of these ends is highly controversial,

---

* David P. Ausubel, Ph. D., M.D., is a Professor of Psychology and Education
in the Ontario Institute for Studies in Education, Toronto, Canada. He points out
that educational research, as a field in its own right, is immature and characterized
by dilemmas which confusedly oscillate between "basic science" research, "extrapolated" research, and "applied" research. Drawing on his training and experience in
medical research, he points toward a possible development of research methodology
in pedagogy which may give education status as a scientific discipline.

[1] The term "applied" is used here to distinguish between sciences which are
oriented toward practical ends as opposed to "basic" sciences which do not serve
this function. *Applied* does not imply that the content of the practical disciplines
consists of applications from the "basic" disciplines. The problems rather than
the knowledge of applied sciences are "applied."

in terms of both substance and relative emphasis. To some individuals the function of education is to transmit the ideology of the culture and a core body of knowledge and intellectual skills. To others, education is primarily concerned with the optimal development of potentiality for growth and achievement—not only with respect to cognitive abilities, but also with respect to personality organization and adjustment. Disagreement with respect to ends, however, neither removes education from the category of science nor makes it any less of an applied branch of knowledge. It might be mentioned in passing that automobile engineers are also not entirely agreed as to the characteristics of the "ideal" car; and physicians disagree violently in formulating a definition of health.

Regardless of the ends it chooses to adopt, an applied discipline only becomes a science when it seeks to ground proposed means to ends on empirically validatable propositions. The operations involved in such an undertaking are commonly subsumed under the term "research." The question under discussion relates to the nature of search in applied science, or, more specifically, in education. Is educational research a field in its own right with theoretical problems and a methodology of its own, or does it merely involve the operation of applying knowledge from "pure" scientific disciplines to practical problems of pedagogy?

RESISTANCE TO EDUCATIONAL RESEARCH

It should be noted at the outset that there is both little general acceptance of the need for educational research and little appreciation of the relevance of such research for the improvement of education. A tradition of research does not exist in education as it does, for example, in medicine or in engineering, where both professionals and consumers commonly agree that research and progress are almost synonymous. This much is clearly evident from the marked resistance which educational researchers encounter from school boards, school administrators, teachers and parents.

Generally speaking, educational research institutions and public school systems have not succeeded in working out orderly and systematic procedural machinery providing for long-term research programs in the schools. In most cases, each individual researcher is obligated to conduct his own separate negotiations with school authorities every time he wishes to work on a problem; and more often than not he meets with indifference or outright resistance. He has learned that it is more effective to carry on research activities through personal "contacts" in the schools than to obtain the necessary permission through official channels. This chaotic situation is in marked contrast to the well established working agreements which all medical schools have with hospitals relative to the conducting of clinical research.

In addition to, or perhaps reflective of the lack of, perceived relevance of educational research to educational progress are other frequently encountered resistances to the performance of research in the public schools. It is alleged, for example, that research utilizes time urgently needed for subject matter or other purposes, that children are "exploited" by being cast in the role of "guinea pigs," and that irreparable psychological or educational damage is inflicted on some children to further "experiments" of questionable value. Furthermore, some educators demand to know how such research is going to help them solve their immediate problems.

Satisfactory answers to such questions can easily be given once the importance of educational research itself is accepted. It can be pointed out that research projects are not so demanding of pupil or teacher time that they interfere with the curricular program of the school; that the school spends time on many things of less intrinsic value; that the ethical standards of educational researchers are generally high enough to preclude harmful or dangerous experimentation; that many research programs are educational in themselves and can be made enjoyable to children. Finally it can be shown that the criterion of *immediate* value and utility is unreasonable and is not applied in other engineering sciences.

NON-RESEARCH APPROACHES TO THE IMPROVEMENT OF PEDAGOGY

If so much resistance to educational research exists, how do educators and others commonly propose to further pedagogical methodology? A time-honored method employed by many "successful" teachers is to examine their own practices, to abstract what seems to them the basis for their success, and to advocate that these practices be universally emulated. The weaknesses of this approach are obvious. The claimed success of these teachers is rarely verified by objective means, the factors to which success is attributed are merely subjective impressions which have not been objectively identified or measured, and no control data are available as a basis for comparison. Often such teachers are successful for entirely different reasons than those of alleged superior methodology. Some have good teaching personalities, others have unusually good students, and still others teach under atypically favorable conditions. To remedy these shortcomings, some teachers have conducted crude classroom experiments. But since the vast majority of these experiments fail to control relevant variables (i.e., significant characteristics of the experimental population, of the proposed method, of the teacher, of the school environment), do not utilize reliable measuring instruments, and do not subject results to tests of statistical significance, they contribute little to the science of pedagogy.

Another less rational approach merely relies on the authority of presumed expert opinion. Some educators are convinced that after twenty-five years of experience in the profession they are entitled to make dogmatic pronouncements on pedagogic method which require no rationalization whatsoever and are valid by fiat alone, i.e., because of the wisdom which extended experience or high status in an administrative or university hierarchy presumably confers.

A third approach places greater weight on logic than on experience. Method A is inferred to be superior to Method B because it is more compatible (a) with certain theoretical considerations that have logical or face validity or (b) with indirectly related empirical findings. Such thinking is obviously necessary as a preliminary step in the formulation of hypotheses to be tested, and is probably the only approach possible in deciding upon the ends that education should pursue. Clearly, however, it cannot constitute an adequate approach in itself with respect to providing a scientific basis for the means employed toward such ends.

EMPIRICAL (RESEARCH) APPROACHES TO PEDAGOGIC METHODOLOGY

Three different kinds of research orientations have been adopted by those who are concerned with scientific progress in applied disciplines such as education: (a) basic science research,[2] (b) extrapolated research in the basic sciences, and (c) research at an applied level.

The "basic science" research approach is predicated on the very defensible notion that applied sciences are ultimately related to knowledge in the underlying sciences on which they are based. It can be

---

[2] The term "basic" refers to the distinction between "basic" and applied sciences made earlier. It does not mean "fundamental." In the latter sense applied research is just as "basic" as research in the pure sciences.

convincingly demonstrated, for example, that progress in clinical medicine is intimately related to progress in biochemistry and bacteriology; that progress in engineering is intimately related to progress in physics and chemistry; and that progress in education is similarly dependent upon advances in psychology, statistics, sociology and philosophy. However, two important kinds of qualifications have to be placed on the value of basic science research for the applied sciences: qualifications of purpose or orientation, and qualifications of level of applicability.

By definition, basic science research is concerned with the discovery of general laws of physical, biological, psychological and sociological phenomenology as an end in itself. Researchers in these fields have no objection, of course, if their findings are applied to practical problems which have social value; in fact there is reason to believe that they are motivated to some extent by this consideration. But the design of basic science research bears no *intended* relation whatsoever to problems in the applied disciplines, the aim being solely to advance knowledge. Ultimately, of course, such knowledge is applicable in a very broad sense to practical problems; but since the research design is not oriented to the solution of these problems, this applicability is apt to be quite indirect and unsystematic, and relevant only over a time period which is too long to be meaningful in terms of the short-range needs of the applied disciplines.

The second qualification has to do with the level at which findings in the basic sciences can be applied once their relevancy has been established. It should be self-evident that such findings enjoy a much higher level of generality than the problems to which they can be applied. At the applied level, specific ends and conditions are added which demand additional research to make manifest the precise way in which the general law operates in the specific case. That is, the applicability of general principles to specific problems is *not given* in the statement of the general principle, but must be specifically worked out for each individual problem. Knowledge about nuclear fission for example does not tell us how to make an atomic bomb or an atomic-powered airplane.

In fields such as education the problem of generality is further complicated by the fact that the practical problems often exist at higher levels of complexity with respect to the order of phenomenology involved than the basic science findings requiring application. That is, new variables are added which may qualitatively alter the general principles from the basic science to such an extent that at the applied level they only have substrate validity but no explanatory or predictive value. For example, antibiotic reactions that take place in test tubes do not necessarily take place in living systems; methods of learning employed by animals in mazes do not necessarily correspond to methods of learning children use in grappling with verbal materials in classrooms.

The basic science approach in educational research, therefore, is subject to many serious disadvantages. Its relevancy is too remote and indirect because it is not oriented toward solving educational problems, and its findings, if relevant, are applicable only if much additional research is performed to translate general principles into the more specific form they have to assume in the task-specialized and more complex contexts of pedagogy.

These limitations would not be so serious if they were perceived. If the limitations of this approach were perceived, it would be defensible for educational institutions to set aside a *small* portion of their research funds for basic science research as a long-term investment. But since these limitations are *not* perceived, some bureaus of educational research confidently invest their major resources in such programs, and then complacently expect that the research findings, which emerge will be both relevant and applicable in their original form to the problems of education.

Naivete with respect to the second premise, i.e., of immediate applicability, is especially rampant and has led to very serious distortions in our knowledge of the psychology of learning that is relevant for pedagogy. The psychology of learning that teachers study is based on findings in general psychology which have been borrowed wholesale without much attempt to test their applicability to the kinds of learning situations that exist in classrooms. It would be a shocking situation indeed if a comparable procedure were practiced in medicine, i.e., if physicians employed therapeutic techniques validated only *in vitro* or by animal experimentation.

The second general research approach in the applied disciplines is "extrapolated basic science research." Unlike pure basic science research it is oriented toward the solution of practical or applied problems. It starts out by identifying significant problems in the applied field, and designs experiments pointed toward their solution on an analogous but highly simplified basic science level. In this way it satisfies the important criterion of relevance, but must still contend with the problem of level of applicability. The rationale of this approach is that many practical problems are so complex that before one can develop fruitful hypotheses leading to their solution they must first be reduced to simpler terms and patterned after simpler models. Thus simplified, problems of control and measurement are rendered more manageable.

Depending on the nature of the problem under investigation, this approach may have genuine merit providing that the resulting research findings are only regarded as "leads" or hypotheses to be tested in the applied situation rather than as definitive answers *per se* to problems in pedagogy. As already noted, however, educational researchers have a tendency to extrapolate basic science findings to pedagogical problems without conducting the additional research necessary to bridge the gap between the two levels of generality involved. Also, when it is necessary to cross levels of phenomenological complexity in extrapolating, this approach has very limited usefulness for the reasons already given above.

The third approach to educational research, research at the applied level, is the most relevant and direct of the three, yet paradoxically is utilized least by professional research workers in the field. When research is performed in relation to the actual problems of education, at the level of complexity in which they exist, that is, *in situ* (under the conditions in which they are to be found in practice), the problems of relevance and extrapolation do not arise.[3] Most rigorous research in applied disciplines other than education is conducted at this level. The research program of a hospital or medical school would be regarded as seriously unbalanced if most of its funds and efforts went into biochemical or bacteriological research instead of into clinical research. The major responsibility for furthering research in the former areas belongs to graduate departments of chemistry and bacteriology. On the other hand, unless medical schools undertake to solve their own clinical problems who else will? And the same analogy obviously holds for education as well.

Although applied research presents greater difficulties with respect to research design, control, and measurement, the rewards are correspondingly greater when these problems are solved. Certainly such problems cannot be solved when they are avoided. If other applied disciplines have been able to evolve satisfactory research methodologies, there is no reason why education cannot also do so. In fact, if any applied discipline with unique and distinctive problems of its own is to survive as a science it has no choice in the matter—it is obliged to do so.

---

[3] Applied research is also directed toward the discovery of general laws within the framework of its applied ends. The generalizations it discovers, therefore, exist at a different plane of generality than those of "basic" science research.

DIFFERENTIATION BETWEEN PSYCHOLOGICAL AND EDUCATIONAL RESEARCH PROBLEMS

Since both psychology and education deal with the problem of learning, how can we distinguish between the special research interests of each discipline in this area? As an applied science, education is not concerned with the general laws of learning *per se*, but only with those properties of learning that can be related to efficacious ways of deliberately effecting stable changes in individuals which have social value. Education, therefore, refers to guided or manipulated learning deliberately directed toward specific practical ends. These ends may be defined as the long-term acquisition of a stable body of knowledge (ideas, concepts, facts), values, habits, skills, ways of perceiving, adjusting, and aspiring, and of the capacities needed for acquiring them.

The psychologist's interest in learning, on the other hand, is much more general. Many other aspects of learning apart from the efficient achievement of designated competencies and capacities for growth in a directed context concern him. More typically, he investigates the nature of current, fragmentary, or short-term learning experiences rather than the kinds of long-term learning involved in assimilating extensive and organized bodies of knowledge, values, habits and skills.

The following kinds of learning problems, therefore, are particularly indigenous to educational research: (a) discovery of the nature of those aspects of the learning process affecting the long-range stability and meaningfulness of organized bodies of knowledge, skills, etc. in the learner; (b) long-range modification (improvement) of learning capacities; (c) discovery of those personality and cognitive aspects of the learner and of the interpersonal and social aspects of the learning environment that affect motivation for learning and characteristic ways of assimilating material; and (d) discovery of appropriate and maximally efficient practices and ways of organizing and presenting learning materials, of deliberately motivating and directing learning toward specific goals.

CONCLUSION

The failure of education to acquire status as an applied scientific discipline can be largely ascribed to two contrasting approaches to the discovery of pedagogical knowledge. One approach has relied on empirically untested theoretical propositions, on dogmatic assertion, or on the unwarranted generalization of subjective impressions from personal teaching experience. The other approach, going to the opposite extreme, has avoided coming to grips with the fundamental research problem of education as an applied science, i.e., the discovery of how pupils assimilate and grow in ability to assimilate symbolical materials in a social and interpersonal environment, and what the optimal conditions for these processes are. Instead it has become preoccupied with basic science research, failing to recognize important limitations of this approach with respect to relevancy and level of generality and complexity, and uncritically extrapolating findings from one level to another without performing the intervening research operations that are necessary.

If the profession of education is open to attack, it is vulnerable on the grounds of failing to make the progress it could reasonably have been expected to make in providing a scientific basis for pedagogy. It is vulnerable because of its complacency, its resistiveness to applied educational research, its tendency to spend more time and effort on dogmatically disseminating unvalidated hypotheses than on endeavoring to secure validation through painstaking research activity. Unfortunately, criticism of professional education is not directed along these lines, but is usually based on the fallacious notions that a science of pedagogy is unnecessary for teaching, that children are not learning as much as they used to, and that the only proper aim of education is the acquisition of factual knowledge and of intellectual skills.

The best defense that education could make to these latter baseless charges is to admit that a science of pedagogy does not yet exist, and to direct its attention toward formulating a research methodology in pedagogy at the applied level of operations at which it functions.

Francis G. Cornell

Productive Methods in Research

In the previous article, Ausubel categorized research in terms of the use to which it is to be put. In this article, Cornell categorizes research according to the techniques involved in carrying it out. The two methods of categorization are not incompatible, since the techniques discussed by Cornell would fit, in almost all cases, into any of the Ausubel categories. Consider, as you read this article, how each technique would fit into the category of "Applied Research," and how, in particular, experimental research could—within the framework of applied research—be used to further knowledge in education.

Francis G. Cornell, "Productive Methods in Research," *Phi Delta Kappan,* 35:29-34, October, 1953. Reprinted with permission.

The term "technique" is considered here to mean specific procedures followed in the execution of some act. A catalogue of procedural details pursued in educational research in its half-century history would be encyclopedic—and probably not very useful. For example, we could describe and catalogue some 50 different "techniques" for determining the correlation between two variables. This, obviously, would be inappropriate, and we shall discuss procedural details *per se* very little. Instead, we shall try to present one view of the more general methods of attack, or research approaches, which appear, in the literature, to have been the most dominant.

FROM "GADGETRY" TO RESEARCH ENDS

No universal system of mutually exclusive and exhaustive categories for the classification of research-approaches will be established. That sort of thing, common in the "how-to-do-research" publications of pre-

War II, seemed to lead nowhere. Moreover, it gave the fledgling graduate student the notion that once he had chosen a problem, all he had to
do was to select, "cookbook" fashion, the appropriate technique, i.e.,
correlational, normative-survey, historical, experimental, etc.; "do a
thesis" and win a degree.

In several of the multifarious areas of educational research there
appears to be a shift from the "gadgetry" emphasis to the major purposes or ends of the research process. This certainly is not general, for
the vast majority of educational literature seems doubtfully to pursue
methods of science,[1] or any other orderly and logical approach, but
not to stem from a theoretical or a conceptual frame which might lead
to an advancement in knowledge.

RESEARCH TECHNIQUES CLASSIFIED

The trend, however, is clear, particularly in the educational-psycho-
logical sphere. Indeed, the trend is not so much a trend in educational
research-methodology as it is in the field of psychology, on which so
much in education depends. Much research of a psychological variety
in education is of the "theoretically derived" type. This is certainly
true of research on learning and at least somewhat true in the general
area of child study.[2] Any discussion, therefore, of research technique
or research method should emphasize the emergence of systems of
thought, which themselves define approaches to which specific techniques become subservient.

To catalogue current and past methods, however, much less sophisticated rubrics must be used. For our purposes, we shall discuss research
technique in education under the following headings: (1) Descriptive,
(2) Metric, (3) Clinical, (4) Correlational, and (5) Experimental. To
this might be added a sixth, which would be those types of techniques
which are theoretically derived and which consist of theory construction or model building and the verification of theoretical systems.[3]

---

[1] B. O. Smith. "Science of Education." *Encyclopedia of Educational Research.*
Revised edition. (Edited by Walter S. Monroe.) New York: The Macmillan Co.,
1950. pp. 1145-52.

[2] O. Hobart Mowrer. "Learning Theory." *Review of Educational Research* 22:
475-95; December, 1952. See also Boyd McCandless and Sidney Rosenblum. "Psychological Theory as a Determiner of Experimental Pattern in Child Study." *Review
of Educational Research* 22: 496-525; Dec., 1952.

[3] Quite recently there has been some thought on the verbal level and some preliminary empirical work stemming therefrom on social theory applied to educa-

These developments are mostly for the future, however, and are the subject of the next article in this issue.

Descriptive Methods

A good proportion of research in the past half century in education may be classed as "descriptive." In this category are all of the so-called normative and survey techniques. Much of this has been essential and important, but much of it has been painfully mundane and inconsequential. Among the useful contributions from the census-like enumerative studies in this category are the word-lists and word-counts made a generation ago. These provided a sound basis for improvement of instruction as well as improvement of textbooks and reading materials.

Fletcher H. Swift, among the earliest of scholars to study school finance, undertook historical descriptive studies of sources of revenue and methods of allocation and apportionment in the several states.[4] There is ample justification for such descriptive documentary research in early phases of research in an area. It is also important, in such fields as school finance, to have current and continuous "fact-getting" of essential data. Thus, the Office of Education and the Research Division of the NEA regularly assemble essential information and facts on the operation of educational programs in the 48 states. Tremendous advances have been made in techniques for the collection and statistical treatment of data.[5]

Much more information may be collected, and more efficiently, by virtue of practical sample survey techniques now available to educational researchers who have had adequate statistical training.[6] With advances in techniques of measurement of attitudes, opinions, and the

---

tional organization and administration. See Francis G. Cornell and Darrell J. Inabnit. "Administrative Organization as Social Structure." *Progressive Education* 30: 29-35; Nov., 1952. Jack W. Getzels. "A Psycho-Sociological Framework for the Study of Educational Administration." *Harvard Educational Review.* 22: 235-46; Fall 1952. W. W. Charters, Jr. "The School as a Social System." *Review of Educational Research* 22: 41-50; Feb., 1952. Aspects of mathematical theories, such as the theory of games, have been subjected to study experimentally. See Frederick Mosteller and Philip Nogee. "An Experimental Measurement of Utility." *The Journal of Political Economy* 59: 371-404; Oct., 1951.

[4] Fletcher H. Swift. *A History of Public Permanent Common School Funds in the United States, 1795-1905.* New York: Henry Holt and Co., 1911. 493 pp.

[5] Nicholas A. Fattu. "Computational Technics." *Review of Educational Research* 21: 415-31; Dec., 1951.

[6] A recent publication on this subject is William G. Cochran. *Sampling Techniques.* New York: John Wiley and Sons, Inc. 1953. 330 pp.

like, new and more dependable information is available to the educationist.[7]

An example of sampling in a national survey reported by Cornell[8] and an example of modern sample methods and opinion measurement in connection with a state reorganization program reported by Massanari[9] are two of several examples of progress in "scientific" descriptive research. But, much survey and descriptive research in education is repetitive and of doubtful value.[10]

Metric Methods

Since the spelling tests of Rice, literature dealing with the production of educational and psychological measures has become prolific. Recent publication of Gulliksen's *Theory of Mental Tests*,[11] and *Educational Measurement*[12] edited by Lindquist, bring together test development techniques and measurement theory evolved over the past half century.

Advances in psychometric methods have given us improved measures of general mental ability, aptitude, personality, and many other individual traits. Psychometric methods have been developed to assist in studying and diagnosing the interrelations of groups of persons. Projective techniques have supplemented older methods for studying personality characteristics of groups and individuals. Progress has been achieved in techniques of item preparation, item analysis, the determination of reliability, test validation, methods of scoring, and methods of scaling. Yet there are many unsolved difficulties in these areas. And there continue to be many aspects of human behavior of

---

[7] Jerome S. Bruner. "Social Psychology and Group Processes." *Annual Review of Psychology, Vol. I (1950)*. (Edited by Calvin P. Stone.) Stanford, Calif.: Annual Reviews, Inc. 1950. pp. 125-40. And, Daniel Katz. "Social Psychology and Group Processes." *Annual Review of Psychology, Vol. II (1951)*. Stanford, Calif.: Annual Reviews, Inc. 1951. pp. 165-68.

[8] Francis G. Cornell. "A Stratified-Random Sample of a Small Finite Population." *Journal of the American Statistical Association* 42: 523-32; Dec., 1947.

[9] Karl L. Massanari. "Public Opinion as Related to the Problem of School District Reorganization in Selected Areas in Illinois." *Journal of Experimental Education* 17: 389-458; June, 1949.

[10] George D. Stoddard. "Educational Research Lacks Impact; It Avoids Controversies and Human Values." *The Nation's Schools* 49:44; May, 1952.

[11] Harold Gulliksen. *Theory of Mental Tests.* New York: John Wiley and Sons, Inc. 1950. 486 pp.

[12] Everet F. Lindquist, Ed. *Educational Measurement.* Washington, D. C.: the American Council on Education, 1951. 819 pp. See also, Oscar K. Buros. *Third Mental Measurements Yearbook (1940-1947).* New Brunswick, N. J.: Rutgers University Press, 1949. 1047 pp.

importance in learning and teaching not easily subjected to measurement.

"Foundation" Programs Based on Measurement

Though techniques of measurement which have developed in education are chiefly psychological, it is often overlooked that there has been considerable research on other types of measurement problems in the educational field. Examples are studies measuring population growth and forecasting population as a basis for planning school buildings, studies measuring the needs of various types of pupil stations in schoolhouse construction problems, and various measurement problems in the field of school finance. The uniquely American scheme of "foundation program" state aid to local districts was made possible only after studies which produced measures of educational need, measures of cost, the development of adequate cost units, and measures of taxpaying ability.[13]

Measurement Research Misused

Without question, measurement research in education has been productive. A good proportion of research work in education has been either the development of a test or a measure, or research on developing tests or measures. On the negative side, there has been much poor measuring in terms of presently available technical standards, and there has been much misuse in the application of tests. Moreover, measurement research has tended to expand horizontally. That is, we seem to do more and more research with more refined critiques or development of technique on specific phases of item analysis or reliability or homogeneity, rather than to advance to new theory or new measurement frontiers.

However, measurement studies appear to be more and more related to purpose. Yet the testing movement has been criticized because it emphasizes measurement for the sake of measurement. In a review of tests as research instruments by Thorndike, in the *Review of Educational Research* covering a three-year period, he stated that he had

---

[13] See Francis G. Cornell and William P. McLure. *"The Foundation Program and the Measurement of Educational Needs."* Chapter 6, pp. 149-216; and R. L. Johns. "Local Ability and Effort to Support Schools." Chapter 7, pp. 219-240 in National Conference of Professors of Educational Administration. *Problems and Issues in Public School Finance.* (Edited by R. L. Johns and E. L. Morphet.) New York: Teachers College, Columbia University, 1952.

"not identified . . . any instances of especially noteworthy advance in test invention or in test theory."[14]

Clinical Methods

There is a category of research involving almost all the techniques of descriptive methods, metric methods, and experimental methods, but which differs from other researches in that the primary emphasis is not on a population of subjects, i.e., pupils, teachers, classrooms, and school systems, but only on one or a very small number. These are usually intensive studies of individual cases. In general, therefore, the interest is "clinical" rather than "actuarial."

This, of course, involves all of the techniques of clinical psychology valuable in the field of educational guidance and counseling, and in individual child study. Of particular recent interest have been projective methods of psycho-diagnosis. There has been considerable use of such instruments as the Rorschach Test, the Thematic Apperception Test, picture interpretation tests, and drawing tests. More objective methods such as inventories and questionnaires are used, as well as less systematic schemes of observation and recording. Among types of technique involved in intensive studies of individuals or groups are ratings, analysis of biographies, both directive and non-directive interviews, controlled systems of observation, analysis of writings, artistic productions, and other products of performance, recorded speech, specialized diary techniques and so on.[15]

"Case-Study" Types of Research

We use this category not simply because of the clinical psychological technique. There are large numbers of reports of experience (somewhat better than haphazardly documented) that someone has had in working with some behavioral aspects of a group of individuals in a classroom or in a school system. A good proportion of reports covered in the *Review of Educational Research* on many topics, such as the elementary school curriculum, the teaching of various subjects, school budgets, the administration of teaching personnel, the financing of state school systems, and child behavior, are reports of experiences of individuals with individual cases. Some of these, like many studies in

---

[14] Robert L. Thorndike. "Tests as Research Instruments." *Review of Educational Research* 21: 450-62; Dec., 1951.

[15] See Saul B. Sells and Robert W. Ellis. "Observational Procedures Used in Research." *Review of Educational Research* 21: 432-49; Dec., 1951.

the descriptive or survey category, are difficult to assess, as purposes are not clear or techniques are not possible which permit generalizations to other situations even though masses of data are assembled.

This area should not, however, be ignored for there has clearly been a movement toward research in the actual situations of schools which does not suffer from the unreality and abstraction of the laboratory experiment. The school study council movement has been in this direction. The emphasis is upon action. Such research as is done, as a by-product of these programs, is of the "clinical" or "case-study" type.[16]

"Action Research" Defined

A recent term in the literature of educational research is "action research," defined by Corey as "research undertaken by practitioners in order that they may improve their practices."[17]

The techniques of action research are not especially unique. The distinction is in the motivation of the person doing the work, and in the substance for study. Actually the action research movement appears to be largely a campaign for more systematic evaluation and the applications of more rigorous methods to the improvement of actual operating situations of school systems. While the traditional researcher is interested only in finding an answer to a generalizable question, the action researcher is motivated to improve practices in an individual school situation.

Some studies in the "clinical" category are undertaken by those motivated in the traditional research sense, the motivation being that of studying the growth and development of individuals or groups by relating one or several variables to the variable of time, or to test hypotheses in the sense of the scientific experiment. There is undoubtedly a great deal of justification for such "one-trial experiments" for the simple reason that so little is known about so many aspects of education. Furthermore, large-scale experimental designs involving an adequate number of properly selected groups of students or school systems is costly and beyond the scope of the resources available in educational research at the present time. The "case study" or "single-subject-experiment" is one of the alternatives to the researcher who wishes to study human phenomena in the totality of the real situation.

---

16 See Norton L. Beach. "Control and Change of School Functions at the Community Level." *Review of Educational Research* 22: 32-40; Feb., 1952.

17 Stephen M. Corey. *Action Research to Improve School Practices.* New York: Bureau of Publications, Teachers College, Columbia University, 1953. 161 pp.

Trial and Error Experiments

This is the type of research which Greenwood in his classification of sociological experiments would call "the trial and error experiment,"[18] an experiment involving trying out something with a single person or group or institution. For instance, a teacher may "try out" (or she may say "conduct an experiment") by various methods of supplementing the textbook in a general science class for purposes of, she hopes, enhancing motivation and of broadening opportunities for learning, with achievement of outcomes not expected from the more or less assignment-study-recite method. She may systematically employ measurements at different periods during the course of the "experiment" in the single class. Scores on tests will reveal certain gains or absences of gain in measured outcome. Yet she will be unable to say how outcomes would have compared with outcomes had the same group been exposed to the conventional method, or many other possible types or methods of instruction. Moreover, it will be impossible for her to attribute changes in pupils to specific causes. In other words, the "single-trial" may not be subjected to the "controls" of the factorial experiment discussed in the section below and in the following article.

However, many tryouts are being made with sufficiently sophisticated experimental design and sufficiently systematic evaluations so that considerable useful knowledge, either as an immediate guide to action or as a clue to future research, is forthcoming.[19]

Correlational Methods

As indicated in the introduction, it is difficult to find a scheme for mutually exclusive classification of research techniques used in education. The bundle of methodological tools, embracing techniques of correlation and multivariate analysis now to be discussed, illustrates the point. In almost any type of research or in almost any specialized research technique, there is some form of relating one phenomenon or variable to another phenomenon or variable. Even in general purpose,

---

[18] E. Greenwood. *Experimental Sociology: A Study in Method*. New York: Kings Crown Press, 1945.

[19] An example of the use of refined techniques in experiment limited administratively in opportunities for scientific control is a study by Carl W. Proehl. *An Experimental Study of the Effects of Two Patterns of Professional Education in the Preparation of Secondary School Teachers*. Doctor's thesis. Urbana, Ill.: University of Illinois, 1953. 156 pp. (Typewritten).

census-type survey-research, relationships are portrayed, for instance, between type of school and size of school, or between characteristics of the school population and location.

Even in the most useful of evidently non-statistical descriptive research, such as the so-called historical studies, "trends," contrasts, and comparisons are emphasized. All of these are techniques definable in statistical symbols of correlation. It should be noted also that correlation has been the handmaiden of measurement practice and theory.

"Correlation Bound" Until Recently

Without a doubt, techniques of correlation have permitted us to advance our knowledge about education considerably. On the other hand, it may be that this device has been a mixed blessing. There is some evidence that until recently educational research was somewhat "correlation bound." Long after the Fisherian view of chi-square had been available, for instance, educational literature, including textbooks in educational statistics, treated chi-square chiefly in connection with the Pearsonian coefficient of contingency, a sort of approximation to the correlation coefficient.

For some time, a decade or two ago, educators used the partial correlation coefficient as if it were the answer to difficulties in designing properly controlled experiments. Multiple regression methods have been, and continue to be, useful in the handling of batteries of tests and in problems of prediction. Correlation, curve-fitting, and multiple regression methods have been strategic techniques in the measurement problems which opened up "scientific" school finance.

Factor Analysis Most Recent Method

Most recent of multivariate methods to assume importance in educational research is factor analysis. In general, factor methods permit an investigator with a matrix of inter-correlations of several variables to answer the question "what goes with what," in a manner which usually simplifies the number of "factors" which must be taken into account to explain phenomena.[20]

There are many variations in methods of factor analysis. There is considerable controversy as to which of several approaches is best and

---

[20] For a recent review of this subject with a bibliography see John B. Carroll and Robert F. Schweiker. "Factor Analysis in Educational Research." *Review of Educational Research* 21: 368-82; Dec., 1951.

about conditions under which factor analysis is generally suitable. It has been pointed out that factor analysis methods may be used for (a) statistical description, (b) suggesting hypotheses, and (c) supporting or disproving hypotheses.[21] The chief difficulties of factor analytic methods are in (1) the variation of results with different sets of measures and with different sets of subjects, and (2) the subjective judgments involved on the part of those applying the techniques.

No Substitute for Careful Definition

In general, multivariate analysis methods are among the indispensable tools of educational research. There is a danger that they may be viewed over-enthusiastically as some form of research magic which will answer all problems. This is not true of any technique which is employed in education. Moreover, multivariate methods have the disadvantage that for some they become an easy escape from the difficult and onerous first step in research—that of careful definition of problems, so that purposes and objectives are clear and that *finally* techniques may be selected which are appropriate to the research goal of the investigator.

Correlation methods have tended to encourage the "shot-gun" approach to problems, a method by which variables are piled up and the investigator grinds figures to see what sense he can make of his complex data. Such research is weak in theory or there is no very clear-cut problem. Instead it involves preoccupation with "numbers," often of doubtful validity and of doubtful educational significance.

Experimental Methods

Fifteen or twenty years ago, the "single variable" experiment was a popular device for educational research. Pupils in an experimental class were "matched" on certain variables, such as achievement and intelligence and age, by a control group. The control group would be instructed in some subject, such as spelling, by the conventional method, and the experimental group would be instructed in the same subject by the experimental method. Gains in the two groups were then compared in the belief that they were identical or that conditions were controlled in all other respects. Observable differences were, therefore, attributed to the single variable of differences in method of instruction,

---

[21] H. J. Eysenck. "The Logical Basis of Factor Analysis." *The American Psychologist* 8: 105-13; Mar., 1953.

and all of the evidence was based upon the tests or measures used as the dependent variable.[22]

There were several objections to this procedure. One of these was that a break from atomistic theories of education began to lead educators to ask more complex questions than could be answered in such a simple design. Another was that the design itself, in many respects, was inadequate statistically, since it actually failed to control many variables, such as the differences in motivations of teacher and pupils in the experimental group (the Hawthorne effect), and many other matters. Since the monumental contributions of Fisher,[23] there has been a vast accumulation of improvements in method of experimental design and statistical analysis, not available earlier in the century.[24] It is far beyond the scope of the present writing to discuss these advances in technique. [A further discussion of this subject is found in the following article by Johnson.] It is of interest to note, however, that the best references digesting them, other than that of the mathematical and biological sciences, may be found in psychological publications.[25]

Techniques Often Not Known

It is somewhat surprising that educational research has responded so slowly to the opportunities which efficient statistical methods make for the maximizing of information from experiments. In a recent three-year review of experimental methods in education, Norton and Lindquist[26] report little evidence that the typical research worker in education thoroughly understands the techniques he uses, or is familiar with recent developments in experimental methods. Indeed, there are limits to which we may expect even the best statistical methods to yield satisfactory experiments in education. A school or a community or a

---

[22] For a brief survey see Francis G. Cornell and Walter S. Monroe. "Experiment." *Encyclopedia of Educational Research.* Revised edition. (Edited by Walter S. Monroe.) New York: The Macmillan Co., 1950. pp. 414-16.

[23] R. A. Fisher. *Statistical Methods for Research Workers.* Eleventh edition. Edinburgh: Oliver and Boyd, Ltd., 1950. 356 p. See also R. A. Fisher. *The Design of Experiments.* Fifth edition. Edinburgh: Oliver and Boyd, Ltd., 1949. 242 p.

[24] A recent treatment of this subject in one volume in the context of educational research is Everet F. Lindquist. *Design and Analysis of Experiments in Psychology and Education.* Boston: Houghton-Mifflin Co., 1953. 393 p.

[25] See for instance chapters on "Statistical Theory and Research Design" by D. A. Grant, A. L. Edwards, and Q. McNemar, in the 1950, 1951, and 1952 volumes of the *Annual Review of Psychology. op. cit.*

[26] Dee W. Norton and Everet F. Lindquist. "Applications of Experimental Design and Analysis." *Review of Educational Research* 21: 350-67; Dec., 1951.

family in the complex of factors cannot be brought into a laboratory situation or selected according to the dictates of most sampling models in any manner which does not, to some extent, contaminate results. In this respect education shares a dilemma with the field of sociology, in which the "natural situation" experiment involving a rigged-up control has been dignified recently by the term "ex post facto experiment."[27] Despite objections to it, the experiment will undoubtedly continue as one of the most important techniques in educational research.

Experimentation Most Likely Hope

In dealing with human behavior, as Freud once put it, a man of science must bear uncertainty. Correlational techniques show us that we may expect thus and so concerning variable X if we have thus and so in variables Y and Z. Practitioners often err in interpreting such studies, as though student A, with a given intelligence test score, unquestionably will achieve in a certain way in school, or, since correlation is high between expenditure and quality of educational program, that if we spend more money we most assuredly shall get better education.

Experimental methods, likewise, are interpretable only in probabilistic terms. The experimental approach, however, at least where manipulation and control are possible, comes much closer to establishing cause and effect than does simple correlation.

All types covered in this review are essential and important in educational research. In the judgment of the writer, however, greater contributions to building a science of education may come from the rigorous methods of experimentation. I suspect that many questionnaire studies and many "psuedo experiments" are conducted simply because our economy has not been sold on supporting either the disciplined training of the research worker or the execution of studies stemming from clear-cut definition of objectives imbedded in a contest of theory, and utilizing efficient hypothesis-testing and verification.

---

[27] F. S. Chapin. *Experimental Designs in Sociological Research*. New York: Harper & Row, Publishers, 1941.

Fred P. Barnes

We Are All Researchers

Frequently research is seen as a mysterious and mystical process that can only be carried out by those especially initiated into its rites. The first two articles in this chapter may well give that impression. However, for educational research to have any impact, it must eventually be used in a practical setting by a practitioner; that is, in a classroom by a teacher. The presumed gulf between the "researcher" and the "teacher" may be more apparent than real. In this article, Barnes makes a case for the teacher as a researcher. Although Barnes may be guilty, to some extent, of oversimplification, he is persuasive. His chart showing similarities between reflective thinking, teaching, and research is particularly worth consideration.

Fred P. Barnes, "We Are All Researchers," *The Instructor*, 69:6-7, June, 1960. Reprinted with permission.

Every teacher knows that educational research is presumed to have a great influence on what schools do. Within recent years both the public and the professional mind have come to respond with attitudes of approbation and esteem to the very word *research*. While our increasingly scientific world has been enlarging everybody's awareness of the effects of research on our everyday living, the profession of teaching has turned to research findings for more adequate answers to its pressing and complicated problems. Belief in the superiority of research-based information about teaching has come to be characteristic of the modern teacher.

"WHAT RESEARCH SAYS"

This preference for research-based information may be observed in many current educational activities, such as the projects sponsored by the U.S. Office of Education through the National Defense Educa-

tion Act of 1958. But one of the clearest illustrations of how this kind
of information is being brought to the teacher may be found in the
National Education Association's production of professional literature.
The current N.E.A. *Catalogue of Publications* lists more than seventy
books and pamphlets which report research findings on numerous
questions commonly asked by teachers working at all grade levels of
the schools. Prominent among these publications is a series of eighteen
pamphlets ($.25 each) grouped together under the title, *What Research
Says to the Teacher*. This series is jointly sponsored by the Department
of Classroom Teachers and the American Educational Research Association. The individual titles deal with the teaching of reading, arithmetic, spelling, handwriting, mathematics, and science, with class composition, audio-visual instruction, homework, the learning process, and
other areas of concern.

Publications like the foregoing seem to imply that educational
research has sufficiently matured to make possible the compiling of
scientific knowledge on teaching, which, in turn, will lead speedily to
improved schools. The theory is that the schools will be improved if
such knowledge is widely disseminated among the teachers. And,
certainly, twenty-five-cent pamphlets represent a step in such dissemination. No one who would like to see better teaching can help but
applaud the work going on in this direction.

PRODUCERS AND CONSUMERS

But teachers and observers of the schools know that mere acquaintance with "what research says" offers no guarantee at all for improvement in teaching. Numerous students of education have noted that
while research findings seem to influence the production of textbooks
and other instructional materials, their *direct* influence on the ways
teachers teach is surprisingly scant. The educational literature is filled
with laments that teachers can be told, but they seem not to hear or
care. Brilliant research findings can be duly reported, but they cannot
be found later in what the schools do.

This seemingly unbridgeable chasm between what the researchers
discover and what the teachers do about the discoveries has long
presented an apparent dilemma to all those interested in the schools.
Does the difficulty lie in our willingness to perpetuate an "unresearched"
assumption about the role of research findings in teaching? We separate
the researchers from the teachers and call them the research *producers*.
They are the specialists whose responsibility it is to come up with new,

exciting, and validated ideas. The teachers are the ones who are expected to use the exciting new ideas. We call them the research *consumers.* Such a neat formula! We have the specialist researchers to produce the new ideas and the practitioner teachers to consume, comprehend, and use them. Associated with the formula are familiar justifications which serve to maintain it: Specialists are essential for the conduct of research, and teachers have not been especially trained for that work.

AN UNWORKABLE FORMULA

But in spite of our tenacious clinging to this time-honored formula, apparently it does not work, and never has worked. What can be wrong? Certainly something essential is missing. What can this absent ingredient be?

We might start with the observation that the product of educational research consists of *ideas.* The products of industrial research may require nothing more complicated than pushing a button where we used to move a lever or learning a preference for a detergent instead of a soap, but there is something personal about the care and feeding of ideas!

Maybe researchers in education should talk to teachers about their new ideas much as they talk to fellow researchers. This way teachers could criticize ideas, and try them experimentally in real situations, much as researchers insist on doing themselves. Such an approach would avoid the danger of teachers accepting research findings as bits of authoritative "truth" (a completely unscientific attitude). And in such a "colleague-type" situation, teachers would have a fine opportunity to help perfect and round out ideas coming from research studies.

Even more important questions concerning the traditional formula are: Can teachers who have never tried to do research really comprehend, consume, and effectively use ideas which have been developed by researchers? Isn't one of the major and most valuable purposes of research findings to stimulate more extensive experimentation and research? Should not teachers use research findings selectively as incentives for their own experimentation in the classroom?

Again, is the simple dissemination of knowledge an effective way to change teachers' perception and accustomed teaching practices? Most of the findings coming from the behavioral sciences tend to indicate that changes in knowledge are not enough to change behavior. Active involvement in personally rewarding projects is needed.

TEACHERS ARE LIKE RESEARCHERS

Consider the argument that teachers are not equipped to do active research. Is it true that a scientific approach to teaching requires special, concentrated preparation? Thomas Henry Huxley, noted naturalist, wrote on this subject to people in general:

> It is imagined by many that the operations of the common mind can be by no means compared with (the cunning skill of men of science; their hypotheses and theories). To hear all these large words, you would think that the mind of a man of science must be constituted differently from that of his fellow men; but if you will not be frightened by terms, you will discover that you are quite wrong, and that all these terrible apparatus are being used by yourselves every day and every hour of your lives.

Huxley's words apply with particular force to teachers, whose work takes them every day into an environment devoted to making changes in human behavior; an environment where the common currency consists in ideas and experimentation.

There is very little to differentiate the thoughtful teacher from the inquisitive researcher, since both predict the results of planned actions, and then test the actions to determine the adequacies of the results. The researcher may employ more formality in the reasoning, planning, observing, and reporting of his investigations, but teachers can easily become good researchers in this more formal sense. And the more creative and inventive they are, the better researchers they may become.

AN EXAMPLE

An instance of teacher research occurred at Halloween time in a first grade. The teacher became interested in the drawings of jack-o'-lanterns made by the children in her room. She observed that the drawings closely resembled dime-store variations of the jack-o'-lantern motif. More particularly, all the jack-o'-lanterns seemed to have one characteristic in common—a triangular nose. It seemed reasonable to conclude that the children had arrived at this preference through imitation.

The teacher guessed that one way to stimulate variations in the drawings would be to substitute an alternative nose for the children to imitate. She also guessed that this substitution would eventually lead to other and more original patterns. So, she drew a jack-o'-lantern of her own (with a *round* nose) and showed it to the children. This was followed by the suggestion that jack-o'-lanterns would make a good Halloween decoration for the schoolroom.

Obligingly, twice more the children produced jack-o'-lanterns. The teacher labeled the three sets of decorations A (first set), B (second set), and C (third set).

After Halloween the teacher collected the decorations; marked each drawing with a symbol: X = triangular nose, Y = round nose, and Z = other nose; and made a chart summarizing the results.

Group	X	Y	Z
A	21	0	1
B	8	12	2
C	7	10	4
	36	22	7

Total No. of Drawings = 65

The teacher observed, among other things, that it required only one alternative suggestion to produce a 66 percent shift in the children's drawings from their stereotyped model. She made a note of this fact and began planning additional ways to encourage creativity in their drawing.

SIMILARITIES IN TEACHING AND RESEARCHING

This teacher, like most teachers, had learned a preference for planning her teaching along the lines of reflective thinking, or problem solving. This is a kind of thinking which rules out mere capricious choice of possible actions to be taken and depends instead on the anticipation of probable consequences as a guide to the contemplated action.

The methodologies of reflective thinking and of the teaching act are highly similar to the steps in the research process. There is reason to assume that good teachers are much better prepared for research activities than is commonly supposed. (See following chart for comparison.)

The acquiring of new knowledge and skill can be personally rewarding and satisfying. The teacher who steps through the forbidding curtain of misconceptions that make scientific procedures seem mysterious will find a new world waiting. And of equal importance, such a teacher will greatly help to realize the power of research-oriented teaching.

COMMON ELEMENTS IN REFLECTIVE THINKING, THE TEACHING PROCESS, AND THE RESEARCH PROCESS

1	2	3	4	5	6	7
5 Steps in Reflective Thought						
Awareness of perplexing situation	Defining the difficulty	Proposing a hypothesis for problem solution	Reasoning out implications of the hypothesis	Testing the hypothesis against experience		
7 Steps in the Teaching Process						
Awareness of general goal-directed teaching-learning object	Assessing state of affairs & diagnosing needs within the group	Selection of activities to meet these needs	Carrying through the activities planned	Evaluating the success (or failure) of the activities	Reassessing the activities	Replanning
7 Steps in the Research Process						
Sensing the problem area	Defining the specific problem	Formulating a hypothesis	Designing the test of the hypothesis	Obtaining evidence	Challenging and generalizing data	If necessary, retest

Stephen M. Corey

A Perspective on Educational Research

Like Barnes, Corey makes a plea for research done at the local level rather than for what he seems to feel is the more generalized research done by "educational researchers." He points out that the research attitude is equally as important as the methodology of research, and that developing this attitude in the local practitioners could have vast rewards. Of some interest is the implication that frequently the educational researcher is more interested in the method than in the result, while the real test of the value of research is the change it makes at the local level.

Stephen M. Corey, "A Perspective on Educational Research," *Phi Delta Kappan*, 35: 21-24, October, 1953. Reprinted with permission.

In the last analysis, the worth of all educational research is judged by its contributions to the improvement of educational practice. These contributions may be rather immediate, or, as in the case of research undertaken primarily to develop educational techniques, or instruments, or theory, somewhat delayed. In either case, the ultimate test of value is the degree to which educational practice is improved by the research.

An educational inquiry, whether philosophical, historical, psychological, or administrative in nature, is conducted in conformity with certain generally accepted operational principles. These, educational investigators have learned to value for good reasons: To the degree the inquiry is disciplined, the consequences are more dependable, are in closer approximation to reality, and hence provide better bases for decisions.

THE RESEARCH PROCESS

A number of authors have written extensively about the principles of inquiry which, when applied to problems in education, constitute educational research.(1, 2, 4, 5, 6, 8) Great emphasis is placed upon the importance of (a) objectivity on the part of the investigator, (b) a careful formulation of hypotheses or predictions to be put to test, (c) an adequate design for testing these hypotheses, (d) procuring valid and reliable evidence, and (e) judicious and careful conclusions based upon the evidence.

Progress in educational research has resulted, in considerable measure, from the invention and development of procedures, techniques, and instruments enabling the investigator to increase his objectivity, to better the design of his inquiries, to improve the reliability and validity of his evidence, and to deepen the sagacity and wisdom of the inferences he derives from his evidence. Concrete examples of such inventions are the tape recorder, used instead of hand notes to eliminate subjective factors in recording class discussions, the standardized intelligence test, used instead of teachers' judgments to procure a more reliable and valid measure of mental ability, and numerous experimental designs and statistical operations to improve the pertinence of data, and the quality of inferences from them.

To the degree that research procedures, techniques, and instruments are viewed as ends, and valued for themselves, unfortunate things happen. The niceties of research can usually be observed most meticulously in minor and insignificant investigations. It is easier to be rigorously scientific, for example, when studying the relationship between the height and weight of children at the time of school entrance than when studying the processes of abstract thinking.

RESEARCH PROCEDURES ARE BUT INSTRUMENTS

This overvaluing of certain established research methods has disposed some educational investigators to hunt for problems amenable to study by those methods. The invention of standardized tests of achievement or intelligence, for example, resulted in a great amount of research that involved little more than administering these tests to various populations under various circumstances and subjecting the scores to statistical manipulations. Similarly, the invention by Pearson and others of methods that made it possible to determine rather exactly the degree of relationship among variables led to a great number of studies involving little more than the computations of coefficients of correlation. Few of these studies made important contributions to educational practice or theory.

Educational research has most significant results when attention is directed first to an important problem about which too little is known. Instruments and procedures are then sought or invented because they are necessary to the study of this problem. Of central importance are the questions to be answered, rather than the techniques that lie at hand for answering them. As has been said, progress in educational research is hastened by the invention of new techniques and instruments making possible more discriminating and more valid inquiry. Progress is retarded by over-dedication to existing techniques and instruments, often resulting in a neglect of problems not lending themselves to study by the use of these techniques and instruments.

RESEARCH AND COMMON SENSE

The scientific method of inquiry in education is not an absolute process, sharply and clearly differentiated from the common sense way in which instructional, supervisory, and administrative problems are attacked by teachers, supervisors, principals and superintendents.(2, ch. 4) Research methods of problem solving in education are more realistically viewed as refinements of procedures that have long characterized man's attempts to understand himself and his environment in order that he might better predict and control future events. (3, ch. 4) These refinements result in better definition of problems, in more creative hypothesizing regarding solutions to these problems, in more ingenious designs for testing these hypotheses, in procuring better evidence throughout the process of problem solving, and in generalizing more carefully and thoughtfully from this evidence.

Despite the fact that methods used in educational research differ primarily in degree of refinement from methods used by teachers and administrators in coping with their day by day problems, there has been a strong tendency for educational research to be thought of as the special province of the professional investigator. The administrative set-up has encouraged this view. The researcher usually is a staff member of a university or college department of education, or of a research bureau, either state or local.

It is regrettable that educational research is generally thought to be the prerogative of a relatively small group of professional educational investigators.(2, ch. 1) The assumption is that if the professional investigators, employing research methods, report the results of their investigations, the practitioners will be able to modify their behavior to conform to them. Thus practitioners are considered to be primarily consumers of research.

While events have given some support to this assumption, there is general dissatisfaction, both among practicing school people and professional educational investigators, with the great gap between what *is* done in education and what research studies indicate *should* be done.

RESEARCH FOR PRACTITIONERS

The scientific method of inquiry will not have the pervasive influence upon practice that its advocates continuously predict until practitioners, teachers, supervisors, and school administrators, learn to conduct research as a way of dealing with day by day problems.(2) It is not enough for professional investigators to study scientifically the problems other people must do something about, and to publish the results. Making research reports more lucid and specifying applications will undoubtedly result in reducing the gap between what is known to be better and what is done. But most practitioners already know better than they do. An effective way to improve what is done is actually to try practices that seem *a priori* more promising and to determine the consequences. This, too, can be a kind of research—research undertaken by educational practitioners to improve their own decisions and their own actions.

This operational or action research, like the research undertaken by the professional investigator and about which so much has been written, is of superior quality in the degree to which it is (a) objective, (b) carefully designed, (c) procures reliable and valid evidence, and (d) employs judicious and careful generalization.

RESEARCHING FOR RESEACHERS

These somewhat different types of educational research, the one undertaken by professional investigators to discover generalizations of wide applicability, the other by the practitioner to guide his decisions and improve his practices, have much in common. To the degree that each is disciplined and conforms to generally accepted principles of inquiry, the findings will be more dependable. Reports of professional researchers can serve as rich sources of hypotheses to be tested in action situations by teachers, supervisors, and administrators. This is quite different from the conventional idea of "consuming research findings." It involves conducting research in specific and unique local situations in order to determine the worth of findings of inquiries undertaken to establish generalizations or principles of broad applicability. The process and results of operational or action investigations by practitioners, focused as they are on real problems, might help professional investigators to avoid the pitfall of inconsequential but methodologically precise inquiry.

RESEARCH VS. CONTROVERSY

At the present time, when public inquiry into public education is common, the need is great for practical, action oriented research conducted in specific communities to test the worth of old or new practices and materials. If this research is cooperative, involving the collaboration of as many as possible of the various persons or groups that are affected by the question at issue, and what might be done about it, so much the better.

Argument about the relative merits of various types of curricular organization or teaching methods rarely involves any research evidence that both speaks for itself and is specifically appropriate to the community in which the controversy is taking place. Sometimes evidence is sought, after the battle lines have been formed, and the word research is used, but adversaries tend to look for what they want to see. Studies or surveys may be conducted to support or to attack current practices but the research attitude, the attiude of scientific inquiry, is lacking.

THE RESEARCH ATTITUDE

Improvement in the quality of educational research over the past two generations has been, in large measure, a consequence of two factors: First, and this was noted above, the discovery and development of methodological procedures making the research process itself more rigorous, more discriminating, and more dependable; second, and a more subtle factor, an attitude of dedication to research as the best way to study educational problems as well as to improve decisions and actions in respect to them.

It seems to be easier to learn research procedures, per se, than to become committed to the research attitude. Mankind has not come by this commitment easily nor have educators.(3, ch. 4, 4, 7) While there have been many discussions of the use of the scientific method in the study of educational problems, there have been, to my knowledge, no research studies isolating and studying the factors influential in the development of the research attitude among educators themselves.

LEARNING TO VALUE RESEARCH

The value placed upon research methodology is undoubtedly learned in much the same fashion as are other values. In the individual case, commitment to the research method of studying educational problems develops as one engages in research, as one experiences consequences perceived to be rewarding. The most intrinsic consequence is intimate experience with improvement in the educational difficulty that the research was designed to ameliorate. For example, the research method of dealing with a teaching problem is most apt to be viewed as good by the teacher who uses this method and by so doing is able to teach more satisfactorily.(10)

This kind of intimate experience with the consequences of using the research method is usually denied the great majority of men and women who view themselves, and are viewed by others, as professional educational researchers. This refers again to the fact that research activities in education have been concentrated in the hands of a relatively small number of men and women, most of whom have little or no responsibility for doing anything about the problems they study. For example, those who have conducted most of the research designed to improve children's reading usually have not been intimately associated with boys and girls as they learn to read. Consequently, the most realistic rewards for significant research in this field are not available to the researchers as first-hand, intimate experiences. The professional educational investigator spends so much of his time investigating that he has little time or energy or inclination left to engage in the practices that his research was designed to improve.

REWARDS PSYCHOLOGICALLY EXTRINSIC

A complex system of rewards for educational research activity has developed that, in general, is psychologically extrinsic. The research method is valued because it brings increased prestige among other professional investigators. It leads to membership in professional organizations devoted to research, to service on their committees, and to publication frequency, one basis for advancement and promotion in the profession.

The development of an extrinsic value system is almost inevitable, and it certainly is not a phenomenon unique to education, but some of its consequences are undesirable. Attaching so much value to practicing the research process often results in insufficient consideration of the importance of the problem investigated, namely, that the inquiry gives reasonable promise of improving significant educational practices, and reasonable indications of doing so economically.

THE PRACTICAL CONSEQUENCES OF RESEARCH

The methods of research are of little help in isolating problems most in need of investigation. This probably is one reason why researchers whose greatest allegiance is to method are unwilling to have practicality judgments made upon their investigations. This point of view is frequently defended by reference to research in the physical sciences. It is argued that the best research is basic or pure research, undertaken without any thought of its practical consequences. The analogy is drawn that no amount of research undertaken to improve the quality of kerosene lamps would ever have resulted in the discovery of the incandescent electric light. Or, that no amount of research undertaken to improve dynamite would have resulted in the discovery of practical ways of releasing atomic energy.

These claims are probably true, but their relation to educational research is only approximate. The fact that reference is rarely if ever made to analogies in social science, in developing this argument for pure (impractical?) inquiry in education, suggests that the conception of pure research as used in the physical sciences may not be appropriate to education. It is interesting, too, that statements in opposition to practical research justify pure or basic research because, in due course, it is more practical. This is not, of course, as paradoxical as it seems.

CONCLUSION

As a conclusion to this statement of perspectives on educational research, I should like to re-emphasize one central idea: The methods of research are not only of value in *studying* educational problems (although this has seemed to be the dominate rationale for educational research during the past fifty years); they can also be of great value to practitioners as they try, not only to *study* their problems but to *do something* about them. It is not as easy to assume the scientific attitude under the pressures of day by day operations of a school as it is to be scientific in the laboratory. But when steps are taken to improve the quality of the research the practitioner engages in as he wrestles with his practical problems, his solutions to these problems will be better ones.

References

1. Barr, Arvil S., Davis, Robert A., and Johnson, Palmer O. *Educational Research and Appraisal*. New York: J. B. Lippincott Co., 1953. 362 pp.

2. Corey, Stephen M. *Action Research to Improve School Practices*. New York: Bureau of Publications, Teachers College, Columbia University, 1953. 161 pp.

3. Dewey, John. *Logic: The Theory of Inquiry*. New York: Holt, Rinehart and Winston, Inc., 1933. 301 pp.

4. Dewey, John. *The Sources of a Science of Education*. New York: Liveright Publishing Corp., 1929. 77 pp.

5. Good, Carter V., Barr, A. S., and Scates, Douglas E. *The Methodology of Educational Research*. New York: D. Appleton-Century, 1936.

6. Lindquist, E. F. *Design and Analysis of Experiments in Psychology and Education*. New York: Houghton Mifflin Co., 1953. 393 pp.

7. Lundberg, George A. *Can Science Save Us?* New York: Longmans, Green and Company, 1947. 122 pp.

8. Monroe, Walter S. and Engelhart, Max D. *The Scientific Study of Educational Problems*. New York: The Macmillan Company, 1936. 504 pp.

9. Rice, J. M. *Scientific Management in Education*. New York: Publisher's Printing Company, 1913. 282 pp.

10. Wann, Kenneth. "Teacher Participation in Action Research Directed Toward Curriculum Change." Unpublished Ed. D. Project. New York: Bureau of Publications, Teachers College, Columbia University, 1950. 240 pp.

Henry James Masson

An Outline of
Certain Processes
of Reasoning in Research

All too often research gets completely confounded with methodology or, even more narrowly, with data analysis. Research requires much more than the design of the experiment and the analysis of the data, although these factors are admittedly crucial. Masson approaches the research process from a slightly different track, as he looks at the reasoning underlying the various activities that make up the process. He points out ways of thinking that will be most fruitful in leading the investigator to formulate reasonable plans that should lead to worthwhile conclusions. For this reason alone, the article is worth careful reading.

H. J. Masson, "An Outline of Certain Processes of Reasoning in Research," *Journal of Engineering Education*, 43:410-19, March, 1953. Reprinted with permission.

The tremendous growth of research in the last thirty years has directed attention to its organization, management, and procedures. Because of the large sums of money, facilities, and personnel involved, and the desire to use these effectively and efficiently, examination and analysis of all procedures in use are constantly appropriate. Although a substantial literature is developing in the area of the management of research and development, the strictly technical literature of the various experimental sciences is almost barren of specific information concerning research procedures, except occasionally a vague reference to the scientific method without, however, amplification as to how it is used as part of the research process. However, in the field of philosophy and logic, there is available an extensive literature on the scientific method, but comparatively few students, planning a career in scientific

41

research, elect courses in these fields as part of their formal training. When such courses are elected, there may develop a feeling of frustration or nonapplicability of subject matter, due to the abstractness of treatment. Many of the more philosophical writers on the subjects are not experimental scientists, and as a result, their language, illustrations, and approach may seem unfruitful to the eager young scientist interested in research.

Such frustration is neither necessary nor desirable. The modern concept of the scientific method, when properly considered, includes a multiplicity of sequences from an awareness of a problem to be solved to its successful conclusion and constitutes a disciplinary and directive philosophy of substantial value. We are concerned here, however, only with certain complex reasoning processes and their influence on the design of experiments and the selection of an experimental path leading to the solution of a problem.

Because of the appeal of research as a means of satisfying the curiosity of individuals and the desire to add to our knowledge of man and his environment, an increasing number of individuals are entering the field and are beginning to learn something of its philosophy and practices. This paper has been prepared in order to stimulate more extensive study by this young group of the literature related to the scientific method in general, and that of logic in particular, and at the same time, to present certain aspects of the methodology of research from a fresh viewpoint. Although these remarks are directed principally to this new group, the experienced investigator may find here and there a point of interest or basis for reflection. An effort has been made to winnow some fundamental principles from a vast amount of material and establish a framework for use in the design of experiments. It has been undertaken with apprehension, because of its departure from the standard presentation and the somewhat unrestrained interpretation and application of classical concepts. Certain ideas will be presented by means of arbitrary, diagrammatic representations, which have been introduced, because most researchers have high structural visualization, and, therefore, may give clarity to the subject.

INSTANCES AND THEIR TREATMENT

All fields of knowledge employ certain terms to describe particular concepts. Various expressions from the field of logic will be used frequently and defined as they occur. One of these, of immediate interest, is the term "instances," which may be defined as any single fact pertaining to a thing, a physical or chemical property, an attribute, or event, which may be investigated scientifically and used to form an hypothesis or theory. A related number of instances may be grouped so as to form a phenomenon, or several groups combined to give the phenomena.

Through chance observation and as the result of designed experiments man has learned various facts. Over the course of time, these facts have been verified, experimentally or otherwise, and allowed to accumulate to form a reservoir or storehouse of knowledge. It is from this accumulation that man, by varying degrees of sagacity, has chosen those single instances, or combination thereof, which intuitively he suspects will lead to a solution of a problem.

CLASSIFICATION

Among the various traits which characterize investigators is the desire for classification—the ambition to bring order out of apparent confusion and establish a basis for convenient use and understanding of facts and their relationships. The desire for an orderly arrangement of facts—a form of "factual tidiness" is inherent in the make-up of the true scientist who wants to have his knowledge organized in a readily available and usable form. Neatness and apportionment are essential to the peace of mind of the scientist, so that his reasoning processes will be unencumbered by any disturbing disarray. Scientists are not content with facts when seen in isolation.

A mere collection or accumulation of instances—facts—does not constitute a science any more than a pile of bricks is a house or other useful structure. Since research is a form of human action which results usually in the discovery of new facts, a sound and fruitful method must be found to group, or bind, the facts together for useful purposes. The aptitudes of the investigator are concerned not only with discovering new and isolated facts, but should go beyond, and be so developed as to extend to the perception of wholes or patterns and consequences thereof.

As classification is an important element of reasoning in research, a few comments may be helpful to indicate its significance. Classification is a mental process carried out by an individual and consists of noticing or detecting certain similarities in attributes or qualities of things or phenomena considered in determining the classification. Or, classification may be described as the process of recognizing or identifying at least one trait or point of similiarity shared in common by a number of instances or phenomena, and mentally associating these in a single group or class. The system of classification used may be based upon established or acceptable concepts or a working definition tentatively postulated for purposes of exploration. A classification may be depicted by a diagram, chart, figure, or in tabular form, as, for example, in the Periodic classification of the chemical elements.

In making the classification, an appraisal of value may be applied. It is rated of high value if there are many significant points of similarity and of low value if there are only a few similarities. The more points of similarity the more homogeneous and satisfactory will be the classification.

It is a matter of common knowledge that some individuals, on rare occasions, and more frequently in the case of experienced investigators, have the uncanny faculty to select, from a vast array of diversified instances, those having certain common similarities and bring them into a given classification. In some cases, based upon their selections and reflections, prediction may be made of what will probably be observed in a designed experiment or indication of the path to be followed toward the solution of a given problem. Apparently, detecting similarities or likenesses is, in some aspects, more difficult than recognizing dissimilarities. In any case, the attempt to establish order among facts is a difficult task at which few succeed significantly. It cannot be reduced to a set of procedures which, when faithfully followed, will guarantee success. Classification will be considered later as part of the process of hypothesis formation.

PRELIMINARIES TO EXPERIMENTAL RESEARCH

A number of preliminary procedures are usually involved prior to the physical design of any experiments as, for example, the application of dimensional and statistical analysis. We are concerned at this point, however, only with certain procedures which usually come before the application of these important mathematical tools. One of the first steps in a research, in which the objective is clearly defined, is to determine which elements of the solution are available in the literature, but have not as yet been correlated or treated as part of the approach to the solution of the designated goal. The procedure to be immediately described applies particularly to the individual who is just about to begin his first research and who, although well grounded in the fundamentals of the broad field of the research, has not worked sufficiently long in the limited area of the research to have become familiar, as part of his working knowledge, with the particular instances that are involved.

It is well to realize that the purpose of carrying out an investigation is based upon the desire to add to knowledge, irrespective of whether or not the results are to be applied immediately or perhaps in the future. In any case, the researcher is operating at the frontiers of knowledge and hopes, through a successful solution, to expand a limited portion of these frontiers.

One of the initial steps undertaken by the researcher with a problem to investigate is that generally known as the "literature search," the mechanics of which may be represented graphically as follows—Fig. 1:

Figure 1

In Fig. I–A, the solid line xy represents an arbitrary designation separating the area of knowledge, represented by crosses, from the unknown area. The dotted line lmn indicates a part of the unknown area circumscribed by the objective of the research. That is, if the investigation is successful, the new frontier of knowledge will be represented by a solid line xlmny. The boundary line xy is indefinite, located in a penumbra region and positioned by the skill (knowledge) and experience of the investigator. The line lmn is more so, the whole being a tentative arrangement for more solid construction. In Fig. 1-B, the instances from the known area, which the investigator suspects are part of the solution to the problem, have been transferred in a purposeful manner to the proposed area of investigation and thereby to begin the population of the region to be added to knowledge. Fig. 1–C represents a segregation of related instances in the new area, thereby disclosing, both in magnitude and nature, known portions and unknown gaps to be filled. In other words, as a result of a careful study of the literature, it is disclosed that what was thought at first to be an area of which nothing definite was known now reduces to one of which certain portions are more clearly defined and other areas which must be investigated experimentally to develop the necessary information for completeness and inclusion within the new frontiers of knowledge.

HYPOTHESIS FORMATION

This leads to a consideration of certain mental processes related to the design of an experiment and selection of experimental paths toward the solution of the problem. Whereas the various processes of classification operate on a certain intellectual plane, the intensive exercise of the same general analytical aptitudes can, in certain groups of individuals, give rise to syntheses and inferences of importance through the processes of reflective thinking and reasoning. In analyzing these processes, we may use a graphical approach, but with objectives and consequences of an heuristic nature.

It has been suggested that by means of classification a working basis may be established for extending the frontiers of knowledge. Occasionally, certain individuals, capable of varying degrees of significant thinking, and under free will, economic and other pressures, have gone an important step beyond classification and through uncanny insight, sometimes referred to as a flash of genius, discernedly take instances from this, that, or the other field, which, when fused together, result in a formulation which may be used as a basis for further exploration —the hypothesis.

Although the term hypothesis is frequently used in research parlance, it is desirable to review briefly its formulation, significance, and importance in the sequences of research procedures. An hypothesis is defined as a comprehensive but tentative interpretation of certain phenomena, to be considered as possibly true until there has been an opportunity, experimentally or otherwise, to bring all related instances into comparison. The initial hypothesis, pending verification, may be regarded as a "working" hypothesis, so that it may serve for immediate purposes of correlation and suggestive of a method of solution of a given problem. It is a tentative guess, or a scaffold, to aid in the construction of a more permanent structure.

A good hypothesis should: (1) bring together, in a simple manner, a given number of instances and interpret the connection between them; (2) be fruitful—fertile—that is, suggestive of significant deductions which are testable; (3) be comprehensible and not inconsistent.

In describing the creation and use of hypotheses, several terms are used. Two of these, induction and deduction, present difficulties in defining, because of the complexities involved and the evolution of interpretation which has taken place over the course of time by many minds. Both are concerned with thought processes. In its simplest form "induction" may be described as the process of reasoning whereby a selected group of instances are synthesized into a hypothesis and "deduction," the process whereby consequences are inferred from the hypothesis. On the basis of the foregoing, it has been advanced that induction is the reverse of deduction, but this is only true in the sense of convergence and divergence as illustrated by what follows. Many thought processes are both in fact inductive and deductive, depending upon the point of view during interpretation.

Classification has been treated as though it was an independent operation on the mind which stopped at mere classification. Actually, in many cases, while the process of classification is in process, the mind is not only seeing relations between instances, but also a possible interpretation of some phenomenon—that is, forming an hypothesis. The two operations may proceed simultaneously, so that in certain cases, particularly in new fields, the two processes are inseparable.

The relation between the processes of classification, inductive reasoning, hypothesis formation, deductive reasoning, and inferences is shown graphically in Fig. 2.

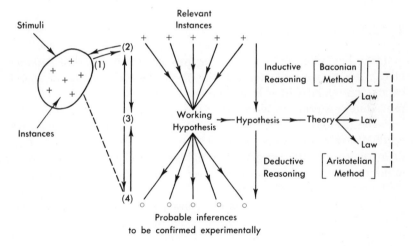

Figure 2

The above tends toward oversimplification. It is a condensation product which could readily be expanded to encyclopedic proportions. In the abridging process, certain concepts have been submerged and fine shades of meaning blended in the microdiagram.

In any case, it is not an expression of reasoning in the nature of a final product, but rather a mobile equilibrium product or condition in dynamic harmony with the state of knowledge at the time of formulation and the grasp of relations by the reasoner at the time of reflection. It consists of a multiplicity of reversible mental processes involving the sagacious selection and rejection of instances and consequences until a usable, consistent, fertile, and workable hypothesis is established which the mind (tentatively) feels is valid and which appears to give promise that it will be helpful in attaining the objective. However, the type of mind we are describing is probably never completely satisfied, but continues the process of selection, sorting and joining facts (jigsaw fashion) in an attempt to construct a composite picture in which all parts fit. One has no measure of the conscious or subconscious trials and errors which have taken place on a mental blackboard of some investigator until a flash thought—a mental leap (inductive)—points the way toward a simple formulation (hypothesis) in which all relevant instances are harmoniously absorbed or consolidated. It is a method of approximation. Hypotheses are tentative and cannot, in many cases, be exhaustively verified. Therefore, the frequent use of the word "probable" in connection with hypotheses.

REASONING PROCESS

In the beginning of the reasoning process, interchange of instances takes place between (1) and (2) (Fig. 2) until a combination or classification is attained which is amenable to inductive reasoning. The next procedure, resulting in a hypothesis, is represented by the interaction between (2) and (3). These operations or thought processes may proceed instantly, or extend over varied and sometimes long periods, depending upon the complacency of the conceiver. However, such a mind, once started, and perhaps in a state of mental momentum is not contented to stop at (3). Whether, as indicated, through an idea momentum or vision, one may suspect consequences of the generalization or hypothesis. This leads to the process of deductive reasoning and the proliferation of consequences as represented by step (3) to (4). If, as the result of deductive reasoning, the consequences appear illogical, improbable, impossible, unreasonable, or contrary to experience and scientific law, the mind (the true scientific and unbiased) re-examines each deduction, reasons and modifies the hypothesis, until eventually complete harmony exists between (3) and (4). In this process, it may be necessary, and usually is, to examine all aspects. In other words, before the mind is satisfied, complete inferential agreement must exist between all phases and stable equilibrium prevails between stages (1), (2), (3), and (4).

Due to the limited comprehensiveness of the normal intellect, all consequences of an hypothesis are usually not deduced by a single mind and confirmed by recourse to memory. Additional significant deductions may be suggested by co-workers. All consequences are, therefore, listed and confirmation sought in the literature or experimentally. This brings us to an important observation. As the result of the foregoing treatment of instances, a new and unsuspected experiment to be tried may be indicated, or even a new field for research suggested. As indicated, a good hypotheses should not only weld together, in homogeneous agreement, a given number of instances, but should also suggest consequences of importance. Such consequences, when confirmed experimentally and their validity established, become instances to be added to the storehouse of knowledge and form the basis for a further expansion of the frontiers of knowledge.

The greater the number and impressiveness of instances included initially, the broader and more fundamental will be the resulting hypothesis. If based upon a sufficiently comprehensive number of instances and confirmed by an adequate number of experimentally proven consequences, the initial "working hypothesis" assumes the status of a valid hypothesis, and upon further confirmation, gives rise to various theories. If, over a long period of time and exposure to testing, no exceptions are found to a given relationship, a law of science may be formulated.

LAWS OF NATURE AND SCIENCE

A law of nature is an order or relationship detected in nature by some human observer based upon his investigations of an area of nature. It is a simple statement of facts, which may, in some cases, be expressed in mathematical form. The laws of science, in general, are not directly concerned with specific things, but rather with abstractions from them. For example, the law of gravitation is concerned with the forces acting between bodies, but there are numerous physical and chemical properties about which the law is silent, or uncommunicative. A law of nature is a summarization, or integration of a number of facts, the relationship or significance of which may be explained or clarified by a theory.

The nascent hypothesis and deductions therefrom are, up to this point, the product usually of one mind with its limitations, inadequacies, and importantly, prejudices. The originator, having exhausted all combinations and processes of reasoning and confident of his conclusions, and having faith in the integrity and sympathetic understanding of his fellow workers and the mutual desire for the advancement of knowledge, exposes and discloses the results of his reasoning processes by publication or otherwise.

Now the whole process begins anew. Compatible minds, interested and expertly familiar with the field of knowledge involved, dissect, analyze, reorient their views and allow an independent reasoning process free rein to evaluate the results of the creator of the new hypothesis. If we look upon the original hypothesis as representing equilibrium, we now find, unless all who study it agree with the premises and conclusions, that conditions (criticisms) will be advanced which have the effect of disturbing the equilibrium, which, in turn, will result in a shift to a new equilibrium (modified hypothesis). The extent of the resulting modification of the original hypothesis will depend upon the nature of each criticism and the number of confirming investigations involved. If, in time, general agreement of a modified hypothesis is reached, the resulting product will probably be superior.

Because of the interest developed, study of the hypothesis does not cease at this stage. Other minds, ordinarily not concerned with the field of research represented by the hypothesis, become interested and see applications in their particular field, and undertake investigations to determine its applicability. This transfer to another field may result in further modification. And so it will be seen that any hypothesis may undergo a sort of fission process.

At times, several rival hypotheses may be extant. Under these circumstances, a crucial experiment (experimentum crucis) is undertaken. It is a critically designed experiment to provide data with which one hypothesis is consistent and which is inconsistent with another.

A given number of instances may be selected to constitute a particular field of knowledge. The number of such instances may be large. One investigator may choose a certain group of instances and formulate an hypothesis while another investigator may choose another group from the same field and formulate what appears to be a different and unrelated hypothesis. But this is not necessarily so. All the instances involved in each case came from the same classification and from the nature of the classification process must have had some characteristics in common. This leads to the suspicion that both hypotheses are related and may be integrated into a single super-hypotheses. This development is illustrated by the contributions of Copernicus, Galilei, Newton, and Einstein.

There remains another situation which illustrates a still different mechanism of reasoning and which has been very fruitful as a means of formulating a working hypothesis to aid in the experimental design of some investigation or establish a basis of explanation for consequences not verifiable experimentally. In the cases studied thus far, the conscious mind is the one considered as functioning. We must give some consideration now to the role of the subconscious mind, although the distinction between the two is very indefinite. In this discussion, the subconscious mind is considered as exerting an effect when the body is completely dissociated from environmental factors disturbing to thinking and engaged in the automatic operations involved in the performance of familiar actions. While in such a state, and in search for a solution to a given problem, instances may be assumed which are not found in any literature or recalled from memory, and with intuitive faith in the reasonableness of the assumptions, the mind proceeds inductively to create an hypothesis and deduce consequences. The consequences may be constructive or fantastic. On the basis of such assumptions, substantial advances were made by earlier thinkers. This is illustrated by the kinetic molecular hypothesis.

The foregoing suggests another approach to hypothesis formation. This is the use of analogy. We may not observe a direct or structural relationship of instances to form an hypothesis, but there appears to be similarities from which others may be inferred. An analogy is a resemblance of relations which may be used for reasoning and from the likeness in certain respects we may infer that other and more important relations exist.

We refer to the flow of liquids as analogous to the flow of electricity, the structure of the atom as analogous to the solar system and cybernetics reasons by analogy between the mechanisms of control and of communication in the animal and various mathematical machines. Such analogical reasoning may be fruitful and help to visualize relationships, but there are dangers. We must, however, distinguish between circumstantial evidence and direct evidence which may lead to a false analogy. Analogy invades and influences our thinking and, although helpful in research, it should be used with caution and not allowed to lead to hasty generalization.

There is a last approach used occasionally and not always looked upon with favor, but, nevertheless, it may indirectly result in valuable contributions and may give some encouragement to the novice and act as an expedient to the experienced investigator. This is the "wild" experiment. The impression exists, and soundly, that the larger the accumulation of instances (knowledge) of the investigator, the greater the probability of his success in solving a given problem. But this is not necessarily so. Too much knowledge may lead to complacency and too much faith in the inviolability of generally accepted hypotheses, theories, or laws, and may result in the rejection of any suggested experiment which is an apparent conflict with them. Valuable discoveries were made by men who did not know they were violating some established theory. Such reckless suggestions leading to "wild" experiments have resulted in unusual discoveries. It is pleasant to have a deduction confirmed experimentally, but it is an experimental result which is at variance with theory, which may be productive of new knowledge and new fields to explore and which points to a path for the advancement of civilization.

CONCLUSION

In conclusion, it should be emphasized that hypotheses usually have a short life, theories come and go, but the facts with which they are concerned remain the same. The properties of benzene have not changed since it was first discovered, but the suggested arrangement of the atoms in the molecule, the interpretations of the formula and the various theories advanced to explain its action have changed—but again, not the properties.

Although an hypothesis may be rejected in due time, its formulation may not have been a complete waste of time and mental effort for experience and a study of discarded hypotheses have shown that when such hypotheses meet the usual specifications and are properly worked upon, they frequently produce more useful results than unguided observations. In fact, a constructive advancement has been made when new experimental evidence indicates the untenableness of a given hypothesis and it is replaced by one more in accordance with the newer evidence.

No scientific law or theory has ever given an explanation of why anything happens, that is, what makes it happen. They explain how things happen, but not why. Although much has been written on the theory of causation, it is sufficient to state, at least in this treatment, that the so-called cause is just a statement of the set of conditions which precedes or accompanies an effect.

SUMMARY

Because of the limited scope of this paper, of necessity many details and issues have not been included. The principal concepts, conditions and procedures outlined for the idea formulation phase of an investigation may be summarized as follows:

(1) An environment satisfactory for research—social, political, economic, and technological.

(2) An individual, or organization, interested and qualified for research and adequately sponsored.

(3) Sources of problems for research which act as "thought starters" and create an awareness of a subject to be investigated—an incitation.

(4) The selection and definition of a problem to be investigated.

(5) The concentration of the mental faculties of an investigator on the objective and scope of the problem until it is thoroughly understood and feasibility determined.

(6) The gathering of all information related to the problem by means of the literature and other surveys in anticipation of the disclosure of instances, hypotheses, theories, and methods which are suspected to be related to and suggest a solution of the problem. The information should be recorded on 3×5 cards and in a notebook.

(7) The sorting, rearranging and classification of the information as a basis for the determination of the known and unknown portions of the circumscribed area of the proposed research. See Fig. 1.

(8) In the case of the unknown areas and in the absence of any hypothesis, theory, or law suggestive of an experimental approach toward the objective, the synthesis of a "working hypothesis" the deductions from which may indicate an attractive path of high certainty toward a solution of the problem.

(9) The discriminate sorting and purposeful selection and classification of instances as a basis for reasoning. It will be helpful generally if these are arranged as in Fig. 2, thereby bringing more of the reasoner's faculties into action.

(10) The implanting of this conception—mental image, together with the objective sought, in the mind of the investigator for his reasoning powers to work upon. This is an "incubating" period.

(11) The elimination of all distractive influences or environmental factors, which, during reflective thinking, would prevent concentration on the purpose at hand.

(12) The period of "digestion" during which the conscious and subconscious mind is constantly and unrelentingly pressing for a simple formulation—hypothesis.

(13) Do not strain for a solution to the point of mental and physical exhaustion. When not making progress set the problem aside com-

pletely and allow the mind to wander and the investigator to engage in a non-related, diverting, and pleasant activity stimulating to the imagination and emotions.

(14) After a period of rest and relaxation, the gradual emergence of an idea for a semitangible synthesis—to be written down—as an initial working hypothesis. Such ideas may emerge unexpectedly at any time, place, or under normal or unusual circumstances.

(15) Making deductions—written down—as in Fig. 2, and then an interplay between (1), (2), (3), and (4), but without losing sight of the purpose of the investigation. One of the inferences should indicate a solution to the problem. At times, the mind may by-pass this step and go directly to the solution of the problem.

(16) The design of experimental equipment and procedures to confirm inferences which indicate a solution of the problem or confirm the solution suggested in 15.

There can never be any guarantee that the faithful application of the foregoing procedures will lead to a successful solution of a problem. However, when through constant application, they become an integral part of the investigator's "working tools," they eliminate careless thinking and help to establish a basis for a possible solution. That is, the mind follows an operative technique which can be learned, applied, but always under control. We may learn the fundamentals of an art or procedure under competent guidance, but it is only through constant practice or application that a high degree of skill is attained. Therefore, the only path to success in research is the constant practice of research.

Suggested Collateral Reading

(1) "How we think." John Dewey. D. C. Heath & Company, N. Y., 1933.
(2) "Scientific Method." F. W. Westaway. Blackie & Son, London, 1924.
(3) "A Philosophy of Science." W. K. Werkmeister. Harper & Row, Publishers, N. Y., 1940.
(4) "The Basis and Structure of Knowledge." W. K. Werkmeister. Harper & Row, Publishers, N. Y., 1948.
(5) "An Introduction to Logic and Scientific Method." M. R. Cohen and E. Nagel. Harcourt, Brace & Co., 1936.
(6) "The Principles of Reasoning." D. S. Robinson. Appleton-Century-Crofts, 3rd ed., N. Y., 1936.
(7) "Introduction to Reflective Thinking." By Columbia Associates in Philosophy. Houghton Mifflin Company, 1923.

(8) "Philosophy, an Introduction." J. H. Randall and J. Buchler. Barnes & Noble, N. Y., 1942.

(9) "The Genius of Industrial Research." D. Killeffer. Reinhold Pub. Co., 1948.

(10) "The Path of Science." K. Mees. John Wiley & Sons, Inc., 1946.

(11) "The Art of Scientific Investigation." W. I. B. Beveridge. W. W. Norton & Co., N. Y.

(12) "The Way of an Investigator." W. B. Cannon. W. W. Norton & Co., N. Y., 1945.

(13) "The Scientist in Action." W. B. George. Emerson Books, Inc., N. Y., 1938.

(14) "How to Solve It." G. Polya. Princeton University Press, Princeton, N. J., 1948.

James D. Raths

Plausible Logic in Educational Research

Underlying all research is the logical argument upon which the strength of the conclusion must be evaluated. A magnificent hypothesis, a superb design, and completely valid and reliable data-gathering instruments may all go for naught if the logic tying everything together is faulty. The educational researcher must, therefore, look to his logical inference patterns if he is to come up with results that contribute to the body of knowledge upon which professional education is based. In this article, Raths points out the difficulty in applying classical, formal logic to educational research and then offers an alternative in the form of plausible logic based on the work of Polyá. The significance of this logic is particularly important when considered along with the relationship of the hypotheses and deduced consequences treated by Masson.

James D. Raths, "Plausible Logic in Educational Research," paper delivered at the American Educational Research Association Convention, February, 1964. Reprinted with permission.

Though research shares purposeful search, conviction and conclusions with other forms of inquiry, it is unique in its use of logical argument. Research cannot be evaluated solely upon its hypotheses, evidence, or conclusions, but rather upon the cogency of the logic it utilizes to connect these elements.

Research makes use of many logical patterns to make passages from evidence to conclusions. Some of these patterns are rather straight forward and familiar to both the doers and consumers of research. On the other hand, other patterns are obscure, not only in the minds of the readers of research, but perhaps in the minds of the researchers themselves. This paper will attempt to formalize a pattern of logic prevalent in research today and to illustrate its application in current educational research literature.

Perhaps we can introduce the notion of an argument with an example. Let us say that a researcher wants to find evidence to test an hypothesis. He may argue: If the experimental group scores significantly better on pertinent criterion measures than the control group, then the hypothesis is true. Presumably, the pattern of logic utilizing this major premise would be as follows:

PATTERN I

Statement	Logical Pattern	Source
If the experimental group does significantly better than the control group, the hypothesis is true.	If A, then B	Assumption
The experimental group does do significantly better than the control group.	A is true.	Experimental evidence
Therefore: The hypothesis is true.	B is true.	Law of detachment(1)

While this argument is logically valid, its truth value depends upon the truth value of its premises. Let us assume that the experimental design has controlled sources of internal validity and the findings that make up the minor premise can be considered true. How confident can we be in the truth of the major premise? Regardless of how well designed the experiment may have been, it is difficult to accept this major premise as true. So many other hypotheses may explain the experimental findings. Because of the doubt cast upon the major premise of this argument, its conclusion must be considered tenuous at best.

What other major premises may this researcher adopt for use in his argument? He may assert: If the hypothesis is true, then the experimental group will score significantly higher on pertinent criterion measures than the control group. Certainly, this major premise has a greater truth value than its converse considered above. But unfortunately the researcher runs into a new obstacle, as can be seen in the following pattern of logic:

PATTERN II

Statement	Logical Pattern	Source
If the hypothesis is true, then the experimental group will do significantly better than the control group.	If A, then B	Assumption
The experimental group does do significantly better than the control group.	B is true.	Experimental evidence
Therefore: ????	????	

In this argument, the major premise is worthy of respect as a true statement, but according to the rules of formal logic, no conclusion can validly be reached.(1) The researcher is faced with a dilemma. He can either argue logically from premises whose truth values are suspect (Pattern I) or he can adopt premises in which he is more confident but from which he can draw no logical conclusions (Pattern II). It is the position of this paper that most researchers do not recognize this dilemma formally in their papers or reports. In their researches, using the second pattern outlined above, experimenters tend with some confidence to conclude that their hypotheses are supported by the evidence. How do they arrive at this conclusion logically?

A source that will help us understand the formal reasoning that is taking place tacitly in these cases is the rather recent work of Polyá(4) in mathematical induction and logic. He asserts that because of the inaccessibility of the antecedents (if-clauses) of many premises to mathematicians, and presumably to experimenters in education, we and they must be satisfied at times to work with the consequents (then-clauses) of a premise. As the consequent of a true if-then statement is confirmed we may feel more confident in the truth value of its antecedent. Of course the degree of confidence varies from situation to situation. The basic plausible inference pattern of Polyá, of which there are many variations, can be applied as follows to our original example:

PATTERN III

Statement	Logical Pattern	Source
If the hypothesis is true, then the experimental group will do better than the control group.	If A, then B.	Assumption
The experimental group does do better than the control group.	B is true.	Experimental evidence
Therefore: The truth of the hypothesis *is more credible.*	A is more credible.	Polyá's paradigm(4)

Of course, the qualification of the conclusion is crucial. A more definite conclusion could only be drawn by going beyond the data available in this research.

Let us turn to other more specific examples in educational research —the application of operational definitions. We may use intelligence test measures to gauge intellectual ability. If a student scores high on an intelligence measure, may we conclude that he is bright? How would we logically reach this conclusion? We may argue: If a student scores high on an intelligence test, then he is bright. On the other hand we may adopt for a major premise: If a student is bright, then he will score high on an intelligence measure. It seems clear that psychometrists would feel more confident in the truth value of the second premise. It is equally clear that the second premise is not amenable to the application of formal logic. It does not follow logically that since a student did score high on an intelligence test, he is therefore intelligent. Using the logical pattern advocated by Polyá, it may be concluded that it is now only *more credible* to say that the student with a high score on an intelligence test is bright.

According to Polyá, this basic pattern of plausible inference may be strengthened by the addition of other minor premises. To illustrate this pattern, we may add to the argument above the minor premise: To score high on an intelligence test without being bright is extremely unlikely. Of course, as for all premises in logical arguments, the truth value of this statement must be supported. From what we know of the sampling distributions of attempts to guess correct answers on group intelligence tests, it seems reasonable to accept this additional premise. The pattern of this argument would be:

PATTERN IV

Statement	Logical Pattern	Source
If a student is bright, he will score high on an intelligence test.	If A, then B.	Assumption
To score high on an intelligence test without being bright is extremely unlikely.	B without A is extremely unlikely.	Assumption
A student does score high on an intelligence test.	B is true.	Experimental evidence
Therefore: That this student is bright is *very much more credible*.	A is very much more credible.	Polyá's paradigm(4)

Notice that with the additional premise and with confidence in the truth value of all of the premises, it is possible to assert the truth value of the conclusions in much stronger terms than when the basic plausible inference pattern (Pattern III) was used.

We may illustrate the application of this pattern of logic to a research study by Ausubel(3) testing the efficacy of organizing meaningful learning material in such a way that teachers make use of advance organizers in their teaching. He tested the hypothesis "that the learning and retention of unfamiliar but meaningful verbal material could be facilitated by the advance introduction of relevant subsuming concepts (organizers)." He concluded that the evidence of his research "unequivocally supports the hypothesis." What pattern of logic did

Ausubel use in arriving at this conclusion? Before answering this question, it is important to point out that in any deductive process, identical conclusions may be reached by many combinations of major and minor premises. Because of this, whenever we attempt to reconstruct a researcher's argument, we are in fact attributing a logic pattern to him that in fact *may not be the one he used*. When an author has not made his argument explicitly clear, the best source of information *vis-a-vis* the argument is the author himself. However, it would appear to me that Ausubel's pattern of logic is as follows:

Statement	Logical Pattern	Source
If the hypothesis (above) is true, then the experimental group will score significantly higher than the control group.	If A, then B.	Assumption
For the experimental group to score significantly higher than the control group without the hypothesis being true is extremely unlikely.	B without A is extremely unlikely.	Assumption
The experimental group did score higher than the control group.	B is true.	Experimental evidence
Therefore: The hypothesis is *very much more credible*.	A is very much more credible.	Polyá(4) (Pattern IV)

Two comments seem in order, First, Ausubel by presenting additional data and by including theoretical considerations admirably supported his premises. Secondly, the conclusion is not qualified, in the manner of Polyá's paradigms except in the use of the word "supports" rather than the word "proves."

This analysis has attempted to identify the implicit assumptions that are involved in the research logic of Ausubel's study. In this case, the assumptions seem tenable.

Another example may further illustrate the value of this analysis. A study designed to determine whether problems which teachers recognize in pupil behaviors agree with those which pupils themselves identify, was reported by Amos and Washington.(2) They concluded that the teachers in their study "appeared especially unaware of the extent of student problems in the areas of Money, Work, the Future, and Health and Physical Development." What series of arguments led to this conclusion? Again, it must be said that attributions of arguments is a risky business, but let us assume that the researchers may have argued: If teachers are unaware of the extent of students' problems in certain areas, then there will be a discrepancy between teachers' marking of the Mooney Problem Check List and the students' own responses. On the other hand, the researchers may have asserted: If there is a discrepancy between the teachers' and students' scores on specific areas on the Mooney Problem Check List, then teachers are unaware of the extent of student's problems in these areas. Which premise seems more likely to be true? The second seems to suffer from the fact that many other hypotheses may explain observed discrepancies between the teachers' and the students' scores. The first statement seems more likely to inspire our confidence, if either does. From this premise, the researchers may argue:

PATTERN V

Statement	Logical Pattern	Source
If teachers are unaware of the extent of students' problems in specific areas, then there will be a discrepancy between the teachers' and students' marking of the Mooney Problem Check List.	If A, then B.	Assumption
There is a discrepancy.	B is true.	Experimental evidence
Therefore: It is credible that teachers are unaware of the extent of students' problems in specific areas.	A is credible.	Polyá's paradigm (Pattern III)

Again some comments are in order. First, the authors did qualify their conclusions to the extent that they used the word "appeared" in their report of findings. But unlike the Ausubel study, Amos and Washington were unable to include the additional premise of the form; B without A is extremely unlikely. The reasons for their being unable to include this statement in their argument are made abundantly clear in their discussion. Since their inference pattern is Polyá's basic one (Pattern III), unsupported by additional minor premises, one wonders if their conclusions should not be more severely qualified.

Perhaps I have attributed arguments to Ausubel or to Amos and Washington that were not the ones they were utilizing. In any case, it would seem important that researchers make their arguments explicit so that we may better understand their research and so that they may take precautions to defend their assumptions with additional evidence or logic. In this way, researchers may make their research more readable and more rigorous.

References

(1) Allendoerfer, C. B., and C. O. Oakley. *Principles of Mathematics* New York: McGraw-Hill Book Company, 1955.

(2) Amos, Robert T., and R. M. Washington. "A Comparison of Pupil and Teacher Perceptions of Pupil Problems" *The Journal of Educational Psychology*, 51:5 October, 1960.

(3) Ausubel, David. "The Use of Advance Organizers in the Learning and Retention of Meaningful Verbal Material" *The Journal of Educational Psychology*, 51:5 October, 1960.

(4) Polyá, G. *Patterns of Plausible Inference Mathematics and Plausible Reasoning* Volume II. Princeton, New Jersey: Princeton University Press, 1954.

John R. Platt

Strong Inference

Frequently research follows the pattern of formulating a hypothesis, deducing a consequence, testing the consequence, and using the result of the test as support for the hypothesis, or—if the results were negative—saying that the hypothesis was not supported (but rarely giving up the hypothesis). This process is what Platt would call weak inference. He is an advocate of strong inference: the process by which the results of an experiment may be used to eliminate an alternative hypothesis. The vast bulk of educational research falls into the weak inference pattern. If educational research is to make the kind of impact that is necessary to further the process of education, it appears reasonable that we may have to adopt the procedures implicitly advocated by Platt in order to make the kind of strides that he indicates can be, and have been made, in other areas.

John R. Platt, "Strong Inference," *Science*, 146:347-52, October 16, 1964. Reprinted with permission.

Scientists these days tend to keep up a polite fiction that all science is equal. Except for the work of the misguided opponent whose arguments we happen to be refuting at the time, we speak as though every scientist's field and methods of study are as good as every other scientist's, and perhaps a little better. This keeps us all cordial when it comes to recommending each other for government grants.

But I think anyone who looks at the matter closely will agree that some fields of science are moving forward very much faster than others, perhaps by an order of magnitude, if numbers could be put on such estimates. The discoveries leap from the headlines—and they are real advances in complex and difficult subjects, like molecular biology and high-energy physics. As Alvin Weinberg says (1), "Hardly a month goes by without a stunning success in molecular biology being reported in the Proceedings of the National Academy of Sciences."

Why should there be such rapid advances in some fields and not in others? I think the usual explanations that we tend to think of—such as the tractability of the subject, or the quality or education of the men drawn into it, or the size of research contracts—are important but inadequate. I have begun to believe that the primary factor in scientific advance is an intellectual one. These rapidly moving fields are fields where a particular method of doing scientific research is systematically used and taught, an accumulative method of inductive inference that is so effective that I think it should be given the name of "strong inference." I believe it is important to examine this method, its use and history and rationale, and to see whether other groups and individuals might learn to adopt it profitably in their own scientific and intellectual work.

In its separate elements, strong inference is just the simple and old-fashioned method of inductive inference that goes back to Francis Bacon. The steps are familiar to every college student and are practiced, off and on, by every scientist. The difference comes in their systematic application. Strong inference consists of applying the following steps to every problem in science, formally and explicitly and regularly:

(1) Devising alternative hypotheses;

(2) Devising a crucial experiment (or several of them), with alternative possible outcomes, each of which will, as nearly as possible, exclude one or more of the hypotheses;

(3) Carrying out the experiment so as to get a clean result;

(1′) Recycling the procedure, making subhypotheses or sequential hypotheses to refine the possibilities that remain; and so on.

It is like climbing a tree. At the first fork, we choose—or, in this case, "nature" or the experimental outcome chooses—to go to the right branch or the left; at the next fork, to go left or right; and so on. There are similar branch points in a "conditional computer program," where the next move depends on the result of the last calculation. And there is a "conditional inductive tree" or "logical tree" of this kind written out in detail in many first-year chemistry books, in the table of steps for qualitative analysis of an unknown sample, where the student is led through a real problem of consecutive inference: Add reagent A; if you get a red precipitate, it is subgroup alpha and you filter and add reagent B; if not, you add the other reagent, B′; and so on.

On any new problem, of course, inductive inference is not as simple and certain as deduction, because it involves reaching out into the unknown. Steps 1 and 2 require intellectual inventions, which must be cleverly chosen so that hypothesis, experiment, outcome, and exclusion will be related in a rigorous syllogism; and the question of how to generate such inventions is one which has been extensively discussed elsewhere (2, 3). What the formal schema reminds us to do is to try to make these inventions, to take the next step, to proceed to the next fork, without dawdling or getting tied up in irrelevancies.

It is clear why this makes for rapid and powerful progress. For exploring the unknown, there is no faster method; this is the minimum sequence of steps. Any conclusion that is not an exclusion is insecure and must be rechecked. Any delay in recycling to the next set of hypotheses is only a delay. Strong inference, and the logical tree it generates, are to inductive reasoning what the syllogism is to deductive reasoning, in that it offers a regular method for reaching firm inductive conclusions one after the other as rapidly as possible.

"But what is so novel about this?" someone will say. This is *the* method of science and always has been; why give it a special name? The reason is that many of us have almost forgotten it. Science is now an everyday business. Equipment, calculations, lectures become ends in themselves. How many of us write down our alternatives and crucial experiments every day, focusing on the *exclusion* of a hypothesis? We may write our scientific papers so that it looks as if we had steps 1, 2, and 3 in mind all along. But in between, we do busywork. We become "method-oriented" rather than "problem-oriented." We say we prefer to "feel our way" toward generalizations. We fail to teach our students how to sharpen up their inductive inferences. And we do not realize the added power that the regular and explicit use of alternative hypotheses and sharp exclusions could give us at every step of our research.

The difference between the average scientist's informal methods and the methods of the strong-inference users is somewhat like the difference between a gasoline engine that fires occasionally and one that fires in steady sequence. If our motorboat engines were as erratic as our deliberate intellectual efforts, most of us would not get home for supper.

MOLECULAR BIOLOGY

The new molecular biology is a field where I think this systematic method of inference has become widespread and effective. It is a complex field; yet a succession of crucial experiments over the past decade has given us a surprisingly detailed understanding of hereditary mechanisms and the control of enzyme formation and protein synthesis.

The logical structure shows in every experiment. In 1953 James Watson and Francis Crick proposed that the DNA molecule—the "hereditary substance" in a cell— is a long two-stranded helical molecule (4). This suggested a number of alternatives for crucial test. Do the two strands of the helix stay together when a cell divides, or do they separate? Matthew Meselson and Franklin Stahl used an ingenious isotope-density-labeling technique which showed that they separate (5). Does the DNA helix always have two strands, or can it have three, as atomic models suggest? Alexander Rich showed it can have either, depending on the ionic concentration (6). These are the kinds of experiments John Dalton would have liked, where the combining entities are not atoms but long macromolecular strands.

Or take a different sort of question: Is the "genetic map"—showing the statistical relationship of different genetic characteristics in recombination experiments—a one-dimensional map like the DNA molecule (that is, a linear map), as T. H. Morgan proposed in 1911, or does it have two-dimensional loops or branches? Seymour Benzer showed that his hundreds of fine microgenetic experiments on bacteria would fit only the mathematical matrix for the one-dimensional case (7).

But of course, selected crucial experiments of this kind can be found in every field. The real difference in molecular biology is that formal inductive inference is so systematically practiced and taught. On any given morning at the Laboratory of Molecular Biology in Cambridge, England, the blackboards of Francis Crick or Sidney Brenner will commonly be found covered with logical trees. On the top line will be the hot new result just up from the laboratory or just in by letter or rumor. On the next line will be two or three alternative explanations, or a little list of "What he did wrong." Underneath will be a series of suggested experiments or controls that can reduce the number of possibilities. And so on. The tree grows during the day as one man or another comes in and argues about why one of the experiments wouldn't work, or how it should be changed.

The strong-inference attitude is evident just in the style and language in which the papers are written. For example, in analyzing theories of antibody formation, Joshua Lederberg (8) gives a list of nine propositions "subject to denial," discussing which ones would be "most vulnerable to experimental test."

The papers of the French leaders François Jacob and Jacques Monod are also celebrated for their high "logical density," with paragraph after paragraph of linked "inductive syllogisms." But the style is widespread. Start with the first paper in the *Journal of Molecular Biology* for 1964 (9), and you immediately find: "Our conclusions . . . might be invalid if . . . (i) . . . (ii) . . . or (iii). . . . We shall describe experiments which eliminate these alternatives." The average physicist or chemist or scientist in any field accustomed to less closely reasoned articles and less sharply stated inferences will find it a salutary experience to dip into that journal almost at random.

RESISTANCE TO ANALYTICAL METHODOLOGY

This analytical approach to biology has sometimes become almost a crusade, because it arouses so much resistance in many scientists who have grown up in a more relaxed and diffuse tradition. At the 1958 Conference on Biophysics, at Boulder, there was a dramatic confrontation between the two points of view. Leo Szilard said: "The problems of how enzymes are induced, of how proteins are synthesized, of how antibodies are formed, are closer to solution than is generally believed. If you do stupid experiments, and finish one a year, it can take 50 years. But if you stop doing experiments for a little while and *think* how proteins can possibly be synthesized, there are only about 5 different ways, not 50! And it will take only a few experiments to distinguish these."

One of the young men added: "It is essentially the old question: How *small* and *elegant* an experiment can you perform?"

These comments upset a number of those present. An electron microscopist said, "Gentlemen, this is off the track. This is philosophy of science."

Szilard retorted, "I was not quarreling with third-rate scientists: I was quarreling with first-rate scientists."

A physical chemist hurriedly asked. "Are we going to take the official photograph before lunch or after lunch?"

But this did not deflect the dispute. A distinguished cell biologist rose and said, "No two cells give the same properties. Biology is the science of heterogeneous systems." And he added privately, "You know there are *scientists;* and there are people in science who are just working with these over simplified model systems—DNA chains and in vitro systems —who are not doing science at all. We need their auxiliary work: they build apparatus, they make minor studies, but they are not scientists."

To which Cy Levinthal replied: "Well, there are two kinds of biologists, those who are looking to see if there is one thing that can be understood, and those who keep saying it is very complicated and that nothing can be understood. . . . You must study the *simplest* system you think has the properties you are interested in."

As they were leaving the meeting, one man could be heard muttering, "What does Szilard expect me to do—shoot myself?"

Any criticism or challenge to consider changing our methods strikes of course at all our ego-defenses. But in this case the analytical method offers the possibility of such great increases in effectiveness that it is unfortunate that it cannot be regarded more often as a challenge to learning rather than as a challenge to combat. Many of the recent triumphs in molecular biology have in fact been achieved on just such "oversimplified model systems," very much along the analytical lines laid down in the 1958 discussion. They have not fallen to the kind of men who justify themselves by saying, "No two cells are alike," regardless of how true that may ultimately be. The triumphs are in fact triumphs of a new way of thinking.

HIGH-ENERGY PHYSICS

This analytical thinking is rare, but it is by no means restricted to the new biology. High-energy physics is another field where the logic of exclusions is obvious, even in the newspaper accounts. For example, in the famous discovery of C. N. Yang and T. D. Lee, the question that was asked was: Do the fundamental particles conserve mirror-symmetry or "parity" in certain reactions, or do they not? The crucial experiments were suggested; within a few months they were done, and conservation of parity was found to be excluded. Richard Garwin, Leon Lederman, and Marcel Weinrich did one of the crucial experiments. It was thought of one evening at suppertime; by midnight they had rearranged the apparatus for it; and by 4 a.m. they had picked up the predicted pulses showing the nonconservation of parity (10). The phenomena had just been waiting, so to speak, for the explicit formulation of the alternative hypotheses.

The theorists in this field take pride in trying to predict new properties or new particles explicitly enough so that if they are not found the theories will fall. As the biologist W. A. H. Rushton has said (11), "A theory which cannot be mortally endangered cannot be alive." Murray Gell-Mann and Yuval Ne'eman recently used the particle grouping which they call "The Eightfold Way" to predict a missing particle, the Omega-Minus, which was then looked for and found (12). But one alternative branch of the theory would predict a particle with one-third the usual electronic charge, and it was not found in the experiments, so this branch must be rejected.

The logical tree is so much a part of high-energy physics that some stages of it are commonly built, in fact, into the electronic coincidence circuits that detect the particles and trigger the bubble-chamber photographs. Each kind of particle should give a different kind of pattern in the electronic counters, and the circuits can be set to exclude or include whatever types of events are desired. If the distinguishing criteria are sequential, they may even run through a complete logical tree in a microsecond or so. This electronic preliminary analysis, like human preliminary analysis of alternative outcomes, speeds up progress by sharpening the criteria. It eliminates hundreds of thousands of the irrelevant pictures that formerly had to be scanned, and when it is carried to its limit, a few output pulses, hours apart, may be enough to signal the existence of the antiproton or the fall of a theory.

I think the emphasis on strong inference in the two fields I have mentioned has been partly the result of personal leadership, such as that of the classical geneticists in molecular biology, or of Szilard with his "Midwest Chowder and Bacteria Society" at Chicago in 1948–50, or of Max Delbrück with his summer courses in phage genetics at Cold Spring Harbor. But it is also partly due to the nature of the fields themselves. Biology, with its vast informational detail and complexity, is a "high-information" field, where years and decades can easily be wasted on the usual type of "low-information" observations or experiments if one does not think carefully in advance about what the most important and conclusive experiments would be. And in high-energy physics, both the "information flux" of particles from the new accelerators and the million-dollar costs of operation have forced a similar analytical approach. It pays to have a top-notch group debate every experiment ahead of time; and the habit spreads throughout the field.

INDUCTION AND MULTIPLE HYPOTHESES

Historically, I think, there have been two main contributions to the development of a satisfactory strong-inference method. The first is that of Francis Bacon (*13*). He wanted a "surer method" of "finding out nature" than either the logic-chopping or all-inclusive theories of the time or the laudable but crude attempts to make inductions "by simple enumeration." He did not merely urge experiments, as some suppose; he showed the fruitfulness of interconnecting theory and experiment so that the one checked the other. Of the many inductive procedures he suggested, the most important, I think, was the conditional inductive tree, which proceeded from alternative hypotheses (possible "causes," as he calls them), through crucial experiments ("Instances of the Finger-post"), to exclusion of some alternatives and adoption of what is left ("establishing axioms"). His Instances of the Fingerpost are explicitly at the forks in the logical tree, the term being borrowed "from the fingerposts which are set up where roads part, to indicate the several directions."

Many of his crucial experiments proposed in Book II of *The New Organon* are still fascinating. For example, in order to decide whether the weight of a body is due to its "inherent nature," as some had said, or is due to the attraction of the earth, which would decrease with distance, he proposes comparing the rate of a pendulum clock and a spring clock and then lifting them from the earth to the top of a tall steeple. He concludes that if the pendulum clock on the steeple "goes more slowly than it did on account of the diminished virtue of its weights . . . we may take the attraction of the mass of the earth as the cause of weight."

Here was a method that could separate off the empty theories!

Bacon said the inductive method could be learned by anybody, just like learning to "draw a straighter line or more perfect circle . . . with the help of a ruler or a pair of compasses." "My way of discovering sciences goes far to level men's wit and leaves but little to individual excellence because it performs everything by the surest rules and demonstrations." Even occasional mistakes would not be fatal. "Truth will sooner come out from error than from confusion."

It is easy to see why young minds leaped to try it.

Nevertheless there is a difficulty with this method. As Bacon empha-sizes, it is necessary to make "exclusions." He says, "The induction which is to be available for the discovery and demonstration of sciences and arts, must analyze nature by proper rejections and exclusions; and then, after a sufficient number of negatives, come to a conclusion on the affirmative instances." [To man] it is granted only to proceed at first by negatives, and at last to end in affirmatives after exclusion has been exhausted."

Or, as the philosopher Karl Popper says today, there is no such thing as proof in science—because some later alternative explanation may be as good or better—so that science advances only by disproofs. There is no point in making hypotheses that are not falsifiable, because such hypotheses do not say anything; "it must be possible for an empirical scientific system to be refuted by experience" (*14*).

The difficulty is that disproof is a hard doctrine. If you have a hypothesis and I have another hypothesis, evidently one of them must be eliminated. The scientist seems to have no choice but to be either soft-headed or disputatious. Perhaps this is why so many tend to resist the strong analytical approach—and why some great scientists are so disputatious.

Fortunately, it seems to me, this difficulty can be removed by the use of a second great intellectual invention, the "method of multiple hypotheses," which is what was needed to round out the Baconian scheme. This is a method that was put forward by T. C. Chamberlin (15), a geologist at Chicago at the turn of the century, who is best known for his contribution to the Chamberlin-Moulton hypothesis of the origin of the solar system.

Chamberlin says our trouble is that when we make a single hypothesis, we become attached to it.

"The moment one has offered an original explanation for a phenomenon which seems satisfactory, that moment affection for his intellectual child springs into existence, and as the explanation grows into a definite theory his parental affections cluster about his offspring and it grows more and more dear to him. . . . There springs up also unwittingly a pressing of the theory to make it fit the facts and a pressing of the facts to make them fit the theory. . . .

"To avoid this grave danger, the method of multiple working hypotheses is urged. It differs from the simple working hypothesis in that it distributes the effort and divides the affections. . . . Each hypothesis suggests its own criteria, its own means of proof, its own method of developing the truth, and if a group of hypotheses encompass the subject on all sides, the total outcome of means and of methods is full and rich."

Chamberlin thinks the method "leads to certain distinctive habits of mind" and is of prime value in education. "When faithfully followed for a sufficient time, it develops a mode of thought of its own kind which may be designated the habit of complex thought. . . ."

This charming paper deserves to be reprinted in some more accessible journal today, where it could be required reading for every graduate student—and for every professor.

It seems to me that Chamberlin has hit on the explanation—and the cure—for many of our problems in the sciences. The conflict and exclusion of alternatives that is necessary to sharp inductive inference has been all too often a conflict between men, each with his single Ruling Theory. But whenever each man begins to have multiple working hypotheses, it becomes purely a conflict between ideas. It becomes

much easier then for each of us to aim every day at conclusive disproofs—at *strong* inference—without either reluctance or combative-
ness. In fact, when there are multiple hypotheses which are not anyone's "personal property" and when there are crucial experiments to
test them, the daily life in the laboratory takes on an interest and
excitement it never had, and the students can hardly wait to get to work
to see how the detective story will come out. It seems to me that this
is the reason for the development of those "distinctive habits of mind"
and the "complex thought" that Chamberlin described, the reason for
the sharpness, the excitement, the zeal, the teamwork—yes, even
international teamwork—in molecular biology and high-energy physics
today. What else could be so effective?

When multiple hypotheses become coupled to strong inference,
the scientific search becomes an emotional powerhouse as well as an
intellectual one.

Unfortunately, I think, there are other areas of science today that
are sick by comparison, because they have forgotten the necessity
for alternative hypotheses and disproof. Each man has only one branch
—or none—on the logical tree, and it twists at random without ever
coming to the need for a crucial decision at any point. We can see from
the external symptoms that there is something scientifically wrong.
The Frozen Method. The Eternal Surveyor. The Never Finished. The
Great Man With a Single Hypothesis. The Little Club of Dependents.
The Vendetta. The All-Encompassing Theory Which Can Never Be
Falsified.

Some cynics tell a story, which may be apocryphal, about the theoretical chemist who explained to his class.

"And thus we see that the C-Cl bond is longer in the first compound
than in the second because the percent of ionic character is smaller."

A voice from the back of the room said, "But Professor X, according
to the Table, the C-Cl bond is shorter in the first compound."

"Oh, is it?" said the professor. "Well, that's still easy to understand,
because the double-bond character is higher in that compound."

To the extent that this kind of story is accurate, a "theory" of this
sort is not a theory at all, because it does not exclude anything. It predicts everything, and therefore does not predict anything. It becomes
simply a verbal formula which the graduate student repeats and believes because the professor has said it so often. This is not science,
but faith; not theory, but theology. Whether it is hand-waving or
number-waving or equation-waving, a theory is not a theory unless it
can be disproved. That is, unless it can be falsified by some possible
experimental outcome.

In chemistry, the resonance theorists will of course suppose that I am criticizing *them*, while the molecular-orbital theorists will suppose I am criticizing *them*. But their actions—our actions, for I include myself among them—speak for themselves. A failure to agree for 30 years is public advertisement of a failure to disprove.

My purpose here, however, is not to call names but rather to say that we are all sinners, and that in every field and in every laboratory we need to try to formulate multiple alternative hypotheses sharp enough to be capable of disproof.

SYSTEMATIC APPLICATION

I think the work methods of a number of scientists have been testimony to the power of strong inference. Is success not due in many cases to systematic use of Bacon's "surest rules and demonstrations" as much as to rare and unattainable intellectual power? Faraday's famous diary (*16*), or Fermi's notebooks (*3, 17*), show how these men believed in the effectiveness of daily steps in applying formal inductive methods to one problem after another.

Within 8 weeks after the discovery of x-rays, Roentgen had identified 17 of their major properties. Every student should read his first paper (*18*). Each demonstration in it is a little jewel of inductive inference. How else could the proofs have gone so fast, except by a method of maximum effectiveness?

Organic chemistry has been the spiritual home of strong inference from the beginning. Do the bonds alternate in benzene or are they equivalent? If the first, there should be five disubstituted derivatives; if the second, three. And three it is (*19*). This is a *strong*-inference test— not a matter of measurement, of whether there are grams or milligrams of the products, but a matter of logical alternatives. How else could the tetrahedral carbon atom or the hexagonal symmetry of benzene have been inferred 50 years before the inferences could be confirmed by x-ray and infrared measurement?

We realize that it was out of this kind of atmosphere that Pasteur came to the field of biology. Can anyone doubt that he brought with him a completely different method of reasoning? Every 2 or 3 years he moved to one biological problem after another, from optical activity to the fermentation of beet sugar, to the "diseases" of wine and beer, to the disease of silkworms, to the problem of "spontaneous generation," to the anthrax disease of sheep, to rabies. In each of these fields there were experts in Europe who knew a hundred times as much as Pasteur, yet each time he solved problems in a few months that they had not been able to solve. Obviously it was not encyclopedic knowledge that produced his success, and obviously it was not simply luck, when it was repeated over and over again; it can only have been the systematic power of a special method of exploration. Are bacteria falling in? Make the necks of the flasks S-shaped. Are bacteria sucked in by the partial vacuum? Put in a cotton plug. Week after week his crucial experiments build up the logical tree of exclusions. The drama of strong inference in molecular biology today is only a repetition of Pasteur's story.

The grand scientific syntheses, like those of Newton and Maxwell, are rare and individual achievements that stand outside any rule or method. Nevertheless it is interesting to note that several of the great synthesizers have also shown the strong-inference habit of thought in their other work, as Newton did in the inductive proofs of his *Opticks* and Maxwell did in his experimental proof that three and only three colors are needed in color vision.

A YARDSTICK OF EFFECTIVENESS

I think the evident effectiveness of the systematic use of strong inference suddenly gives us a yardstick for thinking about the effectiveness of scientific methods in general. Surveys, taxonomy, design of equipment, systematic measurements and tables, theoretical computations—all have their proper and honored place, provided they are parts of a chain of precise induction of how nature works. Unfortunately, all too often they become ends in themselves, mere time-serving from the point of view of real scientific advance, a hypertrophied methodology that justifies itself as a lore of respectability.

We praise the "lifetime of study," but in dozens of cases, in every field, what was needed was not a lifetime but rather a few short months or weeks of analytical inductive inference. In any new area we should try, like Roentgen, to see how fast we can pass from the general survey to analytical inferences. We should try, like Pasteur, to see whether we can reach strong inferences that encyclopedism could not discern.

We speak piously of taking measurements and making small studies that will "add another brick to the temple of science." Most such bricks just lie around the brickyard (20). Tables of constants have their place and value, but the study of one spectrum after another, if not frequently re-evaluated, may become a substitute for thinking, a sad waste of intelligence in a research laboratory, and a mistraining whose crippling effects may last a lifetime.

To paraphrase an old saying, Beware of the man of one method or one instrument, either experimental or theoretical. He tends to become method-oriented rather than problem-oriented. The method-oriented man is shackled; the problem-oriented man is at least reaching freely toward what is most important. Strong inference redirects a man to problem-orientation, but it requires him to be willing repeatedly to put aside his last methods and teach himself new ones.

On the other hand, I think that anyone who asks the question about scientific effectiveness will also conclude that much of the mathematicizing in physics and chemistry today is irrelevant if not misleading.

The great value of mathematical formulation is that when an experiment agrees with a calculation to five decimal places, a great many alternative hypotheses are pretty well excluded (though the Bohr theory and the Schrödinger theory both predict exactly the same Rydberg constant!). But when the fit is only to two decimal places, or one, it may be a trap for the unwary; it may be no better than any rule-of-thumb extrapolation, and some other kind of qualitative exclusion might be more rigorous for testing the assumptions and more important to scientific understanding than the quantitative fit.

I know that this is like saying that the emperor has no clothes. Today we preach that science is not science unless it is quantitative. We substitute correlations for causal studies, and physical equations for organic reasoning. Measurements and equations are supposed to sharpen thinking, but, in my observation, they more often tend to make the thinking noncausal and fuzzy. They tend to become the object of scientific manipulation instead of auxiliary tests of crucial inferences.

Many—perhaps most—of the great issues of science are qualitative, not quantitative, even in physics and chemistry. Equations and measurements are useful when and only when they are related to proof; but proof or disproof comes first and is in fact strongest when it is absolutely convincing without any quantitative measurement.

Or to say it another way, you can catch phenomena in a logical box or in a mathematical box. The logical box is coarse but strong. The mathematical box is fine-grained but flimsy. The mathematical box is a beautiful way of wrapping up a problem, but it will not hold the phenomena unless they have been caught in a logical box to begin with.

What I am saying is that, in numerous areas that we call science, we have come to like our habitual ways, and our studies that can be continued indefinitely. We measure, we define, we compute, we analyze, but we do not exclude. And this is not the way to use our minds most effectively or to make the fastest progress in solving scientific questions.

Of course it is easy—and all too common—for one scientist to call the others unscientific. My point is not that my particular conclusions here are necessarily correct, but that we have long needed some absolute standard of possible scientific effectiveness by which to measure how well we are succeeding in various areas—a standard that many could agree on and one that would be undistorted by the scientific pressures and fashions of the times and the vested interests and busywork that they develop. It is not public evaluation I am interested in so much as a private measure by which to compare one's own scientific performance with what it might be. I believe that strong inference provides this kind of standard of what the maximum possible scientific effectiveness could be—as well as a recipe for reaching it.

AIDS TO STRONG INFERENCE

How can we learn the method and teach it? It is not difficult. The most important thing is to keep in mind that this kind of thinking is not a lucky knack but a system that *can* be taught and learned. The molecular biologists today are living proof of it. The second thing is to be explicit and formal and regular about it, to devote a half hour or an hour to analytical thinking every day, writing out the logical tree and the alternatives and crucial experiments explicitly in a permanent notebook. I have discussed elsewhere (3) the value of Fermi's notebook method, the effect it had on his colleagues and students, and the testimony that it "can be adopted by anyone with profit."

It is true that it takes great courtesy to teach the method, especially to one's peers—or their students. The strong-inference point of view is so resolutely critical of methods of work and values in science that any attempt to compare specific cases is likely to sound both smug and destructive. Mainly one should try to teach it by example and by exhorting to self-analysis and self-improvement only in general terms, as I am doing here.

But I will mention one severe but useful private test—a touchstone of strong inference—that removes the necessity for third-person criticism, because it is a test that anyone can learn to carry with him for use as needed. It is our old friend the Baconian "exclusion," but I call it "The Question." Obviously it should be applied as much to one's own thinking as to others'. It consists of asking in your own mind, on hearing any scientific explanation or theory put forward, "But sir, what experiment could *dis*prove your hypothesis?"; or, on hearing a scientific experiment described, "But sir, what hypothesis does your experiment *dis*prove?"

This goes straight to the heart of the matter. It forces everyone to refocus on the central question of whether there is or is not a testable scientific step forward.

If such a question were asked aloud, many a supposedly great scientist would sputter and turn livid and would want to throw the questioner out, as a hostile witness! Such a man is less than he appears, for he is obviously not accustomed to think in terms of alternative hypotheses and crucial experiments for himself; and one might also wonder about the state of science in the field he is in. But who knows? —the question might educate him, and his field too!

On the other hand, I think that throughout most of molecular biology and nuclear physics the response to The Question would be to outline immediately not one but several tests to disprove the hypothesis—and it would turn out that the speaker already had two or three graduate students working on them!

I almost think that government agencies could make use of this kind of touchstone. It is not true that all science is equal, or that we cannot justly compare the effectiveness of scientists by any method other than a mutual-recommendation system. The man to watch, the man to put your money on, is not the man who wants to make "a survey" or a "more detailed study" but the man with the notebook, the man with the alternative hypotheses and the crucial experiments, the man who knows how to answer your Question of disproof and is already working on it.

There are some really hard problems, some high-information problems, ahead of us in several fields, problems of photosynthesis, of cellular organization, of the molecular structure and organization of the nervous system, not to mention some of our social and international problems. It seems to me that the method of most rapid progress in such complex areas, the most effective way of using our brains, is going to be to set down explicitly at each step just what the question is, and what all the alternatives are, and then to set up crucial experiments to try to disprove some. Problems of this complexity, if they can be solved at all, can be solved only by men generating and excluding possibilities with maximum effectiveness, to obtain a high degree of information per unit time—men willing to work a little bit at thinking.

When whole groups of us begin to concentrate like that, I believe we may see the molecular-biology phenomenon repeated over and over again, with order-of-magnitude increases in the rate of scientific understanding in almost every field.

References and Notes

1. A. M. Weinberg, *Minerva* 1963, 159 (Winter 1963); *Phys. Today* 17, 42 (1964).

2. G. Polyá, *Mathematics and Plausible Reasoning* (Princeton Univ. Press, Princeton, N. J., 1954), vol. 1, *Induction and Analogy in Mathematics;* vol. 2, *Patterns of Plausible Inference.*

3. J. R. Platt, *The Excitement of Science* (Houghton Mifflin Co., Boston, 1962); see especially chapters 7 and 8.

4. J. D. Watson and F. H. C. Crick, *Nature* 171, 737 (1953).

5. M. Meselson and F. Stahl, *Proc. Natl. Acad. Sci. U. S.* 44, 671 (1958).

6. A. Rich, in *Biophysical Science: A Study Program*, J. L. Oncley *et al.*, Eds. (John Wiley & Sons, Inc., New York, 1959), p. 191.

7. S. Benzer, *Proc. Natl. Acad. Sci. U.S.* 45, 1607 (1959).

8. J. Lederberg, *Science* 129, 1649 (1959).

9. P. F. Davison, D. Freifelder, B. W. Holloway, *J. Mol. Biol.* 8, 1 (1964).

10. R. L. Garwin, L. M. Lederman, M. Weinrich, *Phys. Rev.* 105, 1415 (1957).

11. W. A. H. Rushton, personal communication.

12. See G. F. Chew, M. Gell-Mann, A. H. Rosenfeld, *Sci. Am.* 210, 74 (Feb. 1964); *ibid.* 210, 60 (Apr. 1964); *ibid.* 210, 54 (June 1964).

13. F. Bacon, *The New Organon and Related Writings* (Liberal Arts Press, New York, 1960), especially pp. 98, 112, 151, 156, 196.

14. K. R. Popper, *The Logic of Scientific Discovery* (Basic Books, New York, 1959), p. 41. A modified view is given by T. S. Kuhn, *The Structure of Scientific Revolutions* (Univ. of Chicago Press, Chicago, 1962), p. 146; it does not, I believe, invalidate any of these conclusions.

15. T. C. Chamberlin, *J. Geol.* 5, 837 (1897). I am indebted to Professors Preston Cloud and Bryce Crawford, Jr., of the University of Minnesota for correspondence on this article and a classroom reprint of it.

16. M. Faraday, *Faraday's Diary 1820-62* (Bell, London, 1932-36).

17. H. L. Anderson and S. K. Allison, *Rev. Mod. Phys.* 27, 273 (1955).

18. E. C. Watson [*Am. J. Phys.* 13, 281 (1945)] gives an English translation of both of Roentgen's first papers on x-rays.

19. See G. W. Wheland, *Advanced Organic Chemistry* (John Wiley & Sons, Inc., New York, 1949), chapter 4, for numerous such examples.

20. B. K. Forscher, *Science* 142, 339 (1963).

chapter 2

Educational Research: Problem Identification and Hypothesis Development

Although it is apparent to all college advisors that the field of education is "just bristling with problems" to be selected and solved, no such clarity of insight is given the poor student, who too often finds that all of his ideas about research topics fall in the category of "too big," "too small," "already done," "incapable of solution," "beyond his resources and talents," and so on.[1]

Mouly's concern for the poor student ("poor" is defined as pathetic both in this discussion and in Mouly) is neither uncommon nor exactly accurate. Smith, in a study of research proposals submitted to the United States Office of Education (USOE) Cooperative Research program, presents data which imply that "all college advisors" are not so enlightened. He found problem statements submitted by college and university faculty members to have the following frequency of inadequacies.[2]

Inadequacy	*Percentage*
Problem insignificant	66
Theoretical framework inadequate or lacking	87
Problem not delimited	25
Problem unclear or incomplete	26
Key definitions lacking	32

---

[1] George J. Mouly, *The Science of Educational Research* (New York: American Book Company, 1963), p. 77.

[2] Gerald R. Smith, "Inadequacies in a Selected Sample of Unpublished Research Proposals," unpublished doctoral dissertation, Teachers College, Columbia University, 1964, p. 71.

The finding that college professors have the same weaknesses as their students in selecting and developing a research problem should come as no surprise. After all, many graduate students become professors. Unless something different is attempted in the educational program the second generation will look very much like the first.

In an attempt to develop an instrument for evaluating the methodological adequacy of research reports,[3] one of the editors of this volume examined the bulk of the literature on current research process. In light of this examination of the several ways the concept problem is treated, it is not surprising that college faculty members and their students do not easily see the problems with which the field of education is "just bristling." For example Van Dalen says:

> Since identifying the exact nature of a problem is of major importance in research, it is essential that an investigator learn how to recognize and define one. How does one locate problems? What conditions give rise to them? John Dewey answered these questions by suggesting that a problem arises out of some felt-difficulty. Something puzzles or disturbs an individual; a gnawing dissatisfaction nibbles at his peace of mind until he can locate precisely what is bothering him and find some means of solving it.[4]

Unfortunately, as Smith's findings and Mouly's student categories indicate, just any "felt-difficulty" will not do. The problem has to be "significant," not "too big," nor "too small," or the like. The editors believe that failure to define these quality qualifiers does more to create the problem-blindness illusion than any inherent characteristic of the potential researcher. What is "significant"? Whose value system shall we accept? Until such questions are answered the potential researcher has a rubber ruler with which to measure the existence of a researchable problem, for by one set of standards it may be "significant," while by another set it will be "insignificant."

A second means of communicating about what a problem is can be seen in the here-are-problems-that-have-been-studied approach

---

3 William J. Gephart, "Development of an Instrument for Evaluating Reports of Educational Research," unpublished doctoral dissertation, The Ohio State University, 1965. (Also, U. S. Department of Health, Education, and Welfare, Office of Education, Cooperative Research, Project No. S-014, University of Wisconsin-Milwaukee, 1964.)

4 Deobold B. Van Dalen, *Understanding Educational Research: An Introduction* (New York: McGraw Hill Book Company, Inc., 1962), p. 109.

used by many authors. Unfortunately, these authors typically follow such a listing with an admonishment that the real scholar seeks an area in which to make an original contribution to the body of knowledge.

For at least two reasons, the listing of previously studied problems fails to provide the student with the meaning of the term "problem." First, the cryptic phrases or single sentences that typically make up such a listing fall far short of identifying and defining a problem. For example, a part of a list of typical studies is:

1. The holding power of schools
2. The participatory costs for pupils
3. The participation level of pupils
4. What the public thinks of its schools

        . . .

20. Recreation practices of youths and adults in the community.[5]

None of these titles define problems until much more information is known. The public may, for example, think its schools are just fine, which either *is* a problem if the schools are not fine and need major changes, or *is not* a problem if the schools are good and do not need to be radically changed.

Even if this first difficulty were rectified, that is, if the student were given greater detail as to what the research area is, he still would not understand what a problem is. This assertion is based upon the belief that the elements of each of the problems in any such list are extremely different: In one case we lack descriptive information about a variable, in another conflicting evidence seems to exist, and so on. Thus it is all but impossible for even the most analytical student to reach the conclusion that when conditions A, B, and C are in evidence, a researchable problem exists.

A third approach in communicating about research problems is that employed by Travers.[6] In this case four general areas of education or education-related activities are identified. Although this approach helps the student know problems exist in this area and in that one, it has weaknesses. Since he still has no criteria for defining a problem, he is not sure what he is reaching for. Further, once he has decided

---

[5] G. D. McGrath, James J. Jelnek, and Raymond E. Wochner, *Educational Research Methods* (New York: The Ronald Press Company, 1963), p. 8.

[6] Robert M. W. Travers, *An Introduction to Educational Research: Second Edition* (New York: The Macmillan Company, 1964), pp. 59-77.

upon something in the area, the previously described "significance" bugaboo raises its head.

Three discussions in the literature give promise of generic definition of the term "problem." Unfortunately two of them[7] are found in material which has a discussion of the scientific method as the focal point and thus only offhand emphasis is given to the definition of the term "problem." Both texts indicate that the scientific method is valuable when we:

1. lack a means for achieving an end;
2. have difficulty in identifying the character of an object;
3. cannot explain an unexpected event.

The third piece of literature which attempts a generative definition of the term "problem" also is not conveniently available. Clark, Guba, and Smith established an outline for a text on the research process which at this writing has not been completed.[8] They define a problem as one of four things: an anomaly, an uncharted area, unverified "facts," and a situation involving conflicting evidence. Hopefully, from these latter foci a cogent definition for the term "problem" will soon be developed so that for future generations of researchers, the problem will not be the problem.

The articles which comprise this chapter were selected to achieve three things. Through the articles by Carroll and Barber and Fox, we hope to develop a mind set to the existence of problems in a specific area and a discussion of the kinds of events that lead two persons to different ends in a problem-recognition situation. Next, a series of four articles is presented that describes the identification, choice, and definition of a specific problem. Finally, in the belief that Platt's strong inference proposal has direct relevance for educational research, two articles are included on hypotheses. The concentration in the first two portions of this chapter leads to a clearly defined problem. At such a point the researcher should be able to conjecture about the existence of additional variables or about relationships between already identified variables. The discussion of the role of such hypothesizing and the need for multiple hypotheses rounds out these selections.

---

[7] McGrath, op. cit., p. 24; Van Dalen, op. cit., p. 23.

[8] David L. Clark, Egon G. Guba, and Gerald R. Smith, "Functions and Definitions of Functions of a Research Proposal or Research Report," Unpublished mimeo (Columbus, Ohio: The Ohio State University, 1962).

John B. Carroll

Neglected Areas in Educational Research

This selection serves as a bridge between Chapters 1 and 2. Chapter 1 represents the discussion of the kind of research that is being carried out in education—the "regressive maneuvers" as Carroll calls them. Chapter 2 is represented by the areas that are identified as neglected in educational research. Even if one does not totally agree with Carroll, a careful reading of the article would yield some notions as to the type of research that might be the most productive and the areas in which this research might be done.

John B. Carroll, "Neglected Areas in Educational Research," Phi Delta Kappan, 42:339-46, May, 1961. Reprinted with permission.

For the past year, at the request of James B. Conant, I have been engaged in surveying the field of educational research in a special way. Instead of simply trying to summarize what educational psychology and educational research have accomplished, I started out with a series of questions about educational policies and practices which I have tried to answer on the basis of research results. The questions I asked were suggested partly by Mr. Conant himself, and partly by my own precognitions as to fundamental issues in the study of school learning processes. What most of these questions have been will, I believe, become evident as you read.

My success in answering the questions I have posed has been far from ideal. To be sure, I have confirmed what we all know—that there are a number of issues and questions to which we can give definite and useful answers. We know a good deal about how to measure mental abilities, scholastic achievements, and certain aspects of interest, attitude, and even personality. We can describe the course of the child's physical, mental, and emotional development and we can give a reasonably satisfactory account of the nature, course, and conditions of learning. We can point to research answers to a good number of specific questions about how we should teach reading, spelling, arithmetic, and other school subjects.

But having mentioned these and a few other topics, we just about reach the limits of our knowledge. Currently available techniques and findings, however valuable they may be for many purposes, do not in my opinion constitute a truly adequate scientific basis for formulating educational policy or for improving the practice of education. In fact, it seems to me that educational psychology has failed to provide sufficient knowledge about some of the central problems in school learning, and I intend to indicate what I believe these problems are. You will see that what I call "neglected areas" in educational research cannot be described as "off-beat" or highly original topics which nobody appears to have thought of, but problems so persistent and fundamental that everybody is at least subconsciously aware of them.

Then why have they been neglected? They have not been completely neglected, of course; there have been numerous studies which could be called relevant to these areas. I call them neglected chiefly because educational research workers have thus far not been able to mobilize the resources and talent required to provide satisfactorily complete answers. But they can also be called "neglected" because certain habits of thinking and research procedure have deflected investigators from making direct assaults on them.

Ideally, educational psychology ought to result in statements about what effects various teaching procedures and other actions would have upon the kinds of student behaviors we do or do not desire as outcomes of education. To be complete, they need to have built into them any relevant qualifications concerning the characteristics of students, the antecedent conditions under which the statements have validity, and so forth. Since education is a life-long process, our statements ought to refer to the expected course of events over time periods of respectable length.

The neglected problems I shall speak about require statements of this general kind for their solution. It is exceedingly hard to find such statements in research literature.

REGRESSIVE MANEUVERS, NOT EXPERIMENTS

One reason it is hard to find them is the fact that educational research workers have been prone to make what might be called "regressive maneuvers" in their contacts with these problems. The establishment of a scientific statement of the kind I have mentioned requires the execution of investigations which are true *experiments*. That is, one must set up an adequate experimental design and arrange for a series of experimental treatments or manipulations. The first regressive maneuver occurs when the investigator decides to do not an experimental study but a correlational study—an after-the-fact description of the results of treatments over which one has no real control.[1] For example, we have recently had a rash of *post hoc* studies purporting to show the "effects" of certain high-school courses on college grades; we cannot tell to what extent the effects are actually due to sampling biases. Perhaps the regressive maneuver which takes one from an experimental study to a correlational study is not seriously wrong, for with proper statistical controls one can often derive useful information from correlational studies of effects, and indeed there are some problems that can probably be studied only in this way.

The next regressive maneuver is more serious—the decision to concentrate simply on methods of measuring phenomena. Measurement studies are indeed needed, but even at this level there is another possible regressive maneuver—the decision to study phenomena by indirect methods of measurement rather than more direct ones. Examples of regressive strategies in research are the use of supervisors' ratings of teaching effectiveness rather than indices of student gain and the use of questionnaires and self-inventories rather than observations of behavior. The final regressive strategy—and a most honored one—is to abandon any attempt to deal with empirical data and retreat into the cloisters which harbor those who concern themselves exclusively with methodological problems—with statistical theory, computational techniques, or mathematical rationales.

Please understand that I do not intend to disparage the activities to which there is regression. I have spent long, happy, and (I believe) productive periods in the methodological cloisters. I am disparaging the fact that the maneuvering in educational research is chiefly *regressive* rather than *progressive*. There has been too much retreat to measurement and methodological studies without a corresponding sign of progression to the kinds of descriptive and experimental studies which are at the real cutting edge of our science. Our journals are full of measurement and methodological studies; it can hardly be said that

---

[1] It is of interest to note that in the first twenty-eight volumes of the *Journal of Experimental Education,* only approximately 20 per cent of the articles can properly be considered reports of *experimental* studies, and there was no perceptible trend towards an increasing proportion of such studies.

they are cluttered with reports of experimental studies. I suspect that we have come to honor methodological rigor and finesse more than we honor substantiality and relevance of results. Most of our progress has been in developing ways of measuring phenomena and treating data.

Investigators also have certain bad habits which have caused their research studies to be inadequately executed and reported, and interpretable with difficulty. One of these is the failure to specify in tangible terms the actual referents of results of educational and psychological measurements. Instead of attempting to state these meanings in something approaching absolute terms, we resort to the use of relative terms. We report percentiles rather than behavior. We report central tendencies without describing the corresponding points on the statistical continuum. The habit of using arbitrary, relative scales of measurement is so ingrained that one can actually find studies which fail to indicate which end of a scale is which. I feel that measurement people have been neglectful in the fact that they fail to indicate what scores really mean in terms of amounts of knowledge or levels of skill attained. Even in the case of personality and interest tests it should be possible to make an approximate translation of test scores into the kinds of behavior they signify.

INCOMPLETE REPORTS

The investigator who reports results even in relative terms on an arbitrary scale is not as delinquent as the investigator who fails to report central tendencies at all. There is an all-too-frequent practice of reporting coefficients of correlation, for example, without at the same time reporting the univariate statistics for the distributions of the underlying variables. One has no way of appraising the general level of phenomena observed, or of assessing the possibilities of restriction of range.

I could not have identified neglected areas if I had not started with a certain field of inquiry. My field of inquiry was defined in terms of a conceptual model of the school learning process. The model states, in quasi-mathematical terms, that for a given individual and a given educational objective or task, the amount of learning is a function of the individual's basic aptitude for learning the task (defined in terms of the amount of time he will require to achieve a specified criterion of performance), his willingness to engage actively in learning for the amount of time necessary to achieve the criterion of performance, the quality of the instruction given him, his ability to understand this instruction, and the amount of time he is allowed to have for learning. This model, I believe, covers the learning of knowledges, skills, and understandings —which constitute a large part of the educational objectives we hold to be desirable—and it can be adapted to cover the learning of attitudes and other behaviors which cannot precisely be conceptualized as performances. And we can give the model a time dimension which allows us to study remote outcomes of learning such as retention and transfer. Presumably, if we knew how the various parts of the model interact— and if we knew what parameters and conditions apply to this model— we would have a large part of the knowledge we need to guide the course of learning in our schools or anywhere else that learning occurs.

An examination of this model and a survey of what light is shed upon it by educational and psychological research has brought me to at least five major neglected areas.

First, I find that we know little about the relation between *learning rates* and *aptitude*. This problem will be more familiar to you, perhaps, if I speak of it as that of the effect of practice or training on individual differences, or as the problem of the relation between intelligence and learning ability. Call it what you will, it is at the root of many issues of educational policy. The propriety and wisdom of any form of ability grouping or individualization of instruction depends partly upon whether in fact there are substantial differences in learning rates and whether these differences are a function of measurable characteristics of the learner such as his "aptitude," or his previous learning experiences.

The problem involves more than a mere observed relation. What is needed is more information than we now have about the *maximal* learning rates for individuals of given aptitude levels, given *optimal* conditions for learning. Obtaining such information implies a vigorous search for optimal learning conditions in school learning, and thus an extensive series of experimental studies on methods of instruction. There are several possible definitions of "optimal" conditions: they could be "optimal" in the sense of yielding maximal learning rates, or in the sense of yielding maximal retention and transfer, or in the sense of yielding greatest satisfaction and confidence on the part of the learner.

NO GENERAL STATEMENTS POSSIBLE

As matters stand now, we cannot begin to make general statements about this problem. For example, we cannot satisfactorily account for the fact that (as Anderson, Roff, and others have apparently demonstrated[2]) there is a zero correlation between mental age status of a child and the amount of mental age he will gain in the ensuing year. Does this mean that intelligence has nothing to do with learning rates? Does it mean that children of low IQ can learn just as fast as those of higher IQ? Will this be true regardless of the type of learning that is involved? To what extent can measured abilities—for example, those on the Thurstone Primary Mental Abilities Test—be modified by appropriate training, and at what rate can such changes take place? Are learning rates correlated with the asymptotes (if any) of the learning curve? Questions such as these have not been completely neglected, to be sure; Herbert Woodrow[3] and J. W. Tilton[4] have worked on them, and more recently, Harold Holloway[5] did a small study on the trainability of "primary mental abilities." While they were at Educational Testing Service, Robert Stake[6] and Roger Allison[7] did factorial studies of learning parameters in relation to measured aptitudes. The "coaching" studies supported by the College Entrance Examination Board are of some relevance.[8] All these studies, however, can be regarded as only a beginning. We need a broad enough series of investigations to indicate in detail and in depth what rates and courses of learning we may expect for individuals of various measured aptitude levels, for various types of learning, and for various conditions of instruction. We need to determine whether "aptitude level" is just another way of stating "point on a learning curve" or whether it is a way of expressing the slope parameter of the curve. We need to determine these things for

---

[2] John E. Anderson, "The Prediction of Terminal Intelligence from Infant and Preschool Tests," *39th Yearbook, National Society for the Study of Education*, 1940, Part I, 385-403.

Merrill Roff, "A Statistical Study of Intelligence Test Performance," *Journal of Psychology*, 1941, 11, pp. 371-386.

[3] Herbert Woodrow, "The Relation Between Abilities and Improvement with Practice," *Journal of Educational Psychology*, 1938, 29, pp. 215-230.

[4] J. W. Tilton, "The Intercorrelations Between Measures of School Learning, *Journal of Psychology*, 1953, 35, pp. 169-179.

[5] Harold D. Holloway, "Effects of Training on the SRA Primary Mental Abilities (Primary) and the WISC," *Child Development*, 1954, 25, pp. 253-263.

[6] Robert E. Stake, *Learning Parameters, Aptitudes, and Achievements*. Princeton, N. J.: Princeton University Psychology Department, June, 1958.

[7] Roger B. Allison, Jr., *Learning Parameters and Human Abilities*. Princeton, N. J.: Educational Testing Service and Princeton University, May, 1960.

[8] R. E. Dear, "The Effects of a Program of Intensive Coaching on SAT Scores, *Research Bulletin RB-58-5*. Princeton, N. J.: Educational Testing Service, 1958.

all the important types of school learning, not just for the kinds of clerical tasks and parlor games that are utilized in many experiments on learning.

What has been said about the need to study learning rates in relation to aptitude levels applies equally well to the study of outcomes of learning such as retention and transfer. It is exceedingly difficult to find any studies on the amount of retention that can be observed after various amounts of time elapsed from initial school learning. I am speaking here not of short-term retention, as after a summer vacation, but of retention over long periods of time. Perhaps it would be difficult to separate transfer from other learnings and all kinds of "refresher" effects, but even so, we have very little idea, from empirical measurement, about how well students typically retain learnings in arithmetic, social studies, or foreign languages.

More could be said about this, but I must move on to other areas of neglect.

WE KNOW LITTLE ABOUT MOTIVATION

Research has told us little about the role of motivation in school learning. Let us take it for granted, despite the long-standing controversy in the theory of learning, that motivation—in the sense of a willingness on the part of the learner to engage in learning—is indeed a condition of learning. We know little about what actually motivates children to learn, or how to arouse motivation. Research literature reports that motivation as measured by interest tests and questionnaires is rarely related either to aptitude or to school achievement. Our knowledge of the true dynamics of the school learning process is too limited to enable us to account for these low relationships, which on their face seem to contradict the theory of learning. Maslow[9] and others have made a beginning in identifying need systems, but my impression is that these systems are inadequate as yet to explain or to predict how individual pupils approach learning. The study of the motivation of school learning is more than simply the study of systems of rewarding students; the question of what are adequate rewards— and what needs these rewards would presumably fulfill—is too often left open. Studies of both intrinsic and extrinsic motivation are needed.

---

[9] A. H. Maslow, *Motivation and Personality*. New York: Harper & Row, Publishers, 1954.

RESEARCH TO IMPROVE INSTRUCTION

A third large and neglected area in educational research is that of how we can improve the quality of instruction. By this I mean the effectiveness of the procedures which teachers (or textbooks, or workbooks, or laboratory exercises, or teaching machines) employ to communicate knowledge, skill, and understanding to students. One of the virtues and the promises of the recent surge of interest in programed instruction is that at long last it has brought the attention of educational psychologists to the basic issues of how subject matter can be best organized and communicated, how concepts are to be developed and illustrated, and how skills are to be introduced and refined. Gradually a technology of instruction is being forged, but we are in danger of allowing this to occur solely within the context of instruction programed for machines or their close relatives. There is just as much need to develop an instructional technology for teachers, textbooks, films, and other aspects of our total educational enterprise. Only a few psychologists have looked into such questions as what sequences of positive and negative instances of a concept should be presented for optimal concept attainment, or what arrangements of wholes and parts of a complex subject matter are best presented. The didactic principles followed by our teachers and textbook writers are derived more from traditional rhetoric than from modern psychology, and it is at least debatable whether this should be the case.

Another aspect of the need for more information about how to improve the quality of instruction is the study of how empirical laws of learning can be applied in the classroom situation. Let us call this, in fact, a fourth "neglected area" of educational research. I take the position that "learning theory," so-called, is presently concerned with advanced scientific questions relating to the explication of learning phenomena and hence is of little interest to educational psychologists, but that most of the empirical laws of learning which are readily applicable in the classroom have already been discovered and well attested. The teacher's problem, therefore, is the organization of teaching procedures in such a way that the full benefits of these empirical laws of learning can be realized. I was surprised to find that the research literature discloses only a handful of studies which explore how principles of learning can be applied in the classroom. For example, we need more studies concerning how we can use the fact that learning is dependent upon the immediate reinforcement of correct responses, or in what situations we can employ the fact that skills may be shaped by gradual incrementing of response standards. There is no point in testing these principles all over again, as some investigators seem to have tried to do, but there is a need to study the feasibility of their application.

BETTER TEACHER COMPETENCE STUDIES NEEDED

This brings me to a fifth area of neglect in educational research. It is with some trepidation that I claim there has been neglect in the study of teacher competence, in view of the enormous amounts of effort that have been lavished on this field. I nevertheless make this claim, because one can find so very little research on what kinds of behaviors on the part of teachers make for desirable changes in student behavior. I would underline the necessity of using pupil change as a criterion of teacher effectiveness, for after reviewing so many studies which have resorted to the regressive maneuver of utilizing only subjective ratings of teachers I am convinced that we might just as well scrap all such ratings. We find neglect also in the related matter of teacher education —it is virtually impossible to find sound studies of either what changes can be made to occur in student teachers through professional education or of what effects these changes may bring when these teachers enter service. Consideration of what things should be taught to prospective teachers and what actions they should take as teachers sometimes seem to proceed as if educational research never existed.

This sketch of some of the shortcomings of educational research obviously has the limitations of one observer's perspective. You may feel it is distorted. I submit, however, that it is important that periodic assessments of educational research, such as this, be made and widely discussed, to ensure that we are adequately covering the ground and fulfilling the responsibilities we have implicitly taken upon ourselves.

Bernard Barber and Renée C. Fox

The Case of the
Floppy-Eared Rabbits:
An Instance of
Serendipity Gained and
Serendipity Lost

This charming and interesting article was included in this chapter because it represents, to some extent, a problem that wanted investigation. Because of the many factors frequently found in a given bit of educational research, we might expect to find many instances of potential serendipity. This article may alert us to some of the ways in which we may follow up these interesting but incidental findings rather than merely noting them and forgetting them—thus having still another case of serendipity lost.

Bernard Barber and Renée C. Fox, "The Case of the Floppy-Eared Rabbits: An Instance of Serendipity Gained and Serendipity Lost," *American Journal of Sociology,* 54:128-36, September, 1958. Reprinted with permission.

As with so many other basic social processes, the actual process of scientific research and discovery is not well understood.[1] There has been little systematic observation of the research and discovery process as it actually occurs, and even less controlled research. Moreover, the form in which discoveries are reported by scientists to their colleagues in professional journals tends to conceal important aspects of this process. Because of certain norms that are strongly institutionalized in their professional community, scientists are expected to focus their reports on the logical structure of the methods used and the ideas

---

[1] For an account of what is known see Bernard Barber, *Science and the Social Order* (Glencoe, Ill.: Free Press, 1952), chap. ix, "The Social Process of Invention and Discovery," pp. 191-206.

discovered in research in relation to the established conceptual framework of the relevant scientific specialty. The primary function of such reports is conceived to be that of indicating how the new observations and ideas being advanced may require a change—by further generalization or systematization—in the conceptual structure of a given scientific field. All else that has occurred in the actual research process is considered "incidental." Thus scientists are praised for presenting their research in a way that is elegantly bare of anything that does not serve this primary function and are deterred from reporting "irrelevant" social and psychological aspects of the research process, however interesting these matters may be in other contexts. As a result of such norms and practices, the reporting of scientific research may be characterized by what has been called "retrospective falsification." By selecting only those components of the actual research process that serve their primary purpose, scientific papers leave out a great deal, of course, as many scientists have indicated in their memoirs and in their informal talks with one another. Selection, then, unwittingly distorts and, in that special sense, falsifies what has happened in research as it actually goes on in the laboratory and its environs.

Public reports to the community of scientists thus have their own function. Their dysfunctionality for the sociology of scientific discovery, which is concerned with not one but all the components of the research process as a social process, is of no immediate concern to the practicing research scientist. And yet what is lost in "retrospective falsification" may be of no small importance to him, if only indirectly. For it is not unlikely that here, as everywhere else in the world of nature, knowledge is power, in this case power to increase the fruitfulness of scientific research by enlarging our systematic knowledge of it. The sociology of scientific discovery would seem to be an especially desirable area for further theoretical and empirical development.

One component of the actual process of scientific discovery that is left out or concealed in research reports following the practice of "retrospective falsification" is the element of unforeseen development, of happy or lucky chance, of what Robert K. Merton has called "the serendipity pattern."[2] By its very nature, scientific research is a voyage

---

[2] For discussions of serendipity see Walter B. Cannon, *The Way of an Investigator* (New York: W. W. Norton & Co., 1945), chap. vi, "Gains from Serendipity," pp. 68-78; and Robert K. Merton, *Social Theory and Social Structure* (rev. ed.; Glencoe, Ill.: Free Press, 1957), pp. 103-8. Our colleagues, Robert K. Merton and Elinor G. Barber, are now engaged in an investigation and clarification of the variety of meanings of "chance" that are lumped under the notion of serendipity by different users of that term.

into the unknown by routes that are in some measure unpredictable and unplannable. Chance or luck is therefore as inevitable in scientific research as are logic and what Pasteur called "the prepared mind." Yet little is known systematically about this inevitable serendipity component.

For this reason it seemed to us desirable to take the opportunity recently provided by the reporting of an instance of *serendipity gained* by Dr. Lewis Thomas, now professor and chairman of the Department of Medicine in the College of Medicine of New York University and formerly professor and chairman of the Department of Pathology.[3] Then, shortly after hearing about Dr. Thomas' discovery, we learned from medical research and teaching colleagues of an instance of *serendipity lost* on the very same kind of chance occurrence: unexpected floppiness in rabbits' ears after they had been injected intravenously with the proteolytic enzyme papain. This instance of serendipity lost had occurred in the course of research by Dr. Aaron Kellner, associate professor in the Department of Pathology of Cornell University Medical College and director of its central laboratories. This opportunity for *comparative* study seemed even more promising for our further understanding of the serendipity pattern. Here were two comparable medical scientists, we reasoned, both carrying out investigations in the field of experimental pathology, affiliated with distinguished medical schools, and of approximately the same level of demonstrated research ability (so far as it was in our layman's capacity to judge). In the course of their research both men had had occasion to inject rabbits intravenously with papain, and both had observed the phenomenon of ear collapse following the injection.

In spite of these similarities in their professional backgrounds and although they had both accidentally encountered the same phenomenon, one of these scientists had gone on to make a discovery based on this chance occurrence, whereas the other had not. It seemed to us that a detailed comparison of Dr. Thomas' and Dr. Kellner's experiences with the floppy-eared rabbits offered a quasi-experimental opportunity to identify some of the factors that contribute to a positive experience with serendipity in research and some of the factors conducive to a negative experience with it.

We asked for and were generously granted intensive interviews with

---

[3] Lewis Thomas, "Reversible Collapse of Rabbit Ears after Intravenous Papain, and Prevention of Recovery by Cortisone," *Journal of Experimental Medicine*, CIV (1956), 245-52. This case first came to our attention through a report in the *New York Times*. The pictures printed in Dr. Thomas' original article and in the *Times* will indicate why we have called this "the case of the floppy-eared rabbits."

Dr. Thomas and Dr. Kellner.[4] Each reported to us that they had experienced both "positive serendipity" and "negative serendipity" in their research. That is, each had made a number of serendipitous discoveries based on chance occurrences in their planned experiments, and on other occasions each had missed the significance of like occurrences that other researchers had later transformed into discoveries. Apparently, both positive and negative serendipity are common experiences for scientific researchers. Indeed, we shall see that one of the chief reasons why Dr. Kellner experienced serendipity lost with respect to the discovery that Dr. Thomas made was that he was experiencing serendipity gained with respect to some other aspects of the very same experimental situation. Conversely, Dr. Thomas had reached a stalemate on some of his other research, and this gave him added incentive to pursue intensively the phenomenon of ear collapse. Partly as a consequence of these experiences, in what were similar experimental situations, the two researchers each saw something and missed something else.

On the basis of our focused interviews with these two scientists, we can describe some of the recurring elements in their experiences with serendipity.[5] We think that these patterns may also be relevant to instances of serendipity experienced by other investigators.

SERENDIPITY GAINED

Dr. Thomas.—Observing the established norms for reporting scientific research, in his article in the *Journal of Experimental Medicine*, Dr. Thomas did not mention his experience with serendipity. In the manner typical of such reports he began his article with the statement, "For reasons not relevant to the present discussion rabbits were injected intravenously with a solution of crude papain." (By contrast, though not called by this term, serendipity was featured in the accounts of this research that appeared in the *New York Times* and the *New York Herald Tribune.* "An accidental sidelight of one research project had the startling effect of wilting the ears of the rabbit," said the *Times*

---

[4] These interviews lasted about two hours each. They are another instance of the "tandem interviewing" described by Harry V. Kincaid and Margaret Bright, "Interviewing the Business Elite," *American Journal of Sociology*, LXIII (1957), 304-11.

[5] In this paper we shall concentrate on the instances of serendipity gained by Dr. Thomas and lost by Dr. Kellner and give somewhat less attention to elements of negative serendipity in Dr. Thomas' experiments and elements of positive serendipity in those of Dr. Kellner.

article. "This bizarre phenomenon, accidentally discovered . . ." was the way the *Herald Tribune* described the same phenomenon. The prominence accorded the "accidental" nature of the discovery in the press is related to the fact that these articles were written by journalists for a lay audience. The kind of interest in scientific research that is characteristic of science reporters and the audience for whom they write and their conceptions of the form in which information about research ought to be communicated differ from those of professional scientists).[6]

Although Dr. Thomas did not mention serendipity in his article for the *Journal of Experimental Medicine*, in his interview he reported both his general acquaintance with the serendipity pattern ("Serendipity is a familiar term. . . . I first heard about it in Dr. Cannon's class . . .") and his awareness of the chance occurrence of floppy-eared rabbits in his own research. Dr. Thomas first noticed the reversible collapse of rabbit ears after intravenous papain about seven years ago, when he was working on the effects of proteolytic enzymes as a class:

> I was trying to explore the notion that the cardiac and blood vessel lesions in certain hypersensitivity states may be due to release of proteolytic enzymes. It's an attractive idea on which there's little evidence. And it's been picked up at some time or another by almost everyone working on hypersensitivity. For this investigation I used trypsin, because it was the most available enzyme around the laboratory, and I got nothing. We also happened to have papain; I don't know where it had come from; but because it was there, I tried it. I also tried a third enzyme, ficin. It comes from figs, and it's commonly used. It has catholic tastes and so it's quite useful in the laboratory. So I had these three enzymes. The other two didn't produce lesions. Nor did papain. But what the papain did was always produce these bizarre cosmetic changes. . . . It was one of the most uniform reactions I'd ever seen in biology. It always happened. And it looked as if something important must have happened to cause this reaction.

Some of the elements of serendipitous discovery are clearly illustrated in this account by Dr. Thomas. The scientific researcher, while in

---

[6] Further discussion of this point lies beyond the scope of this paper. But in a society like ours, in which science has become "front-page news," some of the characteristics and special problems of science reporting merit serious study. A recently published work on this topic that has come to our attention is entitled *When Doctors Meet Reporters* (New York: New York University Press, 1957). This is a discussion by science writers and physicians of the controversy between the press and the medical profession, compiled from the record of a series of conferences sponsored by the Josiah Macy, Jr., Foundation.

pursuit of some other specific goals, accidentally ("we also happened to have papain . . .") produces an unusual, recurrent, and sometimes striking ("bizarre") effect. Only the element of creative imagination, which is necessary to complete an instance of serendipity by supplying an explanation of the unusual effect, is not yet present. Indeed, the explanation was to elude Dr. Thomas, as it eluded Dr. Kellner, and probably others as well, for several years. This was not for lack of trying by Dr. Thomas. He immediately did seek an explanation:

> I chased it like crazy. But I didn't do the right thing. . . . I did the expected things. I had sections cut, and I had them stained by all the techniques available at the time. And I studied what I believed to be the constituents of a rabbit's ear. I looked at all the sections, but I couldn't see anything the matter. The connective tissue was intact. There was no change in the amount of elastic tissue. There was no inflammation, no tissue damage. I expected to find a great deal, because I thought we had destroyed something.

Dr. Thomas also studied the cartilage of the rabbit's ear, and judged it to be "normal" (". . . The cells were healthy-looking and there were nice nuclei. I decided there was no damage to the cartilage. And that was that . . ."). However, he admitted that at the time his consideration of the cartilage was routine and relatively casual, because he did not seriously entertain the idea that the phenomenon of ear collapse might be associated with changes in this tissue:

> I hadn't thought of cartilage. You're not likely to, because it's not considered interesting. . . . I know my own idea has always been that cartilage is a quiet, inactive tissue.

Dr. Thomas' preconceptions about the methods appropriate for studying the ear-collapsing effect of papain, his expectation that it would probably be associated with damage in the connective or elastic tissues, and the conviction he shared with colleagues that cartilage is "inert and relatively uninteresting"—these guided his initial inquiries into this phenomenon. But the same preconceptions, expectations, and convictions also blinded him to the physical and chemical changes in the ear cartilage matrix which, a number of years later, were to seem "obvious" to him as the alterations underlying the collapsing ears. Here again, another general aspect of the research process comes into the clear. Because the methods and assumptions on which a systematic investigation is built selectively focus the researcher's attention, to a certain extent they sometimes constrict his imagination and bias his observations.

Although he was "very chagrined" about his failure, Dr. Thomas finally had to turn away from his floppy-eared rabbits because he was "terribly busy working on another problem at the time," with which he was "making progress." Also, Dr. Thomas reported, "I had already used all the rabbits I could afford. So I was able to persuade myself to abandon this other research." The gratifications of research success elsewhere and the lack of adequate resources to continue with his rabbit experiments combined to make Dr. Thomas accept failure, at least temporarily. As is usually the case in the reporting of scientific research, these experiments and their negative outcome were not written up for professional journals. (There is too much failure of this sort in research to permit of its publication, except occasionally, even though it might be instructive for some other scientists in carrying out their research. Since there is no way of determining what might be instructive failures and since space in professional journals is at a premium, generally only accounts of successful experiments are submitted to such journals and published by them.)

Despite his decision to turn his attention to other, more productive research, Dr. Thomas did not completely forget the floppy-eared rabbits. His interest was kept alive by a number of things. As he explained, the collapse of the rabbit ears and their subsequent reversal "was one of the most uniform reactions I'd ever seen in biology." The "unfailing regularity" with which it occurred is not often observed in scientific research. Thus the apparent invariance of this phenomenon never ceased to intrigue Dr. Thomas, who continued to feel that an important and powerful biological happening might be responsible. The effect of papain on rabbit ears had two additional qualities that helped to sustain Dr. Thomas' interest in it. The spectacle of rabbits with "ears collapsed limply at either side of the head, rather like the ears of spaniels,"[7] was both dramatic and entertaining.

In the intervening years Dr. Thomas described this phenomenon to a number of colleagues in pathology, biochemistry, and clinical investigation, who were equally intrigued and of the opinion that a significant amount of demonstrable tissue damage must be associated with such a striking and uniform reaction. Dr. Thomas also reported that twice he "put the experiment on" for some of his more skeptical colleagues. ("They didn't believe me when I told them what happened. They didn't really believe that you can get that much change and not a trace of anything having happened when you look in the microscope.") As so often happens in science, an unsolved puzzle was kept in mind

---

[7] Thomas, *op. cit.*, p. 245.

for eventual solution through informal exchanges between scientists, rather than through the formal medium of published communications.

A few years ago Dr. Thomas once again accidentally came upon the floppy-eared rabbits in the course of another investigation:

> I was looking for a way . . . to reduce the level of fibrinogen in the blood of rabbits. I had been studying a form of fibrinoid which occurs inside blood vessels in the generalized Schwartzman reaction and which seems to be derived from fibrinogen. My working hypothesis was that if I depleted the fibrinogen and, as a result, fibrinoid did not occur, this would help. It had been reported that if you inject proteolytic enzyme, this will deplete fibrinogen. So I tried to inhibit the Schwartzman reaction by injecting papain intravenously into the rabbits. It didn't work with respect to fibrinogen. . . . But the same damned thing happened again to the rabbits' ears!

This time, however, Dr. Thomas was to solve the puzzle of the collapsed rabbit ears and realize a complete instance of serendipitous discovery. He describes what subsequently happened:

> I was teaching second-year medical students in pathology. We have these small seminars with them: two-hour sessions in the morning, twice a week, with six to eight students. These are seminars devoted to experimental pathology and the theoretical aspects of the mechanism of disease. The students have a chance to see what we, the faculty, are up to in the laboratory. I happened to have a session with the students at the same time that this thing with the rabbits' ears happened again. I thought it would be an entertaining thing to show them . . . a spectacular thing. The students were very interested in it. I explained to them that we couldn't really explain what the hell was going on here. I did this experiment on purpose for them, to see what they would think. . . . Besides which, I was in irons on my other experiments. There was not much doing on those. I was not being brilliant on these other problems. . . . Well, this time I did what I didn't do before. I simultaneously cut sections of the ears of rabbits after I'd given them papain *and* sections of normal ears. This is the part of the story I'm most ashamed of. It still makes me writhe to think of it. There was no damage to the tissue in the sense of a lesion. But what had taken place was a quantitative change in the matrix of the cartilage. The only way you could make sense of this change was simultaneously to compare sections taken from the ears of rabbits which had been injected with papain with comparable sections from the ears of rabbits of the same age and size which had not received papain. . . . Before this I had always been so struck by the enormity of the change that when I didn't see something obvious, I concluded there was nothing. . . . Also, I didn't have a lot of rabbits to work with before.

Judging from Dr. Thomas' account, it appears that a number of factors contributed to his reported experimental success. First, his teaching duties played a creative role in this regard. They impelled him to run the experiment with papain again and kept his attention focused on its implications for basic science rather than on its potentialities for practical application. Dr. Thomas said that he used the experiment to "convey to students what experimental pathology is like." Second, because he had reached an impasse in some of his other research, Dr. Thomas had more time and further inclination to study the ear-collapsing effect of papain than he had had a few years earlier, when the progress he was making on other research helped to "persuade" him to "abandon" the problem of the floppy-eared rabbits. Third, Dr. Thomas had more laboratory resources at his command than previously, notably a larger supply of rabbits. (In this regard it is interesting to note that, according to Dr. Thomas' article in the *Journal of Experimental Medicine*, 250 rabbits, all told, were used in the experiments reported.) Finally, the fact that he now had more laboratory animals with which to work and that he wanted to present the phenomenon of reversible ear collapse to students in a way that would make it an effective teaching exercise led Dr. Thomas to modify his method for examining rabbit tissues. In his earlier experiments, Dr. Thomas had compared histological sections made of the ears of rabbits who had received an injection of papain with his own mental image of normal rabbit-ear tissue. This time, however, he actually made sections from the ear tissue of rabbits which did *not* receive papain, as well as from those which did, and simultaneously examined the two. As he reported, this comparison enabled him to see for the first time that "drastic" quantitative changes had occurred in the cartilaginous tissue obtained from the ears of the rabbits injected with papain. In the words of the *Journal* article,

> The ear cartilage showed loss of a major portion of the intercellular matrix, and complete absence of basophilia from the small amount of remaining matrix. The cartilage cells appeared somewhat larger, and rounder than normal, and lay in close contact with each other. . . .

Immediately thereafter, Dr. Thomas and his associates found that these changes occur not only in ear cartilage but in all other cartilaginous tissues as well.

How significant or useful Dr. Thomas' serendipitous discovery will be cannot yet be specified. The serendipity pattern characterizes small discoveries as well as great. Dr. Thomas and his associates are currently investigating some of the questions raised by the phenomenon of papain-collapsed ears and the alterations in cartilage now known to underlie it. In addition, Dr. Thomas reported that some of his "biochemist and clinical friends" have become interested enough in certain of his findings to "go to work with papain, too." Two of the major problems under study in Dr. Thomas' laboratory are biochemical: the one concerning the nature of the change in cartilage; the other, the nature of the factor in papain that causes collapse of rabbits' ears and lysis of cartilage matrix in all tissues. Attempts are also being made to identify the antibody that causes rabbits to become immune to the factor responsible for ear collapse after two weeks of injection. The way in which cortisone prolongs the reaction to papain and the possible effect that papain may have on the joints as well as the cartilage are also being considered. Though at the time he was interviewed Dr. Thomas could not predict whether his findings (to date) would prove "important" or not, there was some evidence to suggest that certain basic discoveries about the constituents and properties of cartilaginous tissue might be forthcoming and that the experiments thus far conducted might have "practical usefulness" for studies of the postulated role of cortisone in the metabolism of sulfated mucopolysaccharides and of the relationship between cartilage and the electrolyte imbalance associated with congestive heart failure.

In the research on reversible ear collapse that Dr. Thomas has conducted since his initial serendipitous discovery, the planned and the unplanned, the foreseen and the accidental, the logical and the lucky have continued to interact. For example, Dr. Thomas' discovery that cortisone prevents or greatly delays the "return of papain-collapsed ears to their normal shape and rigidity" came about as a result of a carefully planned experiment that he undertook to test the effect of cortisone on the reaction to papain. On the other hand, his discovery that "repeated injections of papain, over a period of two or three weeks, brings about immunity to the phenomenon of ear collapse" was an unanticipated consequence of the fact that he used the same rabbit to demonstrate the floppy ears to several different groups of medical students:

> I was so completely sold on the uniformity of this thing that I used the same rabbit [for each seminar]. . . . The third time it didn't work. I was appalled by it. The students were there, and the rabbit's ears were still in place. . . . At first I thought that perhaps the technician had given him the wrong stuff. But then when I checked on that and

gave the same stuff to the other rabbits and it *did* work I realized that the rabbit had become immune. This is a potentially hot finding. . . .

SERENDIPITY LOST

Dr. Kellner.—In our interview with Dr. Thomas we told him that we had heard about another medical scientist who had noticed the reversible collapse of rabbits' ears when he had injected them intravenously with papain. Dr. Thomas was not at all surprised. "That must be Kellner," he said. "He must have seen it. He was doomed to see it." Dr. Thomas was acquainted with the reports that Dr. Kellner and his associates had published on "Selective Necrosis of Cardiac and Skeletal Muscle Induced Experimentally by Means of Proteolytic Enzyme Solutions Given Intravenously" and on "Blood Coagulation Defect Induced in Rabbits by Papain Solutions Injected Intravenously."[8] He took it for granted that, in the course of these reported experiments which had entailed papain solution given intravenously to rabbits, a competent scientist like Dr. Kellner had also seen the resulting collapse of rabbits' ears, with its "unfailing regularity" and its "flamboyant" character. And, indeed, our interview with Dr. Kellner revealed that he had observed the floppiness, apparently at about the same time as Dr. Thomas:

> We called them the floppy-eared rabbits. . . . Five or six years ago we published our first article on the work we were doing with papain; that was in 1951 and our definitive article was published in 1954. . . . We gave papain to the animals and we had done it thirty or forty times before we noticed these changes in the rabbits' ears.

Thus Dr. Kellner's observation of what he and his colleagues dubbed "the floppy-eared rabbits" represents, when taken together with Dr. Thomas' experience, an instance of independent multiple observation, which often occurs in science and frequently leads to independent multiple invention and discovery.

Once he had noticed the phenomenon of ear collapse, Dr. Kellner did what Dr. Thomas and any research scientist would have done in

---

[8] See, Aaron Kellner and Theodore Robertson, "Selective Necrosis of Cardiac and Skeletal Muscle Induced Experimentally by Means of Proteolytic Enzyme Solutions Given Intravenously," *Journal of Experimental Medicine*, XCIX (1954), 387-404; and Aaron Kellner, Theodore Robertson, and Howard O. Mott, "Blood Coagulation Defect Induced in Rabbits by Papain Solutions Injected Intravenously," abstract in *Federation Proceedings*, Vol. X (1951), No. 1.

the presence of such an unexpected and striking regularity: he looked for an answer to the puzzle it represented. "I was a little curious about it at the time, and followed it up to the extent of making sections of the rabbits' ears." However, for one of those trivial reasons that sometimes affect the course of research—the obviously amusing quality of floppiness in rabbits' ears—Dr. Kellner did not take the phenomenon as seriously as he took other aspects of the experimental situation involving the injection of papain.

In effect, Dr. Kellner and his associates closed out their interest in the phenomenon of the reversible collapse of rabbits' ears following intravenous injection of papain by using it as an assay test for the potency and amount of papain to be injected. "Every laboratory technician we've had since 1951," he told us in the interview, "has known about these floppy ears because we've used them to assay papain, to tell us if it's potent and how potent." If the injected rabbit died from the dose of papain he received, the researchers knew that the papain injection was too potent; if there was no change in the rabbit's ears, the papain was not potent enough, but "if the rabbit lived and his ears drooped, it was just right." Although "we knew all about it, and used it that way . . . as a rule of thumb," Dr. Kellner commented, "I didn't write it up." Nor did he ever have "any intention of publishing it as a method of assaying papain." He knew that an applied technological discovery of this sort would not be suitable for publication in the basic science–oriented professional journals to which he and his colleagues submit reports of experimental work.

However, two factors apparently were much more important in leading Dr. Kellner away from investigating this phenomenon. First, like Dr. Thomas, Dr. Kellner thought of cartilage as relatively inert tissue. Second, because of his pre-established special research interests, Dr. Kellner's attention was predominantly trained on muscle tissue:

> Since I was primarily interested in research questions having to do with the muscles of the heart, I was thinking in terms of muscle. That blinded me, so that changes in the cartilage didn't occur to me as a possibility. I was looking for muscles in the sections, and I never dreamed it was cartilage.

Like Dr. Thomas at the beginning of his research and like all scientists at some stages in their research, Dr. Kellner was "misled" by his preconceptions.

However, as we already know, in keeping with his special research interests, Dr. Kellner noticed and intensively followed up two other serendipitous results that occur when papain is injected intravenously into rabbits: focal necrosis of cardiac and skeletal muscle and a blood coagulation defect, which in certain respects resembles that of hemophilia.[9]

It was the selective necrosis of cardiac and skeletal muscle that Dr. Kellner studied with the greatest degree of seriousness and interest. Dr. Kellner told us that he is "particularly interested in cardio-vascular disease," and so the lesions in the myocardium was the chance observation that he particularly "chose to follow . . . the one closest to me." Not only did Dr. Kellner himself have a special interest in the necrosis of cardiac muscle, but also his "laboratory and the people associated with me," he said, provided "the physical and intellectual tools to cope with this phenomenon." Dr. Kellner and his colleagues also did a certain amount of "work tracking down the cause of the blood coagulation defect"; but, because this line of inquiry "led [them] far afield" from investigative work in which they were especially interested and competent, they eventually "let that go" as they had let go the phenomenon of floppiness in rabbits' ears. Dr. Kellner indicated in his interview that the potential usefulness of his work with the selective necrosis of cardiac and skeletal muscle cannot yet be precisely ascertained. However, in his article in the *Journal of Experimental Medicine* he suggested that this serendipitous finding "has interesting implications for the pathogenesis of the morphological changes in rheumatic fever, periarteritis nodosa, and other hypersensitivity states."

Thus Dr. Kellner did not have the experience of serendipity gained with respect to the significance of floppiness in rabbits' ears after intravenous injection of papain for a variety of reasons, some trival apparently, others important. The most important reasons, it seems, were his research preconceptions and the occurrence of other serendipitous phenomena in the same experimental situation.

In summary, although the ultimate outcome of their respective laboratory encounters with floppiness in rabbits' ears was quite different, there are some interesting similarities between the serendipity-gained experience of Dr. Thomas and the serendipity-lost experience of Dr. Kellner. Initially, the attention of both men was caught by the striking uniformity with which the collapse of rabbit ears occurred after intravenous papain and by the "bizarre," entertaining qualities of this cosmetic effect. In their subsequent investigations of this phenomenon, both were to some extent misled by certain of their interests and preconceptions. Lack of progress in accounting for ear collapse, combined with success in other research in which they were engaged at the time, eventually led both Dr. Thomas and Dr. Kellner to discontinue their work with the floppy-eared rabbits.

---

[9] See Kellner and Robertson, *op. cit.*, and Kellner, Robertson, and Mott, *op. cit.*

However, there were also some significant differences in the two experiences. Dr. Thomas seems to have been more impressed with the regularity of this particular phenomenon than Dr. Kellner and somewhat less amused by it. Unlike Dr. Kellner, Dr. Thomas never lost interest in the floppy-eared rabbits. When he came upon this reaction again at a time when he was "blocked" on other research, he began actively to reconsider the problem of what might have caused it. Eventual success was more likely to result from this continuing concern on Dr. Thomas' part. And Dr. Kellner, of course, was drawn off in other research directions by seeing other serendipitous phenomena in the same situation and by his success in following up those other leads.

These differences between Dr. Thomas and Dr. Kellner seem to account at least in part for the serendipity-gained outcome of the case of the floppy-eared rabbits for the one, and the serendipity-lost outcome for the other.

Experiences with both serendipity gained and serendipity lost are probably frequent occurrences for many scientific researchers. For, as Dr. Kellner pointed out in our interview with him, scientific investigations often entail "doing something that no one has done before, [so] you don't always know how to do it or exactly what to do":

> Should you boil or freeze, filter or centrifuge? These are the kinds of crossroads you come to all the time. . . . It's always possible to do four, five, or six things, and you have to choose between them. . . . How do you decide?

In this comparative study of one instance of serendipity gained and serendipity lost, we have tried to make inferences about some of the factors that led one investigator down the path to a successful and potentially important discovery and another to follow a somewhat different, though eventually perhaps a no less fruitful, trail of research. A large enough series of such case studies could suggest how often and in what ways these factors (and others that might prove relevant) influence the paths that open up to investigators in the course of their research, the choices they make between them, and the experimental findings that result from such choices. Case studies of this kind might also contribute a good deal to the detailed, systematic study of "the ways in which scientists actually . . . think, feel and act," which Robert K. Merton says could perhaps teach us more "in a comparatively few years, about the psychology and sociology of science than in all the years that have gone before."[10]

---

[10] See his Foreword to *Science and the Social Order* by Bernard Barber, p. xxii.

C. M. Lindvall

The Review of
Related Research

One place to seek problems in education is in the research literature. This is not to suggest that one enters the research literature blindly, hoping that a problem will materialize. Rather, one can sharpen the problem by a careful scrutiny of the related research.

Lindvall suggests that this problem sharpening is the true purpose of the review of related research. He further suggests that, if properly done, the review may make some small contribution toward theory building.

C. M. Lindvall, "The Review of Related Research," *Phi Delta Kappan*, 40:179-80, January, 1959. Reprinted with permission.

The written reports of research undertaken to fulfill a requirement for a master's or doctor's degree in education usually include a section presenting a review of related research. However, in many cases the careful reader will be somewhat puzzled as to how this review is related to the rest of the report or what exact purpose it is expected to serve. Too often it seems to be more of an appendage than an integral part of the total report. In some cases it appears that the researcher has a feeling that every candidate for an advanced degree has a responsibility for preparing an annotated bibliography of researches somewhat related to his own and is attaching his contribution to his research report. No real attempt is made to show the exact relationship between the reviewed research and the project of the candidate.

Most persons planning a thesis or dissertation probably look upon the review of related research as one of the easier tasks with which they are faced. They realize that it will involve quite a bit of their time but feel that it shouldn't require a great deal of original thinking and planning such as will be called for in the major part of their study. This project should be relatively simple. However, these same persons may also have only a hazy idea as to the purpose of the review and are probably influenced by certain misconceptions. It may well be suggested that these misconceptions and the related misuse of the review of research are one of the fundamental weaknesses in educational research.

COMMON MISCONCEPTIONS

One of the erroneous ideas concerning the purpose of the review has already been mentioned. This is the feeling that every candidate is responsible for producing an annotated bibliography of some length. This is, of course, not the reason for the review. The candidate's responsibility is to plan, to pursue, and to report a significant piece of research. Other agencies can do a much more extensive and satisfactory job of preparing annotated bibliographies. This is the major purpose of various encyclopedias, review journals, and volumes of abstracts. Duplicating some small part of the work of these agencies is no contribution.

Another, and perhaps even more common, misconception is the idea that the review is presented to show that the candidate's research has not been done previously by someone else. But any necessarily limited review cannot provide this proof of originality. At best it can only show that no piece of research reviewed by the candidate is exactly the same as his study. With educational research being carried on at a multitude of educational institutions and by numerous other agencies, it is extremely doubtful that any candidate can even discover references to any considerable portion of the studies that have been carried out in his area of interest. Also, in an area such as education where problems are so numerous and so complex and where the application of scientific methods is relatively new, it is doubtful that the question of the uniqueness of research is nearly as important as many other questions. It might be suggested that finding the ways in which studies are comparable and in which they are related to one another is a more important problem. In any case, the relatively small number of researches that can be reviewed by any one candidate cannot provide conclusive proof of originality. The review of related research can serve a more important and a more feasible purpose than this.

TRUE PURPOSE OF THE REVIEW

The problems which must be the subject of educational research are many and complex. No great contribution to their solution can be made by isolated research findings. As with other areas of scientific study, real solutions can be expected only when a cooperative attack is made, when the findings of one researcher can be combined with those of many others. This requires that studies be related to one another. It means that the person contemplating a research study should not think of himself as a lone pioneer making an original and independent attack in some problem area. Rather, it means that he should thoroughly familiarize himself with what is already known in that area. He must become acquainted with the significant research findings. In this way he can identify some of the exact spots where there is a void in existing knowledge. He can ask the important questions and formulate significant research problems. This will also enable him to see how his problem and his findings will relate to other researches and how his efforts, when combined with those of others, can help to complete some total picture. It is this fitting of a particular project into a broader scheme, enabling one to see its importance and to relate it to many other studies, that is the real purpose of the review of related research. Through this study of existing research, the candidate locates and defines his exact problem. Then, in writing up this review, he so organizes these previous findings that the reader can see just why the problem is important and how it is going to fit into a wider pattern of research results.

THE REVIEW AS A CONTRIBUTION TO THEORY

This purpose of the review of research may also be viewed in another manner. It may be considered as a small contribution to the building of research theory.

If one reads very much in research journals or in books dealing with principles of research, particularly in the behavioral sciences, he will repeatedly encounter the charge that a major weakness of research in these areas is the lack of any framework of theory to serve as the base for research problems. Despite the recurrence of this criticism, however, few of the critics offer any suggestions as to how the condition might be improved. The typical candidate for a graduate degree is probably quite puzzled as to what he can do about this situation. In many cases it is even likely that he has no clear conception of what is meant by theory when the term is used in this connection.

Of course, one of the classic models of what is meant by a framework of theory is the periodic table and its accompanying concepts of atomic weights and atomic and molecular structure. Here a combination of speculation and of known facts produced by research has resulted in a theory regarding the structure of elements and of how they combine to form compounds. This has served as the basic point of origin for countless research problems. It has served as the basis for hypotheses of this type: "If these two elements have these properties, it should be possible to combine them through this process to form this compound." The resulting research has, in turn, served to strengthen, to clarify, or to modify the theory. This is the way in which good theory functions. It serves as a source for meaningful research problems and logical hypotheses and also provides an organized system which permits new research results to make a contribution to some total picture.

We are forced to admit that the critics are correct in that there is little, if any, of this in education. Perhaps a major reason for this is the complexity of the relationships that must be studied. However, it is probably also due to the fact that not enough persons have made serious attempts to do this type of thinking and planning. Certainly we cannot expect the average candidate for an advanced degree to make any major contribution to theory building; but we should expect him to make some attempt in this direction. He should do this in his review of related research. Here he should bring together the results of existing research, show how the results are related, and thereby provide some type of organization of the existing knowledge in his area of interest. In this way he can provide a framework which shows that there is a certain void which his study will attempt to fill. This framework will serve to justify the meaningfulness of his problem and will show how it will help to supplement others in enlarging knowledge in a particular area. This type of review can make the research much more meaningful to the reader and should also suggest additional important research problems.

It is unlikely that any one student is going to produce a very complete or a fully satisfactory framework of theory. However, if every person obtaining an advanced degree makes a real effort to organize the research and thinking in some limited area, we will have a vast number of persons working at this important task. Their efforts will, at least, be a step in the right direction.

With any research study the review of related research can serve its proper function only if it is an integral part of the total project. It cannot be a loosely related supplement. It must provide the framework of thought which produces an important problem, documents its significance, and fits it into its proper place in an organized field of knowledge. If every thesis and dissertation includes this type of review, educational research should increase in significance and usefulness.

Wilse B. Webb

The Choice of the Problem [1]

The Raths article in the previous chapter suggested that research results were worthwhile only to the extent of the strength of the logical argument that demonstrated their probable truth or falsity. In this article Webb suggests another criterion of worthwhile research—a worthwhile problem. If the problem is insignificant then, no matter how precise the logical argument and how elegant the design and techniques, the results will be insignificant. Webb suggests that the usual criteria applied to the problem will not necessarily yield significant problems, and further offers three general criteria which he feels will yield more significant problems and thus more significant research.

Wilse B. Webb, "The Choice of the Problem," *American Psychologist*, 16:223-27, May, 1961. Reprinted with permission.

The matter of how to judge the goodness or badness of a result, particularly when this result is a theoretical formulation, has received considerable attention in recent years. Today in psychology, such decisions are increasingly necessary. Our subject matter has become quite boundless: muscle twitches and wars, the sound of porpoises and problems of space, the aesthetic qualities of tones and sick minds, psychophysics and labor turnover. The range of organisms involved in the studies of these problems extends from pigeons to people, from amoebas to social groups. Further the techniques of measurement have been honed and sharpened by electronic tubes, computing machines, mathematical niceties, and imaginative testing procedures. Too often, in this lush environment, we as researchers may find after some months of toil and research that our findings, although in accord with nature and beautifully simple, are utterly petty and we ourselves are no longer interested in them much less anyone else being interested.

---

[1] An abridged version of the Presidential Address to the Southern Society for Philosophy and Psychology given at the fifty-second Annual Meeting in Biloxi, Mississippi, April 15, 1960.

This problem of carefully selecting and evaluating a problem does not involve the researcher alone. In our complex beehive of today, this is a question for the teacher of research, the thesis and dissertation director, the research director of laboratories or programs, and the dispensers of research funds—in a small way, department chairmen and deans, and in a large way, the guardians of the coffers of foundations and government agencies.

We are not without criteria, of course. Either implicitly or explicitly we seek justification for what we do. Certainly when grants are involved we seek for some reasons to justify the getting or the giving of money. For our consideration, I have rummaged around and turned up six widely used bases for doing an experiment: curiosity, confirmability, compassion, cost, cupidity, and conformability—or, more simply, "Am I interested," "Can I get the answer," "Will it help," "How much will it cost," "What's the payola," "Is everyone else doing it?"

I believe you will find that these are the things that enter our minds when we evaluate a student's problem, dispense a sum of research money, or decide to put ourselves to work. To anticipate myself, however, I will try to establish the fact that these bases, used alone or in combination although perhaps correlated positively with a "successful" piece of research, will probably have a zero or even negative correlation with a "valuable" piece of research.

Before proceeding to examine these criteria, however, let me introduce a clarifying footnote. Although I am concerned about selecting a problem beyond the routine and "successful" experiment—and here I shall use completely indiscriminately (with apologies to the philosophers) such terms as "good," "valued," "enduring," "worthwhile"—I do not wish to disparage the necessary place of routine experiments, i.e., well conducted experiments which fill in and extend those more creative ones. I think that even the most cursory consideration of the history of science reveals that the "original" or the "important" experiment almost inevitably pushes out from routine work that has preceded it and is further dependent upon the supportive routine experiments for their fruition into the field. Most definitely, I would contend that it is far more important to do a routine experiment than no experiment at all.

But back to the problem before us: Are our reasons for experimenting sufficient guidelines to decide about experiments? The first of these, *curiosity*, is the grand old man of reasons for experimentation and hence, justification for our experimentation. In the days when knighthood was in flower, this was the most familiar emblem on the scientist's shield. It was enough to seek an answer to "I wonder what would happen if . . . ." This was sometimes formalized with the dignified phrase, "knowledge for knowledge's sake."

Today this is not a strong base of operation. Perhaps costs have outmoded whimsey; perhaps the glare of the public stage has made us too self-conscious for such a charming urge. Or, perhaps more forebodingly, we are less curious—or, perhaps a combination of these has made curiosity less defensible. More critically, when we look more closely at this justification for doing, or proposing to do an experiment, it does not turn out to be one. Clearly a person can be curious about valuable things, trivial things, absurd things, or evil things. I think we would all find it a little difficult to judge the relative merits of two pieces of completed research by trying to decide which of the two experimenters was the most curious. Perhaps wisely, then, it seems more and more difficult to convince deans or directors of research, or dispensers of funds that a problem is worth investigating because we, personally, happened to be puzzled by it.

The criterion of *confirmability* as a criterion of worthiness of the pursuit of a topic has two sides: a philosophic one and a pragmatic one. Philosophically, this criterion reached its glory in the '30s and '40s when the voice of a logical positivist was heard throughout the land. In no uncertain terms, they told us that the criterion for a problem was "that the question asked could be answered." On the pragmatic side, this criterion is interpreted to mean: "Pick variables which are likely to be statistically significant." Undoubtedly, the philosophical point of view has done much to clear up our experimental work by hacking through a jungle of undefined and ambiguous terms. From the pragmatic point of view, this has been a much valued criterion for the graduate student with several kids who must finish his thesis or dissertation to get out and start earning a living. However, it is just this criterion that may be voted the most likely to result in a pedestrian problem. It demands problems which have easily measurable variables and clearly stated influences. It discourages the exploration of new, complex, or mysterious areas. To exercise this criterion alone would force one to choose an experiment of measuring age as related to strength of grip on the handle of the dynamometer against exploring variables associated with happiness. Both may be quite worthwhile, but the latter has less of a chance of being approached so long as we exercise the criterion of confirmability alone.

The problem of *costs* must enter into considerations of undertaking an experiment. In the real, live world, determining the value of a thing is very simple. Find out how much it costs. Clearly, anything that costs a lot is very valuable. A car or house which costs more than another car or another house is naturally worth more. One pays for what one gets and one gets what one pays for. This thinking carries over into the world of scientific affairs. Space probes are obviously important because they cost a lot; a project which can get a large grant must be a good one or else it would not cost so much.

Certainly this is very faulty reasoning. That methodologies differ in their costs is quite obvious; the more expensive the methodology, the more valuable and important the activity is not a direct derivative. Einstein undoubtedly used less equipment than his dentist but we may suspect that Einstein attacked the more valuable problem. Departments of Philosophy are far less expensive than Departments of Veterinary Medicine but I do not believe them to be necessarily less valuable.

It is quite true that when a large sum of money is expended on a particular project that some decisions have been made that the desirability or the value of that project justifies the expenditure of this large sum. Money may serve as a crude index of where to look for decision bases that justify large expenditures but cannot serve as judgment bases themselves. If a person says, "To do this piece of research will cost x amount of money and will occupy x amount of my life," he has merely brought his problem into focus and has raised the critical question more clearly, i.e., is such an expenditure worth it? He has not solved the problem of how valuable his experiment is, but raised the question—some other criterion must be sought for an answer to that question.

A somewhat new criterion has entered into thinking today: *compassion*. As we have moved into the applied world, this rather new criterion has come into increasing use—at least this seems true of psychology. A person asks himself as he begins an experiment, "Will the results make things better?" and implicitly assumes that an affirmative answer will make his experiment or his project more valuable. The problem then is assessed in terms of its solutions or answers resulting in the patient's improvement, a reduction in prejudice, a happier or a healthier world, etc. A variation on this question, as it is asked in the market place and in some of the other sciences directly, is in a slightly cruder form: "Will this be useful; what service will this finding perform?"

H. G. Wells has a comment in this guideline for performance in his book *Meanwhile:*

> The disease of cancer will be banished from life by calm, unhurrying, persistent men and women working with every shiver of feeling controlled and suppressed in hospitals and in laboratories. . . . Pity never

made a good doctor, love never made a good poet, desire for service never made a discovery.

In one sense of the word, this criterion is a form of the old, applied vs. basic issue that plagues all sciences that live with one foot in technology and the other foot in theory. I cannot begin to resolve this issue here. I can, however, I believe, say this: it is quite possible for a piece of research undertaken in compassion or for utility to be quite valuable, enduring, well thought of, etc. It is also quite possible that it be trivial, superficial, limited, useless, etc. The same may be said for any given piece of basic research in which utility or compassion was never an issue. I am not one who believes that because a piece of research has no relevant use, it then by definition is valuable; or that a finding because it is useful is worthless. If these statements may be granted, it would appear then that some more fundamental criteria must be applied.

Cupidity is a variation on the criterion of compassion. Here, however, the "pay-off" is not for others but for oneself. Very simply the research is evaluated in terms of whether it will get one a promotion, favorable publicity, peer applause. Well, sometimes, undoubtedly what is good for you is good for others, and hence of general value.

However, the contrary is just as likely to be true: namely, what is good for you is not necessarily good for others at all. For example, making the natural assumptions that deans cannot read and department chairmen do not, the greater the number of papers, then the greater the probability of promotion. This results in a whirling mass of fragmented, little, anything printables to be constantly turned out instead of mature, integrated, programmatic articles. In being good to yourself you have done little or no good for others. The most casual recall would suggest that the impelling motives behind most significant advances in thought have not been cupidity, rather to the contrary such advances seemed to be more "selfless" than "selfish."

The last of my "useful" criteria is that of *conformity*. In these days of togetherness, it is not at all surprising to find conformity and its cousin, comfortableness, serving as guidelines for determining the should or should not of experimentation. We mean, by conformity, the choice of the currently popular problem, i.e., one within an ongoing and popular system, for example, operant conditioning, statistical learning theory; or a currently popular area of investigation, for example, sensory deprivation, or the Taylor Manifest Anxiety Scale.

As with all of our preceding criteria for deciding about a research project, conformity clearly has its merits. It would be foolish to turn one's back on new methods or a recent breakthrough of ideas which have been developed and certainly the interactive stimulation of mutual efforts in the same area are helpful factors in research. These, however, seem to be more means than ends to be sought for. One must be cautioned against becoming overenamored by the availability of a method at the expense of thoughtfulness or being charmed by the social benefits of working in an active area at the expense of the scientific implications of such work. More simply, some things that a lot of people are doing are quite worthwhile, and some are quite ridiculous.

Unfortunately, however, the assiduous cultivation of all these virtuous goals may still, it would seem, even in combination result in the most pedestrian of problems. We must then search further for means of assuring ourselves that the problem is a good one. The usual criteria do not seem to answer.

I am going to say that there are three fundamentals which form the basis for good experiments or good problems. None of these are new. By disclaiming originality, however, I can claim that they are profound and that their presence or absence makes a significant effect in the value of the problem to an individual. Two of these are characteristics of the person, and one of the problem. The most common tags for my trio are: knowledge, dissatisfaction, and generalizability. The first two of these, of course, refer to the individual himself and the third to the problem itself.

I think that there is very general agreement that one can only work effectively in an area when he has a thorough understanding of this general area of concern. It is quite often that the significant finding comes from a fusion of quite a number of simple studies or a perception of gaps in the detailed findings or the methodologies and procedures of others. I am quite sure that the vaunted, creative insight of the scientist occurs more frequently within a thorough knowledge of one's area than as a bolt from the blue.

In a quite mechanical sense, a failure to obtain all knowledge possible about one's problem area is to fail to profit from the errors of thought of the past, if they be errors, or the knowledges obtained, if such knowledges are correct. Either represents an arrogance of a witless kind. Moreover, in this very practical sense, unless these backgrounds are well assessed by the worker, one may find oneself both discovering a most well-known discovery and be in the embarrassing position of arriving at the party dressed in full regalia a day late. Or perhaps, more tragic for the world of ideas, such a person without knowledge may remain unheard, being incapable of gaining the attention of competent workers through an ineptitude of expression or lack of relation to the field.

Secondly, however, to avoid the sins of conformity, suggested previously—for specialized knowledge groups can become more ingroupish than a band of teenagers—a healthy opposition must be present. I have designated this as dissatisfaction. Other terms to be used are skepticism, negativism, or perhaps more charmingly, iconoclasm.

It is, of course, quite possible that I am very wrong in emphasizing the necessity of an opposing set to the existent knowledges and methodologies in one's time. Clearly the most convenient position would be to invoke the concept of "genius" or "insight," leading to important problems as a result of broad surveys of the literature, or efficiency in employing procedures. This, however, would hardly be useful as a guideline. One can hardly suggest to a person that they strain and have an insight, or try hard and be a genius.

There are, on the other hand, considerable empirical evidences, or at least examples, to substantiate the fact that original discoveries contain an element of active revolution. Skipping lightly through psychological history, we can point to Helmholtz' classical rate of nerve conduction experiments which flew in the face of established knowledge about immediate conductivity, Freud defied the reign of conscious thought, Watson negated mentalism, Köhler set against the tide of trial and error learning, in recent times Harlow has spoken not so much for positive adient motivation as against avoidant motives as the prime mover of man.

Logically, and psychologically (and happily they conjoin occasionally) this seems to make good sense. A significant research problem is a creative act. One can hardly be creative if one is avidly listening to the voice of others. We have good evidence from such experimentations as the Luchin's jar experiments that developed sets can clearly block solutions to problems. More simply, if one agrees with everything that everyone else says, one's role is automatically limited to feeding the fires, applauding the words or, at best, carrying the word. None of these are actions that lead to truly important research activities.

We may have, however, great knowledge and object quite violently to the items of this knowledge and proceed to conduct small experiments to substantiate our objections and still be doing little more than picking at a pimple on the face of one's science, to use a vulgar analogy. A further critical requirement must be recognized—a critical requirement that is most difficult to capture in words: to be an important result, one's findings require "extensity." Another word used here is that one's results must be generalizable. Poincaré, in his *Methods of Science*, states most clearly the reasoning underlying this requirement:

> What, then, is a good experiment? It is that which informs us of something besides an isolated fact. It is that which enables us to foresee, i.e.,

that which enables us to generalize. . . . Circumstances under which one has worked will never reproduce themselves all at once. The observed action then will never recur. The only thing that can be affirmed is that under analogous circumstances, analogous action is produced.

A further quotation from the same book amplifies this point of view:

. . . it is needful that each of our thoughts be as useful as possible and this is why a law will be the more precious the more general it is. This shows us how we should choose. The most interesting facts are those which may serve many times.

Very simply, this boils down to being able to evaluate the probable consequence of your findings with the question which goes something like this: "In how many and what kind of specific circumstances will the relationships or rules that hold in this experiment hold in such other instances?" If the answer to this is only in instances almost exactly replicable of this particular circumstance, the rules that we obtain are likely to be of little consequence. If, however, the rule applies to what apparently is a vast heterogeneity of events in time and space, in varieties of species and surrounds, this rule is likely to have great value. Stated otherwise, the extent to which our variables and situations are unique and rare in contrast to universal and common largely determines the extent to which the findings are likely to be considered trivial or tremendous in their implications.

My summary can be quite simple:

Research today is both complex and costly. Guidelines are needed to sort among these complexities to enhance our chances of a sound investment, be this personal, financial, or temporal.

Six criteria may be, and often are, applied to judge a project's "success" potential: curiosity, confirmability, cost, compassion, cupidity, and conformability. There is probably a good probability that studies meeting the guidelines will "pay off" in some form of coinage—perhaps small change.

However, for a study to be an enduring and critical one for the history of ideas or to enter into that stream, three further items seem involved:

1. You must know thoroughly the body of research and the techniques of experimentation which are related to a given problem area. Naivete may be a source of joy in an artistic field but this is not the case in valued research efforts.

2. You should be able to disbelieve, be dissatisfied with, or deny the

knowledge that you have. (This is no paradox in relation to our first statement. Recognize that the first requirement is propaedeutic to this one. This is an active, not a passive state; this is to know and then know differently, rather than a know-nothing state.) Valued research seems to grow from dissatisfactions with the way things are, rather than agreeable perpetuation of present ways of proceeding.

3. You should, very simply, look for the forest beyond the tree, test the generality of your proposed finding. If your finding is referent to a rat in a particular maze, a patient on a particular couch, or a refined statistical difference, then that rat, that patient, or a captive statistician may listen to you. This would be a skimpy and disappointing audience to my way of thinking.

It is quite likely that we cannot all become geniuses. We can at least try to be less trivial. Learn as much as we can, believe in new ways, seek as great extensity in our variables as we can.

Carter V. Good

Criteria for Selection
of the Research Problem

In the previous selection Webb suggests three general criteria for the selection of the problem, criteria that would lead to more worthwhile research. In this selection Good suggests ten specific criteria that will help the researcher determine whether or not his problem may be worthwhile. Good's criteria extend beyond those of Webb; that is, they consider more than the significance of the problem. It might be interesting to evaluate Good's criteria to determine how many deal with the actual significance of the problem and how many might be considered more in a practical vein—and then see if any contradictions exist between Good and Webb.

Carter V. Good, "Criteria for Selection of the Research Problem," *Peabody Journal of Education*, 19:242-56, March, 1942. Reprinted with permission.

These suggestions are offered to candidates for graduate degrees, to field workers interested in problem solving, and to other students of research. Most of the illustrations are drawn from the areas of education, psychology, and the social sciences.

Factors to be considered in selection of a thesis or research problem are both external and personal. External criteria have to do with such matters as novelty and importance for the field, availability of data and method, and institutional or administrative cooperation. Personal criteria involve such considerations as interest, training, cost, and time. A more detailed list of criteria for selection of the problem follows:

1. Novelty and avoidance of unnecessary duplication
2. Importance for the field represented
3. Interest and intellectual curiosity
4. Training and personal qualifications
5. Availability of data and method
6. Special equipment and working conditions

7. Sponsorship and administrative cooperation
8. Costs and returns
9. Hazards and penalties
10. Time factor

NOVELTY AND AVOIDANCE OF UNNECESSARY DUPLICATION

Students of research have recognized as a source of problems the repetition of experiments or the extension of investigations; however, this means deliberate, planned repetition rather than accidental or blind duplication through ignorance of the area and literature represented.

An almost unexplainable example of duplication is found in the thesis projects of two professors in different state universities of Ohio, both of whom were working on the certification of teachers in Ohio, one at a graduate school in the same state and the other at a university on the eastern seaboard. In 1935 the dissertation of one candidate was published at the eastern school, to the great surprise and chagrin of the other investigator, who then took up another problem. The latter candidate could have found the thesis of the successful doctorate investigator listed as under way in the January, 1933, number of the *Journal of Educational Research*, well before he began work. This instance of duplication is all the more surprising in view of the fact that both men were in the same state, were engaged in similar occupational pursuits, and no doubt were using many of the same records of the state department of education and of other agencies or institutions interested in certification.

Even great scientists and able scholars have been negligent and sometimes contemptuous of the literature and earlier investigations in their fields of specialization. Pasteur blundered in representing himself as the first to discover that microscopic animals could live without breathing, since Leeuwenhoek two centuries earlier and Spallanzani a hundred years before Pasteur had found the same thing. Pasteur also rediscovered the fact that microbes cause meat to spoil, without giving proper credit to Schwann, who was the first to make that observation.[1]

The problem of novelty or newness is not merely one of duplication of earlier investigations. It involves the recency of the data interpreted,

---

[1] T. A. Boyd, *Research*, pp. 74-75. New York: D. Appleton-Century Co., 1935.

especially in the case of survey studies made during a period of great economic, educational, or social change. The city superintendent of schools and doctorate candidate who early in 1940 made an industrial survey of his community, a youth and employment survey of the high school graduates, and a canvass of parents and high school pupils concerning attitudes toward the curriculum found the data inadequate as a basis for curriculum reorganization late in 1941. In the intervening period great industrial changes as a result of the national defense program had taken place, with marked effects on employment, attitudes, and the school program.

The question of duplication arises when two graduate students propose a joint thesis, a type of cooperative effort seldom permitted, although many wives of candidates have well earned a share in the graduate degrees awarded their husbands. It is true that there are many commissions, surveys, and research agencies with large programs of investigation in which graduate studies are worked out as complementary parts of a research pattern. Also, in certain historical areas, different chronological periods are treated separately in graduate theses; for example, the constitutional and legal basis of education in Ohio, 1800-1850, by one doctorate candidate; 1850-1900 by a second doctorate student; and 1900-1930 in a Master's thesis. The problem of pupil transportation requires a series of studies for regions with different geographic, climatic, population, and road conditions, as in Wyoming, Ohio, and West Virginia.

It frequently happens that two or more scholars, scientists, or inventors may be working simultaneously on the same problem, each without knowledge of the other, and may announce their findings at almost the same time. In such instances, history has viewed the discovery as a joint contribution; for example, James and Lange, a theory of the emotions; Darwin, Spencer, and Wallace, a theory of evolution; Lancaster and Bell, a system of monitorial instruction; Newton and Leibnitz, the calculus as a general method and a system of notation for it; the Wright brothers and Langley, heavier-than-air flying; Bell and Gray, the telephone; Faraday and Henry, the principles of electromagnetic induction; Mendelyeev and Meyer, similar classifications of the chemical elements; and Mayer, Mohr, Helmholtz, and Golding, the generalization of the conservation of energy.[2]

---

[2] E. G. Boring, *A History of Experimental Psychology*, pp. 165, 502-3. New York: Century Co., 1929.

T. A. Boyd, *op. cit.*, p. 280.

IMPORTANCE FOR THE FIELD REPRESENTED

This criterion for choice of a problem involves such matters as significance for the field involved, timeliness, and practical value in terms of application and implementation of the results. Scientific work in education, psychology, and the social sciences in general has an especially urgent obligation to play a social role in rendering service to society and humanity.[3] It is high time that the social responsibilities of scientists and of research workers be recognized and accepted.

Francis Bacon was aiming at the invention of a method that would solve not only particular scientific problems, but also provide for the adaptation of the results to the social process. The core of Bacon's work was not so much science as the social relations of science. He was critical of Galileo's method of abstracting problems entirely from their general and social context. Scientists, in the main, have followed Galileo for three centuries, accumulating discoveries in areas of research artificially isolated from the general body of knowledge and social affairs.[4]

An illustration of failure to recognize a socially valuable problem is found in the case of two research students who went to investigate a racial conflict in a certain community. They returned with the statement that everything was harmonious between Orientals and Americans, a race riot having just been settled amicably, hence there was nothing to investigate. They overlooked an excellent opportunity to study an accommodation process, an adjustment between races.[5]

J. G. Crowther, *The Social Relations of Science*, p. 450. New York: The Macmillan Co., 1941.

Charles A. Ellwood, *A History of Social Philosophy*, pp. 437-41. Englewood Cliffs, N.J.: Prentice-Hall, Inc., 1938.

Gardner Murphy, *An Historical Introduction to Modern Psychology*, pp. 121, 216-17. New York: Harcourt, Brace & World, Inc., 1932.

[3] Carter V. Good, "Educational Progress During the Year, 1940," *School and Society*, LIII (March 15, 1941), 330-37.

For extended recent discussions of this problem see:

J. D. Bernal, *The Social Function of Science*. New York: The Macmillan Co., 1939. pp. xvi., 482.

J. G. Crowther, *The Social Relations of Science*. New York: The Macmillan Co., 1941. pp. xxxiv., 665.

Florian Znaniecki, *The Social Role of the Man of Knowledge*. New York: Columbia University Press, 1940. pp. viii., 212.

[4] J. G. Crowther, *op. cit.*, pp. 351-52.

[5] Emory S. Bogardus, *Introduction to Social Research*, p. 5. Los Angeles: Suttonhouse, 1936.

The element of timeliness is illustrated by studies of the tuitional value of motion pictures, an important problem about 1922. If similar studies were undertaken today for the simple purpose of ascertaining whether children secure value received for time spent in viewing an instructional film, the problem would be considered relatively unimportant, since an affirmative answer is already well known.[6]

The research worker is not expected, as a general rule, to implement the results of his studies, however desirable this consummation may be; he is not even compelled to point out the practical applications of his findings, although this step seems essential, especially in the social sciences. It is suggested that the scientist in education cannot leave himself out of his own picture and that research in education is part of the process of education itself.[7] Even in the physical aspects of child development, traits cannot be measured as if they were independent entities growing without some central control on the part of the organism. In reading, research has advanced from study of relatively mechanical factors toward the purpose of the reader and the social uses of the process. Guidance investigations have moved away from the notion of fitting a pattern of aptitudes into a pattern of demands to a consideration of the individual in relation to society. Research in educational finance must concern itself with forces of public opinion and common desire. Survey testing is now of secondary importance as compared with functional use of measurement for segregation or classification, diagnosis, prediction or prognosis, evaluation, and standardization of desirable practices. "When it comes to education there is no avoiding the step from the study of the elements of a problem, objectively considered, to the study of what can be done to acquaint the individual or the group with the situation. Educational research leads into education. How to implement research is a part of research itself."[8]

Even where applications of scientific discoveries are clearly indicated, there are almost countless examples of the thwarting of science in such fields as health, nutrition, medicine, housing, recreation, education, industry, and invention, owing to economic and social factors, tradition, competition, the profit motive, war, and prejudice.[9]

---

[6] Douglas E. Scates and Charles F. Hoban, Jr., "Critical Questions for the Evaluation of Research," *Journal of Educational Research*, XXXI (December, 1937), 241-54.

[7] H. W. Holmes and Others, *Educational Research*, pp. 181-82. Washington: American Council on Education, 1939.

[8] H. W. Holmes and Others, *op. cit.*, p. 182.

[9] J. G. Crowther, *op. cit.*, pp. 576-91.

INTEREST AND INTELLECTUAL CURIOSITY

The history of science is studded with the names of scholars led (and sometimes driven) to their discoveries by consuming intellectual curiosity. One of the personal motives for research most frequently mentioned by scientists themselves is pure curiosity, accompanied by genuine interest and a derived satisfaction or enjoyment. Only an insatiable curiosity and driving interest could have compelled Aristotle to undertake so varied a program of activities, which identify him in the language of today as professor, philosopher, psychologist, logician, moralist, political thinker, biologist, founder of literary criticism, and author of books on all these subjects.[10] Herschel was a musician until the age of forty, but his curiosity and strong interests in astronomy and in the making of telescopes led to the spectacular discovery of the planet Uranus, origination of descriptive astronomy, and a lasting impetus to the construction of large telescopes. Galileo's interests cropped out in his freshman days at the University of Pisa; he soon gave up premedical work in favor of mathematics and natural science. While poor, he evidently was not interested in monetary rewards; a professor of medicine then received the equivalent of about $2,000 a year, and a professor of mathematics only about $65.

The desire to understand fully and to construct a completely coherent system of ideas that will explain phenomena frequently is so strong that scientists go to extremes in concentration, withdrawal from human contacts, and in reluctance to publish anything short of perfect solutions of problems.[11] Cavendish had his meals placed through a hole in the wall of his room, to avoid speaking to anyone and to reduce interruptions to a minimum. He failed to publish his invention of electrical condensers, which was rediscovered by Faraday. Newton asked that his first paper, the solution of a problem in annuities, be published without his name attached, for fear of increasing the number of his acquaintances. Darwin worked on the *Origin of Species* for more than twenty years, and might never have published it without pressure from Lyell.

Striking differences in intellectual curiosity and scientific interests are noted in the work of Huxley, a great propagandist for science,

---

[10] Frederick Slocum, "Intellectual Curiosity," *School and Society*, XLVIII (August 6, 1938), 157-63.

[11] J. G. Crowther, *op. cit.*, pp. 511-16.

and of Darwin, a great research worker.[12] Huxley's diary of the voyage on the *Rattlesnake* is concerned with personal psychological problems and resistance to fits of depression, while Darwin's diary of the voyage on the *Beagle*, in spite of his poor health, is devoted to the collection of facts and the development of scientific ideas.

It follows that the graduate student's choice of area, problem, or method will depend to a large extent on his interests, as well as on such criteria as novelty, importance for the field represented, training, etc.

TRAINING AND PERSONAL QUALIFICATIONS

It should be recognized that such fields as education, psychology, and sociology are greatly indebted to workers with specialized training in other disciplines, especially during the stages when the foundations are being laid for a new science. To use psychology as an example, contributors to the early development of psychology include: Descartes, philosopher and physiologist; Leibnitz and Locke, philosophers and men of political affairs; Berkeley, philosopher, bishop, and educator; Hume, philosopher, historian, and politician; Hartley, learned physician; James Mill, historian and diplomatist; John Stuart Mill, philosopher, logician, and political economist; Charles Bell, Flourens, Johannes Muller, and E. H. Weber, physiologists; Lotze, metaphysician; Helmholtz, physiologist and physicist; Bain, really a psychologist but formally a logician; Fechner, physicist and philosopher; and finally Wundt, physician and physiologist who in 1875 accepted a chair of philosophy at Leipzig, although his experiments and work make it possible without reservation to call him the senior psychologist in the history of psychology.[13] Many later psychologists have continued to pursue special training in medicine and physiology. Graduate students may well interpret the preceding illustrations as a suggestion to avoid over specialization or narrowness in their programs of training.

The versatility of Leonardo da Vinci should be interpreted in the light of his training as an apprentice in the shop of Verrocchio, a distinguished painter, goldsmith, and craftsman who had some knowledge of sculpture, architecture, and engineering.[14]

Gabriel Tarde's contributions to sociology were derived primarily

12 *Ibid.*, p. 516.

13 Edwin G. Boring, *op. cit.*, pp. 223-24, 310.

14 J. G. Crowther, *op. cit.*, p. 253.

from his training for the law and his long period of service as a criminal judge in France. He saw how crime was so frequently the result of contagion and association, and decided that most of the phenomena of human society are socially acquired and socially transmitted.[15]

The worker's physical equipment must be considered in relation to the contemplated field and problem. James Rowland Angell, near the end of his college course, considered the pursuit of medicine, but weak eyes compelled him to forego the arduous microscopic work that was and is an essential feature of the medical training program.[16] If medicine was the loser, psychology and university administration gained a competent worker.

Freedom from bias is an essential prerequisite for successful research in the social sciences.[17] There is the interesting case of the young college woman who undertook to write a hero-worshiping paper on the career of a fascist leader and in despair asked the instructor for an extension of time, because the evidence was "all on the wrong side of the question."[18]

The wise graduate student will consider carefully both the subject-matter content and the treatment of research methodology in his program of training—past, present, and future—in selection of the thesis problem. Through organized courses and seminars, supplemented by independent reading, the necessary background concerning content and research methods can be secured. For example, to write the history of a state department of education, the student should know at least the history of the state and nation, history of education in the state and in the United States, school administration, and the historical method. In this particular instance, the graduate investigator in question has had substantial advanced work in all the fields mentioned. The student may well become acquainted with the different investigational procedures, considering the available courses and seminars where certain of these methods are analyzed in detail, before definitely formulating his thesis problem. It has even been suggested that, if life were longer and time less fleeting, those engaged in edu-

---

[15] Charles A. Ellwood, *op. cit.*, pp. 417-26.

[16] Carl Murchison, Editor, *A History of Psychology in Autobiography*, Volume III, p. 5. Worcester, Mass.: Clark University Press, 1936.

[17] For examples drawn from graduate theses in education see: Carter V. Good, A. S. Barr, and Douglas E. Scates, *The Methodology of Educational Research*, pp. 72-73. New York: D. Appleton Century Co., 1936.

[18] Cecil B. Williams and Allan H. Stevenson, *A Research Manual*, p. 30. New York: Harper & Row, Publishers, 1940.

cational research should know the entire range of research in psychology, biology, and sociology, as well as possess basic training in the humanities, history, philosophy, and science.[19]

It is admitted that classroom instruction is only one source of training. John Stuart Mill never went to school except to his father. What he learned through personal accomplishment and exacting paternal instruction was further impressed on him by later becoming the tutor of his younger sisters and brothers.[20] However, it should be remembered that Mill's native equipment was such as to enable him to begin study of Greek at the age of three years.

AVAILABILITY OF DATA AND METHOD

Closely related to the immediately preceding criterion of training and personal equipment is that of availability of satisfactory data and an appropriate method. The data under consideration must meet certain standards of accuracy, objectivity, and verifiability. The contemplated problem should be viewed in the light of the possible research approaches.

Writers on research methods have emphasized the desirability of becoming familiar with the purposes served by the several investigational procedures before making a definite choice of the thesis topic. One of the things that graduate students in education have had to live down is the questionnaire complex, the tendency to turn to the questionnaire as an instrument before careful formulation of the problem and before thoughtful consideration of an appropriate method. The normative-survey type of research is not expected to yield rigorous data concerning causes. The experimental method is not pointed toward a description of prevailing conditions or practices.

Sometimes a theoretically desirable procedure breaks down under actual field conditions; for example, an experimental investigation of motion pictures in the school, involving 11,000 children in more than 300 classes, taught by nearly 200 teachers.[21] It was impossible for the investigators to keep in close contact with all the centers; consequently conditions could not be kept uniform. In one school keen rivalry

---

[19] Henry W. Holmes and Others, *op. cit.*, pp. 184-86.

[20] Edwin G. Boring, *op. cit.*, p. 217.

[21] Ben D. Wood and Frank N. Freeman, *Motion Pictures in the Classroom.* Boston: Houghton Mifflin Co., 1929. p. 392.

Douglas E. Scates and Charles F. Hoban, *op. cit.*, p. 244.

developed between the control and experimental teachers. In many schools visual aids other than those contemplated in the experiment were used. In other instances teachers were so unfamiliar with the instructional use of motion pictures that exaggerated conditions resulted.

Certain types of problems defy solution, in terms of available data and techniques, because of the vastness and complexity of the problem (for example, the causes of the fall of the Roman Empire) or because of the loss or suppression of evidence. Probably Channing's survey of the entire sweep of American history will be the last attempted by one author. A doctorate candidate gave up a study of the social and educational attitudes of one thousand school board members in a particular state when the interview technique seemed the only feasible approach. In turning to another problem, a survey of secondary school organization in one of the Spanish-speaking countries of South or Central America, he still must consider the availability of data and method in terms of the language factor, necessary travel, and his knowledge of comparative education.

In certain instances the approach to a problem opens through a fortunate combination of circumstances, increased insight on the part of the investigator, or a change in occupational status or professional assignment. Darwin's trip on the *Beagle* through the South Seas, 1831-1836, gave him a magnificent opportunity to observe and collect plants and animals.[22] A graduate student who called on a prominent citizen to investigate a local conflict received the reply that everything was quiet; a more experienced worker, who understood the sense of local pride possessed by the community "booster," found that bitter racial conflicts actually were in progress in the locality.[23] An elementary school principal found the way open to study the departmentalized elementary school when his school board sent him on a field trip to observe the reorganization procedures employed in a selected group of cities. Specialists in music education and in trades and industries were enabled to make state wide surveys of the opportunities in their respective fields on appointment to state supervisory positions.

SPECIAL EQUIPMENT AND WORKING CONDITIONS

Available treatises dealing with the several research methods include descriptions of the special sources, equipment, and working conditions

---

[22] Gardner Murphy, *op. cit.*, p. 119.
[23] Emory S. Bogardus, *op. cit.*, pp. 4-5.

commonly represented in the several types of investigation—historical, survey, experimental, case, and genetic. Consideration is given earlier in this article to personal qualifications and to training in the use of special techniques and material equipment.

It should be emphasized that the quality of scientific work resides not in the ornateness of the laboratory equipment or the complexity of the measuring and recording instruments, but in the soundness of the thinking and the validity of the evidence for solution of the problem. The major purpose of such equipment is to refine the process of observation through control of conditions or through accuracy or permanence of recording. Desirable as elaborate equipment and adequate financial support may be, there are many instances of problem solving outside the laboratory or study.[24] Helmholtz said that, after he had been working on a problem for some time, happy ideas for a solution came to him at some place other than his working table. Darwin was riding in his carriage when his theory of evolution came to him. Watt was walking on Sunday afternoon when he invented the condensing steam engine. Morse conceived the telegraph on a return trip from Europe. The aria of the beautiful quartet in the "Magic Flute" came to Mozart while he was playing billiards.

Improvised laboratories sometimes have produced remarkable results. The Curies conducted their long search for radium in a shed that had been a dissecting room. Bell experimented on his telephone in a Salem cellar and in a Boston attic. Pasteur discovered pasteurization in an old room that had been a cafè. Goodyear stumbled across vulcanization of rubber in a New England kitchen.

Thorndike candidly mentions an extreme ineptitude and distaste on his part for using machinery and physical instruments. He regrets the absence in his training of a systematic course in the use of standard physiological and psychological apparatus and of extended training in mathematics, modestly suggesting that his work might have been better had he been at home with apparatus for exposing, timing, registering, and the like.[25]

Many men of genius, and others of lesser talents, have a drive and a power of concentration to accomplish their tasks in spite of the handicaps of working conditions.[26] Descartes once left Paris in disgust because his friends insisted upon disturbing him in his quarters. During the very productive period of twenty years before his death

---

[24] T. A. Boyd, *op. cit.*, pp. 55-62.

[25] Edward L. Thorndike, *History of Psychology in Autobiography*, Volume III, *op. cit.*, pp. 267-68.

[26] Edwin G. Boring, *op. cit.*, pp. 159, 209-10.

he is said to have lived in thirteen places and in twenty-four houses, with his whereabouts unknown except to a few intimates who respected his seclusion and forwarded communications to him. Driven by financial pressure, James Mill composed several volumes of the *History of India* at one end of a table, while his son, John Stuart Mill, went to school to the father at the other end, among other things learning Greek and interrupting his father for the meaning of every new word.

SPONSORSHIP AND ADMINISTRATIVE COOPERATION

In graduate departments of instruction it is common practice for the thesis to be sponsored by a faculty adviser in whose area of specialization the problem lies. When a committee gives this advice, as is usually the case for the doctorate dissertation, the chairman is the major adviser. In selecting his problem, the candidate will do well to consider the availability of a particular professor for the duration of the graduate program. Leave of absence, a heavy teaching schedule, an already excessive number of advisees, concentration on writing or research, numerous speaking engagements, ill health, or personality difficulties on the part of a particular professor may render him relatively unavailable for additional assignment to the extent that the graduate student may wish to turn elsewhere for thesis guidance or at least to consider the hazards involved in securing the necessary conferences and advice. It is recognized that the beginning graduate student often lacks the factual background to act judiciously in choosing an adviser; however, students have a way of educating each other to the problems of a particular department or institution and to the characteristics and idiosyncrasies of individual professors.

In many instances the sponsorship of a department, institution, or school system is necessary to collect certain types of data or to use special sources. Permission from the responsible school officers usually must be secured to administer tests to children, to interview employees or to distribute questionnaires among them, to observe pupils and teachers at work, to rate school buildings or equipment, to introduce innovations in materials and methods, or to study problem pupils. Official permission ordinarily is necessary to use the minutes of a board of education or the records of a school unit—state, county, city, or smaller local system. Certainly a graduate student would be unwise to attempt a thesis problem where administrative cooperation is withheld. Occasionally an institution or school system is willing to sponsor officially a thesis that relates closely to the work of the sponsoring organization or promises to solve one of its pressing problems, although unfortunate experiences in public relations have rendered most universities and administrative officers wary about too frequent use of this practice.

COSTS AND RETURNS

Graduate instruction and research are expensive. Fortunately for the student, only a part of the cost is passed on to him. Endowments, taxes, and grants from foundations make possible reduced tuition rates as well as scholarships, fellowships, and assistantships. These same sources of revenue have provided financial assistance for certain types of theses, such as those involving large-scale testing programs, extended tabulations, intricate laboratory equipment, or expensive travel. In advance of final selection of the thesis problem, the candidate must consider carefully his own financial resources, in the light of such facilities and assistance as can be provided by the institution.

Graduate students are not alone in encountering financial difficulties in pursuit of their objectives. Thorndike says that he made it a rule early in his career to spend so little and earn so much as to be free from financial worry.[27] It seems the rule rather than the exception for inventors, scholars, and scientists to meet pecuniary problems in connection with their investigations, writing, and research.[28] Newton at one time in his life was so poverty-stricken that he had to ask relief from paying the weekly dues of a shilling to the Royal Society. Charles Goodyear, after discovering how to vulcanize rubber, died in debt to the extent of $200,000. John Fitch, discouraged and poverty-stricken after his series of experiments with the steamboat, took his own life. LeBlanc discovered how to make cheap alkali, but died in a French poorhouse. Comte, after losing his position and suffering other reverses, found his income so reduced that he told John Stuart Mill of his difficulties. Mill, with the aid of Grote, the historian, raised about 20,000 francs as a gift for Comte in order that he might continue study and publication of his books, but after five years Comte was again in financial straits. Herbert Spencer was an invalid most of his life, with

---

27 Edward L. Thorndike, *History of Psychology in Autobiography*, Volume III, *op. cit.*, p. 270.

28 Charles A. Ellwood, *op. cit.*, p. 364.

T. A. Boyd, *op. cit.*, pp. 53-54.

a very uncertain income. He put more into his early books than he received from them, since he usually employed an amanuensis. Only within the last few years of his life did he receive any substantial revenue from his books, and even in those years the publication of *Descriptive Sociology* took from him a large part of his earnings.[29]

Some scientists have had large personal resources, which they used in the pursuit of research.[30] Roger Bacon was a member of a wealthy family and probably earned substantial fees while lecturing in Paris between 1236 and 1251. He spent ten thousand pounds, in modern money, on the purchase of books, experiments and instruments, journeys to meet scholars, and secretaries. Within a period of eighteen years, Lavoisier received an income of sixty thousand pounds, most of which was spent on research. Charles Darwin was an English gentleman of wealth and leisure, which provided favorable conditions for his work.

The illustrations just cited suggest that the work of the scholar or scientist guarantees no fixed monetary return. Often the chief reward is the satisfaction of an intellectual interest in the solution of a problem. Pasteur declared, "I could never work for money, but I would always work for science," while Agassiz said, "I have no time to make money."[31] It is true that the work of both these scientists was supported by educational institutions. For the graduate student, who usually is interested in tangible returns on completion of his program of advanced study, there is reasonable expectation of one or more of the following developments: advancement on the salary schedule, promotion, enhancement of reputation, or cultivation of an area of specialization.

HAZARDS AND PENALTIES

The illustrations of the preceding section indicate the pecuniary hazards that frequently attend the pursuit of scientific work. In the selection of certain types of problems, the worker may well consider other special penalties of a personal, social, or professional character, not necessarily with the thought of avoiding or giving up a particular study but of making the choice with eyes open. For example, there are agencies that have sought to place restrictions on animal experimentation in psychology, medicine, and other fields, with the result that the

---

[29] Charles A. Ellwood, *op. cit.*, pp. 339-40.
[30] J. G. Crowther, *op. cit.*, pp. 208, 436.
[31] T. A. Boyd, *op. cit.*, pp. 283-91.

American Psychological Association finds it desirable to maintain a Committee on Precautions in Animal Experimentation, which has available a printed list of rules and precautions for such research. Pressure groups and institutional taboos have handicapped the investigation of problems of social hygiene and sex in sociology, psychology, and education. Opposition frequently is voiced against the reporting of results that run counter to the beliefs or programs of certain economic, social, patriotic, or religious groups.[32]

When Fechner was suffering from what today might be called a "nervous breakdown," he increased his difficulties by undertaking the study of positive after-images from bright stimuli, particularly the sun. This produced violent pain in his eyes and partial blindness, from which he did not recover for several years.[33]

Galileo was highly praised by some, ridiculed by others, and summoned before the Inquisition at the age of seventy-eight to recant his so-called heretical teachings. With health broken, he returned home to continue productive work. Totally blind at eighty, he continued work, dictating to some of his faithful disciples.

Physical handicaps were encountered by the historians, Parkman and Prescott, who for long periods were almost blind. At one time Parkman used a frame with parallel wires to guide his black crayon.

The type of stern and uncompromising education received by precocious John Stuart Mill from his father meant that he had no boyhood friends, no child's play, and little youthful reading. The son's curriculum included Greek at three years of age; Aesop's *Fables*, the *Anabasis*, all of Herodotus, some of Plato, and many other standard Greek works before eight; and Latin, geometry, and algebra at eight years. Later, there were several years of mental depression when Mill, brought up in austere personal life to scorn all emotion, began to doubt the value of his political and social activities.[34]

To be the butt of ridicule is frequently the price paid by pioneers. People laughed at Fulton's steamboat, Stephenson's locomotive, the

---

[32] H. K. Beale, *Are American Teachers Free?* New York: Charles Scribner's Sons, 1936. pp. xxiv., 855.

William Gellerman, *The American Legion as Educator.* Teachers College Contributions to Education, No. 743. New York: Teachers College, Columbia University, 1938. p. 280.

Bessie L. Pierce, *Citizens' Organizations and the Civic Training of Youth.* New York: Charles Scribner's Sons, 1933. pp. xviii., 428.

Bruce Raup, *Education and Organized Interests in America.* New York: G. P. Putnam's Sons, 1936. p. 238.

[33] Gardner Murphy, *op. cit.,* p. 87.

[34] Edwin G. Boring, *op. cit.,* pp. 217-18.

Wright brothers' flying machine, the horseless carriage, the achievement tests of James M. Rice, and at the I. Q.

These are some of the penalties of pioneering, although in the interest of accurate perspective for the modern student of the social sciences it should be said that he will not ordinarily encounter such difficulties. Many agencies and institutions have contributed toward smoothing the path of the research worker of today.

TIME FACTOR

Graduate students quite properly are interested in the length of time necessary to complete the program for an advanced degree. They are eager to begin or to continue their professional careers and usually have limited financial resources. As a general rule, the minimum amount of graduate work for the Master's degree is one year, and for the Doctor's degree, three years. The time required for completion of the thesis depends on the variables of the student, problem, department, adviser, and institution. Most students have their course work finished before the thesis is completed. Few good Doctors' dissertations are accepted with less than the equivalent of a full year of work, while a Master's thesis of similar quality may require half that time. By their very nature, historical, experimental case, and longitudinal genetic studies frequently require more time than the several types of normative-survey work. Many students have found it profitable both intellectually and professionally to do at least part of their graduate work in full-time residence during the academic school year rather than to depend entirely on the part-time courses of the regular year or the summer-session program.

Lest the beginning graduate student and others become too impatient with the time requirements for careful training and research, a few examples may be cited from the lives and works of famous scholars and scientists.[35] Copernicus worked nearly forty years on his problem and eventually published his only book, on the heliocentric theory of the motions of the planets. Galileo's *Dialogues Concerning Two New Sciences* was published in 1638 when he was seventy-four years of age, after collecting and developing the material for fifty years. John Locke did not attain fame as a philosopher until the publication of his *Essay*

---

[35] Edwin G. Boring, *op. cit.*, pp. 169-70, 179, 186-88, 495.
J. G. Crowther, *op. cit.*, pp. 308, 513.
T. A. Boyd, *op. cit.*, pp. 177-81.

in 1690 (begun in 1671), when he had reached fifty-seven. On the other hand, George Berkeley, Locke's immediate successor in British philosophy, published his two important contributions in successive years, 1709 and 1710, when he was about twenty-five. Berkeley's philosophical successor, David Hume, also matured early, publishing his most important work at twenty-eight; later in life, court fame and society distracted him from greater philosophical accomplishment. Darwin spent more than twenty years in preparation of the *Origin of Species*. William James worked twelve hard years on his *Principles of Psychology*, published in 1890. Pasteur used five years to find his remedy for hydrophobia. Faraday needed ten years to "change magnetism into electricity." Fifteen years of research and five million dollars went into the discovery of synthetic indigo.

When Charles F. Kettering was doing research for the National Cash Register Company, he estimated that a certain project would require a year for completion. When asked to double his force and reduce the time to six months, his reply was: "Do you think that by putting two hens on the nest a setting of eggs could be hatched out in less time than three weeks?"[36]

---

[36] T. A. Boyd, *op. cit.*, p. 177.

T. A. Lamke

A Primer in Research . . .
Lesson I: Defining the Problem

Many would-be researchers are capable of identifying a general problem but incapable of mounting a research effort that contributes to the resolution of that problem. The activity which enables movement, Lamke contends, is the development of operationalized definitions for the factors included in the general problem statement. Operationalizing, he recognizes, moves to a focus on a specific situation and apparently away from the general problem. This moving away is not a major problem, nor a failure to solve the problem, but rather a tactic which fits nicely in the reasoning processes described in Chapter 1. The researcher identifies a general problem, structures specific observations, and generalizes back to the general problem. Lamke acknowledges that the details defined in the process of operationalizing, especially sample selection and treatment, are the determiners of the researcher's ability to generalize.

T. A. Lamke, "A Primer in Research . . . Lesson I: Defining the Problem," *Phi Delta Kappan*, 38:127-29, January, 1957. Reprinted with permission.

The research worker (often a student working on a thesis or dissertation) may at first attack his problem vigorously, and feel that he is making progress. But if he is inexperienced, and after the momentum generated by his initial enthusiasm dies away, he often finds himself slowing to a halt, breathing heavily, despite his continued earnest efforts.

The difficulty is usually with the statement of his problem.

The researcher will ordinarily find it quite easy to decide on a broad area within which he wishes to work. His experience, training, and the necessities of the moment will all point to one or several general problem areas. But he will not find a concrete research problem—a problem which may actually be solved—no matter how congenial the general area, until he realizes that ideas and relations specified with sufficient

143

exactness to serve (generally) for purposes of communication will not often be found usable for doing anything other than sketching a research problem in broadest outline.

For example, the problem of interest may be the effectiveness of the mathematics curriculum in the secondary school. The problem as stated is put into sufficiently specific terms so that individuals may understand it in a broad sense, and communicate with each other about it in a general way. Because this is true, the inexperienced researcher may not see the urgent necessity of further specification of the problem. He will attempt to find methods of answering the question as it stands. He will finally recognize that any methods he can think of to solve the problem or answer the question will be inadequate; he may finally conclude that he simply cannot do research work.

But in this case, what is meant by "curriculum"? By "secondary school"? By "effectiveness"? Definitions appropriate for research work will not usually be supplied by the dictionary. For example, *Webster's New International Dictionary*, second edition, defines curriculum as:

> A. A course, especially a specified fixed course of study, in a school or college, as one leading to a degree. B. The whole body of courses offered in an educational institution, or by a department thereof;—the usual sense.

This definition is not helpful to the researcher; he must here (and often) supply his own definition. The definition which will be of most help to him will usually be obtained in two steps: (1) pointing at the things involved; and (2) describing those things and indicating how they were identified.

This process may seem to be a considerable retrogression from the practice of the well-educated man who, when he wishes to define a word, uses *Webster* or perhaps the *Oxford Dictionary*. Yet it provides the key to progress on the research problem.

In this case, then, what must "curriculum" mean to the researcher? In general terms, and for ordinary people, the curriculum is indeed a formal sequence of certain school experiences; or, perhaps, all experiences associated with the school. But to the researcher, the curriculum must be these activities (pointing), perhaps to algebra, geometry and arithmetic; in these (pointing) courses, perhaps science, mathematics, mechanical drawing, industrial arts, and business.

It goes without saying that these "operational definitions" must not be in disagreement with *Webster* or other authorities; they need always be such that they can be defended.

The operational definition given above is completely in accord with *Webster;* to the student who is not reflective or thoughtful, there may seem to be no real difference. But the difference between the two is very significant for the researcher; it lies in the fact that with *Webster's* definition no action on the part of the researcher is indicated; with the operational definition certain things are clearly indicated for the researcher to *do* as he proceeds to solve his problem (for example, he must examine courses with specific titles).

Again, what is meant by "secondary schools"? *Webster* says a secondary school is " . . . a school providing secondary education, as an American high school, an English public school, a French lycee, and a German Gymnasium or Realschule." This is not useful to the researcher. He must say, for example (pointing), that he means *these* secondary schools in Iowa, in Blackhawk County, or in Waterloo.

Again, what is meant by "effective"? *Webster* tells us " . . . 2. Producing a decided or decisive effect; efficient; hence, brilliant; striking . . . " This is all well and good, but the researcher needs to be able to *point* to something which indicates effectiveness: to scores on standardized test A, perhaps, or grades in specified courses in specified colleges.

If he defines the terms in the original problem in this fashion, he may arrive at something like this: "The relationship between the amount of high school mathematics and achievement in college mathematics of graduates of East Waterloo High School, 1945-1955."

The novice in the field of research may find this outcome disappointing. It is not the question he wishes to answer. He may say that he is not interested in grades in college mathematics as a measure of the effectiveness of a high school curriculum, or that he has no special interest in the graduates of East Waterloo High School. He may say that he "really wants to find the answer" to the original problem posed.

It is at this point that the student who will be able to finish a piece of research and the student who finds it impossible to do so begin to part ways. The researcher tries to find answers to important problems in such a way that his findings have the widest possible application. He realizes, however, that any generalizations which may result from his study are *based on specific operations at specific times in specific places with specific materials.* A well-trained and experienced research worker may design an investigation from which many valid and broad generalizations may result. The beginner in research often is able to produce a study from which only limited generalizations may be drawn. *The difference is in the design of the study, in the selection and treatment of the specifics.* The difference does not lie in the fact that one deals with specifics but not the other. Both do so.

The process of solving the original problem, of "really getting the answer" to the question, must certainly involve activity of some kind with certain materials in certain places at certain times. Any research worker can only isolate the specifics about which he knows and which he can get at, and try to put them together so that the broadest generalizations can be drawn from his results. If he succeeds in "finding the answer," excellent. If because of the resources and techniques available to him, he is able to answer the question only for certain places at certain times under certain conditions, he has still made a contribution if the facts were not known before and have some significance.

The extent of the generalization made possible by a researcher's solution to a problem is made possible because of the way he dealt with selected specifics: it did not result alone from a general consideration of the general problem. It is at the latter point that the neophyte may stop; if he does, he never gets to specifics; he never solves his problem, nor any part of it.

In the example cited, namely, a study of the relationship between the amount of high school mathematics taken and subsequent achievement in college mathematics, of graduates of East Waterloo High School, 1945-1955, the researcher has his work indicated with some clarity. He will examine the amount (courses, hours of class, texts covered—whatever it is, he will specify) taken by individuals who graduated from East Waterloo High School during the period (as listed in school records). He will obtain from college records the grades they made in college mathematics (college and courses specified). He will compare the two. Either he can follow up every graduate or he cannot; if not, he would probably insert "selected" before "graduates" in the statement of the problem. He has yet to decide how he will relate the two sets of data. He will probably examine the various methods previously used for establishing relationships between two sets of data; he will choose one or several, and so, operationally, "relationship" will mean this (pointing) mathematical operation.

He has not answered the original question. He is not alone. Who has, once and for all? He may be satisfied if he has contributed objective evidence in a manner permitting the widest generalization possible.

Before anything can be presented, there must be something to present. Before anything can be examined, there must be something specific to examine. It is the researcher's task to define and delimit the original broad problem area which attracted him, so that he will be able to deal in specifics.

In summary, the trick is to so state, define, and delimit a problem that the subsequent action which must be taken to solve it is clearly specified. Implicit in the definition and delimitation should be specific action with certain concrete materials to be found in definite places at given times.

D. B. Van Dalen

The Role of Hypotheses in Educational Research

Published research without stated hypotheses can be found. One suspects, however, when this type of research is found, that data were collected and explanations sought later—rather than the other way around. In the previous chapters, Masson, Raths, and Platt have at least implicitly indicated the importance of hypotheses. In this article Van Dalen clearly indicates the importance of the hypothesis. It might be valuable to evaluate research that appears to be done without a hypothesis to determine whether it might not have been improved by the inclusion of a specific hypothesis.

D. B. Van Dalen, "The Role of Hypotheses in Educational Research," *Educational Administration and Supervision,* 42:457-60, 1956. Reprinted with permission.

Educational research is of a relatively recent origin. Nevertheless, a review of the studies reveals that considerable work has been done. Moreover, members of the profession are gradually grasping a deeper understanding of scientific procedures. Their improvements in technical precision and refinements in methodology have considerably strengthened the foundations of the profession. Despite the progress they have made, however, many educators do not fully understand one important aspect of the scientific method: the need for hypotheses.

No scientific undertaking can proceed effectively without well-conceived hypotheses—any attempt to do so is like working in the dark. For, according to John Dewey, hypotheses regulate "the selection and weighing of observed factors and their conceptual ordering." Hypotheses, therefore, are indispensable tools for research workers who aspire to be scientific in their investigations. To draw attention to this often overlooked aspect of research methodology, the following discussion defines hypotheses and reviews their more significant functions.

DEFINITION

A hypothesis is a suggested solution to a problem. A hypothesis consists of elements expressed in an orderly system of relationships which seek to explain a condition that has not yet been verified by facts. In a hypothesis, some of the elements or relationships between the elements are known facts. But other elements or relationships are conceptual. That is, they are products of the research worker's imagination. They leap beyond known facts and experiences. Thus, a hypothesis logically relates known facts to intelligent guesses about unknown conditions in an effort to extend or enlarge our knowledge. The conceptual and factual elements and relationships must be formulated in such a precise and objective manner that the research worker can test the implications of the hypothesis.

Hypotheses as a Means of Stating Assumptions

A hypothesis is a means of stating the essential assumptions underlying the proposition in an all-encompassing statement. This statement is the end product of a thorough analysis of all the factual and conceptual elements that are relevant to the problem and their proper relationship to one another. The isolating and combining of all relevant phenomena into a conceptual context provides a solid base for a successful investigation of the problem. Before concluding a study, the research worker prepares a report giving a complete background of the facts and explanations that led up to the structuring of the specific hypothesis. Such a presentation helps the reader (who may not possess the investigator's observational or reading background) grasp the connections between the hypothesis and its underlying assumptions.

Hypotheses as Means of Presenting Explanations

Providing explanations is one of the primary functions of a hypothesis. Science strives to supply the reasons for the occurrence of events or conditions. Thus, scientific inquiry goes beyond the amassing of facts or the mere describing and classifying of them in accordance with their superficial properties. Research seeks the underlying patterns or general principles that explain the structural interrelations of the phenomena under observation. In searching for the possible factors giving rise to an event or condition, the research worker engages in a high order of conceptualization. That is, he relies on his reasoning process to build schemes of explanation that account for the factors he is trying to understand.

An analysis of a problem usually reveals that the observable data are vague and incomplete, some elements do not appear to be related to other known elements or to fit into any particular order, and there are not adequate interpretations for some phenomena. The nature of the work before the investigator is to complete the data, systematize the information, and give some interpretations that will explain the unknown factors. A hypothesis provides the explanations necessary to accomplish these tasks. A hypothesis may provide the conceptual elements that complete the known data, conceptual relationships that systematize unordered elements, and conceptual meanings and interpretations that explain the unknown phenomena. Thus, through conceptualization, which makes it possible to introduce elements and relationships that are not directly observable, the investigator can go beyond the known data and set up a possible solution to a problem.

Hypotheses as Determiners of the Relevancy of Facts

Selecting the facts necessary to conduct research is a matter of crucial concern to the investigator. Aimlessly collecting a mass of facts on a given subject is futile, for the infinity of possibilities prohibits any rational manipulation of them. The strategic facts needed to solve a problem do not automatically label themselves as relevant to it. If facts are to serve the research worker, they must be carefully and significantly selected. The hypothesis serves as the organizing principle that makes it possible to accomplish this task. The hypothesis provides the structural framework around which pertinent data can be organized. It guides the investigator in ascertaining what facts to collect and enables him to decide how many facts he needs to test its implications adequately. Without a hypothesis, research is unfocused, haphazard, and accidental.

Hypotheses as Determiners of the Research Design

A hypothesis helps the investigator determine what research procedures and methods to use. Owing to the manner in which the hypothesis points up the pertinent issues at stake, it immediately rules out many methods as irrelevant to the testing of the postulated solution. Moreover, a well-constructed hypothesis leads the investigator to the particular modes of attack that will meet its specific demands. For instance, a hypothesis often suggests what subjects or data are sufficient; what instruments or operations are adequate; what statistical methods are appropriate; or what events, facts, or circumstances are required to evaluate its implications satisfactorily. Thus, the hypothesis reveals what procedures are appropriate and adequate for testing the suggested solution to the problem.

Hypotheses as the Framework of the Conclusions

A hypothesis aids the research worker in presenting the conclusions of his study. A hypothesis is a tentative principle or generalization that accounts for some given phenomena. It retains the character of a guess until some facts are found to support it. Through appropriate testing situations, the necessary facts are collected. In the conclusion of the study, these findings are organized in terms of the purposes that initiated the investigation. If the factual evidence agrees with the original proposal, it confirms the hypothesis; if it disagrees with the original proposal, it discredits the hypothesis. If an investigator does not establish a hypothesis but merely collects facts on a subject and cites them *per se* or classifies them according to his whims in the conclusions of the study, he does not necessarily advance knowledge appreciably. The hypothesis provides a framework for stating the conclusions of the study in a meaningful manner.

Hypotheses as Sources for the Formulation of New Hypotheses

An explanatory hypothesis enables us to extend and unify our knowledge. A well-conceived hypothesis offers a general principle that renders more understandable the phenomena under consideration. Yet, a hypothesis is regarded not as an end in itself but as a means to further understanding. It serves as an intellectual lever by which investigators can pry loose more facts to be fitted into other or more inclusive explanations. Therefore, a hypothesis serves as a base from which new lines of investigations branch out in various directions. Through its implications, a hypothesis raises additional questions that need explanations. The explanation proposed by the investigator creates a need for formulating other hypotheses. These, in turn, lead to new investigations and thus to the discovery of additional knowledge. A hypothesis is not advanced as a final statement; it asks to be outdated and surpassed.

SUMMARY

Without a hypothesis, a research worker often wastes time in directionless investigations; if he produces meaningful results it is largely due to chance. Knowledge cannot be advanced appreciably by those who engage in ineffectual fumbling. In research work, a hypothesis is needed to clarify the issues at stake and to crystallize the problem for investigation. However, a hypothesis is not spontaneously created. It can only be established after a thorough analysis of the theoretical and factual background of the problem. Formulating a hypothesis requires imagination and the ability to see relationships. The hypothesis the researcher actually investigates usually is constructed only after he has rejected several trial drafts. Nevertheless, spending energy on this difficult task is time well invested, for the hypothesis helps the investigator determine what facts to locate, what procedures and methods to employ in conducting the study, and how to organize and present his findings in the conclusion of the study. A hypothesis serves as a powerful beacon that lights the way for the research worker.

T. C. Chamberlin*

The Method of
Multiple Working Hypotheses

This article is old, first published in 1897 in the *Journal of Geology* (Vol. 5, pp. 837-848). The author of the article was a famous geologist who has been dead for nearly 40 years. It would appear that these facts, a 70-year-old article by a man dead 40 years, would strongly incline against the article's inclusion in a book like this. Yet you will find it referred to in glowing terms by Platt in his article on strong inference in Chapter 1. After reading this article evaluate it against some of the more modern ones you may have read. Couldn't the method of multiple working hypotheses be applied to education? Perhaps even more strongly—shouldn't the method be applied to education? In light of what Platt says about inference and Van Dalen about hypotheses, the Chamberlin article could have been written yesterday (or tomorrow) and yet it has been around for 70 years.

T. C. Chamberlin, "The Method of Multiple Working Hypotheses," *Scientific Monthly*, 59:357-62, November, 1944. Reprinted with permission.

There are two fundamental modes of study. The one is an attempt to follow by close imitation the processes of previous thinkers and to acquire the results of their investigations by memorizing. It is study of a merely secondary, imitative, or acquisitive nature. In the other mode the effort is to think independently, or at least individually. It

---

* Professor T. C. Chamberlin of the University of Chicago, who died in 1928, was a famous geologist and a former president of the American Association for the Advancement of Science. He was noted for his rigorous application of the scientific method. In 1897 he published in the *Journal of Geology* (vol. 5, pp. 837-848) the paper that is here reprinted with permission of the University of Chicago Press. Because the demand for it continued through the years, it was reprinted in 1931 in the *Journal of Geology* (vol. 39, pp. 155-165). Such evidence of the importance of this essay to geologists suggested that it should be made available to other scientists, all of whom should be acquainted with "The Method of Multiple Working Hypotheses."

is primary or creative study. The endeavor is to discover new truth or to make a new combination of truth or at least to develop by one's own effort an individualized assemblage of truth. The endeavor is to think for one's self, whether the thinking lies wholly in the fields of previous thought or not. It is not necessary to this mode of study that the subject matter should be new. Old material may be reworked. But it is essential that the process of thought and its results be individual and independent, not the mere following of previous lines of thought ending in predetermined results. The demonstration of a problem in Euclid precisely as laid down is an illustration of the former, the demonstration of the same proposition by a method of one's own or in a manner distinctively individual is an illustration of the latter, both lying entirely within the realm of the known and old.

Creative study, however, finds its largest application in those subjects in which, while much is known, more remains to be learned. The geological field is pre-eminently full of such subjects; indeed, it presents few of any other class. There is probably no field of thought which is not sufficiently rich in such subjects to give full play to investigative modes of study.

Three phases of mental procedure have been prominent in the history of intellectual evolution thus far. What additional phases may be in store for us in the evolutions of the future it may not be prudent to attempt to forecast. These three phases may be styled "the method of the ruling theory," "the method of the working hypothesis," and "the method of multiple working hypotheses."

In the earlier days of intellectual development the sphere of knowledge was limited and could be brought much more nearly than now within the compass of a single individual. As a natural result those who then assumed to be wise men, or aspired to be thought so, felt the need of knowing, or at least seeming to know, all that was known, as a justification of their claims. So also as a natural counterpart there grew up an expectancy on the part of the multitude that the wise and the learned would explain whatever new thing presented itself. Thus pride and ambition on the one side and expectancy on the other joined hands in developing the putative all-wise man whose knowledge boxed the compass and whose acumen found an explanation for every new puzzle which presented itself. Although the pretended compassing of the entire horizon of knowledge has long since become an abandoned affectation, it has left its representatives in certain intellectual predilections. As in the earlier days, so still, it is a too frequent habit to hastily conjure up an explanation for every new phenomenon that presents itself. Interpretation leaves its proper place at the end of the intellectual procession and rushes to the forefront. Too often a theory is promptly born and evidence hunted up to fit it afterward. Laudable as the effort at explanation is in its proper place, it is an almost certain source of confusion and error when it runs before a serious inquiry into the phenomenon itself. A strenuous endeavor to find out precisely what the phenomenon really is should take the lead and crowd back the question, commendable at a later stage, "How came this so?" First the full facts, then the interpretation thereof, is the normal order.

The habit of precipitate explanation leads rapidly on to the birth of general theories.[1] When once an explanation or special theory has been offered for a given phenomenon, self-consistency prompts to the offering of the same explanation or theory for like phenomena when they present themselves, and there is soon developed a general theory explanatory of a large class of phenomena similar to the original one. In support of the general theory there may not be any further evidence or investigation than was involved in the first hasty conclusion. But the repetition of its application to new phenomena, though of the same kind, leads the mind insidiously into the delusion that the theory has been strengthened by additional facts. A thousand applications of the supposed principle of levity to the explanation of ascending bodies brought no increase of evidence that it was the true theory of the phenomena; but it doubtless created the impression in the minds of ancient physical philosophers that it did, for so many additional facts seemed to harmonize with it.

For a time these hastily born theories are likely to be held in a tentative way with some measure of candor or at least some self-illusion of candor. With this tentative spirit and measurable candor, the mind satisfies its moral sense and deceives itself with the thought that it is proceeding cautiously and impartially toward the goal of ultimate truth. It fails to recognize that no amount of provisional holding of a theory, no amount of application of the theory, so long as the study lacks in incisiveness and exhaustiveness, justifies an

---

[1] I use the term "theory" here instead of hypothesis because the latter is associated with a better controlled and more circumspect habit of the mind. This restrained habit leads to the use of the less assertive term "hypothesis," while the mind in the habit here sketched more often believes itself to have reached the higher ground of a theory and more often employs the term "theory." Historically also, I believe the word "theory" was the term commonly used at the time this method was predominant.

ultimate conviction. It is not the slowness with which conclusions are arrived at that should give satisfaction to the moral sense, but the precision, the completeness and the impartiality of the investigation.

It is in this tentative stage that the affections enter with their blinding influence. Love was long since discerned to be blind, and what is true in the personal realm is measurably true in the intellectual realm. Important as the intellectual affections are as stimuli and as rewards, they are nevertheless dangerous factors in research. All too often they put under strain the integrity of the intellectual processes. The moment one has offered an original explanation for a phenomenon which seems satisfactory, that moment affection for his intellectual child springs into existence; and as the explanation grows into a definite theory, his paternal affections cluster about his offspring and it grows more and more dear to him. While he persuades himself that he holds it still as tentative, it is none the less lovingly tentative and not impartially and indifferently tentative. As soon as this parental affection takes possession of the mind, there is apt to be a rapid passage to the unreserved adoption of the theory. There is then imminent danger of an unconscious selection and of a magnifying of phenomena that fall into harmony with the theory and support it and an unconscious neglect of phenomena that fail of coincidence. The mind lingers with pleasure upon the facts that fall happily into the embrace of the theory, and feels a natural coldness toward those that assume a refractory attitude. Instinctively, there is a special searching-out of phenomena that support it, for the mind is led by its desires. There springs up also unwittingly a pressing of the theory to make it fit the facts and a pressing of the facts to make them fit the theory. When these biasing tendencies set in, the mind rapidly degenerates into the partiality of paternalism. The search for facts, the observation of phenomena, and their interpretation are all dominated by affection for the favored theory until it appears to its author or its advocate to have been overwhelmingly established. The theory then rapidly rises to a position of control in the processes of the mind and observation; induction and interpretation are guided by it. From an unduly favored child it readily grows to be a master and leads its author whithersoever it will. The subsequent history of that mind in respect to that theme is but the progressive dominance of a ruling idea. Briefly summed up, the evolution is this: a premature explanation passes first into a tentative theory, then into an adopted theory, and lastly into a ruling theory.

When this last stage has been reached, unless the theory happens perchance to be the true one, all hope of the best results is gone. To be sure, truth may be brought forth by an investigator dominated by a false ruling idea. His very errors may indeed stimulate investigation on the part of others. But the condition is scarcely the less unfortunate.

As previously implied, the method of the ruling theory occupied a chief place during the infancy of investigation. It is an expression of a more or less infantile condition of the mind. I believe it is an accepted generalization that in the earlier stages of development the feelings and impulses are relatively stronger than in later stages.

Unfortunately the method did not wholly pass away with the infancy of investigation. It has lingered on, and reappears in not a few individual instances at the present time. It finds illustration in quarters where its dominance is quite unsuspected by those most concerned.

The defects of the method are obvious and its errors grave. If one were to name the central psychological fault, it might be stated as the admission of intellectual affection to the place that should be dominated by impartial, intellectual rectitude alone.

So long as intellectual interest dealt chiefly with the intangible, so long it was possible for this habit of thought to survive and to maintain its dominance, because the phenomena themselves, being largely subjective, were plastic in the hands of the ruling idea; but so soon as investigation turned itself earnestly to an inquiry into natural phenomena whose manifestations are tangible, whose properties are inflexible, and whose laws are rigorous, the defects of the method became manifest and an effort at reformation ensued. The first great endeavor was repressive. The advocates of reform insisted that theorizing should be restrained and the simple determination of facts should take its place. The effort was to make scientific study statistical instead of causal. Because theorizing in narrow lines had led to manifest evils, theorizing was to be condemned. The reformation urged was not the proper control and utilization of theoretical effort but its suppression. We do not need to go backward more than a very few decades to find ourselves in the midst of this attempted reformation. Its weakness lay in its narrowness and its restrictiveness. There is no nobler aspiration of the human intellect than the desire to compass the causes of things. The disposition to find explanations and to develop theories is laudable in itself. It is only its ill-placed use and its abuse that are reprehensible. The vitality of study quickly disappears when the object sought is a mere collocation of unmeaning facts.

The inefficiency of this simply repressive reformation becoming apparent, improvement was sought in the method of the working hypothesis. This has been affirmed to be *the* scientific method. But it is rash to assume that any method is *the* method, at least that it is the ultimate method. The working hypothesis differs from the ruling theory in that it is used as a means of determining facts rather than as a proposition to be established. It has for its chief function the suggestion and guidance of lines of inquiry—the inquiry being made, not for the sake of the hypothesis, but for the sake of the facts and their elucidation. The hypothesis is a mode rather than an end. Under the ruling theory, the stimulus is directed to the finding of facts for the support of the theory. Under the working hypothesis, the facts are sought for the purpose of ultimate induction and demonstration, the hypothesis being but a means for the more ready development of facts and their relations.

It will be observed that the distinction is not such as to prevent a working hypothesis from gliding with the utmost ease into a ruling theory. Affection may as easily cling about a beloved intellectual child when named a "hypothesis" as if named a "theory," and its establishment in the one guise may become a ruling passion very much as in the other. The historical antecedents and the moral atmosphere associated with the working hypothesis lend some good influence, however, toward the preservation of its integrity.

Conscientiously followed, the method of the working hypothesis is an incalculable advance upon the method of the ruling theory, but it has some serious defects. One of these takes concrete form, as just noted, in the ease with which the hypothesis becomes a controlling idea. To avoid this grave danger, the method of multiple working hypotheses is urged. It differs from the simple working hypothesis in that it distributes the effort and divides the affections. It is thus in some measure protected against the radical defect of the two other methods. In developing the multiple hypotheses, the effort is to bring up into view every rational explanation of the phenomenon in hand and to develop every tenable hypothesis relative to its nature, cause, or origin, and to give to all of these as impartially as possible a working form and a due place in the investigation. The investigator thus becomes the parent of a family of hypotheses; and by his parental relations to all is morally forbidden to fasten his affections unduly upon any one. In the very nature of the case, the chief danger that springs from affection is counteracted. Where some of the hypotheses have been already proposed and used, while others are the investigator's own creation, a natural difficulty arises; but the right use of the method requires the impartial adoption of all alike into the working family. The investigator thus at the outset puts himself in cordial sympathy and in parental relations (of adoption, if not of authorship) with every hypothesis that is at all applicable to the case under investigation. Having thus neutralized, so far as may be, the partialities of his emotional nature, he proceeds with a certain natural and enforced erectness of mental attitude to the inquiry, knowing well that some of his intellectual children (by birth or adoption) must needs perish before maturity, but yet with the hope that several of them may survive the ordeal of crucial research, since it often proves in the end that several agencies were conjoined in the production of the phenomena. Honors must often be divided between hypotheses. One of the superiorities of multiple hypotheses as a working mode lies just here. In following a single hypothesis, the mind is biased by the presumptions of its method toward a single explanatory conception. But an adequate explanation often involves the co-ordination of several causes. This is especially true when the research deals with a class of complicated phenomena naturally associated but not necessarily of the same origin and nature, as, for example, the Basement complex or the Pleistocene drift. Several agencies may not only participate but their proportions and importance may vary from instance to instance in the same field. The true explanation is therefore necessarily complex, and the elements of the complex are constantly varying. Such distributive explanations of phenomena are especially contemplated and encouraged by the methods of multiple hypotheses and constitute one of its chief merits. For many reasons we are prone to refer phenomena to a single cause. It naturally follows that when we find an effective agency present, we are predisposed to be satisfied therewith. We are thus easily led to stop short of full results, sometimes short of the chief factors. The factor we find may not even be the dominant one, much less the full complement of agencies engaged in the accomplishment of the total phenomena under inquiry. The mooted question of the origin of the Great Lake basins may serve as an illustration. Several hypotheses have been urged by as many different students of the problem as the cause of these great excavations. All of these have been pressed with great force and with an admirable array of facts. Up to a certain point we are compelled to go with each advocate. It is practically demonstrable that these basins were river valleys antecedent to the glacial incursion. It is equally demonstrable that there was a blocking-up of outlets. We must conclude then that the present basins owe their origin in part to the pre-existence of river valleys and to the blocking-up of their outlets by drift. That there is a temptation to rest here, the history of the question shows. But, on the other hand, it is demonstrable that these basins were occupied by great lobes of ice and were important channels of glacial movement. The leeward drift shows much material derived from their bottoms. We cannot, therefore, refuse assent to the doctrine that the basins owe something to glacial excavation. Still again it has been urged that the earth's crust beneath these basins was flexed downward by the weight of the ice load and contracted by its low temperature and that the basins owe something to crustal deformation. This third cause tallies with certain features not readily explained by the others. And still it is doubtful whether all these combined constitute an adequate explanation of the phenomena. Certain it is, at least, that the measure of participation of each must be determined before a satisfactory elucidation can be reached. The full solution therefore involves not only the recognition of multiple participation but an estimate of the measure and mode of each participation. For this the simultaneous use of a full staff of working hypotheses is demanded. The method of the single working hypothesis or the predominant working hypothesis is incompetent.

In practice it is not always possible to give all hypotheses like places, nor does the method contemplate precisely equable treatment. In forming specific plans for field, office, or laboratory work, it may often be necessary to follow the lines of inquiry suggested by some one hypothesis rather than those of another. The favored hypothesis may derive some advantage therefrom or go to an earlier death, as the case may be, but this is rather a matter of executive detail than of principle.

A special merit of the use of a full staff of hypotheses co-ordinately is that in the very nature of the case it invites thoroughness. The value of a working hypothesis lies largely in the significance it gives to phenomena which might otherwise be meaningless and in the new lines of inquiry which spring from the suggestions called forth by the significance thus disclosed. Facts that are trivial in themselves are brought forth into importance by the revelation of their bearings upon the hypothesis and the elucidation sought through the hypothesis. The phenomenal influence which the Darwinian hypothesis has exerted upon the investigations of the past two decades is a monumental illustration. But while a single working hypothesis may lead investigation very effectively along a given line, it may in that very fact invite the neglect of other lines equally important. Very many biologists would doubtless be disposed today to cite the hypothesis of natural selection, extraordinary as its influence for good has been, as an illustration of this. While inquiry is thus promoted in certain quarters, the lack of balance and completeness gives unsymmetrical and imperfect results. But if, on the contrary, all rational hypotheses bearing on a subject are worked co-ordinately, thoroughness, equipoise, and symmetry are the presumptive results in the very nature of the case.

In the use of the multiple method, the reaction of one hypothesis upon another tends to amplify the recognized scope of each. Every hypothesis is quite sure to call forth into clear recognition new or neglected aspects of the phenomena in its own interests, but ofttimes these are found to be important contributions to the full deployment of other hypotheses. The eloquent expositions of "prophetic" characters at the hands of Agassiz were profoundly suggestive and helpful in the explication of "undifferentiated" types in the hand of the evolutionary theory.

So also the mutual conflicts of hypotheses whet the discriminative edge of each. The keenness of the analytic process advocates the closeness of differentiating criteria, and the sharpness of discrimination is promoted by the co-ordinate working of several competitive hypotheses.

Fertility in processes is also a natural sequence. Each hypothesis suggests its own criteria, its own means of proof, its own method of developing the truth; and if a group of hypotheses encompasses the subject on all sides, the total outcome of means and of methods is full and rich.

The loyal pursuit of the method for a period of years leads to certain distinctive habits of mind which deserve more than the passing notice which alone can be given them here. As a factor in education, the disciplinary value of the method is one of prime importance. When faithfully followed for a sufficient time, it develops a mode of thought of its own kind which may be designated "the habit of parallel thought," or "of complex thought." It is contradistinguished from the linear order of thought which is necessarily cultivated in language and mathematics because their modes are linear and successive. The procedure is complex and largely simultaneously complex. The mind appears to become possessed of the power of simultaneous vision from different points of view. The power of viewing phenomena analytically and synthetically at the same time appears to be gained. It is not altogether unlike the intellectual procedure in the study of a landscape. From every quarter of the broad area of the landscape there come into the mind myriads of lines of potential intelligence which are received and co-ordinated simultaneously, producing a complex impression which is recorded and studied directly in its complexity. If the landscape is to be delineated in language, it must be taken part by part in linear succession.

Over against the great value of this power of thinking in complexes there is an unavoidable disadvantage. No good thing is without its drawbacks. It is obvious, upon studious consideration, that a complex or parallel method of thought cannot be rendered into verbal expression directly and immediately as it takes place. We cannot put into words more than a single line of thought at the same time, and even in that the order of expression must be conformed to the idiosyncrasies of the language. Moreover, the rate must be incalculably slower than the mental process. When the habit of complex or parallel thought is not highly developed, there is usually a leading line of thought to which the others are subordinate. Following this leading line the difficulty of expression does not rise to serious proportions. But when the method of simultaneous mental action along different lines is so highly developed that the thoughts running in different channels are nearly equivalent, there is an obvious embarrassment in making a selection for verbal expression, and there arises a disinclination to make the attempt. Furthermore, the impossibility of expressing the mental operation in words leads to their disuse in the silent processes of thought; and hence words and thoughts lose that close association which they are accustomed to maintain with those whose silent as well as spoken thoughts predominantly run in linear verbal courses. There is, therefore, a certain predisposition on the part of the practitioner of this method to taciturnity. The remedy obviously lies in co-ordinate literary work.

An infelicity also seems to attend the use of the method with young students. It is far easier, and apparently in general more interesting, for those of limited training and maturity to accept a simple interpretation or a single theory and to give it wide application, than to recognize several concurrent factors and to evaluate these as the true elucidation often requires. Recalling again for illustration the problem of the Great Lake basins, it is more to the immature taste to be taught that these were scooped out by the mighty power of the great glaciers than to be urged to conceive of three or more great agencies working successively in part and simultaneously in part and to endeavor to estimate the fraction of the total results which was accomplished by each of these agencies. The complex and the quantitative do not fascinate the young student as they do the veteran investigator.

The studies of the geologist are peculiarly complex. It is rare that his problem is a simple unitary phenomenon explicable by a single simple cause. Even when it happens to be so in a given instance, or at a given stage of work, the subject is quite sure, if pursued broadly, to grade into some complication or undergo some transition. He must therefore ever be on the alert for mutations and for the insidious entrance of new factors. If, therefore, there are any advantages in any field in being armed with a full panoply of working hypotheses and in habitually employing them, it is doubtless in the field of the geologist.

chapter 3

Educational Research: Design and Analysis

The assertion in the introductory statement of Chapter 1 that research is a logical reasoning process provides the basis for considering both the topics—design and analysis. Typically the researcher strives to determine the degree of truth inherent in a statement. He hypothesizes and he seeks support for his hypothesis. Unfortunately he seldom is able to observe directly the truth value of the hypothetical statement. For example, he might hypothesize that a given child is highly intelligent, but no way exists to open up that child's head to observe directly his intelligence. Instead the researcher finds himself observing indicators of the child's level of intelligence, usually his ability to provide specified answers to equally specified questions. If predicted responses are seen, the hypothesis—that the child is highly intelligent—is deduced to be true.

The research process has many links and, like the proverbial chain, is no stronger than its weakest link. The previous chapter indicated that the researcher must attend to the assumption of the relationship of a property being studied (in our example, intelligence) and the indicants of the property (in our example, predicted responses to specified questions). If such an assumption is not generally acceptable, the study fails to contribute evidence to the truth value of the hypothetical statement.

Two additional crucial links to the research process chain can be identified at this point—design and analysis. Design refers to those plans made by the investigator to ensure the generation of the most appropriate data for testing the hypothesis or answering the questions posed. Analysis refers to those techniques by which the researcher examines the data to reach a decision about what was observed. These two aspects of the research process are the focus of this chapter.

The word *appropriate* in the definition of design stated above needs elaboration. Its use infers that some observations are better than others, a fact easy to substantiate. Consider our hypothesis that a child is highly intelligent. Some data could be generated for the test of this hypothesis by asking the nonprofessional adults with whom the child comes into contact, "Is this a highly intelligent child?" Most professional educators would consider such data inappropriate since the relation between intelligence and perceptions of untrained observers has not been established. Suppose we shift our data generation. Now we employ questions from an accepted standardized intelligence test as the data generation technique. Do we now have an "appropriate" set of data for inferring truth or lack of truth of our hypothesis? The answer to our question is, "It depends." The answers to questions stated in English by a child raised in a French-speaking environment would not provide "appropriate" data about the hypothesis. If an English-speaking child is told the answers shortly before being given the test, his responses are not "appropriate" data.

In these negative examples, hypotheses which rival the hypothesis being investigated must be considered as an explanation for what is observed. The failure of the one child to respond correctly is just as likely to be due to the language barrier as it is to a lack of intelligence. In the other case proper responses might be attributed to the cueing rather than intelligence. Thus the manner in which data were generated in these two cases gave rise to rival hypotheses, rival explanations for what was observed. Appropriate data for the test of a given hypothesis are those data generated in a manner which eliminates all the possible rival hypotheses. Thus, to conduct a test of a hypothesis, a researcher must plan data generation activities which will (1) produce data logically acceptable as consequences of the truth of the hypothesis, and (2) rule out the possibility of explanations of the data by hypotheses other than the one being tested.

Three factors shape the generation of data: the nature of the units involved in the study, the treatments experienced by those units, and the nature of the observation or measurement process. If in the study of a given problem we change one of these factors, we change the data. For example, if we are conducting a study of anxiety in a test-taking situation, we might select the first fifty available classes of students as our subjects. Or we might specify a population in which we are interested, say all high school juniors and seniors in a given system, and randomly select subjects. In the first of these cases we would generate one set of anxiety responses; in the second, another. The former would provide data representative of some unknown group. The latter would provide data representative of a specified population of high school juniors and seniors.

Similarly, differing treatments generate differing data. Suppose that in one case in the test anxiety problem, the treatment is the administration of a test containing items that are expected to be too difficult for the vast majority of persons tested. In another case we administer a test with instructions indicating the extreme importance of the test to the individuals' opportunity for engaging in a desired future behavior. In both cases the study is focused on anxiety but the differences in the treatments would cause behavior displayed by the subjects to be quite different, thus generating quite different sets of data.

Finally, the manner in which the behavior of the units is observed shapes the data. Using our anxiety example, if we administer a paper and pencil test (for example, the Sarrazon Test of Anxiety) after the treatment is applied, our data will take one form. If we electrically wire each student and measure his galvanic skin response, our data will take another form.

A quality scale can be structured for each of the three factors listed above. For the units factor this scale would range from the highest possible extreme, perfect representation of a specified population, down to zero or unknown representativeness. Perfect representation can be achieved only by the involvement of the entire population. Even then individual differences would create an observation that probably would not be representative of the group at a subsequent time. Through the use of random selection and—in case of several treatments—random assignment, the probability is high that generated data will be representative of that which would be obtained from the population of interest. At the other extreme are those research efforts which proceed through the use of units that happen to be available. In such cases the representativeness of the responses is, at worst, zero and, at best, unknown.

The quality scale for the treatment factor in data generation has similar range. A situation in which we can not be sure what happened to the units involved is at the zero end of the scale while a study in which both the content and sequence of the events are carefully programed is at the other end. The former is often the case when two curricula, a new program and a traditional program, are involved. Such an investigation too often fails to describe carefully the details of the new program and equally often assumes that the details of the traditional program are known by the reader. The careful specification of treatments can be seen in studies of computer-assisted instruction. In such cases the investigator must detail the treatment in order to program the computer.

Measurement of responses of selected units during or after experiencing a treatment also can be thought of along a scale of quality. At the zero quality end are those observations that are highly subjective with very questionable validity and reliability. Anecdotal records written by teachers frequently have these characteristics. They are measurements, however; a record of some event has been made. Too often we are unsure of the meaning. We do not know what they measure, a child's behavior or a teacher's perception. Just as often we have doubts whether a similar observation would result in a similar anecdotal record. In this case, our concern is for the reliability of the anecdotal measure. In contrast to the anecdotal record with its subjectivity, invalidity, and unreliability are some of the measures found in the student health records. Measures of student height are usually objective, valid, and reliable. That is, different measures using a height scale would be expected to display near perfect agreement in observing a given student's height (objectivity); we are convinced that the height scale in feet and inches really is a measure of height and not some other factor (validity); and finally, a student who is measured as 5 feet 3 inches would be measured as 5 feet 3 inches if the measurement was repeated the next day (reliability). Such a measure is at the opposite

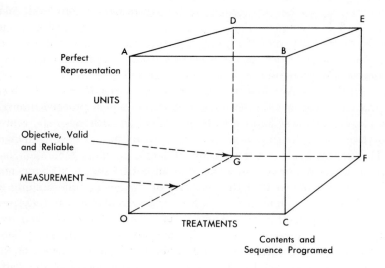

Figure 1.   *The Research Quality Cube*

end of the measurement quality scale. Most measurements in education fall somewhere between these two extremes.

If the units, treatment, and measurement factors of data generation are considered as the three dimensions of a cube, a model for conceptualizing about the quality of the data generation techniques in a given research project is depicted (Fig. 1). The scale of unit quality runs along the dimension OA, treatment quality OC, and measurement quality OG. A project which selected a sample perfectly representative of a population of interest would be located at Point A on the cube. If, in that same study, a thorough programing of the content and sequence of the treatments was employed in generating data, the project would be conceptualized as being at Point B on the quality cube. Finally, if our study employed perfectly objective, valid, and reliable measuring techniques, it would be located at Point E on the cube.

A given study infrequently reaches this level of data generation quality. Studies often are less than perfect in sample representativeness, and thus fall somewhere between points O and A. Similarly the study may lack control over all the aspects of the treatment. In such an instance our study is not located at Point E, but rather somewhere within the cube depending on the nature of our data generation failures.

In considering the location of a given study within the quality cube, our goal is not to demean a study for its position. Rather our objective is to understand the strengths and weaknesses of the study in order to gauge the strength of its conclusions, *and* to speculate on the methodological advancements necessary to move toward excellence in data generation. Such understanding will result in the development of sounder data, the basis for greater credence in our decisions about the truth or falsity of our hypotheses.

The research quality cube has one more use that should be discussed before turning to the analysis aspect of research. The literature on the research process presents four general research methodologies: historical, descriptive, quasi-experimental, and experimental. Each of these methods has characteristics that restrict position within the research quality cube. For example, a descriptive study focuses a researcher's efforts on unit selection, measuring the existing status of those units, and inferring the status of the population those units represent. A descriptive researcher should strive for perfect population representation and objective, valid, and reliable measurement. Although he may be interested in describing a particular population because something has happened to it, he does not know for sure what that something is. If we wish to describe the educational background of school superintendents, we do so *because* something happened to them; they became superintendents. We cannot know the content of that treatment nor sequence. Just some treatment was experienced. Similar statements can be made about other descriptive studies, thus confining them to the zero point on the treatment scale. Given this point, a descriptive study is confined to the left-hand face of the quality cube (OADG). A perfect descriptive study would be located at Point D, and any lesser descriptive study would be somewhere on the face of the cube.

The quasi-experimental method[1] includes those experiments conducted in situations which deny the opportunity of sample or unit selection. We must use available intact groups without knowledge of the population represented. By definition this method is at the zero point on the unit scale. Thus the quasi-experiment is always located on the base of the cube. A perfect study employing this methodology would be located at Point F, while a lesser project would be somewhere on the base (OCFG), depending upon the nature of its measurement and treatment deficiencies.

True experimentation involves control over all three factors. Thus the perfect experiment would be located at Point E. A given experiment would locate somewhere *within* the quality cube depending upon the particular sampling, treatment, or measurement problems it contains.

The historian works at the opposite corner of the cube. He investigates events or treatments that occurred to an unspecified population and were recorded or measured in some manner. His task involves ferreting out what the treatment was, the population which experienced it, the representativeness of the sample on which he has data, and the objectivity, validity, and reliability of the records he collects as evidence. The historian, then, finds himself starting at the zero point and charged with moving up within the quality cube to achieve sound conclusions.

The discussion thus far has focused upon two faces of the data quality cube (OADG and OCFG) which touch the zero point. A third surface also touches this point (OABC). On this face would be located studies in which unit selection and treatment can be managed by the researcher, while no control is possible over measurement. To date no formal methodology exists with these characteristics. However, several recent developments seem to imply that one is developing. These in-

---

[1] Campbell, Donald T., and Julian C. Stanley, "Experimental and Quasi-Experimental Designs for Research on Teaching," in *Handbook of Research on Teaching*, N. L. Gage, editor, Chicago: Rand McNally, 1963.

clude the Rand McNally publication entitled *Unobtrusive Measures*,[2] the work of Barker and Gump,[3] and the experimental method proposed by Egon Guba.[4] In *Unobtrusive Measures*, Campbell *et al* discuss the use of "Natural Measures" citing the case of the folk song waitress who knew that her customer ". . . was a logger and not just a common bum, cause nobody but a logger stirs his coffee with his thumb." Baker and Gump have been studying children by observing and recording all that happens to the child. In such an effort care could be taken in selecting representative children and in controlling the setting, to have knowledge of the nature of the treatment. In this "stream of behavior" approach the investigator cannot be sure of what he is measuring in the observations he makes. In fact, the major concern in this type of study is the development of analytical methods which will increase validity, objectivity, and reliability. Guba's experimental method was proposed for the study of educational change. Its first application was a situation in which the control of unit selection would have been possible and in which treatment was controlled. Several elementary schools throughout the country were selected to receive a large supply of films and filmstrips plus an abundance of projection equipment. An observer was placed in each of these schools to record what happened. In this case some control over measurement was asserted. The investigator had specified what measurements were to be collected but he was unable to specify completely when they would be obtained. In citing these three events, the authors of this publication are attempting to suggest that a new methodology is emerging, a methodology that should be employed, examined, and improved as educators continue their search for empirical knowledge.

The use of the research quality cube in this manner leads to direct inferences about the nature of the findings of different research methods as well as a basis for evaluating the adequacy of the data generated in a given study.

Final statements about the quality of a given research effort must be deferred until the appropriateness and accuracy of the employed data analysis techniques are considered. This statement is based upon the

[2] Webb, E. J., D. T. Campbell, R. C. Schwartz, and L. B. Sechrest, *Unobtrusive Measures: Nonreactive Research in the Social Sciences*. Chicago: Rand McNally, 1966.

[3] As exemplified in Roger G. Barker, "Explorations in Ecological Psychology," *American Psychologist*, 20, 1-14, 1965.

[4] Egon G. Guba, "Methodological Strategies for Educational Change," paper presented at the Conference on Strategies for Educational Change, Washington, D.C., 1965.

assumption that casual examination of data is often misleading. An example may help make this point. Imagine an experiment in which two randomly selected samples of five students each received different treatments. A test at the end of that treatment produced scores upon which a decision is to be reached regarding the relative effectiveness of the two treatments. The individuals' scores were as shown below along with the averages for the groups.

Treatment A	Treatment B
19	26
23	30
18	24
14	27
26	28
$\overline{X}_A = 20$	$\overline{X}_B = 27$

Since the number of scores is relatively small, a visual examination leads to the recognition that Treatment B produced higher scores. This recognition is enhanced by ranking the scores from high to low in both groups, a simple data-analysis procedure, as shown below.

Treatment A	Treatment B
26	30
23	28
19	27
18	26
14	24

Again a visual examination convinces us that Treatment B gives higher scores because only one of the students receiving Treatment A scored as high as any of the students receiving Treatment B. Simplifying the welter of data by ranking the scores has led us to a stronger conclusion.

Suppose we repeated our experiment and got the scores shown below.

Treatment A	Treatment B
19	25
25	42
14	20
10	14
32	34
$\overline{X}_A = 20$	$\overline{X}_B = 27$

If we visually examine these scores again we might conclude that Treatment B is the more effective. The mean scores indicate that the two groups differ just as did the first two groups. If we rank these scores we get:

Treatment A	Treatment B
32	42
25	34
19	25
14	20
10	14

Now our conclusion that B is higher is not so clear in spite of the difference in means. Each score in Column B is higher than the adjacent score in Column A. But, in both Column A and B, the scores are similar. If we move the highest score under Column B from the top to the bottom of the list we have:

Treatment A	Treatment B
32	34
25	25
19	20
14	14
10	42

Our visual examination now leads us to the conclusion that these treatments were not different. Only one pair of scores (10 and 42) provides the observed difference. When a statistical test of the differences between the means is computed, a significant difference is substantiated in the first experiment ($t = 3.04$; $p = .05$) and not in the second ($t = 1.13$). From this example we can see that a superficial look at data can be misleading.

When the number of scores is increased, the difficulty of making sense out of them without a statistical analysis is tremendously magnified. In such cases researchers must utilize methods to simplify the mass of numbers which provide greater surety of decision.

The appropriateness of an analytic procedure is based upon three factors: the scalor nature of the measurement procedure; the manner in which the data are generated; and the assumptions inherent in the mathematical derivation of the statistic. This introductory statement has partially discussed the manner in which the data are generated. To analyze the appropriateness of a specific statistic, we need to know more about the research design than that discussed heretofore. These design details are discussed in articles by Campbell, Stanley, Chandler, and Shannon which follow. Burke's article focuses on the question of scalor nature necessary in judging appropriateness of a statistic. Cornell's article focuses upon the frequent misuse of statistics by individuals who apply statistics without a clear understanding of how the statistic was derived or how their data were generated.

The articles presented in this chapter were selected to first present some of the general problems of the use of human subjects and their performance in the experimental situation. These problems should be considered as the research design is developed, for not only are ethical and human considerations involved but also the possibilities of rival hypotheses. In this area are articles by Berg on the use of human subjects, and Cook and Orne on the question of rival hypotheses. Secondly, articles are included which discuss research methods. Among these are the writings of Stanley, Carpenter, Corbally, Shannon, and Borgatta. Finally, several articles are presented which discuss data analysis. These articles focus on the interpretation problem in data analysis and neglect specifics about statistics, a focus chosen by the editors in the belief that no shortcut to the understanding of specific statistics is available. The interested educator must undertake a serious and systematic study of the standard statistical texts.

Irwin A. Berg

The Use of Human Subjects in Psychological Research [1]

The problems of design in research are numerous, and one of the fundamental problems involves subjects. If the researcher is content to work with
animals, one type of problem confronts him. If, however, the researcher desires to work with humans, a whole host of problems confronts him. Since educational research is not likely to make vast strides unless work is done with
humans, the educational researcher is faced with the problem of how to handle
his subjects. Berg, in this article, has considered the use of human subjects
in psychological research. Do his criteria apply to educational research as well?
How is the problem of generalizability of results affected by strict application
of these principles?

Irwin A. Berg, "The Use of Human Subjects in Psychological Research," *American
Psychologist*, 9:108-11, 1954. Reprinted with permission.

For some years the APA has had a Committee on Precautions in
Animal Experimentation and has published rules regulating the use of
animals for research purposes. This Committee and the animal experimentation code were established largely as an answer to the wild accu-
sations about "dog torture chambers" hurled by antivivisectionists. The
code provided a clear public statement of how animal experimentation
was carried out, and the Committee could investigate charges that any
of the code's provisions had been violated.

In the past no particular attention appears to have been paid to the
use of human subjects in psychological research, apparently because
no general problem existed as it did for animal experimentation. Of
course, one heard gossip at times about a local uproar in some college

---

[1] One of several reports prepared in connection with the activities of APA's Legal
and Legislative Committee.

community when students were asked to complete questionnaires which dealt with sex, race relations, or other emotionally charged material. Similar protests occasionally followed stress or frustration experiments or somatotype studies in which nude or nearly nude subjects were photographed. But such public outcries were rather rare and chiefly of local concern. Certainly they could in no way be compared to the nationwide clamor about animal research instigated by the antivivisectionists. Indeed, it was not until 1953 that a formal statement was issued by the APA concerning the general welfare of human research subjects. This may be found in *Ethical Standards of Psychologists*, published by the APA.

Like psychology, the medical sciences had no noteworthy problem in the use of human subjects for research purposes. The physician's responsibilities for his individual patient were carefully defined, and it was presumed that a subject in any medical experiment would be treated as if he were a patient. But on the heels of the Allied victory in Europe in World War II came stories of incredibly barbarous medical experiments performed on human subjects by Nazi physicians in the name of science. When the documentation of these atrocities was published (6), the integrity of the entire profession of medicine was challenged; for the German doctors involved were no mere tools or quasi-charlatans. They were leaders in their profession, and they themselves planned and executed their program of deliberate maiming and lingering death. It was out of these findings of the Nuremberg trials that the present concern over the use of human subjects in research grew. While writings on the problem have come chiefly from medical persons, all sciences which use human subjects for research are to some degree involved. As Shimkin put it, "Responsibilities do exist, and it is better to define them and see that they are not abused than to deny their existence and accept the consequences of denial" (7, p. 205).

The psychologist who is engaged in research with human subjects is not likely to get into trouble if he adheres firmly to the principles of *consent, confidence,* and *standard* or *acceptable procedure.* Since it is highly improbable that psychologists direct research which may imperil the lives of subjects, a risk which is present in some medical experimentation, it is believed that these principles will suffice for virtually all research in which psychologists utilize the services of human subjects. However, because psychologists occasionally design research for which a physician assumes responsibility, the basic principles governing medical experiments with human subjects, as set forth by Taylor (8, p. xxiii) after the Nuremberg trials, will be presented here later.

When psychological research has aroused public ire, it has probably occurred most often when the principle of *consent* was violated in connection with some cherished cultural value. The uproars over questionnaires which students found personally obnoxious or the protests against being photographed in the nude are cases in point. Had the subjects been permitted to volunteer for the investigations, it is unlikely that such difficulties would have arisen. Many items of personal information are so trivial that it may appear unnecessary to invite subjects clearly and pointedly to participate, and to permit any to withdraw who wish to do so. Yet what is trivial to one is a threat to another. An innocent question on annual income smacks of internal revenue checkups to some persons, and a question on attitude is reminiscent of the Gestapo to others. The only safe procedure is to invite participation while avoiding any appearance of coercion and to make it easy for any subject to withdraw gracefully. Where the information requested is highly personal or where the experiment involves some pain, discomfort, or risk, the subject should be made fully aware of what he is consenting to, at least in a general way. If the subject is to be whirled in a Barany chair, electrically shocked, or quizzed about his sex practices, prudence dictates that the subject should be told what he is in for. Kidd (5, p. 212) remarked that ". . . the law does not regard trifles"—*de minimis non curat lex;* the public, however, often does. Further, the trifle occasionally has serious consequence. The present writer once saw a subject seized by a convulsion after ice water was squirted in his ear to demonstrate nystagmus. The subject remarked afterward that he never would have served had he known what was going to be done to him.

Upon occasion the consent of the subject himself cannot be obtained because he is legally incapable of giving it, as in the case of mental patients. In such instances the family or the physician or other person responsible for the patient's welfare may grant the necessary permission. Another special occasion concerns the use of case history or psychological test data without obtaining prior consent of the persons involved. Often such records are old and the subjects too numerous or too scattered geographically to make such consent feasible. Yet college and other institutional officials sporadically raise this question. If the persons concerned are not harmed by the use of their records and their identities are not publicly revealed, there is no problem and their consent for the professional use of such existing records is not necessary.

The second principle, that of *confidence*, relates to more than the confidential nature of the personal information concerning the subjects used in research. It also relates to public confidence in psychology itself. The activities of both the research and the practicing psychologist converge closely at this point. If psychology is to be regarded as a mature profession, more than skill and knowledge must be demonstrated. The trust in which the psychologist holds personal information must be taken for granted by the public. This is not merely a legal control in the sense of avoiding libel or slander suits. Indeed, the psychologist could probably disclose any information about his subjects or clients in the performance of a public, legal, or moral duty without fear of legal penalty, provided he did so without malice. This seems to be a generally accepted principle of the law. Thus, the problem is not one of legal immunity, but rather one of guarding personal data concerning a client, patient, or subject in an experiment so closely that such knowledge in the psychologist's possession will be publicly regarded as *privileged*. A number of states have no statute granting privileged communication to physicians; yet because the public assumes that such privilege exists, no problem is encountered. The State of Illinois, for example, has no such statute; but as Guttmacher and Weihofen (3, p. 270) note, the courts have upheld the psychiatrist when he has refused to testify in regard to a patient.

Just what should be regarded as confidential is something of a problem. About the only statement that can be made is that good sense and good taste must prevail. Should occasion arise to disclose the fact, whether a subject is 5 or 6 feet tall is obviously not a matter for secrecy but whether he is afflicted by fetishistic behavior is. A subject's psychological test scores, for example, are properly kept confidential, despite the fact that such data are often handled carelessly. A number of psychological clinics and counseling bureaus, as cases in point, will not transmit any information about a client or patient without his written consent. This procedure should be standard for agencies which disclose such information to persons outside of their own professional organization.

It is significant that Kinsey's sexual behavior studies have not encountered opposition in the areas here under discussion. Kinsey uses only subjects who volunteer and who know what they are in for, and he guarantees confidence. The public reference to coded material, locked strongroom files, etc. enable Kinsey to obtain histories which would otherwise be unavailable to him. The parallel one may draw is that when any information is given in confidence, the welfare and advancement of our science demands that the identity of the subject be completely protected. If material is not given in confidence and if good taste and good sense do not clearly indicate that the information should be treated as confidential, the only rule to follow in such doubtful cases may be put tersely: *hold your tongue and pen.*

The third principle governing the use of human subjects in psychological research is that of *standard* or *acceptable procedure*. This assumes that the experimenter is competent in the area of his research undertaking and the procedure is standard in the sense of having been tried many times previously by many investigators. If the procedure is novel, and many procedures must be novel if we are to advance, the procedure must be regarded as acceptable by competent psychologists. That is, psychologists of established reputation in the field should have examined the proposed new procedure as well as any attendant risks and approved the approach as acceptable. Adherence to this principle of standard or acceptable procedure is a legal safeguard. No one has been successfully sued, so far as the present writer is aware, on grounds that a memory drum drove a subject psychotic or that an electric shock caused mental or bodily harm in a psychological experiment. Nor is there likely to be a successful suit so long as it can be demonstrated that the procedure has been widely used without detriment to other subjects and that obvious precautions were taken, such as using properly insulated wires, having a physician available where physical danger exists, etc. But it should be noted in this connection that some lawyers who specialize in industrial accident claims are quietly reviewing the problem of lawsuits based upon the charge that neurotic or psychotic behavior was produced by the stresses of a particular job. A word to the wise should suffice.

The importance of this third principle goes beyond legal protection in that, like the principles of consent and confidence, the esteem in which the psychological profession is held is directly involved. At least one therapist who personally used sexual intercourse as an experimental treatment for some of his female patients is now languishing in prison. Despite the fact that his procedure could in no sense be regarded as standard or acceptable, the public reaction was one of outrage and psychology suffered a severe blow. Another research study, though it was never actually carried out, is of interest in this reference frame. A counseling psychologist spent considerable time designing a study in which groups of clients would be given varying interpretations of their test results. Some would be given accurate interpretations while others who scored low would be told they scored high and others who scored high would be told they scored low, etc. The study was ingeniously designed and encompassed several critical points by carefully controlling the effects of counseling, motivation, and the like. But however important the study might be, the possible effects upon the subjects are horrible to contemplate. Only a psychopath could execute such research. Furthermore, much the same information could be gathered by controlled studies of counseled versus noncounseled subjects and, most important, without risk to the subject.

In some respects military personnel are in a special category with respect to service as experimental subjects and submission to medical (and presumably psychological) treatment. Of course, any military person has the same right to volunteer or not to volunteer as a civilian subject in an experiment. However, it appears to be essential that such service should not hamper or incapacitate the subject in the performance of his military duties. There is, however, an old tradition of human experimentation in the military services, the most famous example of which is the yellow fever studies of Walter Reed. Currently, the authorized fields of research in the military forces include virtually every field of psychology. The psychologist who is engaged in research with military personnel is urged to read the article by W. H. Johnson (4) of the Judge Advocate Corps, United States Army.

In passing judgment upon the Nazi physicians who were charged with atrocities disguised as medical research, the Nuremberg tribunal laid down 10 basic principles governing permissible medical experiments. These principles are quoted by General Telford Taylor in Mitscherlich and Mielke's *Doctors of Infamy* (6, p. xxiii). These principles are regarded as so basic and so important to psychology that they are herewith quoted in full:

1. The voluntary consent of the human subject is absolutely essential. This means that the person involved should have legal capacity to consent; should be so situated as to be able to exercise free power of choice, without the intervention of any element of force, fraud, deceit, duress, overreaching, or other ulterior form of constraint or coercion; and should have sufficient knowledge and comprehension of the elements of the subject matter involved as to enable him to make an understanding and enlightened decision. This latter element requires that before the acceptance of an affirmative decision by the experimental subject there should be made known to him the nature, duration, and purpose of the experiment; the method and means by which it is to be conducted; all inconveniences and hazards reasonably to be expected; and the effects upon his health or person which may possibly come from his participation in the experiment.

The duty and responsibility for ascertaining the quality of the consent rests upon each individual who initiates, directs, or engages in the experiment. It is a personal duty and responsibility which may not be delegated to another with impunity.

2. The experiment should be such as to yield fruitful results for the good of society, unprocurable by other methods or means of study, and not random and unnecessary in nature.

3. The experiment should be so designed and based on the results of animal experimentation and a knowledge of the natural history of the disease or other problem under study that the anticipated results will justify the performance of the experiment.

4. The experiment should be so conducted as to avoid all unnecessary physical and mental suffering and injury.

5. No experiment should be conducted where there is an a priori reason to believe that death or disabling injury will occur; except, perhaps in those experiments where the experimental physicians also serve as subjects.

6. The degree of risk to be taken should never exceed that determined by the humanitarian importance of the problem to be solved by the experiment.

7. Proper preparations should be made and adequate facilities provided to protect the experimental subject against even remote possibilities of injury, disability, or death.

8. The experiment should be conducted only by scientifically qualified persons. The highest degree of skill and care should be required through all stages of the experiment of those who conduct or engage in the experiment.

9. During the course of the experiment the human subject should be at liberty to bring the experiment to an end if he has reached the physical or mental state where continuation of the experiment seems to him to be impossible.

10. During the course of the experiment the scientist in charge must be prepared to terminate the experiment at any stage, if he has probable cause to believe, in the exercise of the good faith, superior skill, and careful judgment required of him that a continuation of the experiment is likely to result in injury, disability, or death to the experimental subject.

References

1. Anonymous. Regulation of psychological counseling and therapy. *Columbia Law Rev.*, 1951, 51, 474-495.

2. Guttentag, O. E. The physician's point of view. *Science*, 1953, 117, 207-210.

3. Guttmacher, M. S., & Weihofen, H. *Psychiatry and the law.* New York: W. W. Norton & Co., Inc., 1952.

4. Johnson, W. H. Civil rights of military personnel regarding medical care and experimental procedures. *Science*, 1953, 117, 212-215.

5. Kidd, A. M. Limits of the right of a person to consent to experimentation on himself. *Science*, 1953, 117, 211-212.

6. Mitscherlich, A., & Mielke, F. *Doctors of Infamy.* New York: Abelard-Schuman, Ltd., 1949.

7. Shimkin, M. B. The problem of experimentation on human beings. I. The research worker's point of view. *Science,* 1953, 117, 205-207.

8. Taylor, T. Statement pp. xvii-xxvi in Mitscherlich, A., and Mielke, F. *Doctors of Infamy.* New York: Abelard-Schuman, Ltd., 1949.

Martin T. Orne[1]

On the Social
Psychology of the
Psychological Experiment[2]

In the previous article, Berg suggests certain precautions that must be met
when dealing with human subjects, one of which is the permission of the subject.
What happens when a subject voluntarily enters an experimental situation?
Perhaps an even more important question is whether generalizations can be
made from volunteers to nonvolunteers. Orne, in this article, suggests that
experimental situations have certain "demand characteristics" which cause the
subjects to behave in certain ways, ways that differ from behavior where the
"demand characteristics" are not present. Again the question arises as to
what implications the phenomenon has for education. Do we create certain
"demand characteristics" when we experiment in a school classroom? If we do,
what can be done about them?

Martin T. Orne, "On the Social Psychology of the Psychological Experiment: With
Particular Reference to Demand Characteristics and Their Implications," *American
Psychologist*, 17:776-83, 1962. Reprinted with permission.

It is to the highest degree probable that the subject['s] . . . general
attitude of mind is that of ready complacency and cheerful willingness
to assist the investigator in every possible way by reporting to him
those very things which he is most eager to find, and that the very
questions of the experimenter . . . suggest the shade of reply expected
. . . Indeed . . . it seems too often as if the subject were now regarded
as a stupid automaton. . . . (A. H. Pierce, 1908).

[1] I wish to thank my associates Ronald E. Shor, Donald N. O'Connell, Ulric
Neisser, Karl E. Scheibe, and Emily F. Carota for their comments and criticisms in
the preparation of this paper.

[2] This paper was presented at the Symposium, "On the Social Psychology of the
Psychological Experiment," American Psychological Association Convention, New
York, 1961.

The work reported here was supported in part by a Public Health Service
Research Grant, M-3369, National Institute of Mental Health.

Since the time of Galileo, scientists have employed the laboratory experiment as a method of understanding natural phenomena. Generically, the experimental method consists of abstracting relevant variables from complex situations in nature and reproducing in the laboratory segments of these situations, varying the parameters involved so as to determine the effect of the experimental variables. This procedure allows generalization from the information obtained in the laboratory situation back to the original situation as it occurs in nature. The physical sciences have made striking advances through the use of this method, but in the behavioral sciences it has often been difficult to meet two necessary requirements for meaningful experimentation: reproducibility and ecological validity.[3] It has long been recognized that certain differences will exist between the types of experiments conducted in the physical sciences and those in the behavioral sciences because the former investigates a universe of inanimate objects and forces, whereas the latter deals with animate organisms, often thinking, conscious subjects. However, recognition of this distinction has not always led to appropriate changes in the traditional experimental model of physics as employed in the behavioral sciences. Rather the experimental model has been so successful as employed in physics that there has been a tendency in the behavioral sciences to follow precisely a paradigm originated for the study of inanimate objects, i.e., one which proceeds by exposing the subject to various conditions and observing the differences in reaction of the subject under different conditions. However, the use of such a model with animal or human subjects leads to the problem that the subject of the experiment is assumed, at least implicitly, to be a *passive responder* to stimuli—an assumption difficult to justify. Further, in this type of model the experimental stimuli themselves are usually rigorously defined in terms of what *is done* to the subject. In contrast, the purpose of this paper will be to focus on what the human subject *does* in the laboratory: what motivation the subject is likely to have in the experimental situation, how he usually perceives behavioral research, what the nature of the cues is that the subject is likely to pick up, etc. Stated in other terms, what factors are apt to affect the subject's reaction to the well-defined stimuli in the situation? These factors comprise what will be referred to here as the "experimental setting."

Since any experimental manipulation of human subjects takes place within this larger framework or setting, we should propose that the above-mentioned factors must be further elaborated and the parameters of the experimental setting more carefully defined so that

---

[3] Ecological validity, in the sense that Brunswik (1947) has used the term: appropriate generalization from the laboratory to nonexperimental situations.

adequate controls can be designed to isolate the effects of the experimental setting from the effects of the experimental variables. Later in this paper we shall propose certain possible techniques of control which have been devised in the process of our research on the nature of hypnosis.

Our initial focus here will be on some of the qualities peculiar to psychological experiments. The experimental situation is one which takes place within the context of an explicit agreement of the subject to participate in a special form of social interaction known as "taking part in an experiment." Within the context of our culture the roles of subject and experimenter are well understood and carry with them well-defined mutual role expectations. A particularly striking aspect of the typical experimenter-subject relationship is the extent to which the subject will play his role and place himself under the control of the experimenter. Once a subject has agreed to participate in a psychological experiment, he implicitly agrees to perform a very wide range of actions on request without inquiring as to their purpose, and frequently without inquiring as to their duration.

Furthermore, the subject agrees to tolerate a considerable degree of discomfort, boredom, or actual pain, if required to do so by the experimenter. Just about any request which could conceivably be asked of the subject by a reputable investigator is legitimized by the quasi-magical phrase, "This is an experiment," and the shared assumption that a legitimate purpose will be served by the subject's behavior. A somewhat trivial example of this legitimization of requests is as follows:

A number of casual acquaintances were asked whether they would do the experimenter a favor; on their acquiescence, they were asked to perform five push-ups. Their response tended to be amazement, incredulity and the question "Why?" Another similar group of individuals were asked whether they would take part in an experiment of brief duration. When they agreed to do so, they too were asked to perform five push-ups. Their typical response was "Where?"

The striking degree of control inherent in the experimental situation can also be illustrated by a set of pilot experiments which were performed in the course of designing an experiment to test whether the degree of control inherent in the *hypnotic* relationship is greater than that in a waking relationship.[4] In order to test this question, we tried to develop a set of tasks which waking subjects would refuse to do, or would do only for a short period of time. The tasks were intended to be psychologically noxious, meaningless, or boring, rather than painful or fatiguing.

---

[4] These pilot studies were performed by Thomas Menaker.

For example, one task was to perform serial additions of each adjacent two numbers on sheets filled with rows of random digits. In order to complete just one sheet, the subject would be required to perform 224 additions! A stack of some 2,000 sheets was presented to each subject—clearly an impossible task to complete. After the instructions were given, the subject was deprived of his watch and told, "Continue to work; I will return eventually." Five and one-half hours later, the *experimenter* gave up! In general, subjects tended to continue this type of task for several hours, usually with little decrement in performance. Since we were trying to find a task which would be discontinued spontaneously within a brief period, we tried to create a more frustrating situation as follows:

Subjects were asked to perform the same task described above but were also told that when finished the additions on each sheet, they should pick up a card from a large pile, which would instruct them on what to do next. However, every card in the pile read,

> You are to tear up the sheet of paper which you have just completed into a minimum of thirty-two pieces and go on to the next sheet of paper and continue working as you did before; when you have completed this piece of paper, pick up the next card which will instruct you further. Work as accurately and as rapidly as you can.

Our expectation was that subjects would discontinue the task as soon as they realized that the cards were worded identically, that each finished piece of work had to be destroyed, and that, in short, the task was completely meaningless.

Somewhat to our amazement, subjects tended to persist in the task for several hours with relatively little sign of overt hostility. Removal of the one-way screen did not tend to make much difference. The postexperimental inquiry helped to explain the subjects' behavior. When asked about the tasks, subjects would invariably attribute considerable meaning to their performance, viewing it as an endurance test or the like.

Thus far, we have been singularly unsuccessful in finding an experimental task which would be discontinued, or, indeed, refused by subjects in an experimental setting.[5, 6] Not only do subjects continue

---

[5] Tasks which would involve the use of actual severe physical pain or exhaustion were not considered.

[6] This observation is consistent with Frank's (1944) failure to obtain resistance to disagreeable or nonsensical tasks. He accounts for this "primarily by S's unwillingness to break the tacit agreement he had made when he volunteered to take part in the experiment, namely, to do whatever the experiment required of him" (p. 24).

to perform boring, unrewarding tasks, but they do so with few errors and little decrement in speed. It became apparent that it was extremely difficult to design an experiment to test the degree of social control in hypnosis, in view of the already *very high degree of control in the experimental situation itself.*

The quasi-experimental work reported here is highly informal and based on samples of three or four subjects in each group. It does, however, illustrate the remarkable compliance of the experimental subject. The only other situations where such a wide range of requests are carried out with little or no question are those of complete authority, such as some parent-child relationships or some doctor-patient relationships. This aspect of the experiment as a social situation will not become apparent unless one tests for it; it is, however, present in varying degrees in all experimental contexts. Not only are tasks carried out, but they are performed with care over a considerable period of time.

Our observation that subjects tend to carry out a remarkably wide range of instructions with a surprising degree of diligence reflects only one aspect of the motivation manifested by most subjects in an experimental situation. It is relevant to consider another aspect of motivation that is common to the subjects of most psychological experiments: high regard for the aims of science and experimentation.

A volunteer who participates in a psychological experiment may do so for a wide variety of reasons ranging from the need to fulfill a course requirement, to the need for money, to the unvoiced hope of altering his personal adjustment for the better, etc. Over and above these motives, however, college students tend to share (with the experimenter) the hope and expectation that the study in which they are participating will in some material way contribute to science and perhaps ultimately to human welfare in general. We should expect that many of the characteristics of the experimental situation derive from the peculiar role relationship which exists between subject and experimenter. Both subject and experimenter share the belief that whatever the experimental task is, it is important, and that as such no matter how much effort must be exerted or how much discomfort must be endured, it is justified by the ultimate purpose.

If we assume that much of the motivation of the subject to comply with any and all experimental instructions derives from an identification with the goals of science in general and the success of the experiment in particular,[7] it follows that the subject has a stake in the outcome of

---

[7] This hypothesis is subject to empirical test. We should predict that there would be measurable differences in motivation between subjects who perceive a particular experiment as "significant" and those who perceive the experiment as "unimportant."

the study in which he is participating. For the volunteer subject to feel that he has made a useful contribution, it is necessary for him to assume that the experimenter is competent and that he himself is a "good subject."

The significance to the subject of successfully being a "good subject" is attested to by the frequent questions at the conclusion of an experiment, to the effect of, "Did I ruin the experiment?" What is most commonly meant by this is, "Did I perform well in my role as experimental subject?" or "Did my behavior demonstrate that which the experiment is designed to show?" Admittedly, subjects are concerned about their performance in terms of reinforcing their self-image; nonetheless, they seem even more concerned with the utility of their performances. We might well expect then that as far as the subject is able, he will behave in an experimental context in a manner designed to play the role of a "good subject" or, in other words, *to validate the experimental hypothesis.* Viewed in this way, the student volunteer is *not* merely a passive responder in an experimental situation but rather he has a very real stake in the successful outcome of the experiment. This problem is implicitly recognized in the large number of psychological studies which attempt to conceal the true purpose of the experiment from the subject in the hope of thereby obtaining more reliable data. This maneuver on the part of psychologists is so widely known in the college population that even if a psychologist is honest with the subject, more often than not he will be distrusted. As one subject pithily put it, "Psychologists always lie!" This bit of paranoia has some support in reality.

The subject's performance in an experiment might almost be conceptualized as problem-solving behavior; that is, at some level he sees it as his task to ascertain the true purpose of the experiment and respond in a manner which will support the hypotheses being tested. Viewed in this light, the totality of cues which convey an experimental hypothesis to the subject become significant determinants of subjects' behavior. We have labeled the sum total of such cues as the *"demand characteristics of the experimental situation"* (Orne, 1959a). These cues include the rumors or campus scuttlebutt about the research, the information conveyed during the original solicitation, the person of the experimenter, and the setting of the laboratory, as well as all explicit and implicit communications during the experiment proper. A frequently overlooked, but nonetheless very significant source of cues for the subject lies in the experimental procedure itself, viewed in the light of the subject's previous knowledge and experience. For example, if a test is given twice with some intervening treatment, even the dullest college student is aware that some change is expected, particularly if the test is in some obvious way related to the treatment.

The demand characteristics perceived in any particular experiment will vary with the sophistication, intelligence, and previous experience of each experimental subject. To the extent that the demand characteristics of the experiment are clear-cut, they will be perceived uniformly by most experimental subjects. It is entirely possible to have an experimental situation with clear-cut demand characteristics for psychology undergraduates which, however, does not have the same clear-cut demand characteristics for enlisted army personnel. It is, of course, those demand characteristics which are perceived by the subject that will influence his behavior.

We should like to propose the heuristic assumption that a subject's behavior in any experimental situation will be determined by two sets of variables: (a) those which are traditionally defined as experimental variables and (b) the perceived demand characteristics of the experimental situation. The extent to which the subject's behavior is related to the demand characteristics, rather than to the experimental variable, will in large measure determine both the extent to which the experiment can be replicated with minor modification (i.e., modified demand characteristics) and the extent to which generalizations can be drawn about the effect of the experimental variables in nonexperimental contexts [the problem of ecological validity (Brunswik, 1947)].

It becomes an empirical issue to study under what circumstances, in what kind of experimental contexts, and with what kind of subject populations, demand characteristics become significant in determining the behavior of subjects in experimental situations. It should be clear that demand characteristics cannot be eliminated from experiments; all experiments will have demand characteristics, and these will always have some effect. It does become possible, however, to study the effect of demand characteristics as opposed to the effect of experimental variables. However, techniques designed to study the effect of demand characteristics need to take into account that these effects result from the subject's *active* attempt to respond appropriately to the *totality* of the experimental situation.

It is perhaps best to think of the perceived demand characteristics as a contextual variable in the experimental situation. We should like to emphasize that, at this stage, little is known about this variable. In our first study which utilized the demand characteristics concept (Orne, 1959b), we found that a particular experimental effect was present only in records of those subjects who were able to verbalize the experimenter's hypothesis. Those subjects who were unable to do so did not show the predicted phenomenon. Indeed we found that whether or not a given subject perceived the experimenter's hypothesis was a more accurate predictor of the subject's actual performance than his statement about what he thought he had done on the experimental task. It became clear from extensive interviews with subjects that response to the demand characteristics is not merely conscious compliance. When we speak of "playing the role of a good experimental subject," we use the concept analogously to the way in which Sarbin (1950) describes role playing in hypnosis: namely, largely on a nonconscious level. The demand characteristics of the situation help define the role of "good experimental subject," and the responses of the subject are a function of the role that is created.

We have a suspicion that the demand characteristics most potent in determining subjects' behavior are those which convey the purpose of the experiment effectively but not obviously. If the purpose of the experiment is not clear, or is highly ambiguous, many different hypotheses may be formed by different subjects, and the demand characteristics will not lead to clear-cut results. If, on the other hand, the demand characteristics are so obvious that the subject becomes fully conscious of the expectations of the experimenter, there is a tendency to lean over backwards to be honest. We are encountering here the effect of another facet of the college student's attitude toward science. While the student wants studies to "work," he feels he must be honest in his report; otherwise, erroneous conclusions will be drawn. Therefore, if the subject becomes acutely aware of the experimenter's expectations, there may be a tendency for biasing in the opposite direction. (This is analogous to the often observed tendency to favor individuals whom we dislike in an effort to be fair.)[8]

Delineation of the situations where demand characteristics may produce an effect ascribed to experimental variables, or where they may obscure such an effect and actually lead to systematic data in the opposite direction, as well as those experimental contexts where they do not play a major role, is an issue for further work. Recognizing the contribution to experimental results which may be made by the demand characteristics of the situation, what are some experimental techniques for the study of demand characteristics?

---

[8] Rosenthal (1961) in his work on experimenter bias, has reported a similar type of phenomenon. Biasing was maximized by ego involvement of the experimenters, but when an attempt was made to increase biasing by paying for "good results," there was a marked reduction of effect. This reversal may be ascribed to the experimenters' becoming too aware of their own wishes in the situation.

As we have pointed out, it is futile to imagine an experiment that could be created without demand characteristics. One of the basic characteristics of the human being is that he will ascribe purpose and meaning even in the absence of purpose and meaning. In an experiment where he knows some purpose exists, it is inconceivable for him not to form some hypothesis as to the purpose, based on some cues, no matter how meager; this will then determine the demand characteristics which will be perceived by and operate for a particular subject. Rather than eliminating this variable then, it becomes necessary to take demand characteristics into account, study their effect, and manipulate them if necessary.

One procedure to determine the demand characteristics is the systematic study of each individual subject's perception of the experimental hypothesis. If one can determine what demand characteristics are perceived by each subject, it becomes possible to determine to what extent these, rather than the experimental variables, correlate with the observed behavior. If the subject's behavior correlates better with the demand characteristics than with the experimental variables, it is probable that the demand characteristics are the major determinants of the behavior.

The most obvious technique for determining what demand characteristics are perceived is the use of postexperimental inquiry. In this regard, it is well to point out that considerable self-discipline is necessary for the experimenter to obtain a valid inquiry. A great many experimenters at least implicitly make the demand that the subject not perceive what is really going on. The temptation for the experimenter, in, say, a replication of an Asch-group pressure experiment, is to ask the subject afterwards, "You didn't realize that the other fellows were confederates, did you?" Having obtained the required, "No," the experimenter breathes a sigh of relief and neither subject nor experimenter pursues the issue further.[9] However, even if the experimenter makes an effort to elicit the subject's perception of the hypothesis of the experiment, he may have difficulty in obtaining a valid report because the subject as well as he himself has considerable interest in appearing naive.

Most subjects are cognizant that they are not supposed to know any more about an experiment than they have been told and that excessive knowledge will disqualify them from participating, or, in the case of a postexperimental inquiry, such knowledge will invalidate their per-

[9] Asch (1952) himself took great pains to avoid this pitfall.

formance. As we pointed out earlier, subjects have a real stake in viewing their performance as meaningful. For this reason, it is commonplace to find a pact of ignorance resulting from the intertwining motives of both experimenter and subject, neither wishing to create a situation where the particular subject's perfomance needs to be excluded from the study.

For these reasons, inquiry procedures are required to push the subject for information without, however, providing in themselves cues as to what is expected. The general question which needs to be explored is the subject's perception of the experimental purpose and the specific hypotheses of the experimenter. This can best be done by an open-ended procedure starting with the very general question of, "What do you think that the experiment is about?" and only much later asking specific questions. Responses of "I don't know" should be dealt with by encouraging the subject to guess, use his imagination, and in general, by refusing to accept this response. Under these circumstances, the overwhelming majority of students will turn out to have evolved very definite hypotheses. These hypotheses can then be judged, and a correlation between them and experimental performance can be drawn.

Two objections may be made against this type of inquiry: (a) that the subject's perception of the experimenter's hypotheses is based on his own experimental behavior, and therefore a correlation between these two variables may have little to do with the determinants of behavior, and (b) that the inquiry procedure itself is subject to demand characteristics.

A procedure which has been independently advocated by Riecken (1958) and Orne (1959a) is designed to deal with the first of these objections. This consists of an inquiry procedure which is conducted much as though the subject had actually been run in the experiment, without, however, permitting him to be given any experimental data. Instead, the precise procedure of the experiment is explained, the experimental material is shown to the subject, and he is told what he would be required to do; however, he is not permitted to make any responses. He is then given a postexperimental inquiry as though he had been a subject. Thus, one would say, "If I had asked you to do all these things, what do you think that the experiment would be about, what do you think I would be trying to prove, what would my hypothesis be?" etc. This technique, which we have termed the pre-experimental inquiry, can be extended very readily to the giving of pre-experimental tests, followed by the explanation of experimental conditions and tasks, and the administration of postexperimental tests. The subject is requested to behave on these tests as though he had been exposed to the experimental treatment that was described to him. This type of procedure is not open to the objection that the subject's own behavior has provided cues for him as to the purpose of the task. It presents him with a straight problem-solving situation and makes explicit what, for the true experimental subject, is implicit. It goes without saying that these subjects who are run on the pre-experimental inquiry conditions must be drawn from the same population as the experimental groups and may, of course, not be run subsequently in the experimental condition. This technique is one of approximation rather than of proof. However, if subjects describe behavior on the preinquiry conditions as similar to, or identical with, that actually given by subjects exposed to the experimental conditions, the hypothesis becomes plausible that demand characteristics may be responsible for the behavior.

It is clear that pre- and postexperimental inquiry techniques have their own demand characteristics. For these reasons, it is usually best to have the inquiry conducted by an experimenter who is not acquainted with the actual experimental behavior of the subjects. This will tend to minimize the effect of experimenter bias.

Another technique which we have utilized for approximating the effect of the demand characteristics is to attempt to hold the demand characteristics constant and eliminate the experimental variable. One way of accomplishing this purpose is through the use of simulating subjects. This is a group of subjects who are not exposed to the experimental variable to which the effect has been attributed, but who are instructed to act *as if* this were the case. In order to control for experimenter bias under these circumstances, it is advisable to utilize more than one experimenter and to have the experimenter who actually runs the subjects "blind" as to which group (simulating or real) any given individual belongs.

Our work in hypnosis (Damaser, Shor, & Orne, 1963; Orne, 1959b; Shor, 1959) is a good example of the use of simulating controls. Subjects unable to enter hypnosis are instructed to simulate entering hypnosis for another experimenter. The experimenter who runs the study sees both highly trained hypnotic subjects and simulators in random order and does not know to which group each subject belongs. Because the subjects are run "blind," the experimenter is more likely to treat the two groups of subjects identically. We have found that simulating subjects are able to perform with great effectiveness, deceiving even well-trained hypnotists. However, the simulating group is not exposed to the experimental condition (in this case, hypnosis) to which the given effect under investigation is often ascribed. Rather, it is a group faced with a problem-solving task: namely, to utilize whatever cues are made available by the experimental context and the experimenter's concrete behavior in order to behave as they think that hypnotized subjects might. Therefore, to the extent that simulating subjects are able to behave identically, it is possible that demand characteristics, rather than the altered state of consciousness, could account for the behavior of the experimental group.

The same type of technique can be utilized in other types of studies. For example, in contrast to the placebo control in a drug study, it is equally possible to instruct some subjects not to take the medication at all, but to act as if they had. It must be emphasized that this type of control is different from the placebo control. It represents an approximation. It maximally confronts the simulating subject with a problem-solving task and suggests how much of the total effect could be accounted for by the demand characteristics—assuming that the experimental group had taken full advantage of them, an assumption not necessarily correct.

All of the techniques proposed thus far share the quality that they depend upon the active cooperation of the control subjects, and in some way utilize his thinking process as an intrinsic factor. The subject does *not* just respond in these control situations but, rather, he is required *actively* to solve the problem.

The use of placebo experimental conditions is a way in which this problem can be dealt with in a more classic fashion. Psychopharmacology has used such techniques extensively, but here, too, they present problems. In the case of placebos and drugs, it is often the case that the physician is "blind" as to whether a drug is placebo or active, but the patient is not, despite precautions to the contrary; i.e., the patient is cognizant that he does not have the side effects which some of his fellow patients on the ward experience. By the same token, in psychological placebo treatments, it is equally important to ascertain whether the subject actually perceived the treatment to be experimental or control. Certainly the subject's perception of himself as a control subject may materially alter the situation (Orne & Scheibe, 1964).

A recent experiment in our laboratory illustrates this type of investigation. We were interested in studying the demand characteristics of sensory deprivation experiments, independent of any actual sensory deprivation. We hypothesized that the cautious overly treatment of subjects, careful screening for mental or physical disorders, awesome release forms, and, above all, the presence of a "panic (release) button" might be more significant in producing the effects reported from sensory deprivation than the actual diminution of sensory input. A pilot study (Stare, Brown, & Orne, 1959), employing preinquiry techniques, supported this view.   Recently, we designed an experiment to test more rigorously this hypothesis.

This experiment, which we called Meaning Deprivation, had all the *accoutrements* of sensory deprivation, including release forms and a red panic button. However, we carefully refrained from creating any sensory deprivation whatsoever. The experimental task consisted of sitting in a small experimental room which was well lighted, with two comfortable chairs, as well as ice water and a sandwich, and an optional task of adding numbers. The subject did not have a watch during this time, the room was reasonably quiet, but not soundproof, and the duration of the experiment (of which the subject was ignorant) was four hours. Before the subject was placed in the experimental room, 10 tests previously used in sensory deprivation research were administered. At the completion of the experiment, the same tasks were again administered. A microphone and a one-way screen were present in the room, and the subject was encouraged to verbalize freely.

The control group of 10 subjects was subjected to the identical treatment, except that they were told that they were control subjects for a sensory deprivation experiment. The panic button was eliminated for this group. The formal experimental treatment of these two groups of subjects was the same in terms of the objective stress—four hours of isolation. However, the demand characteristics had been purposively varied for the two groups to study the effect of demand characteristics as opposed to objective stress. Of the 14 measures which could be quantified, 13 were in the predicted direction, and 6 were significant at the selected 10% alpha level or better. A Mann-Whitney U test has been performed on the summation ranks of all measures as a convenient method for summarizing the overall differences. The one-tailed probability which emerges is $p = .001$, a clear demonstration of expected effects.

This study suggests that demand characteristics may in part account for some of the findings commonly attributed to sensory deprivation. We have found similar significant effects of demand characteristics in accounting for a great deal of the findings reported in hypnosis. It is highly probable that careful attention to this variable, or group of variables, may resolve some of the current controversies regarding a number of psychological phenomena in motivation, learning, and perception.

In summary, we have suggested that the subject must be recognized as an active participant in any experiment, and that it may be fruitful to view the psychological experiment as a very special form of social interaction. We have proposed that the subject's behavior in an experiment is a function of the totality of the situation, which includes the experimental variables being investigated and at least one other set of variables which we have subsumed under the heading, demand characteristics of the experimental situation. The study and control of demand characteristics are not simply matters of good experimental technique; rather, it is an empirical issue to determine under what circumstances demand characteristics significantly affect subjects' experimental behavior. Several empirical techniques have been proposed for this purpose. It has been suggested that control of these variables in particular may lead to greater reproducibility and ecological validity of psychological experiments. With an increasing understanding of these factors intrinsic to the experimental context, the experimental method in psychology may become a more effective tool in predicting behavior in nonexperimental contexts.

References

Asch, S. E. *Social psychology*. Englewood Cliffs, N.J.: Prentice-Hall, Inc., 1952.

Brunswik, E. *Systematic and representative design of psychological experiments with results in physical and social perception*. (Syllabus Series, No. 304) Berkeley: Univer. California Press, 1947.

Damaser, Esther C., Shor, R. E., & Orne, M. T. Physiological effects during hypnotically requested emotions. *J. psychosom. Med.*, 1963, 25, 334-343.

Frank, J. D. Experimental studies of personal pressure and resistance: I. Experimental production of resistance. *J. gen. Psychol.*, 1944, 30, 23-41.

Orne, M. T. The demand characteristics of an experimental design and their implications. Paper read at American Psychological Association, Cincinnati, 1959. (a)

Orne, M. T. The nature of hypnosis: Artifact and essence. *J. abnorm. soc. Psychol.*, 1959, 58, 277-299. (b)

Orne, M. T., and Scheibe, K. E. The contribution of non-deprivation factors in the production of sensory deprivation effects: The psychology of the "panic button." *J. abnorm. soc. Psychol.*, 1964, 68, 3-12.

Pierce, A. H. The subconscious again. *J. Phil., Psychol., scient. Meth.*, 1908, 5, 264-271.

Riecken, H. W. A program for research on experiments in social psychology. Paper read at Behavioral Sciences Conference, University of New Mexico, 1958.

Rosenthal, R. On the social psychology of the psychological experiment: With particular reference to experimenter bias. Paper read at American Psychological Association, New York, 1961.

Sarbin, T. R. Contributions to role-taking theory: I. Hypnotic behavior. *Psychol. Rev.*, 1950, 57, 255-270.

Shor, R. E. Explorations in hypnosis: A theoretical and experimental study. Unpublished doctoral dissertation, Brandeis University, 1959.

Stare, F., Brown, J., & Orne, M. T. Demand characteristics in sensory deprivation studies. Unpublished seminar paper, Massachusetts Mental Health Center and Harvard University, 1959.

Desmond L. Cook

The Hawthorne Effect in Educational Research

The previous two articles have dealt with problems of human experimentation as they particularly relate to the field of psychology. In each case the question has been asked, "How do these ideas relate to educational research?" The article by Cook answers this question. What difference, if any, is there between the Hawthorne effect discussed by Cook, and "demand characteristics" discussed by Orne? Is the educational researcher in a more fortunate position than the psychological researcher because he can deal more frequently with usual and nonthreatening situations? If the attributes of the experiment are well hidden, does this overcome the Hawthorne effect? Finally, in light of Berg's thesis, are we being ethical in hiding the attributes of an experiment even if we are quite sure no harm will be done?

Desmond L. Cook, "The Hawthorne Effect in Educational Research," *Phi Delta Kappan,* 44:116-22, 1962. Reprinted with permission.

What is the *Hawthorne effect?* When, where, and how did the concept originate? If one seeks answers to these questions in such references as Good's *Dictionary of Education,*[1] the dictionary of psychological terms by English,[2] most of the books on educational research methodology, or the several issues of the *Encyclopedia of Educational Research,* the listings and indexes will not help him. This failure to index the Hawthorne effect concept is rather significant, since the phenomenon is so frequently referred to in explaining either the apparent conclusive or nonconclusive results of educational researches.

Even though not indexed, the term does appear quite frequently in the literature on research methodology, and its general nature is

---

[1] C. V. Good, *Dictionary of Education.* New York: McGraw-Hill Book Company, 1959.

[2] H. B. English, *A Comprehensive Dictionary of Psychological and Psychoanalytical Terms.* New York: Longmans, Green, 1958.

commonly recognized by the researchers. The implications for educational research have not, however, been fully explored. The intent of this paper is to answer three questions: (1) What is the Hawthorne effect? (2) What are its implications for educational research? (3) What methods have been advanced to control the effect in research procedures?

WHAT IS THE HAWTHORNE EFFECT?

So far as I know, the term as it is now generally used first appears in written form in the book *Research Methods in the Behavioral Sciences* by Festinger and Katz.[3] In a discussion of experiments conducted in field settings, French contrasts laboratory and field experimentation settings and points up the problem of generalizing from each type.[4] He indicates that the difference between the two types is not in the nature of the research that takes place but in whether the researcher is working with real or artificial social phenomena. French believes that the laboratory setting is artificial if the subjects behave differently than if they were not in the laboratory. To him, a field experiment is usually not subject to artificiality. Consequently, the problem of generalizing to other real life situations is thus avoided. He goes on, however, to point out an important exception:

> That this is not always the case . . . is well illustrated in the famous Hawthorne experiments. From a methodological point of view, the most interesting finding is what we might call the "Hawthorne Effect."

Let us look at the original Hawthorne experiments for this "interesting finding." In 1924 the Massachusetts Institute of Technology initiated a series of tests under the sponsorship of the National Research Council and the Illuminating Engineering Society to ascertain the relationship between illumination and production in various factory situations. The report by C. E. Snow[5] contains the results of the several investigations. One of the participating firms was the Hawthorne plant of the Western Electric Company. The tests conducted there are of

---

[3] L. Festinger and D. Katz, editors, *Research Methods in the Behavioral Sciences.* New York: Dryden Press, 1953.

[4] John R. P. French, Jr., "Experiments in Field Settings," in L. Festinger and D. Katz, editors, *Research Methods in the Behavioral Sciences.* New York: Dryden Press, 1953, Ch. 3, pp. 98-135.

[5] C. E. Snow, "Research on Industrial Illumination," *Tech Engineering News,* 8:257-282.

immediate concern because it is from them that the term *Hawthorne effect* was eventually derived.

Three separate series of illumination-production tests were conducted at the Hawthorne plant. Space does not permit a detailed report of each series, but because the sequence of the series is important it will be described. In the first series, the investigators manipulated the lighting in three different parts of the plant. A general observation was made that production levels under the different amounts of illumination were always *higher* at the end than at the start and did not fall off even with a decrease in illumination. As a result of this first series, certain necessary modifications in procedure became evident.

> The results of this first winter's test, covering the three departments described, brought out very forcibly the necessity of controlling or eliminating the various additional factors which affected production output in either the same or opposing direction to that which we could ascribe to illumination.[6]

The second and third series of tests have high relevance to the topic, not only because of their subsequent results but also because of the methodological procedures employed. One must first be cognizant of the era in which these studies were conducted. In the early Twenties, industrial psychologists were working under the conviction that the traditional approach to scientific investigation of manipulating a single variable was a means of fruitful investigation. Under this approach, illumination change was to be the independent variable and production the dependent variable. To overcome the limitations of the first series, the investigators set up the two subsequent experimental series using the comparable groups technique. They tried to control as many sources of variation as possible, as witness their physically isolating experimental groups from each other, placing them in separate buildings or parts of the factory. What were the results of these two investigations?

> This test resulted in a very appreciable production increase in both groups and of almost identical magnitude. The difference in efficiency of the groups was so small as to be less than the probable error of the values. Consequently, we were again unable to determine what definite part of the improvement in performance should be ascribed to illumination.[7]

---

[6] *Ibid.*

[7] *Ibid.*

The results of the third experimental series were quite unexpected, since the investigators *decreased* illumination rather than increasing it as in other studies.

> As the level of illumination in the test group enclosure changed to a lower value, the efficiencies of both the test and control groups increased slowly and steadily.[8]

Snow goes on to report the findings observed in other experiments on illumination conducted in other factory situations in several geographical locations. Of all the experiments described in his paper, only the Hawthorne studies have gained any degree of prominence. The reason for this we shall see later. What was the general conclusion from the series of tests conducted under the National Research Council's auspices? Snow points out the significant factor in one of his summary statements:

> Any investigation attempting to evaluate definitely the effect of illumination or some such influence must take the greatest of pains to control or eliminate all factors but the one being studied. Many of them can be controlled or eliminated, but the one great stumbling block remaining is the problem of the psychology of the human individual.[9]

The results of the investigations were such that one could not help feel as Blum does in his book, *Industrial Psychology and its Social Foundations:*

> In most such experimentation the sponsors would have thrown out the evidence and the "crackpots" responsible; it would have been considered a nightmare to be repressed and suppressed.[10]

Why have the Hawthorne investigations become better known than any of the other illumination experiments? Even though the experimental methodology became more and more refined through the successive experiments, the simple answer became more elusive, as Snow concluded. Blum says:

> It was clear that a direct relationship between illumination and production was nonexistent and that the answer would have to be obtained by attacking a different aspect of the problem.[11]

---

[8] *Ibid.*, p. 274.

[9] *Ibid.*, p. 282.

[10] M. L. Blum, *Industrial Psychology and Its Social Foundations* (2nd ed.). New York: Harper & Row, Publishers, 1957, Ch. 2, p. 25.

[11] *Ibid.*, p. 50.

The direction which the research then took is described by two of the Hawthorne researchers, Roethlisberger and Dickson:

Although the results from these experiments on illumination fell short of the expectations of the company in the sense that they failed to answer the specific question of the relation between illumination and efficiency, nevertheless they provided a great stimulus for more research in the field of human relations.[12]

The Hawthorne researchers then undertook a series of investigations designed to develop ways of studying the introduction of variables into work situations. Consequently, rest periods, working hour changes, and wage incentives were introduced and observations made of the workers' reactions to such variables. These studies were similar to the illumination experiments in that unpredicted results accompanied the changes as noted by Pennock.

From these tests have come some startling results, startling because they were unexpected as well as because they were sometimes contrary to accepted opinion. In the first place, there was a gradual yet steady increase in production regardless, to a certain extent, of test conditions imposed. . . . Now this unexpected and continual upward trend in the productivity throughout the periods, even . . . when the girls were put on a full 48-hour week with no rest period or lunch, led us to seek some explanation or analysis.[13]

Three hypotheses were suggested as possible causes and each in turn was subsequently rejected. Pennock's summarization of the results of the investigation begins to develop for us a meaning of the term Hawthorne effect.

We have shown that fatigue is not a governing factor in the performance of the test group, and have partially evaluated the effect of increased incentive due to change in method of pay, which leaves us convinced that the rather remarkable results we have been able to obtain with this group are due mainly to changes in their mental attitude. This we consider a major accomplishment of our entire study.[14]

The impact of this finding was so marked that it led the Western Electric Company to begin a series of investigations designed to

---

[12] F. J. Roethlisberger and W. J. Dickson, *Management and the Worker.* Cambridge, Mass.: Harvard University Press, 1941, p. 18.

[13] G. A. Pennock, "Industrial Research at Hawthorne: An Experimental Investigation of Rest Periods, Working Conditions, and Other Influences," *The Personnel Journal,* 8:296-313, 1929, p. 304.

[14] *Ibid.,* p. 309.

explore the nature of employee attitudes. These investigations were characterized by an employee interviewing program which had a "non-directive" flavor somewhat prior to the work of Carl Rogers. This latter group of studies was to become highly influential in the development of the area of industrial psychology now known as "human relations in industry." A complete account of the various investigations, including the illumination experiments at Hawthorne, is presented in the book, *Management and the Worker*, by Roethlisberger and Dickson.[15] A retrospective view of the investigation and subsequent implications for industry are presented in *Hawthorne Revisited*,[16] by Landesberger.

Two observations can now be made, one relating to the method, the other to definition. Methodologically, the procedure followed by the illumination investigators is not unlike that often observed in educational research. A change is introduced and promising results are secured. This promising lead is followed up by carefully controlled experimentation to study more precisely the effects of the change. The results are too often similar to those obtained in the illumination experiments. Regardless of what is done, we have difficulty in attributing observed changes in the dependent variable directly to the manipulated independent variable.

From the several studies presented, a working definition of the Hawthorne effect can now be developed. French provides a start by stating that the marked increases in production were related not to the manipulated changes but " . . . only to the special social position and social treatment they [the subjects] received."[17] The special social treatment was created in turn by the "artificial" aspects of the experiment.

From this beginning, we might extrapolate the following definition of the concept: *The Hawthorne effect is a phenomenon characterized by an awareness on the part of the subjects of special treatment created by artificial experimental conditions. This awareness becomes confounded with the independent variable under study, with a subsequent facilitating effect on the dependent variable, thus leading to ambiguous results.* To go much beyond this general definition at present is risky, due primarily to the lack of any real evidence derived from direct study of the effect as to its behavioral specifics or components. I trust,

---

15 *Op. cit.*

16 H. A. Landesberger, *Hawthorne Revisited*. Ithaca, New York: Cornell University Press, 1958.

17 French, *op. cit.*, p. 101.

however, that it will provide a frame of reference for the rest of the paper.

WHAT ARE IMPLICATIONS FOR EDUCATIONAL RESEARCH?

Accepting for the moment the definition of the Hawthorne effect as presented, what implication does it have for research in education? One answer to this question can be found in a statement by Paul Rosenbloom in the recent symposium on educational research sponsored by Phi Delta Kappa. In describing recent experimentation with the mathematics curriculum in the state of Minnesota, Rosenbloom writes:

> There is of course in educational experimentation a so-called Hawthorne effect. It is well known that in an experimental situation teachers and pupils are more highly motivated, so this makes a certain problem. You know, for example, that in educational experimentation, no matter what the hypothesis is, the experimental classes do better than the control classes.[18]

Ruth Strang, writing on reading research in the *Educational Forum* for January, 1962, echoes the comments made by Rosenbloom:

> There are always uncontrolled variables that may influence the results. Thus at the end of the experiment, the investigator cannot choose but be apologetic; he cannot say with certainty that a given result was obtained by virtue of a particular teaching method which he wanted to study. The apparent differences in the two sets of results might be attributed to differences in the personality or enthusiasm of the teacher, the learning rate of the children, or any of the other factors we have already mentioned.[19]

The Rosenbloom and Strang quotations reflect the usual way of relating the Hawthorne effect to educational research.

The Hawthorne effect can also be used to account for situations where no differences are observed between the experimental and control groups at the end of an experimental period. How can such a

---

[18] Paul C. Rosenbloom, "Large-Scale Experimentation with Mathematics Curriculum" in *Research Design and Analysis*, R. O. Collier and S. M. Elam, editors, Second Annual Phi Delta Kappa Symposium on Educational Research, 1961, Ch. 1B, p. 11.

[19] Ruth Strang, "Reactions to Research in Reading," *The Educational Forum*, 26:187-192, January, 1962, p. 187.

situation occur? It might occur when an experimenter approaches a classroom to measure student performance before conducting the experiment. The pretesting of not only the experimental but the control group can become a signal to the latter group that they are the subjects of an experiment. They might also be able to identify the experimenter's purpose. Consequently, the control group engages in activities leading to such improvement that the final result is that both groups perform equally well at the end of the experimental period.

The Hawthorne effect has plagued the research methodologist for a good many years. Brownell noted it approximately ten years ago in a critique of research appearing in the *Fiftieth Yearbook of the National Society for the Study of Education:*

> More than once, serious doubt has been cast on the evidence for an experimental program of instruction when attention has been called to seemingly innocuous but actually influential factors. For example, the very novelty of a new system of instruction may make it attractive to teachers and learners alike, thus giving it a special advantage, and perhaps only a temporary advantage over the rival, traditional system of instruction.[20]

He goes on to tell about an investigator who became increasingly irritated at the gains in reading shown under experimental versus control procedures over a short period of time. This investigator said that he would outdo all other investigators by demonstrating even greater gains in still a shorter period of time. The suggested technique was to administer a reading test in the most lackadaisical manner allowed by the test directions and then within a few hours test students with the second form of the test but administered under such conditions as subjects would be at highest possible pitch of zeal.

Retreating still further to the past to demonstrate the researcher's awareness of the problem, one finds reference to the effect appearing in McCall's *How to Experiment in Education*, written in 1923.

> Though evidence on this question is meager, there is some reason to believe that the mere process of experimenting with new methods or materials of instruction attracts such attention to the traits in question as to cause an unconscious concentration, both on the part of teacher and pupil upon progress in these traits. As a result, it is

---

[20] W. A. Brownell, "A Critique of Research on Learning and Instruction in the School." *Fiftieth Yearbook of the National Society for the Study of Education,* Pt. 1, *Graduate Study in Education.* H. B. Henry, editor. Chicago: University of Chicago Press, 1951, Ch. 6, p. 60.

supposed that a large temporary effort is called for, thus causing a large but artificial growth, and that this artificial effort will evaporate if the novel methods or materials were used term after term.[21]

McCall even suggested a way of determining if the effect were present in a given experimental situation:

> If each succeeding term shows a flagging of effort and an elimination or reduction of superiority, the existence of such ephemeral effort may be assumed.[22]

Interestingly enough, the Hawthorne studies showed no such reduction over time and thus novelty as a variable explaining results was rejected during the course of the investigations.

Even with McCall's early warning, many educators have persisted in using the comparable-groups method, with the correlated confounding of experimental variables by what is now called the Hawthorne effect. But the sophisticated research methodologist in education no longer jumps enthusiastically upon the bandwagon of new instructional methods like programed instruction, educational television, language laboratories, team teaching, and other new techniques of instruction. Further, he cannot help but wonder whether recent curriculum revisions, which often show large gains in student knowledge, may not be contaminated by a type of Hawthorne effect.

As an example, I would suggest the recent situation in Wisconsin where the McGuffey Readers were adopted as supplemental texts to the regular basal readers. A news release noted that the pupils in the first four grades were as much as two years ahead of their grade level in reading ability.[23] The principal is quoted as saying that the students in the first grade were able to spell at fourth-grade level, according to nationally accepted tests. He then went on to credit the success of the reading program to a system of phonics as opposed to the whole word method. Has it occurred to the principal that the ruckus created by the McGuffey issue (which included the firing of a principal who objected to adoption of the McGuffey readers) may have caused teachers, students, and parents simply to concentrate more on the reading process than ever before?

---

[21] William A. McCall, *How to Experiment in Education*. New York: The Macmillan Co., 1923, p. 67.

[22] *Loc. cit.*

[23] "Kids with McGuffeys Way Ahead," *Columbus Dispatch*, Columbus, Ohio, June 13, 1962, p. 9A.

WHAT ARE SOME SUGGESTED SOLUTIONS?

Recognizing that our research efforts are often contaminated or confounded by the Hawthorne effect, is there anything we can do about it? If we had a complete answer to the operation and hence control of the Hawthorne effect in educational research, there would of course be no need for this section of the paper. We must recognize, as Roethlisberger has in his book, *Management and Morale*, an inherent difficulty in social science research:

> . . . the working hypotheses of these specialists [social scientists], particularly on their applied side, must be far less clear, distinct, and well formulated than in the more highly developed and exact engineering sciences. There is no simple way of thinking about or putting together the complicated events involved, and there is equally no simple way of dealing with them.[24]

But complexity is no excuse for inaction. Steps should be taken if at all possible prior to the experimentation, so that an apology will not be needed at the end. Levitt, in discussing the possible influence of an experimental climate on research results in clinical psychology, stresses early attention to the problem:

> . . . the experimenter should not lose sight of the possibility of a climate when he is designing his investigation, and should take whatever prophylactic steps are logically necessary to prevent its occurrence. After the data have been obtained, one may be led to suspect the operation of an experimental climate, but there is very little that can be done about it *post hoc*.[25]

The principal problem involved in controlling the Hawthorne effect is the establishment of what is referred to in science as a "closed system." Such a system is one wherein no event outside of it influences events within it. The establishment of a closed system in educational experimentation becomes very difficult because the research activity must be done in psychological or socio-psychological environments, both of which are relative to the structure of the subjects. As B. O. Smith points out,

---

[24] F. J. Roethlisberger, *Management and Morale*. Cambridge, Mass.: Harvard University Press, 1941, p. 145.

[25] E. E. Levitt, *Clinical Research Design and Analysis*. Springfield, Ill.: Charles C Thomas, Publisher, 1961, p. 111.

. . . the psychological environment is what the subject conceives it to be, and what he conceives goes back to his personal structure and the dynamics of his situation.[26]

Thus an experimental situation may be one thing to one subject and a different thing to another subject.

Two general solutions have been presented. The first is to abandon, more or less, the conventional experimental-control group type of research design. This action was recommended by Brownell in 1951 and is re-emphasized by Strang in 1962 in the article on reading research previously cited. Brownell admitted that new advances in statistical analysis would facilitate the use of the comparable-group design but felt that its inherent limitation of failure to control all variables, plus the training needed to become sophisticated with the new statistical procedures, prohibited the widespread use of this design. As an alternative, he suggested a procedure originating largely in the field of developmental psychology. This procedure consists of continuous observation to detect changes in student behavior upon the introduction of certain events by the teacher. In short, it would be carefully documented observation of the teaching-learning process as it was actually carried on in the classroom. Brownell recognized that many persons in education would not accept this as good research methodology, but he felt that it had many possibilities.

Such a technique was not overlooked in the Hawthorne studies. In fact, almost all of the investigations carried on after the illumination experiments were of this type. The investigators in effect abandoned the traditional single-variable approach within the comparable-groups technique and resorted to an observational procedure. The introduction of the observer, however, was not without cost. He became a "confidant" of the girls, who talked with him about their work and personal problems. It was this expression of feelings which confounded again the results of a set of planned studies and led ultimately to the interviewing program.

Strang suggests another procedure:

. . . it would be more useful to adopt the single group comparison type of experiment that is employed in the physical sciences. Here all the factors in the given situation are carefully described. Then one factor is modified and the resultant total factor is recorded. In this way we would gain some insight into the ways in

---

[26] B. O. Smith, "Science of Education," in *Encyclopedia of Educational Research,* W. S. Monroe, editor. New York: The Macmillan Co., 1952, p. 1148.

which learning is affected by various complex conditions, including the pupils' prior experiences.[27]

This procedure, plus the one offered by Brownell, are preferred over the comparable-groups approach by Strang because she feels the attempts to use comparable-group experimentation in educational research represents a premature attempt to be scientific. The result, in reading research, has been misleading conclusions having detrimental effects upon the teaching of reading, she thinks.

The second solution is to continue with comparable-group experimentation but to develop experimental designs which not only are internally valid but are also externally valid. External validity here means that generalizations can be made from the experimental situation to non-experimental situations which the former is said to represent.

Campbell identifies seven categories of variables affecting the internal validity of experimental design.[28] These are history, maturation, testing, instrument decay, regression, selection, and mortality. He then goes on to point out that the interaction of these variables and of the experimental arrangements affect the external validity or generalizability of experimental results. Not all of the interactions are equally strong in various experimental designs, but they must be recognized. In a chapter on experimental design prepared for the AERA *Handbook of Research on Teaching*, Campbell and Stanley[29] indicate that some of the categories identified above can be somewhat discounted in comparable-group designs, but others cannot. They particularly point out the importance of what they call *reactive arrangements*. These are characterized by the " . . . play-acting, out-guessing, up-for-inspection, I'm-a-guinea-pig, or whatever attitudes,"[30] which are generated when the student knows he is participating in an experiment and tend to interfere with the external validity of the design. To overcome this limitation, the authors suggest that the experimental treatments and accompanying instrumentation (i.e., testing) be included whenever and wherever possible as part of the regular classroom procedure, if the results are to be generalized to other classroom units.

---

[27] Strang, *op. cit.*, p. 188.

[28] D. T. Campbell, "Factors Relevant to the Validity of Experiments in Social Settings," *Psychological Bulletin.* 54:297-312, 1957.

[29] D. T. Campbell and J. C. Stanley, "Experimental Designs for Research on Teaching," Mimeographed chapter draft for *Handbook of Research on Teaching.* N. L. Gage, editor, American Educational Research Association.

[30] *Ibid.*, p. 42.

In short, they would attempt to disguise the fact that an experiment is being conducted.

Correlated with this latter suggestion is a recommendation that, to avoid the singling out of individuals to be assigned at random to treatment or control groups and thus arousing their suspicions, regular classroom units with their regular teachers be employed as the means of minimizing individual reactions to experimental situations. Campbell and Stanley feel that such arrangements can be effective, since the process of experimentation is hidden from the student. They recognize, however, that if the *treatments* are other than variations of usual classroom events occurring at regular times in the yearly program, and/or if the *observations* (tests, etc.) are not considered a part of regular examinations, then we are still faced with the basic problem of cueing students.

Berg, however, raises the question whether it is moral and ethical to subject human beings to experimentation without their being aware of the fact.[31] His position is that psychological experimentation, and hence much educational research, must be done with "volunteer" subjects. If this restriction is accepted, we are squarely on the horns of a dilemma. One cannot experiment unless he informs his subjects, but informing the subjects will invalidate experimental results.

Opposed to the Campbell and Stanley position are individuals who suggest that we not try to hide the fact that an experiment is in progress but try instead to give equal exposure to both the experimental and control groups, thus establishing a type of experimental control over the Hawthorne effect. The national Research Council takes this position:

> As much attention must be paid to students and teachers in all treatment groups as in those of particular interest to the experimenter. Equal excitement must be generated and all groups must identify with their respective procedures.[32]

Rosenbloom noted that this procedure was employed to a certain degree in conducting the mathematics experiment in the schools of Minnesota already mentioned. The investigators tried to make it something of a mark of distinction for schools to be considered a part of the experimental program.

---

[31] A. Berg, "The Use of Human Subjects in Psychological Research," *The American Psychologist*. 9:108-111, March, 1954.

[32] *Psychological Research in Education*. Washington, D. C.: National Research Council, Publication 643, National Academy of Sciences, 1958, p. 24.

Travers concurs with the idea that both the experimental and control groups should feel equally singled out, but feels that this technique is inferior to the suggestion that the groups be unaware of the fact that they are participating in an experiment.[33] He makes reference to a technique which has been commonly recommended for controlling the Hawthorne effect, and that is the use of a *placebo* treatment. Studies involving placebo treatments are quite common in the field of medicine, where one group receives the drug to be tested while the other receives a placebo made to appear and taste the same as the drug. This methodology is illustrated in Crest toothpaste experiments, advertised on television, Rosenbloom recognized the possible use of a placebo treatment in his study:

> Now the ideal thing would be to have placebos, consisting of conventional texts in lithographed form and stamped "Experimental Edition." But so far we have not been able to make the necessary arrangements for that. The best we have been able to do this year in our ninth grade classes was to send to all control classes a lithographed pamphlet put out by McGraw-Hill called *Modern Mathematics for High Schools*. We gave instructions to the teachers of control classes to supplement the conventional text with this material, and to tell their classes that we are trying to find out whether a good conventional text, supplemented in this way, is better than the experimental text.[34]

In a discussion of the use of placebo treatments in psychotherapy, Rosenthal and Frank suggest some criteria to test the effectiveness of this procedure:

> To show that a specific form of treatment produces more than a non-specific placebo effect it must be shown that its effects are stronger, last longer, or are qualitatively different from those produced by the administration of placebo, or that it affects different types of patients.[35]

CONCLUSION

The Hawthorne effect is not only a complex problem but also an important one. While the problem has been generally recognized

---

[33] R. M. W. Travers, *An Introduction to Educational Research*. New York: The Macmillan Co., 1958.

[34] Rosenbloom, *op. cit.*, p. 11.

[35] David Rosenthal and Jerome Frank, "Psychotherapy and the Placebo Effect," *Psychological Bulletin*, 53:294-302, 1956, p. 297.

and various solutions have been suggested as noted, there has been little direct experimentation to determine its qualitative and quantitative contributions to the results in research. However, the U. S. Office of Education provided Ohio State University with funds to investigate this problem over a three-year period.[36]

A story related by Herzog seems relevant to our discussion.[37] She tells of the little old lady who did her courting in the Nineties and who liked to tell about her grandmother's efficient chaperoning. Grandmother would just move into the living room where the two young people were sitting on the sofa. She would say, "Now you two young people go right ahead and visit and don't pay any attention to me. Just act as if I weren't here." As Herzog points out, there was some difference of opinion in the family about whether Grandmother thought they were acting as if she weren't there, but there was no doubt in anyone's mind about whether they were really acting that way. It takes a wary eye to be sure the research project is not playing a role like Grandmother's.

---

[36] Cooperative Research Project 1757, "The Impact of the Hawthorne Effect in Experimental Designs in Educational Research," Desmond L. Cook, Director, 1967.

[37] Elizabeth Herzog, *Some Guide Lines for Evaluative Research*, Childrens Bureau, Social Security Administration, 1959.

Finley Carpenter

Wanted: More Descriptive Research in Education

In Chapter 1, both Ausubel and Cornell suggest that the only way educational research will move forward is through the medium of experimental research. Carpenter does not disagree with them but points out that to do experimentation you must have standard terminology and some notion of what the significant variables may be. He suggests that what we need are some thorough and precise descriptive studies so that we can determine what the variables in various situations are. After the variables have been determined, then, through experimentation, they may be manipulated to discover optimum arrangements.

F. Carpenter, "Wanted: More Descriptive Research in Education," *Educational Research Bulletin*, 33:149-54, 1954. Reprinted with permission.

A good case can be made for the argument that we often put the cart before the horse in educational research. We exhibit a tendency to put last things first and first things last. We display an overanxiety to get practical results, sliding over much of the laborious and painstaking pick-and-shovel work. When we look at the better-developed sciences, we find that great labor had been given to descriptive classification of material before experimentation yielded its best fruit. Even a cursory examination of the history of chemistry shows that progress was meager until a method was established for classifying and describing the elements. Zoology and botany are also based on descriptive classification.

But in education, and for that matter the other behavioral sciences, we have not developed description sufficiently to shape our materials in an orderly framework and to define variables as part of a standard language system. The purpose of this paper is twofold: first, to point up the need for more descriptive research; and, second, to call attention to limitations in existing methods which might be identified as response-response correlations (testing research) and controlled experiments.

Research in education can be classified in a number of different ways, but for present purposes only three kinds will be identified:

Response-response correlations.—Data in these studies are scores on tests, usually the paper-and-pencil variety. The researcher sets up a number of correlations and draws conclusions based on the significance level of computed coefficients.

Controlled experimentation.—The researcher is largely concerned here with the effect of manipulated variables upon behavior. In education the experiment often deals with the differential effect of teaching methods upon learning. For example, the experimenter sets up two ways of teaching spelling. One group is taught by Method A and another group by Method B. After both groups are given the same criterion test, difference in average performance is calculated and conclusions are based upon a test of significance.

Descriptive research.—The purpose of this research is to establish a clear description of materials and phenomena under investigation. The ultimate aim is to classify events so that later research can employ an unequivocal terminology and to lessen the confusion coming from *ad hoc* definitions. Observation is emphasized. Intensive and prolonged observation of the complex phenomena in education seems essential for building the necessary order for later research. Experimentation and test correlations have failed to establish such order. Therefore, it is significant to speak of descriptive research as a particular phase and to examine the reasons for giving it emphasis at this time. We may begin by recalling a list of restrictions in research of the first two types named.

Since most of the limitations of response-response correlations are well known, I shall list them without extended treatment.

1. Validity is largely a matter of assumption because most test-correlations studies do not show the relationship between scores and non-paper-and-pencil performance. Intercorrelation of test scores does not necessarily establish that the tests are measuring the more important objectives so often listed.

2. Generalizations are *ad hoc*, that is, they are limited to the specific tests involved. When other tests with equivalent titles are used, the results are quite often different.

3. Tests offer little direct information on how learning develops. Teachers are interested in finding efficient ways of changing response patterns; but tests fail, in the main, to provide such information.

4. Most experience involves learning; behavior is changing continually. And to the extent response patterns are changing, test reliability is attenuated as a function of time between test and retest. Even the interpretative significance of the split-half *r*'s of reliability is reduced.

5. In education we are interested in significant gains, not necessarily in the statistical interpretation of significance, for, if we use large groups, a relatively small difference can be statistically significant. In the practical sense, however, the difference may not merit the expense of making suggested changes.

6. Statements of functional relations are confined to response categories. Only by tenuous and indirect inferences can we generalize about the rôle environmental factors have in learning.

7. The test-correlation approach delimits information because it is largely confined to dichotomous response classes, that is, the student either passes or fails an item. (Even weighting procedures used on multiple-response tests are a doubtful improvement.) Behavior is telescoped into scores, which further limits the range of data. But most importantly, tests yield no detailed information of response changes in process.

8. Tests fail to get at the dynamics of behavior. Again, this is due to the scant descriptive information given by test scores.

9. Test titles suggest linear dimensions which are usually more apparent than real. It is claimed that tests are measuring something, but just what is measured is often a matter of conjecture. Consequently, it is difficult to generalize about test results except in terms of prediction.

10. Tests have contributed little to the development of learning theories. The reason lies largely in the fact that tests do not offer the kind of data that is best for postulating relations between response classes and environmental factors. Test correlations do not deal directly with independent variables, which are vital referents in theoretical statements.

The preceding list is a partial outline of the limitations of response-response correlation research. Our expectancies, therefore, should not exceed the actual outcomes. It is hardly worth while to repeat that tests have been useful, but largely as instruments of prediction.

We need more than prediction, however, to develop a science. We need to improve ways of control and to construct useful theoretical explanations.

Experimentation is the *sine qua non* of most sciences. It is essential for the development of the scientific aspect of education. We need, then, more and better experiments. But much of the difficulty in educational experimentation lies in confused communication. We lack a standard terminology that is precise and inclusive of our important phenomena. In short, description has been poorly developed. Specifically, the difficulties are largely lack of control in the complex situation and lack of clearly identified variables and definition of specific response classes. This suggests a need for more basic experimentation, such as is being done by Mech and others.[1] But the contention here is that all terms do not need experimental definition, in the sense that they can be made precise only as derived from manipulating variables in the controlled situation. Most of our events can be classified by careful observation when a number of competent observers sift data and modify classifications until a fruitful terminology is developed.

It should be emphasized that the criticisms made do not imply that tests and controlled experiments should not be used. The point is that the two approaches often begin without clear descriptions of the materials and processes under scrutiny. Therefore, more could be expected from the usual methods if they were based upon well worked-out descriptions acceptable to most researchers in the field. The intention here is not to say that descriptive research should be considered as opposed to testing and experiments but to emphasize the need for more adequate description as a useful prelude to testing and experimentation, especially the latter.

Suppose a research team is interested in the broad area of teaching-learning effectiveness. They review existing studies and find a host of inconclusive results. They find that attempts to determine personal traits of the effective teacher lead into a blind alley because of the

---

[1] Mech, E. "Resistance to Extinction of Two Patterns of Verbal Reinforcement," *Journal of Experimental Education*, XII (December, 1952), pp. 155-63; Mech, E., Kapos, E., Hurst, F., and Auble, D., "A Mathematical Description of the Relationship between Frequency of Responding (F) and Intertrial Interval in a Motivating Situation," *Journal of Psychology*, XXXVII (January, 1954), pp. 251-56a; Mech, E., and Auble, D., "Quantitative Studies of Verbal Reinforcement in Classroom Situations: I. Differential Reinforcement Related to Frequency of Error and Correct Responses," *Journal of Psychology*, XXXV (April, 1953), pp. 307-12; Mech, E., and Auble, D., "Partial Verbal Reinforcement Related to Distributed Practice in a Classroom Situation," *Journal of Psychology*, XXXVI (July, 1953), pp. 165-86.

difficulty in measuring personality traits and because effective teachers seem to be found at all points on the continua. They look at studies in which methods of instruction are compared and find the problem of control so difficult that virtually nothing can be concluded about differences in outcome. Such controls as equalizing teachers' enthusiasm about methods of instruction assigned to them in an experiment and keeping students in different classes from interacting outside class (contamination effect) are almost overwhelming. These difficulties suggest that a new approach or an intervening phase of research is needed. Our team then takes a look at the possibilities of descriptive research as the best point of departure. So they ask the question, Can the classroom be objectively described? They forego the temptation of determining *a priori* labels for classroom events. Instead they decide to derive categories inductively from a great number of specific operations recorded during observation. They observe classrooms daily and meet periodically to discuss their findings. They evaluate the desirability of building a formal structure for their observations instead of operating under an implicit structure peculiar to the individual observer. But they decide to form the explicit structure by sifting "uncontrolled" observations instead of imposing a logical frame of reference too early in the project. They believe that observation at first should be a freewheeling process, not restricted by a consensus of decisions until considerable data have been reported.

Adoption of a criterion is discussed and the research team decides to choose growth in problem-solving as a worthy objective. As the meaning of problem-solving becomes more clearly worked out, they begin to sharpen their observation for classroom operations that seem to have some bearing upon growth in problem-solving.

Finally, the day arrives when they think that enough data are in the hopper to call for an orderly organization, a determination of categories. They soon learn that their data can be ordered in a variety of ways. For example, they are confronted with the decision of classifying events under psychological headings such as "motivation," "stimulation," "expectancy," "permissiveness," and the like, or by using more pedestrian terms such as "amount of verbal approval," "frequency of problem-solving questions raised by the instructor," "extent to which instructor demonstrates phases of problem-solving during lecture," "amount of group interaction." To avoid the difficulty of deciding upon special definitions of psychological higher-order constructs, they decide to group their events under the more commonly understood phrases. They do this because observation is not yet complete. Psychological labels can be applied later.

Their first draft of a structured instrument for observation finally emerges. Part of it looks like the following:

CHECK LIST OF CLASSROOM OBSERVATIONS

Instructor Behavior

I. Lecture Operations
   A. Organization
      1. Follows a prepared syllabus given to the students
      2. Places an outline on the blackboard
      3. Presents an oral outline
      4. Presents no outline
      5. Summarizes at the end of the hour
   B. Problem-solving content of the lecture
      1. Extent to which instructor demonstrates problem-solving
         a. Identifies specific problems
         b. Identifies appropriate data
         c. Supplies alternative hypotheses
         d. Appraises hypotheses
         e. Draws conclusions
         f. Points out tentative character of conclusions
      2. Amount of time given to delivery of factual information

II. Discussion

   A. Structure
      1. Discussion structured by instructor
      2. Discussion partially structured by students
      3. Discussion predominantly structured by students
   B. Evaluation operations by instructor
      1. Frequency of positive verbal approval
      2. Frequency of negative verbal approval
      3. Frequency of times instructor said nothing about students' recitation
      4. Frequency of frowns and other negative responses associated with recitation
      5. Frequency of times instructor accepts irrelevant responses
      6. Frequency of times instructor accepts (does not correct) wrong responses
   C. Amount of required recitation
      1. Frequency with which instructor calls upon students by name
      2. Frequency with which instructor directs questions to the class as a whole
   D. Problem-solving content of questions raised by instructor
      1. Frequency of "why" questions
      2. Frequency of questions readily answered by short phrases

3. Frequency of questions asking for identification of assumptions
4. Frequency of questions asking for hypotheses
5. Frequency of questions asking for interpretation of data
6. Frequency of questions asking for expression of critical opinion
7. Frequency of questions asking for appraisal of a remark made by another student
8. Frequency of times instructor draws a student out to elaborate on his (student's) remark
9. Frequency of times instructor allows a student called upon to "pass" without making any remark

A comparable list of operations could be inserted under the heading of "Student Behavior." After further refining, our team draws up an instrument that can be used to determine the frequency of certain classroom operations that have some promise of being related to growth in problem-solving.

The next phase of their research is to determine the reliability of their instrument by comparing results of different observers in the same classroom. It is obvious that, to describe a classroom, the same class would have to be observed daily for nearly a whole term. Still later phases would include the relating of different descriptions to prescribed outcomes in problem-solving. From this they could determine what single operations or clusters have significant relations to the criterion measure. Thus, important classroom variables could be named, and an experimental study launched to determine how much the instructor can manipulate the variables and relate changes to outcomes.

The approach just outlined does not exclude the use of tests, but the implication is that, when tests are involved, some clear connection be shown between the measures and their ultimate criteria, actual behavior. Also, there promises to be profit in using tests more freely in the experimental situation, that is, in noting changes in scores as the conditions are changed. This means putting less reliance on correlations between tests that have only assumed validity.

This procedure promises to yield definitions of useful variables that could be handled in the controlled experiment. Names of such variables could become standard terms. Until we have worked in the descriptive phase much more extensively, however, we shall continue to stumble along with the cart before the horse.

John E. Corbally, Jr.

The Critical Incident Technique and Educational Research

Much of educational research has to do with behaviors, both teacher behaviors and pupil behaviors. Individual behaviors are not too difficult to measure, but frequently the most significant behaviors involve interaction behaviors. The technique discussed by Corbally offers some possibilities for the measurement of interaction behaviors. This technique might also have much to offer in the descriptive area that was called for in the previous article.

John E. Corbally, Jr., "The Critical Incident Technique," *Educational Research Bulletin*, 35:57-62, 1956. Reprinted with permission.

Use of the "critical incident technique" has been increasing in educational research. This method, originally developed by industrial psychologists, presents an excellent means of investigating behavior, particularly the effectiveness of specific behavior in fulfilling educational purposes.

The writer, who has recently completed a study[1] utilizing this technique, felt that certain comments regarding its use in educational research would be of value—both in evaluating research using the method and in considering future utilization of the technique. In order to accomplish these tasks, it seems necessary to describe the method briefly, to consider its advantages and disadvantages as a research tool, and to indicate certain refinements which may increase its value for educational research.

---

[1] It is expected that a monograph reporting this study, which is entitled "Critical Elements in School Board and Community Relations," will be published by the College of Education late in 1957.

John C. Flanagan is generally recognized as the originator of the critical incident technique. In an article written in 1949, he outlined the methodology of the technique and certain requirements for its successful use.[2] In brief, the procedure involves job analysis through a study of the total job rather than through an investigation of the separate parts of the job.

In practice, this involves having competent observers watch men on the job and observe the outcomes of their work. When the outcomes seem especially satisfactory or unsatisfactory to the observer in terms of the aims of the job, a report is made of the actual behavior of the worker which led to these results. From a large number of such reports, it is possible to isolate the acts which seem to have the most influence on the effectiveness of the work. Such acts are known as the "critical elements" of the job. The reports of behavior which led to especially satisfactory or unsatisfactory outcomes are known as reports of "critical incidents." The identification of critical elements is valuable in that this indicates behaviors in which workers should strive to reach effectiveness due to the significant effect of the manner in which these elements are performed on the outcomes of the job.

Those acts which do not become classified as the critical elements of a job are considered to be "noncritical" for one of two reasons. Either the performance of these elements varies little from worker to worker or such performances bear little relation to the final outcomes of the job. It should be noted that the first alternative makes it imperative to realize that not all noncritical elements are inconsequential.

In summary, the method consists of: observation of on-the-job behavior, evaluation of significant success or lack of success in meeting the aims of the job, reporting incidents which led to marked success or failure in meeting the aims of the job, and treatment of the data in such incidents to isolate and categorize the critical elements of the job.

An example might well provide an additional summary to this description of the critical incident technique. In this case, a school superintendent was the observer and he was observing his board of education as they performed their varying tasks. He was observing them with particular emphasis on the manner in which their behavior influenced school-community relations. He observed, for example, one incident in which an irate citizen appeared before the board demanding to know why his social club was denied permission to use the school

---

[2] Flanagan, John C. "Critical Requirements: a New Approach to Employee Evaluation," *Personnel Psychology*, II (Winter, 1949), pp. 419-25.

gymnasium for a bazaar. The board members were courteous and tactful as they carefully explained their written and long-established policy regarding community use of school buildings. The citizen was completely satisfied, thanked the board for its time, and complimented the board members on the clarity of their policy.

This was, then, a report of a critical incident with satisfactory results. From this report, the following critical elements could be isolated:

The board adopts written policy to give consistency to its actions.
The board adheres to its written policy.
Board members are courteous and tactful with visitors at board meetings.

From a large number of such incidents, many critical elements may be isolated and subsequently categorized to provide insight into the critical elements of a given task. The best single description of the method as used by Flanagan is found in a report of a study of research personnel.[3]

There are always dangers in adapting a research tool developed in one field for use in another. As originally conceived, this technique was used to study men as they worked with machines (that is, airplanes, scientific instruments, assembly lines).[4] In education, men are studied as they work with men. This introduces a number of variables not present in the first instance. Consequently, care must be taken to ensure that the complexity of the job or task studied, particularly with reference to human interaction, does not invalidate the technique.

Thus, while it seems possible to study effective behavior as one group (school-board members) works with one other group (lay citizens), it does not seem logical to assume that the method could be adapted easily to study a total program such as school-community relations. (School here would include teachers, pupils, administrators, and members of the school board, and community would include indi-

---

[3] Flanagan, John C. "Critical Requirements for Research Personnel." Pittsburgh: American Institute for Research, March, 1949. Mimeographed and microfilmed.

[4] Flanagan, John C. "Job Requirements," *Current Trends in Industrial Psychology*, edited by W. Dennis (Pittsburgh: University of Pittsburgh Press, 1949, pp. 32-54). *See also*, Gordon, Thomas, "The Use of the Critical Incident Technique in the Construction of an Evaluation Procedure for Airline Pilots," *American Psychologist*, IV (July, 1949), p. 301; *and* Preston, Harley O., *The Development of a Procedure for Evaluating Officers in the United States Air Force* (Pittsburgh: American Institute for Research, 1948).

viduals, organizations, neighborhoods, and so forth). The number of variables—already approaching a danger point in the first example—would appear to be completely out-of-hand in the second.

Therefore, the use of the critical incident technique in educational research should be restricted to studies of situations with limited complexity.

Second, the method assumes that observers can report incidents in which outcomes in terms of the aims of the undertaking are clearly recognizable. This leads to two distinct problems. Outcomes in education are often either deferred, unrecognizable, or both. Aims are often unformed, controversial, misunderstood, capable of many interpretations, or any combination of these and other factors.

Therefore, in designing a research project in which the critical incident technique is to be used, great care must be taken to ensure that the problem is one in which aims and outcomes can be recognized by various competent observers with both validity and reliability.

A third problem in the use of this technique lies in the danger that either the researcher, the reader, or both will confuse the frequency of mention of a critical element and a "degree of criticalness." At the present time, the use of the critical incident technique does not in any way indicate that one critical element is more critical than another. Some elements may occur more often in the course of a job than will others, but this frequency of occurrence in no way denotes a degree of criticalness.

Therefore, reports of critical incident studies must stress that the technique is not designed to discriminate between several types of behavior with regard to their criticalness except to indicate that some behaviors are critical and others are noncritical.

The method does depend to a great degree on the subjective judgment of competent observers. To the statistically minded, this fact may lead to some deprecation of the use of the method in research. Too often, however, educational research has suffered from the application of one or both of two assumptions. The first is to assign a high degree of objectivity to anything that can be brought under statistical treatment. The second is to hesitate to push into an area with research unless a method can be devised which at least gives the appearance of complete objectivity. To be sure, objectivity must be sought to the very utmost of the ability of the researcher. However, a method which provides usable and apparently valid results should not be discarded because it seems to have elements of subjectivity.

Therefore, efforts should be made to improve the method, but its use should not be discouraged because it seems to possess elements of subjectivity.

The isolation and categorization of critical elements from critical incident reports is an extremely difficult task. The exact meanings of descriptions supplied by many different observers from many varying locations are often obscure. Ideally, the method functions best when the research design includes the use of a team of well-trained observers. Practically, however, this is often impossible. It becomes necessary, then, for the research worker to develop methods of checking categorization—preferably using some other research worker as an assistant in this process.

One final caution must be stated. In reporting research using this method, great care must be taken to make clear the meaning of such terms as "critical element," "critical incident," or "noncritical elements." While the terms offer little confusion after some use, the casual reader may not assign the proper meanings to the words and may rather easily make false assumptions.

In spite of some disadvantages, the critical incident technique has much to offer the researcher in education and other social-science fields. The technique offers an outstanding method of studying a task in terms of the behavior of those engaged in the task. It provides a means of studying a task in the actual and varying situations where the task must be done day after day. It provides recommendations which can be utilized immediately by practitioners in the field. The data, which are gathered in terms of critical incidents, provide much insight into the problems facing individuals as they attempt to perform certain tasks and provide case-study material for use in training others to perform these tasks. Also, the data provide many examples of good practice in the field which are useful for both in-service and pre-service training. Finally, the findings from critical incident studies have been used to aid in the development of evaluation devices to screen those desirous of entering certain fields of endeavor.[5]

Research in education has placed increased emphasis on behavior, particularly in the areas of teaching and administrative competency. In the furtherance of investigations of this type, no method seems to offer more promise than the critical incident technique.

The preceding section presented several problems which arise in the use of the critical incident technique in educational research. In order to meet certain of these problems, the following suggestions seem appropriate.

---

[5] Whalen, Richard E., Jr. "Effectiveness of Elected and Appointed School Board Members." 1953. An unpublished doctoral dissertation on file in the library of Indiana University. *See also*, American Institute for Research, "The Development of Tests of Aptitude and Proficiency," *The American Institute Research Note*, No. 5, 1951.

The bulk of the reported research in education using this technique has been done by the individual research worker—usually as part of a doctoral study. In view of the problems arising from the choice of observers and the interpretation of observers' reports, it is likely that the team approach can provide more fruitful results than can the individual approach. Research projects using this method might well involve the training of a team of observers as a first step. There can be no doubt that this approach will cause new problems, particularly in observing a wide number of incidents and their results. However, such a method, if properly developed, should increase materially the objectivity of the results.

A second problem involves an extension of the method. As presently used, the technique identifies critical elements, but does not supply information regarding any degree of criticalness. Logic indicates that not all critical elements are "extremely critical." Further study is necessary to permit the development of this next step. An hypothesis of the writer is that this next step can be taken through analysis of the results of critical incidents. At present, the results are only judged to be satisfactory or unsatisfactory in terms of the aims of the undertaking. A more careful analysis of these results might well provide insight into the criticalness of the critical elements found in critical incidents.

A final, and difficult, problem arises in the identification of a critical incident. In most studies in the field of education, a crisis can be identified, but the many significant incidents leading to it are less clear. It is likely that certain critical elements may be overlooked in a study because certain significant incidents are overlooked by observers. Here again, the problem is centered in the selection and training of observers and the time span used for observation.

The critical incident technique appears to offer many advantages for educational research—particularly in studies of behavior. The method presents several difficulties and care must be taken to ensure that it is used only in appropriate research projects. On the other hand, the technique seems to have outstanding advantages for certain types of educational research and, if certain refinements can be made, the technique can have wide application and provide valuable findings.

J. R. Shannon[*]

Experiments in Education: A New Pattern and Frequency of Types

Descriptive research may be important in educational research (see Carpenter, this chapter), but experimental research is still necessary to move education forward. Shannon has analyzed a great number of researches in an effort to determine a pattern for educational experimentation. Although no effort is made to evaluate each type, it might be a valuable exercise for the reader to determine which of the various types seems to offer the most promise for worthwhile educational experimentation.

J. R. Shannon, "Experiments in Education: A New Pattern and Frequency of Types," *Journal of Educational Research*, 48:81-93, October, 1954. Reprinted with permission.

"This is the first book on educational experimentation to be published at home or abroad," wrote Editor M. V. O'Shea in introducing that book thirty years ago.[1] And, being the first book, it, like many "first books," enjoyed prestige, and both led and misled several later writers in its field for many years.

A PATTERN WHICH SET PRECEDENT

The book classified educational experiments into three groups: "one-group method," "equivalent-groups method," and "rotation method."[2]

---

[*] Several graduate students at Sacramento State College assisted in this survey by locating reports of experiments in the library. The writer is grateful for this help, and especially to Sidney A. Inglis, Jr., for a helpful suggestion. Although graduate students helped by locating several of the experiments covered in this analysis, the writer examined every report and classified it by type himself.

[1] William A. McCall, *How to Experiment in Education*. New York: The Macmillan Company, 1923, p. xi.

[2] *Ibid.*, pp. 14-18, 21-29, 140-160, 271; 18-19, 29-31, 161-186, 271; 19-20, 31-36, 187-207, 272.

But the categorization is inadequate, and it is unfortunate that it became the accepted pattern for several later writers who apparently followed it uncritically. In fact, there is evidence both within the book and outside of it suggesting that the classification was made largely from an armchair rather than from an analysis of a representative sampling of reports of experiments.

Internal evidence number one is what the book says about the frequency of use of single-group experimentation, calling it "the most frequently used of all types of investigations or experiments.'[3] Internal evidence number two is the book's classification of types of "scientific educational research," which it says "may be grouped conveniently into three divisions,—descriptive investigations, experimental investigations, and causal investigations."[4]

That these assertions could not be supported long after they were published, even if they could have been at the time, is attested by either a causal or a scientific analysis of types of scientific educational research and of textbooks on how to do such research. All types of educational experiments put together are much less numerous than surveys;[5] the one-group method of experimentation is not the most frequently used method in a large sampling of reports of experiments, as the present survey shows; and later textbooks writers did not follow the McCall organization of types of scientific educational research.[6]

A lot of water has gone over the dam since 1923, and a lot of progress has been made in educational research. That a pattern for research in general, and for experiments in particular, which fitted in 1923— assuming that it fitted then—was inappropriate a few years later, is not to be wondered at. The survey underlying the present report revealed that a number of experiments thirty years ago, by men who later became big names in education, were rather shabby jobs. In fact, many researches called experiments were not experiments at all.

Just as the more inventive authorities have broken away from the 1923 McCall pattern for types of educational research in general, so should they from the 1923 pattern for types of educational experiments in particular. The three McCall types of experiments exist, but there are other types besides. Also, there are variants and subdivisions of the

---

[3] *Ibid.*, p. 14.

[4] *Ibid.*, p. 5.

[5] J. R. Shannon, "The Relative Frequency of Use of Types of Procedure and Sources of Data in Research in Education," *Journal of Educational Research*, 41: 41-46, September, 1947.

[6] J. R. Shannon and Marian A. Kittle, "An Analysis of Eight Textbooks in How to Do Research in Education," *Journal of Educational Research*, 37: 31-36, September, 1943.

three. A new pattern, one based on a survey of a large, representative number of reports of educational experiments, is needed. Instead of making what appears to be an armchair organization of types and then, Procrustes like, making the cloth fit the pattern, it is preferable to devise a new pattern which fits the cloth.

GENESIS OF THE NEW PATTERN

The pattern employed in the present report was devised to fit a presumably representative sampling of 1,000 experiments dating from 1909 to 1952 and emanating from a wide variety of sources. The distribution of the 1,000 experiments by dates of their reports was: 1910 or before, 3; 1911 to 1920, 126; 1921 to 1930, 270; 1931 to 1940, 277; 1941 to 1950, 280; since 1950, 44.

The sources of the sampling of 1,000 were: education magazines, doctoral dissertations, master's theses, and miscellaneous sources. Doubtlessly, several of the magazine articles or miscellaneous reports were dissertations or theses. In fact, it is known that most of the Teachers College, Columbia University, Contributions to Education were doctoral dissertations but none are labeled as such. More specifically, the 1,000 reports of experiments in education or educational psychology were from sources as follows: education magazines, 759 (*Journal of Educational Research*, 229; *Journal of Educational Psychology*, 132; *Journal of Genetic Psychology* or *Pedagogical Seminary*, 80; *School Review*, 72; *Journal of Experimental Education*, 70; *School and Society*, 69; *Elementary School Journal*, 34; *Educational Administration and Supervision*, 19; *Educational and Psychological Measurement*, 12; *Educational Leadership* or *Educational Method* or *Journal of Educational Method*, 11; *California Journal of Educational Research*, 10; *Teachers College Journal*, 5; twelve other education magazines, 16); doctor's dissertations, 63 (University of Minnesota, 17; New York University, 9; State University of Iowa, 9; Yale University, 5; fourteen other universities, 23); master's theses, 61 (Indiana State Teachers College, 22; Kansas State College, 14; Pennsylvania State College, 8; University of Southern California, 6; University of Chicago, 5; three other colleges or universities, 6); miscellaneous sources, 117 (*Educational Research Bulletin*, Ohio State University, 48; Teachers College, Columbia University, Contributions to Education, 21; New York Society for Experimental Education Contributions to Education, 15; *Research Quarterly*, 13; National Society for the Scientific Study of Education *Yearbooks*, 9; *Bulletins* of the Department of Secondary School Principals, 5; four other sources, 6.)

Over seven hundred different research workers were named as authors or co-authors of the reports of the 1,000 experiments. Many of these were nationally or internationally known scholars, among whom were the following fifty arbitrarily selected names of past or present leaders in education: John C. Almack, E. J. Ashbaugh, Bird T. Baldwin, A. S. Barr, Louis P. Benezet, Roy O. Billet, Grace E. Bird, William F. Book, Frederick S. Breed, Thomas H. Briggs, William A. Brownell, Leo J. Brueckner, B. R. Buckingham, William H. Burnham, Harold F. Clark, Ellsworth Collings, S. A. Courtis, C. C. Crawford, Harl R. Douglass, J. B. Edmonson, George W. Frasier, Frank F. Freeman, Arthur I. Gates, Carter V. Good, Harold Hand, Henry Harap, George W. Hartmann, Gertrude Hildreth, Leta S. Hollingsworth, Palmer O. Johnson, Frederick B. Knight, George C. Kyte, William A. McCall, Paul McKee, Ernest C. Moore, Garry Cleveland Myers, Louis A. Pechstein, Rudolph Pintner, Luella Cole Pressey, G. M. Ruch, Douglas E. Scates, P. R. Stevenson, Percival M. Symonds, Edward L. Thorndike, Carleton Washburne, Beth L. Wellman, G. M. Whipple, Guy M. Wilson, Ben D. Wood, and J. Wayne Wrightstone.

Any research which met the criteria for classifying a research as an experiment, which was reported clearly enough and fully enough to afford an understanding of its purpose and procedure, which pertained to education or educational psychology, and which came within the purview of the writer while he made his rather painstaking survey in 1951 and 1952, was included until the arbitrarily predetermined number of 1,000 was obtained. "White-rat" experiments were excluded, but experiments with inanimate materials or instruments used in education, such as chalk, trumpets, or formulae for predicting success in algebra, were included.

CRITERIA FOR CLASSIFYING A RESEARCH AS AN EXPERIMENT

As with most boundaries, the distinctions between historical research and experimental research in education, and between surveys and experiments, are almost arbitrary. Some researches clearly are experiments and some clearly are surveys or histories. For guides in deciding borderline cases in the present survey, the following principles were adopted:

1. There must have been a problem. It was not enough for a writer to simply describe an event or activity in school as a matter of historical record.

2. Something must have undergone trial, rather than just observation, and the performer or experimenter must have been conscious at the time that he was experimenting, with at least a slight semblance of control of factors. If a person marries, he is not experimenting in matrimony, as a rule, although he may be able to conclude after a period of years whether or not the experience was successful.

3. There must have been performance involved. Experimentation is an active process and not a passive one.

4. A researcher in a survey simply takes a picture (or a series of pictures) of a situation (or a number of situations). If he is photographing a pen of guinea pigs, he can shift his position so as to get the most advantageous point of view of the rodents, or select just certain ones for his picture, and still be conducting a survey. But if he gets inside the pen and holds the animals still while the camera is clicked, he is conducting an experiment. The laying on of hands—controlling of factors—therefore, was set as the distinction between an experiment and a survey.

5. There are good experiments and poor experiments. It is not the quality of the job which determines what the job is. An experiment may not be well planned or well controlled but still be an experiment. Therefore, perfection was not a criterion.

6. It was not necessary that the experiment be completed and final conclusions reached at the time of the report.

7. The researcher's word for it was not conclusive. Many writers call things experiments which are not experiments.

CHARACTERISTICS OF THE NEW PATTERN

The analysis of 1,000 reports of experiments unearthed thirteen types. It is not claimed that the thirteen are all the types there are, but an analysis of an additional 1,000 reports would not, in all probability, disclose another thirteen types. The pattern presented in this report became apparent in the analysis of the first 100 reports, and it was not added to in the succeeding 900.

Other types are easily conceivable but did not appear among the 1,000 examples used. Some such are reversed groups, the groups being known not to be equivalent (Type number 8), and reversed single subjects, either equivalent, not known to be equivalent, or known not to be equivalent (Types 14, 15, 16). These four theoretical types fit so perfectly into the pattern that they were included in the outline even though no frequencies were unearthed among the 1,000 examples. It does not require a pathological imagination to see these possibilities or other possibilities.

Furthermore, the present types could be broken down more minutely by recognizing other characteristics in experiments already reported or in ones healthily imagined. For example, all the first sixteen types could be subdivided into *things done by* the subjects or groups and *things done to* the subjects or groups. Type 17 could be broken down into school buildings, school fixtures, teaching equipment, teaching supplies, playground equipment, sanitary supplies, custodial supplies, instruments for measuring, instruments for projecting pictures, instruments for predicting school success, etc. Thus, the total possible number of types could be extended to several dozen.

If a categorization is too detailed, however, it loses its usefulness. A deliberate effort was made, therefore, to keep the number of types as small as the essential characteristics of the 1,000 examples would permit.

The basis of classification in the pattern presented herewith resembles the one used by McCall in 1932, but the present pattern differs from McCall's in three important respects.

First, the present pattern adds two additional major classifications: *single subject* and *materials or instruments*.

Second, it makes a distinction between *parallel* and *equivalent*. Confusion of these two concepts is amusingly illustrated by a 1951 contributor to the *Journal of Experimental Education*.[7] "In the present experiment the 'equivalent-groups' method was used," so he said, but he made it clear that his groups were deliberately chosen so as not to be equivalent in the chief factor concerned. *Parallel* is the word he should have used.

Equivalent, as McCall used the word and Boraas repeated it, evidently means *parallel*. But an experiment can use equivalent groups in either parallel formation or reversed formation. If two equivalent groups are experimented with simultaneously, with a single controlled variable, and conclusions based on comparisons made, the type of procedure is not the same as if the experimenter went farther and reversed the groups with respect to the single variable. *Equivalent* should not be assumed to mean *parallel*, since it can mean *reversed* as well. The

---

[7] Harold Boraas, "Photographic Analysis of Letter Forms with Respect to Speed Changes and Stability," *Journal of Experimental Education*, 20: 87-96, September, 1951.

pattern of types presented herewith recognizes both parallel equivalent groups and reversed equivalent groups.

The third major feature differentiating the new pattern from the old is its use of major headings and subheadings. *Groups* is a basis of classification in both the old and new patterns. The old pattern went beyond groups to incorporate procedures when it recognized "equivalent-groups method" as separate from "rotation method," but it did not go far enough in respect to procedures. A single subject or a single group can be used once without involving a variable factor, or it can be used in a series of two or more performances with a variable factor. This difference in procedure is too basic to be overlooked. Furthermore, parallel groups can be equivalent, not known to be equivalent, or deliberately formed so as not to be equivalent, a distinction too fundamental to slight.

DETAILS OF THE NEW PATTERN

Table I, appearing in a later section of this report, shows the new pattern of types in outline form. In the present section, however, the several types are described serially without reference to major headings and subheadings.

Type 1. A single group (or more groups than one but all treated alike), with no so-called control group, treated once, not in series (or in series with the same act repeated and no changing factor involved), and maybe with comparison with earlier practice or with the mode of practice. No comparisons are made between the members of the group.

Example: Louis P. Benezet, "The Story of an Experiment," *NEA Journal*, 24: 241-244, 301-303; 25: 7-8, November and December, 1935, and January, 1936. In certain grades in certain elementary schools of Manchester, New Hampshire, formal teaching of arithmetic was postponed until the sixth grade. Comparisons were made with normal practice and earlier practice. The subject matter of the experiment was in the area of curriculum, or what to teach.

Type 2. A single group of subjects, such as school children (or more groups than one but all treated alike at each stage of the experiment), with the group experimented with in two or more stages with a changing factor involved, and comparisons made from stage to stage.

Example: Carter V. Good, "The Effect of Mind-Set or Attitude on the Reading Performance of High-School Pupils," *Journal of Educational Research*, 14: 178-186, October, 1926. Five equivalent forms of the Thorndike-McCall Reading Scale were administered to a single group of pupils, one at the outset and one after each of four steps in an experiment involving a changing factor. Comparisons of test results were made from stage to stage. The procedure was in the area of teaching methods.

Type 3. Two or more groups, known to be equivalent in regard to essential characteristics or abilities, are treated in parallel formation with all factors kept constant, presumably, except the single variable which is the topic for investigation. *Parallel* does not necessarily imply that all groups be experimented with simultaneously; they can be in series but with no individual group used more than once.

Example: Edward L. Thorndike and Paul J. Kruse, "The Effect of Humidification of a School Room Upon the Intellectual Progress of Pupils," *School and Society*, 5: 657-660, June 2, 1917. Two sixth-grade groups of 43 pupils each, who were of equal initial ability, were taught for four months in the same manner except for the humidity in their rooms. They were tested at the beginning and at the end in language, reading, and spelling. This experiment illustrates what is called later in this report a topic in administration.

Type 4. This type is just like Type 3 except that the parallel groups are not known to be equivalent. They may be assumed to be, because of grade placement, but not known by objective measurement to be. Type 4 includes also experiments with parallel groups in which the reports do not mention the matter of equivalence, and ones in which the parallel groups are known to be only slightly different.

Example: Hilda Hughes, "Lessons in Supervision of Rural Schools from the Indiana Experiment," *NEA Addresses and Proceedings*, 63: 568-576, 1925. The school children in two whole counties were used as an experimental group and those in two presumably comparable counties were a control group. This was under the auspices of the General Education Board, for the purpose of demonstrating the value of supervision of instruction. It was in the field of administration.

Type 5. Type 5 is like Types 3 and 4 except that the parallel groups are chosen or set up so as to be known to be distinctly different. The differentness between the groups, in this type, is usually the "single variable." Comparisons are made between the groups to see what differences in performance exist between them when teaching, curriculum, and administrative factors are kept uniform.

Example: Arthur E. Traxler, "Group Corrective Reading in the Seventh Grade—An Experiment," *School Review*, 41: 519-530, September, 1933. A group of poor readers were given corrective reading over a period of weeks. Comparison of increased reading competence was made with a parallel group of similar pupils who were not poor readers. The topic was classified in the area of curriculum.

Other Type 5 experiments compared such divergent groups as: bright children and dull ones, successful ones in school work and unsuccessful ones, musically talented ones and untalented ones, morally delinquent ones and normal ones, children and adults, and good penmen versus poor penmen.

Type 6. Equivalent groups in reversed formation, with each group being used as the experimental group at one time and as the control group at another, in respect to a single controlled variable. Comparisons are made between groups at each stage in the experiment instead of between a group at one stage with itself at another stage. (Comparisons of this latter type characterize Type 2.) Type 6 is like 3 except that it goes farther and reverses the situation.

Example: Palmer O. Johnson, "A Comparison of the Lecture-Demonstration, Group Laboratory Experimentation, and Individual Laboratory Experimentation Methods of Teaching High School Biology," *Journal of Educational Research*, 18: 103-111, September, 1928. Three groups of pupils were equated on the basis of the Terman Group Intelligence Test, and "by the rotation plan each section performed eight experiments by each of the demonstration, individual, and group methods." Comparisons were made between sections using different methods. Teaching methods is clearly the area of the experiment.

Type 7. Groups not known to be equivalent are used in reverse formation. The type is like Type 6, except that the groups are not known to be equivalent, and like Type 4, except that it goes farther and reverses the groups.

Example: Thomas H. Briggs, "Praise and Censure as Incentives," *School and Society*, 26: 596-598, November 5, 1927. Two comparable classes not known to be equivalent were compared. One teacher one day used reprimands and threats, while another used commendation and encouragement. The next day, the two teachers rotated in their incentives. Comparisons were made at each stage of the experiment. Teaching method was the area of the research.

Type 8. Groups set up to be non-equivalent are used in reversed formation. This type was not found among 1,000 examples, but it can be imagined. It could not be a well-controlled procedure, however, because it would, by definition, involve two variables.

Types 9 through 16 resemble Types 1 through 8, respectively, except that they deal with single subjects instead of groups of subjects. Educational psychologists are especially prone to experiment with single subjects.

Type 9. A single subject (or more subjects than one but all treated alike) with no control group or control subject, treated once, not in series (or in series with the same act repeated and no changing factor involved), and maybe with comparison with earlier practice or with other measures. No comparison is made between subjects.

Example: Bernice Leland, "Wilbur," *Journal of Educational Research*, 16: 132-135, September, 1927. The title of the report suggests single subject. Wilbur was an intelligent boy whose handwriting was atypical, and his teacher experimented with him "to solve the riddle of his unusual performance." The experiment falls in the area of teaching method.

Type 10. A single subject, such as a school pupil, treated in a series of ways, with a changing factor, and comparisons made from stage to stage.

Example: C. G. Bradford, "An Experiment in Typewriting," *The Pedagogical Seminary*, 22: 445-468, December, 1915. Four adults, each treated as an individual, were subjects of experimentation over a period of two to four months to study the influence of practice, of different stimuli, of distribution of practice, and of such secondary factors as time of day, fatigue, etc. Teaching methods is the area of this experiment.

Type 11. Two or more equivalent single subjects in parallel formation, all treated alike except for the one variable, and comparisons made between individuals.

Example: Paul R. Farnsworth, "Concerning So-Called Group Effects," *Journal of Genetic Psychology*, 35: 587-594, December, 1928. Pairs of college students, equated by Thorndike or Otis intelligence tests, were experimented with to compare the relative effectiveness of working alone and working in the presence of others. The research was classified as teaching method.

Type 12. Two or more single subjects not known to be equivalent, used in parallel formation, and comparison made between them. This differs from Type 11 in that the subjects are not known to be equivalent, and from Type 4 in that single subjects are experimented with instead of groups of subjects.

Example: Herbert Barry, Jr., "The Role of Subject Matter in Individual Differences in Humor," *Journal of Genetic Psychology*, 35: 112-128, March, 1928. Two graduate students at Harvard University, not known to be equivalent, were experimented with to see how they differed in their responses to presumably humorous situations. In spite of the title, the experiment was classified in the area of teaching method.

Type 13. Two or more individual subjects chosen because they are known to be different in some essential respect relating to the topic of investigation, given identical treatment, and compared for difference in results.

Example: Sante De Sanctis, "Visual Apprehension in the Maze Behavior of Normal and Feebleminded Children," *Journal of Genetic Psychology*, 39: 463-467, December, 1931. One normal child and one "abnormal child, characterized as weak and unstable, with mental incapacity of slight degree" were compared as to reactions in a maze "designed . . . expressly to test the capacity of orientation in a situation which offers several possibilities." The experiment reported by De Sanctis was performed by Vera Roncagli. It was classified as teaching method.

Types 14, 15, 16. Single subjects, known to be equivalent, not known to be equivalent, and known not to be equivalent, respectively, used in reverse formation. None of these was discovered but their types seem logical.

Type 17. Materials, material facilities, or instruments relating to schools or to formal instruction. These are inanimate objects or procedures, not live subjects either as individuals or in groups.

Example: J. R. Shannon, "Economics and Aesthetics of Chalk," *American School Board Journal*, 117: 55-56, 58, 61, October, 1948. Four grades of chalk manufactured by the same company were put to a series of tests to see which was the most economical purchase. The experiment was in the area of administration.

FREQUENCY OF TYPES

Table I shows the seventeen types of experimental procedure in outline form with major headings and subheadings, thus affording a better understanding of the pattern as a whole. The three co-ordinate subheadings under *groups of subjects—in single formation, in parallel formation*, and *in reversed formation*—correspond to McCall's "one-group method," "equivalent-groups method," and "rotation method," respectively. But the present pattern adds more major headings, breaks the subheadings into finer categories, and clarifies "equivalent."

As a side issue not essential to the pattern, the table breaks the frequencies down under three subheadings of purpose or area in education. The three are teaching method (*T* in the table), curriculum (*C* in the table), and administration (*A* in the table). The three are

Table I

OUTLINE OF TYPES OF EXPERIMENTS IN EDUCATION,
AND FREQUENCIES OF TYPES

Types of Characteristics	Types by Number	Frequencies by Purposes			
		T	C	A	Totals
Groups of subjects					
In single formation					
Treated once, not in series (or in series with the same act repeated and no changing factor involved), and maybe with comparison with earlier practice or with the mode of practice	1	47	61	54	162
Treated in series with a changing factor and with comparison from stage to stage	2	72	11	47	130
In parallel formation					
Equivalent, with a single variable	3	152	44	43	239
Not known to be equivalent, with a single variable	4	153	62	51	266
Known not to be equivalent, usually with no variable factor, to determine the degree of non-equivalence in performance	5	26	9	19	54
In reversed formation					
Equivalent, with a single variable	6	14	1	1	16
Not known to be equivalent, with a single variable	7	21	1	3	25
Known not to be equivalent	8	–	–	–	–
Single subjects					
In single formation					
Treated once, not in series (or in series with the same act repeated and no changing factor involved), and maybe with comparison with earlier practice or with the mode of practice	9	12	5	7	24
Treated in series with a changing factor and with comparison from stage to stage	10	34	4	10	48

Table I (Continued)

Types of Characteristics	Types by Number	Frequencies by Purposes			
		T	C	A	Totals
In parallel formation					
Equivalent, with a single variable	11	3	–	–	3
Not known to be equivalent, with a single variable	12	7	–	3	10
Known not to be equivalent, usually with no variable factor, to determine the degree of non-equivalence in performance	13	4	–	1	5
In reversed formation					
Equivalent, with a single variable	14	–	–	–	–
Not known to be equivalent	15	–	–	–	–
Known not to be equivalent	16	–	–	–	–
Materials and instruments	17	–	–	18	18
Totals		545	198	257	1,000

based on the assumption that all problems in education can be classified as pertaining to either how to teach, what to teach, or organization and administration. It is admitted that the categorization is a bit far-fetched at times and that some reports of experiments among the 1,000 were classified arbitrarily. An example is Ellsworth Collings, *An Experiment with a Project Curriculum* (Macmillan, 1923). Project teaching involves how to teach, what to teach, and administration, all three. But since Collings called it *curriculum*, it was classified accordingly here. The breakdown into the three areas of purpose or area in education is valuable in that it reveals a peculiarity of experimental research: whereas experiments are not nearly so numerous in education as surveys, they are more likely to be used in the field of teaching method than in curriculum and administration put together.[8]

RELIABILITY OF DATA

Work sheets made in handling the data on the 1,000 experiment, but not reproduced in this report of the survey, show three significant facts substantiating the reliability of the data:

---

[8] Examples of categorizations under *T*, *C*, or *A* were shown at the same time the thirteen procedural types were illustrated in the preceding section of this report. A sentence appears after each example telling how it was classified.

1. As each one hundred experiments was completed in the data-gathering stage of the survey, its frequency of types was recorded separately. The ten sets of data thus tabulated did not agree completely in relative frequency of types, but there was no great difference and no trend or pattern of differences.

2. These tabulations by hundreds showed a consistent distribution between areas or purposes of the experiments. Teaching method was first in every hundred; administration was second in six groups.

3. A separate tabulation by years of publication of reports also showed a consistency. There has been no significant change in the frequency pattern of types in the decades covered by the 1,000 experiments. Parallel groups led in every decade, just as they do for the total time period.

CONCLUSIONS

A survey of published reports of 1,000 experiments in education, equitably distributed by time from 1909 to 1952, selected from a wide variety of sources, and representing the work of over 700 scholars, warrants the following conclusions:

1. Any pattern or categorization of types of experimental procedure should be based on extant reports of experiments and not on general impression or armchair analysis. The pattern should be made to fit the cloth and not the cloth to fit the pattern.

2. The McCall pattern of 1923 was approximately sound as far as it went, but it did not go far enough. There are numerous reputable experiments in education which can not be fitted into his pattern at all.

3. The present pattern, consisting of thirteen types found employed among 1,000 specimens, goes beyond the McCall pattern by:

  a. Adding new types.

  b. Subdividing types.

  c. Clarifying confusion over *equivalent* and *parallel*.

4. Most experiments in education are in the area of teaching method.

5. The dominant types of experimental procedure are parallel groups, with the groups not known to be equivalent (but apparently presumed to be approximately so, at least) or with the experimental factors so well controlled that the groups are known to be equivalent in the significant characteristics concerned. The assertion that the single-group type is most common was not true in 1923 and it is not true today.

6. The single-group type is clearly second in frequency of use in published reports of experiments in education, however.

7. Minor types of experimental procedure—parallel groups known not to be equivalent, reversed groups, single subjects, and materials and instruments—represent a combined total of over twenty per cent of educational experiments and are too important to overlook.

SO WHAT?

Precedent which has prestige is an easy guide for present problems, and it is a safe one when nothing better can be justified. But it is unwise to follow any precedent unquestioningly. Just as soon as any traditional pattern ceases to fit the facts, it should be abandoned and a better one substituted.

The traditional pattern of types of experimental procedure in education does not fit the cloth. A new pattern is proposed which seems more suitable. Research scholars in education would do well to follow the new pattern in their experimenting, and thinking or teaching about experimenting, until future surveys show that it too is outmoded.

Edgar F. Borgatta

Toward a Methodological Codification: The Shotgun and the Saltshaker

In Chapter 1, Platt speaks of strong inference which involves crucial tests which may cast doubt upon alternative hypotheses as well as indicate support for a "favored" hypothesis. In Chapter 2, we find Chamberlin advocating the use of multiple working hypotheses. At what point does the aforementioned technique become the general gathering of data, the "shotgun technique?" In this article, Borgatta offers some defense for the "shotgun technique," pointing out instances where it may be the only method to use. The question then becomes where does the shotgun develop such a wide range that any result becomes useless?

Edgar F. Borgatta, "Toward a Methodological Codification: The Shotgun and the Saltshaker," Sociometry, 24:432-5, 1961.

In an area like social psychology where the idea of theory is highly valued, it is not surprising to find that approaches that do not have the elegance ordinarily expected of "hard theory" are often both disliked and maligned. One of the frequent whipping boys is identified as the "shotgun approach." This paper attempts to outline briefly the basis for use of the shotgun approach.

Consider, as a convenient example, a recent criticism of the shotgun approach in a review of several social psychology monographs. Having indicated that the authors had discussed correlations that had been found, the reviewer proceeded with the following statement (1):

> And this, in turn, is the frightening part of such a 'shotgun approach.' Conservatively estimated, the number of correlation co-

efficients presented in this monograph is 3,963. By chance, one would expect 40 to be significant at the 1%-level and another 160 to be significant at the 5%-level. Conclusions based on such 'statisticizing' must be tenuous at best, even if founded on sound hypotheses. When much of the theorizing is after the fact (as in the present monograph), one wonders whether or not it really has been worth the effort.

Here two questions raised frequently in regard to the shotgun approach are made explicit. The first is that, given the multitude of findings that occur when a great many questions are asked, how does one find out which ones are the stable or important ones? And, second, is it worth theorizing after the fact?

Let us attempt to answer the first question by giving attention to a major alternative. Suppose an investigator is concerned with a given set of facts about which he wishes to know more, say, in terms of concomitants, precursors, and consequences (presuming this includes everything). We have to acknowledge that (a) he must have some information about the facts he wishes to investigate or he wouldn't be able even to raise the issue. Then, being a reasonable scientist, (b) he will go to the literature or to authorities that are otherwise available, and he will find out what the status of knowledge is in regard to the facts. Having looked over the area, he selects what appears to be the "best" theory. Conceivably there may be only one theory covering the facts, but more likely there will be several. The permissiveness of science allows him to take certain liberties and, on the basis of *his* judgment, to formulate his revision of *the* theory.

Obviously, the theory will not be "hard theory." Besides being limited in range, the assumed variables are, of course, inferentially related to the *ad hoc* variables of the researcher, and the goodness of the inference is crucial to hypothesis testing. Having the theory, one he has either accepted or redefined, he may observe phenomena to test the theory; that is, if certain conditions can be specified at a point in time, certain consequences *must* follow by the hypothesis derived from the theory.

Now either of several things can occur. First, the findings may be in accord with the hypothesis and satisfy a given statistical significance for a hypothesis test. Second, the findings may not satisfy the arbitrary test. Third, not only may the second condition obtain, but the findings may appear to contradict the hypothesis. Suppose the results are in accord with his hypothesis. The researcher is then faced with several additional alternatives. For example, he may ask how well he can predict the phenomena that concern him (the consequences) and, if he has not predicted them at the maximum level that would be desired, he must then account for this insufficient prediction. This may mean improvement of measures, or it may mean revision of the theory to take additional factors into account. He is, however, in business. But to improve the prediction of the consequences he must seek further leads. At this point he can go back to his original work of reviewing the literature, speaking with authorities, and in other ways examining what the relevant variables are for his research, and on the basis of these, revise his theory and go over the entire cycle again, ad infinitum. We must emphasize here that this iterative procedure must always refer to the same bases of knowledge that the first trial involved, plus the new experience, although certainly additional things may be added and others dropped in the subsequent procedures. The researcher must also examine the question of what alternate theories could have predicted the results, and exploring this question should lead to further development of hypotheses.

If the research had negative findings, presumably this could occur from errors of measurement, in which case he may wish to revise his procedure. He may have had some faulty logic involved in his hypothesization, or his theory might have been inappropriate. In any event, he has the same problem of going back and revising, just as though he had had findings, except that in this case he is not able purposively to improve the prediction of the consequences, because he has not been able to predict at all.

The last alternative is the one of findings in the direction opposed from those that were hypothesized. This, of course, is the most charming type of result, since it permits a paper in which one blasts away, indicating how foolish others may have been to have had any kinds of findings contrary to this and how gullible they were to have reported them. The virtuosity permitted under findings contrary to those hypothesized is not paralleled in any other way in science. In any event, the researcher must also undertake the iterative procedure, but from this peculiar point, that the empirical facts contradict the "best" theory.

Let us see how *the notion of the shotgun* now relates to the research process. In the elegance of his theory, the investigator has asked only those questions that are necessary to test the theory. If he has findings in accord with the theory, we note that to improve the prediction of the consequences (hypothesized by the theory) or to differentiate his theory from others that would predict similar findings, he must inevitably revert to other measures and possibly go outside his initial scope of inquiry. This inevitable operation also is involved if he gets negative findings. Now the question forcefully arises, "Why did he restrict his initial question asking to what obviously was a prejudgment about the very situation he wished to investigate?"

The shotgun researcher is just as competent as his fellow in reading the literature and in appealing to authorities for leads, but, instead of assuming or formulating a "best" theory as such, he notes the things that have been indicated to be relevant to the class of phenomena he wishes to observe. Among these, let us assume, are those factors that have been built into his colleague's theory. The shotgun researcher, though, does not have the confidence of his colleague, so he says that possibly this rather elegant theory, while brilliant, may still be factually inappropriate. Thus, *without necessarily foregoing preferences*, he observes that there are theories in the speculative sense. His concern becomes one of asking questions relevant within the scope of the problem. In fact, he is not able to define the problem too well; he may even introduce certain alternative definitions of what the problem might be. Therefore, he observes the consequences in not one, but in several ways.

After having done his research, the shotgun researcher has reached the point where he has a mass of data corresponding to the inclusive set of research questions. It can't give answers in accord with the hypothesis or contrary to the hypothesis. At best, what can be said is: These classes of phenomena that might have been called consequences had we had *a* theory appear equivalent and these do not; they appear to be ordered in these ways; then for each of these consequences the predictability is such and such on the basis of these variables. The shotgun researcher, thus, is left with the job of unscrambling his findings. This may not be an elegant procedure, but, on the other hand, why should it be?

At this point the shotgun researcher has a body of empirical generalizations about which he can speculate, just as his colleague might speculate about how to improve his observations after he has found data in accord with his hypothesis. The advantage he has is that he may go to his data immediately to reject much that his colleague must now continue to test in his iterative procedure. Note, however, that the shotgun researcher must, just like any other scientist, ask: "Whither do I go?" He has, however, covered many of the avenues that will plague his colleague for a long time. On the other hand, he must (as must also his colleague) test the stability and generality of his findings through replication.

The second point made earlier was whether or not it is worth while building theory on a *post hoc* basis. The question that really arises is whether there is any alternative to this. In the shotgun method, if all relevant questions that could be included have indeed been included, the findings should represent a substantial and relatively systematic panel of empirical observations. What could be a better basis on which to formulate generalizations and to speculate about additional factors that might be involved?

There is one final point that needs to be clarified. Apparently the most devastating thing that can be said about a researcher who uses something that can be labeled the shotgun method is that occasionally he throws in "everything including the kitchen sink." As in the case of a lot of other straw men, finding the culprit in the literature is more difficult than recalling incidents of hearing this criticism. What is important, however, is that in science, if one cannot predict the criterion (that is, if there is no known variance that can be controlled in regard to an observed class of phenomena), or if the limits of the predictable variance have been found and improvement is not available in the known sources of variance, then by definition the known sources of variance are taken into account. There no longer exists a rationale for testing additional variance except for excluding rejected solutions. By definition, all tests of additional variance are at random within the scope of possible solutions of unknown or untested value until additional variance is encountered, and then, of course, one may again test in the neighborhood of the new source of variance to see if the criterion can be improved. What needs to be emphasized is that, when one is looking for new sources of variance, this is explicitly throwing in the kitchen sink, the garbage pail, or whatever else is available that has not been looked at yet. It seems trivial to emphasize, and yet it is very important: science permits within its scope the prediction of phenomena without necessarily understanding them (say, on a reductionistic base). On the other hand, by definition, it is not possible to understand in a scientific sense without being able to predict.

Reference

1. Dunnette, M. D., "Leadership: Many Stones and One Monument," *Contemporary Psychology*, 1958, 3, 362-363.

Eli S. Marks

Some Sampling Problems in Educational Research *

The problem of working with human subjects has been considered at the beginning of this chapter. When dealing with human subjects an even more fundamental question arises than how to work with them, and that is, how do you get the subjects? The results of an elegantly designed and carried out piece of research can come to naught if the results are applicable to no one, save the small group upon whom the research was carried out. The problem is one of sampling, and Marks deals with some of the more common problems that face educational researchers if they wish to generalize beyond the thirty-or-so students who make up an individual classroom.

E. S. Marks, "Some Sampling Problems in Educational Research," *Journal of Educational Psychology*, 42:85-96, 1951. Reprinted with permission.

In the past few years considerable progress has been made both in the theory and the practice of sampling as a research tool. Possibly the most important development in the field has been the clarification of concepts and the increasing realization that we can get meaningful answers from statistics only when we ask meaningful questions.

I am sure that all of us have had the experience of reading a study which used very elaborate statistical techniques and winding up completely dissatisfied with the conclusions. The mechanical application of analysis of variance, normalization of distributions, chi-square, factor analysis and the like, without a real examination of underlying concepts and assumptions has lead to a situation in which many sincere and intelligent research workers view all statistical analyses as sterile manipulations of meaningless numbers. This situation is not a fault of statistics. It is, rather, an effect of the substitution of techniques for

---

* Paper delivered at the American Educational Research Association meeting at Atlantic City, February 27, 1950.

thought, of a preoccupation with statistical means and an obscuring of statistical ends. While I am sure there are many problems in educational research which require and merit development of new sampling techniques, I should like to emphasize in this paper the need not for new techniques but for a more discerning application of old ones.

All of the sampling techniques mentioned in this paper have been used successfully in fields other than educational research. The present paper is concerned with the feasibility of practical application of these techniques to educational research. An attempt has been made to outline the general nature of the applications but the scope of the paper does not permit the development of details. Modern sampling practice and theory involve using a combination of several sampling methods to secure greater efficiency. The development of an efficient sampling plan will usually require the services of a skilled sampling technician. For the research worker who wishes to develop his own sampling designs, a bibliography is appended to this paper. The bibliography has been purposely restricted to relatively few references, the selection being limited to those references which are likely to be both useful and accessible to workers in the field of educational research.

In designing a sample, a knowledge of sampling techniques can be very helpful and a good sampling statistician will know how to select the most efficient sampling design, but no sampling technician and no book or article on sampling can do anything for you until you have determined the ends to be served by the sample design.

DEFINING THE POPULATION

The matter of definition of a population is fundamental and has, in many statistical studies, been given inadequate attention. All too frequently, research workers draw their samples and their conclusions from different populations. We start with a study of the 'relation between birth order and feelings of insecurity'; secure fifty to one hundred subjects through a sympathetic friend who happens to be superintendent of schools in a conveniently located city and conclude that 'feelings of insecurity are not correlated with birth order.' I have no particular quarrel with such a conclusion—it may well be true for many populations—but it has nothing to do with the data collected. From a group of cases picked up without consideration of what population is represented, we can conclude nothing about any population other than the cases actually observed.

It should be noted that a valid sample and statistically sound conclusions can be drawn from the school system to which our obliging friend, the superintendent, gives us access. A research finding does not have to apply to the whole population of the United States or the whole human race in order to be scientifically valuable. Our difficulties in drawing sound conclusions from samples stem from our own over-ambitiousness. We are not content with reporting our conclusions as applying to our own school or university or local community—we insist on discussing our results as if they apply to every human population.

If our sample is restricted to a school, group of schools, a community, a city or a state, our statistical conclusions must be similarly restricted. If we discuss the significance of a difference or a correlation coefficient or some other sample estimate, we should bear in mind that the conclusion applies only to the population sampled. Speculations on applicability to other populations are entirely proper and may be extremely valuable, but they should be labelled as speculations and not as statistical inferences.

LISTING THE POPULATION

The definition should be explicit enough to permit anyone to say with confidence: "This object or person is in the defined population and this one is not." The next step in selecting a sample is to 'list' the population. Some types of sampling (e.g., simple random sampling) require a listing of each population element. For other types of sampling (cluster sampling) it is sufficient to list the population in groups or clusters and to list the individual elements only for those clusters actually selected for the sample. For example, drawing a simple random sample of the public school children of the United States enrolled on March 1, 1950, would require listing every child. To draw a cluster sample it would be sufficient to list every school and list children only for the schools selected for the sample. Whether we list individual elements or groups of elements, the list from which the sample is drawn must include the entire population.

SIMPLE RANDOM SAMPLING

Whether we draw a sample of elements or a sample of clusters, it is essential that the selection of the sample units be made by some process of known random character. The temptation to substitute personal judgment for a table of random numbers may be great, but yielding to it is dangerous if we hope to apply any form of probability inference to our results. Actually, the statistical techniques outlined in most textbooks are valid only for simple random sampling. For example, the familiar formula for the estimated standard error of a mean or a percentage applies only when all the observations are drawn independently and with equal probability, conditions usually satisfied only by simple random samples.

While simple random sampling is a desirable technique for many purposes, such sampling is in most cases a luxury which few research workers can afford. It requires a complete listing of the individual population elements. Such a listing might be available for some school populations—might, for example, be obtainable for a population of all teachers in a school system—but, in many cases, such listings can be obtained only at extremely high cost. Even where lists are available, simple random sampling may be very expensive (in terms of both money and effort) if data are to be collected by personal contact. If, for example, we plan to interview in their homes a sample of one hundred mothers with children attending the New York City schools, a simple random sample would probably be distributed so that no two mothers were within ten minutes walking distance of each other (except in Manhattan where you might find a couple of mothers only five or six blocks apart). The difficulty is, of course, the requirement that cases be drawn independently, a condition which gives a very small probability of selecting two mothers from the same block.

The condition of equal probability of selection for each element of a simple random sample may also be a disadvantage for some purposes. Suppose, for example, that we wish to estimate the aggregate expenditure for home economics of public schools in the State of Illinois, and plan, for this purpose, to draw a sample of seventy-five schools. Simple random sampling would require that the probability of drawing a school with five thousand enrollment be the same as the probability of drawing one with one hundred twenty enrollment and be the same for high schools as for elementary schools. With a sample of seventy-five schools, selection of only one large high school with a substantial program in home economics might give an estimate two or three times greater than the correct figure.

CLUSTER SAMPLING

For some purposes, simple random sampling will prove most satisfactory. For other purposes, it may be desirable to use cluster sampling and sampling with unequal probabilities. However, when we use cluster sampling or sampling with unequal probabilities, we must make appropriate modifications of our variance formulae.

While sampling of groups is usually easier and cheaper than sampling of individuals, the reduced cost per sample case is not all gain. For a given population, the variance between cluster samples will usually be larger than the variance between samples of individuals. A good example of this is the estimation of the proportion of Negroes living in New York City. If we were to draw several samples of one thousand individuals at random from all persons living in New York, the proportion Negro in these samples would probably vary only slightly from sample to sample. If we were to draw five city blocks and in each block take two hundred persons (giving the same number, one thousand, in the sample), the proportion Negro in different samples might vary tremendously. If we happened to draw a block from one of the areas with high Negro concentration, our sample would be twenty per cent or more Negro. If we happened to draw no such block, we might have no Negroes in the sample. While most cases will be less extreme than this illustration, even a small tendency towards greater homogeneity within clusters than there is over the whole population, can have very substantial effects on the variance of sample estimates when the clusters are large. This fact must be recognized in estimating these variances.

In deciding whether to use cluster sampling or some other sampling technique, relative costs and accuracy must be considered. A cluster sample estimate may have three times the variance of a similar estimate from a simple random sample of the same size, but the cluster sample may cost only one-sixth as much. By tripling the size of the cluster sample we may be able to get the same accuracy as we can with simple random sampling at half the cost.

SAMPLING WITH UNEQUAL PROBABILITIES

Sampling with unequal probabilities also requires a modification of the familiar formulae for sampling errors. One method of using unequal probabilities is stratification. Here, the sampling units are divided into groups (or 'strata') and the sampling is done separately in each stratum, usually with different sampling probabilities in the various strata. Another method of using unequal probabilities is to assign the different probabilities directly to each sampling unit and draw the sample with these probabilities from the whole population. The use of unequal probabilities may require the weighting of individual observations in preparing sample estimates, but this can frequently be avoided by drawing clusters with varying probabilities and subsampling the clusters in a manner which equalizes the probability of selection for individual elements.

Cutting ourselves loose from the strait jacket of simple random sampling does not mean that we go over to haphazard and uncontrolled sampling methods. Cluster sampling and sampling with unequal probabilities preserve the principle of random selection (rather than selection based on judgment or convenience) and give sample results which conform to, and permit the application of probability theory. We must, of course, modify our theory to conform to the sampling techniques actually used. A suitable combination of probability sampling techniques can be used to give unbiased samples with measurable sampling errors and such estimates will be no more expensive than estimates from 'judgment samples' where the sampling errors and biases are not determinable.

AN ILLUSTRATION—SELECTING A NATIONAL SAMPLE OF SECONDARY-SCHOOL STUDENTS

The use of a combination of methods can be illustrated by the situation in which we wish to develop norms for achievement tests to be used in secondary schools. We want to estimate the average scores on these tests for all students attending secondary schools in the United States. Suppose that funds and other resources available for the work indicate that the sample must be restricted to some limited number of school systems and we have available a complete list of all secondary schools in the United States arranged by school system. To draw the sample we could:

(1) Group the school systems of the United States into strata. For maximum efficiency, the strata should contain approximately equal numbers of secondary-school students and should be as internally homogeneous as possible with respect to achievement of secondary-school students. The grouping into strata can be done on a judgment basis using any information which can be obtained regarding the probable achievement of secondary-school students in the system. We might also want to consider in our stratification the cost of giving tests in a school system and the size of the school system. Some of the strata may be established so that they contain only one school system. Since maximum sampling efficiency will call for drawing a single school system from each stratum, the number of strata should be equal to the number of school systems we wish to draw.

(2) Within each stratum, assign to each school system a probability of selection. Usually, we would assign larger probabilities to the larger school systems since the 'weight' of a school system in our population of secondary-school students will be proportional to its size. If data are available on enrollment of secondary-school students, it might be desirable to make the probability of selecting a school system proportional to the number of secondary-students enrolled. There are various ways of assigning unequal probabilities of selection to different school systems. For example, suppose a stratum contained two school systems, A, with an enrollment of 5,000 secondary-school students and B with 10,000. We want to make the probability of selecting B twice that of selecting A. A technique for doing this is to select a five-digit random number from one of the standard tables of random numbers and: (a) select A, if the random number is between 00001 and 05000 ('between' as used here, includes also '1' and '5000'). (b) select B, if the random number is between 05001 and 15,000. (c) draw another random number, if our first number is less than 1 (i.e., zero) or greater than 15,000, and continue until we get a number between 1 and 15,000.

The random number technique can be used quite generally for assigning unequal probabilities (assigning to each school system to be drawn, a block of consecutive numbers equal to the enrollment in the school system).

(3) Use within each of the selected school systems, a similar technique for selecting schools, giving each school in the system a probability of selection proportional to the estimated number of secondary-school students enrolled.

(4) Finally, select secondary-school students at random within the selected schools using the school's records of students enrolled. The proportion of students to be sampled in a given school can be so determined that every secondary-school student in the United States has the same chance of being included in the sample and it will then not be necessary to use weights in preparing the sample estimates.

In determining the number of strata to be set up, the number of schools to be selected, and the number of students to be tested, considerations of cost and desired accuracy are paramount. The sampling technician can tell you which sample design will give you lowest costs for a given level of accuracy or will give you the least error for a fixed expenditure. However, you must first determine what your goals of cost and accuracy are. If you go to a competent sampling technician for advice, he will ask:

(1) Exactly what do you wish to estimate from the sample?

(2) What precision must these estimates have? Is it satisfactory to get an estimated norm within five per cent of the true national average or must it be within one-half or one-tenth per cent?

(3) How much are you willing to spend to achieve the accuracy desired?

IMPORTANCE OF CLEAR STATEMENT OF PURPOSES

Efficiency in sample design depends to some extent on how much you know about the population to be sampled; depends to an even greater extent on how much you know about your own purposes and how clearly you have defined these purposes. In some cases, a clear definition of purpose is the key to an apparently insoluble problem. Consider the problem of determining how well a particular college entrance examination does in predicting which college applicants will succeed. It has been suggested that solution of this problem requires that the college admit an unselected sample of applicants so we may observe which ones succeed and which fail. Such a solution would, however, disrupt college admissions procedures. There are definitions of this problem which make its solution impracticable without drastic interference with normal admissions procedure. There is, however, a definition of the problem which admits of a practical solution; namely, expose the applicants both to the test and to the other selection procedures. Accept all applicants who are satisfactory by all criteria and reject all applicants who are unsatisfactory by all criteria. For these applicants, our test can be no better and no worse than the alternatives since all criteria give the same answer. Since we have eliminated the obviously unsatisfactory applicants, and accepted the obviously satisfactory ones, accepting from the middle group at random will probably not have any serious consequence. If a simple random selection from this group is undesirable, differential selection can be used, still preserving the principle of random (and unbiased) selection. The probabilities can be determined so as to accept a minimum number of applicants from the 'doubtful competence' group but still to have a sufficient number to permit an unbiased comparison of the test with the alternative criteria.

SAMPLING FOR TEST CONTENT

The problem of preparing equivalent forms of the same test is also one which can profit from a re-examination of basic concepts. One method of approaching the problem is to consider that: (1) the items in all forms of a test form a 'universe' of items and (2) the purpose of a particular form of test is to yield estimates of the individual's average or aggregate score on all items in the universe.

With this approach different forms of a test become samples of items from a universe of items. If we use an identical sampling procedure in drawing the sample of items for each form, the forms of the test are automatically 'equivalent.' We replace the difficult problem of determining (after constructing the test forms) whether items were drawn from the same universe by the much simpler problem of drawing items so that you know they are from the same universe. The techniques used in drawing a sample of persons are equally applicable to sampling items and the problem of securing maximum test reliability becomes identical with the problem of securing minimum sampling variance.

The problem of getting equivalent forms of a test is part of the more general problem of sampling a 'behavioral universe.' In general, a test is used as a sample of an individual's behavior or performance in some larger field. The problems of defining the behavioral universe and drawing a sample from it are similar to those of defining and sampling a universe of persons. Principles applicable to the problem of sampling persons are equally applicable to the sampling of performances. It can be seen that the most serious problem in sampling performances will be obtaining an inclusive listing of the universe.

COMMON MISCONCEPTIONS ABOUT SAMPLING

The preceding discussion has touched briefly on some points about which misconceptions are common. One of these misconceptions is, of course, the application of the standard textbook treatment of simple random sampling to situations where the sampling is neither random nor simple; i.e., where groups are sampled rather than individuals or the sample selection is not on a probability basis.

Another area where misconceptions are common is 'stratification.' The most serious error in this field is the idea that stratification removes the need for random selection within strata. This is the fallacy which underlies the quota sampling technique used by many of the opinion polling agencies. The other misconception about stratification is emphasis on proportional sampling from the various strata. The emphasis in this paper has been on using stratification as a device for assigning unequal probabilities of selection to different population elements. There are dangers to assigning unequal probabilities:

(1) With unequal sampling probabilities the sample elements must be weighted by the reciprocal of the probability to obtain unbiased estimates. Failure to weight may result in very serious biases.

(2) By proper assignment of the sampling probabilities, it may be possible to make very substantial gains in the efficiency of a sample. On the other hand, a poor assignment of the sampling probabilities can result in very substantial losses in sampling efficiency.

Thus, inequal sampling probabilities should be used with caution. Nevertheless, the advantages of a more flexible and more efficient sampling design should not be discarded because of the pitfalls resulting from careless use of the design.

Another area of serious misconception is the field of bias in sampling. The very term 'bias' suggests that it is undesirable—and it is. There are, however, conditions where it is better to use a biased estimate rather than accept the even more undesirable alternatives necessary to removing the bias. The criterion should be total error, which is composed of bias and variance. If avoiding a small bias means taking a very large variance, take the bias and keep the total error small. Most of our errors of judgment are, however, in the reverse direction; i.e., we strive for big samples (which mean, usually, small variances) and pay no attention at all to the sizes of the biases. The extremes of attending only to bias or attending only to variance are both undesirable.

Approach to sample design must be flexible, and avoid rote use of techniques regardless of their applicability. We must take into account the factors of the particular sampling situation, remembering that what is most efficient for one situation may be most inefficient for another situation. Above all, sample design must look to the purposes of the study and reject all solutions—no matter how 'elegant' they may be—which do not achieve those purposes.

Bibliography

Cochran, W. G.: "Relative Accuracy of Systematic and Stratified Random Samples for a Certain Class of Population." *Annals of Mathematical Statistics*, vol. 18 (1946), pp. 164-177.

———— "Sampling Theory When the Sampling Units Are of Unequal Sizes." *Journal of the American Statistical Association*, vol. 37 (1942), pp. 199-212.

Cornell, F. G.: "A Stratified Random Sample of a Small Finite Population." *Journal of the American Statistical Association*, vol. 42 (1947), pp. 523-532.

Deming, W. E.: *Some Theory of Sampling.* John Wiley and Sons, Inc., New York, (1950).

Deming, W. E. and Simmons, W.: "On the Design of a Sample for Dealers' Inventories." *Journal of the American Statistical Association,* vol. 41 (1946), pp. 16-33.

Goodman, Roe: "Sampling for the 1947 Survey of Consumer Finances." *Journal of the American Statistical Association,* vol. 42 (1947), pp. 439-448.

Hansen, M. H. and Deming, W. E.: "On Some Census Aids to Sampling." *Journal of the American Statistical Association,* vol. 38 (1943), pp. 353-357.

Hansen, M. H. and Hurwitz, W. N.: "Relative Efficiencies of Various Sampling Units in Population Inquiries." *Journal of the American Statistical Association,* vol. 37 (1942), pp. 89-94.

————— "On the Theory of Sampling from Finite Populations." *Annals of Mathematical Statistics,* vol. 14 (1943), pp. 333-362.

————— "The Problem of Non-Response in Sample Surveys." *Journal of the American Statistical Association,* vol. 41 (1946), pp. 517-529.

————— "On the Determination of Optimum Probabilities in Sampling." *Annals of Mathematical Statistics,* vol. 20 (1949), pp. 426-432.

————— "Dependable Samples for Market Surveys." *Journal of Marketing,* vol. 14 (1949), pp. 363-372.

Hansen, M. H., Hurwitz, W. N., and Gurney, M.: "Problems and Methods of a Sample Survey of Business." *Journal of the American Statistical Association,* vol. 41 (1946), pp. 173-189.

Hauser, P. M. and Hansen, M. H.: "On Sampling in Market Surveys." *Journal of Marketing,* vol. 9 (1944), pp. 26-31.

————— "Area Sampling—Some Principles of Sample Design." *Public Opinion Quarterly,* vol. 8 (1945), pp. 183-193.

Jessen, R. J., et al.: "On a Population Sample for Greece." *Journal of the American Statistical Association,* vol. 42 (1947), pp. 357-384.

King, A. J. and Jessen, R. J.: "Master Sample of Agriculture." *Journal of the American Statistical Association,* vol. 40 (1945), pp. 38-56.

Madow, W. G. and L. H.: "On the Theory of Systematic Sampling." *Annals of Mathematical Statistics,* vol. 15 (1944), pp. 1-24.

Madow, L. H.: "Systematic Sampling and its Relation to Other Sampling Design." *Journal of the American Statistical Association,* vol. 41 (1946), pp. 204-217.

Marks, E. S.: "Sampling in the Revision of the Stanford-Binet Scale." *Psychological Bulletin*, vol. 44 (1947), pp. 413-434.

McVay, F. E.: "Sampling Methods Applied to Estimating Numbers of Commercial Orchards." *Journal of the American Statistical Association*, vol. 42 (1947), pp. 533-540.

Neyman, J.: "Contribution to the Theory of Sampling Human Populations." *Journal of the American Statistical Association*, vol. 35 (1938), pp. 101-116.

Nordin, J. A.: "Determining Sample Size." *Journal of the American Statistical Association*, vol. 39 (1944), pp. 497-506.

Osborne, J. G.: "Sampling Errors of Systematic and Random Surveys of Cover Type Areas." *Journal of the American Statistical Association*, vol. 37 (1942), pp. 256-264.

Sampling Staff, Bureau of the Census: "A Chapter in Population Sampling." Government Printing Office. Washington, D. C. (1947).

Stephan, F. F.: "Representative Sampling in Large-Scale Surveys." *Journal of the American Statistical Association*, vol. 34 (1939), pp. 343-352.

——— "History of the Uses of Modern Sampling Procedures." *Journal of the American Statistical Association*, vol. 43 (1948), pp. 12-39.

——— "Stratification in Representative Sampling." *Journal of Marketing*, vol. 6 (1941), pp. 38-46.

Stock, J. S. and Frankel, L. R.: "The Allocation of Sampling Among Several Strata." *Annals of Mathematical Statistics*, vol. 10 (1939), pp. 288-293.

Yates, F.: "Sampling Methods for Censuses and Surveys." Hafner Publishing Company, New York (1949).

Donald T. Campbell

Factors Relevant to the Validity of Experiments in Social Settings [1]

When an educational researcher has finished his work, how does he know that the variable he has manipulated really caused any difference that may be found? Further, how can he be certain that his results may be generalized beyond the small sample that has been used in the research? The role of sampling has been discussed in the previous selections. In this article Campbell discusses the role of design in eliminating confounding variables that might account for an obtained result or might reduce the generalizability of the result.

Donald T. Campbell, "Factors Relevant to the Validity of Experiments in Social Settings," *Psychological Bulletin*, 54:297-312, 1957. Reprinted with permission.

What do we seek to control in experimental designs? What extraneous variables which would otherwise confound our interpretation of the experiment do we wish to rule out? The present paper attempts a specification of the major categories of such extraneous variables and employs these categories in evaluating the validity of standard designs for experimentation in the social sciences.

Validity will be evaluated in terms of two major criteria. First, and as a basic minimum, is what can be called *internal validity:* did in

---

[1] A dittoed version of this paper was privately distributed in 1953 under the title "Designs for Social Science Experiments." The author has had the opportunity to benefit from the careful reading and suggestions of L. S. Burwen, J. W. Cotton, C. P. Duncan, D. W. Fiske, C. I. Hovland, L. V. Jones, E. S. Marks, D. C. Pelz, and B. J. Underwood, among others, and wishes to express his appreciation. They have not had the opportunity of seeing the paper in its present form, and bear no responsibility for it. The author also wishes to thank S. A. Stouffer (33) and B. J. Underwood (36) for their public encouragement.

fact the experimental stimulus make some significant difference in this specific instance? The second criterion is that of *external validity, representativeness,* or *generalizability:* to what populations, settings, and variables can this effect be generalized? Both criteria are obviously important although it turns out that they are to some extent incompatible, in that the controls required for internal validity often tend to jeopardize representativeness.

The extraneous variables affecting internal validity will be introduced in the process of analyzing three pre-experimental designs. In the subsequent evaluation of the applicability of three true experimental designs, factors leading to external invalidity will be introduced. The effects of these extraneous variables will be considered at two levels: as simple or main effects, they occur independently of or in addition to the effects of the experimental variable; as interactions, the effects appear in conjunction with the experimental variable. The main effects typically turn out to be relevant to internal validity, the interaction effects to external validity or representativeness.

The following designation for experimental designs will be used: *X* will represent the exposure of a group to the experimental variable or event, the effects of which are to be measured; *O* will refer to the process of observation or measurement, which can include watching what people do, listening, recording, interviewing, administering tests, counting lever depressions, etc. The *X*s and *O*s in a given row are applied to the same specific persons. The left to right dimension indicates temporal order. Parallel rows represent equivalent samples of persons unless otherwise specified. The designs will be numbered and named for cross-reference purposes.

THREE PRE-EXPERIMENTAL DESIGNS AND THEIR CONFOUNDED EXTRANEOUS VARIABLES

The One-Shot Case Study

As Stouffer (32) has pointed out, much social science research still uses Design 1, in which a single individual or group is studied in detail only once, and in which the observations are attributed to exposure to some prior situation.

$$X \quad O \qquad \text{1. One-Shot Case Study}$$

This design does not merit the title of experiment, and is introduced only to provide a reference point. The very minimum of useful scientific information involves at least one formal comparison and therefore at least two careful observations (2).

The One-Group Pretest-Posttest Design

This design does provide for one formal comparison of two observations, and is still widely used.

$O_1 \quad X \quad O_2$ 2. One-Group Pretest-Posttest Design

However, in it there are four or five categories of extraneous variables left uncontrolled which thus become rival explanations of any difference between O_1 and O_2, confounded with the possible effect of X.

The first of these is the main effect of *history*. During the time span between O_1 and O_2 many events have occurred in addition to X, and the results might be attributed to these. Thus in Collier's (8) experiment, while his respondents[2] were reading Nazi propaganda materials, France fell, and the obtained attitude changes seemed more likely a result of this event than of the propaganda.[3] By history is meant the specific event series other than X, i.e., the extra-experimental uncontrolled stimuli. Relevant to this variable is the concept of experimental isolation, the employment of experimental settings in which all extraneous stimuli are eliminated. The approximation of such control in much physical and biological research has permitted the satisfactory employment of Design 2. But in social psychology and the other social sciences, if history is confounded with X the results are generally uninterpretable.

The second class of variables confounded with X in Design 2 is here designated as *maturation*. This covers those effects which are systematic with the passage of time, and not, like history, a function of the specific events involved. Thus between O_1 and O_2 the respondents may have grown older, hungrier, tireder, etc., and these may have produced the difference between O_1 and O_2, independently of X. While in the typical brief experiment in the psychology laboratory, maturation is unlikely to be a source of change, it has been a problem in research in child development and can be so in extended experiments

---

2 In line with the central focus on social psychology and the social sciences, the term *respondent* is employed in place of the terms *subject, patient,* or *client.*

3 Collier actually used a more adequate design than this, an approximation to Design 4.

in social psychology and education. In the form of "spontaneous remission" and the general processes of healing it becomes an important variable to control in medical research, psychotherapy, and social remediation.

There is a third source of variance that could explain the difference between O_1 and O_2 without a recourse to the effect of X. This is the effect of *testing* itself. It is often true that persons taking a test for the second time make scores systematically different from those taking the test for the first time. This is indeeed the case for intelligence tests, where a second mean may be expected to run as much as five IQ points higher than the first one. This possibility makes important a distinction between *reactive* measures and *nonreactive* measures. A reactive measure is one which modifies the phenomenon under study, which changes the very thing that one is trying to measure. In general, any measurement procedure which makes the subject self-conscious or aware of the fact of the experiment can be suspected of being a reactive measurement. Whenever the measurement is *not* a part of the normal environment it is probably reactive. Whenever measurement exercises the process under study, it is almost certainly reactive. Measurement of a person's height is relatively nonreactive. However, measurement of weight, introduced into an experimental design involving adult American women, would turn out to be reactive in that the process of measuring would stimulate weight reduction. A photograph of a crowd taken in secret from a second story window would be nonreactive, but a news photograph of the same scene might very well be reactive, in that the presence of the photographer would modify the behavior of people seeing themselves being photographed. In a factory, production records introduced for the purpose of an experiment would be reactive, but if such records were a regular part of the operating environment they would be nonreactive. An English anthropologist may be nonreactive as a participant-observer at an English wedding, but might be a highly reactive measuring instrument at a Dobu nuptials. Some measures are so extremely reactive that their use in a pretest-posttest design is not usually considered. In this class would be tests involving surprise, deception, rapid adaptation, or stress. Evidence is amply present that tests of learning and memory are highly reactive (35, 36). In the field of opinion and attitude research our well-developed interview and attitude test techniques must be rated as reactive, as shown, for example, by Crespi's (9) evidence.

Even within the personality and attitude test domain, it may be found that tests differ in the degree to which they are reactive. For some purposes, tests involving voluntary self-description may turn out to be more reactive (especially at the interaction level to be discussed below) than are devices which focus the respondent upon describing the external world, or give him less latitude in describing himself (e.g., 5). It seems likely that, apart from considerations of validity, the Rorschach test is less reactive than the TAT or MMPI. Where the reactive nature of the testing process results from the focusing of attention on the experimental variable, it may be reduced by imbedding the relevant content in a comprehensive array of topics, as has regularly been done in Hovland's attitude change studies (14). It seems likely that with attention to the problem, observational and measurement techniques can be developed which are much less reactive than those now in use.

Instrument decay provides a fourth uncontrolled source of variance which could produce an O_1-O_2 difference that might be mistaken for the effect of X. This variable can be exemplified by the fatiguing of a spring scales, or the condensation of water vapor in a cloud chamber. For psychology and the social sciences it becomes a particularly acute problem when human beings are used as a part of the measuring apparatus, as judges, observers, raters, coders, etc. Thus O_1 and O_2 may differ because the raters have become more experienced, more fatigued, have acquired a different adaptation level, or have learned about the purpose of the experiment, etc. However infelicitously, this term will be used to typify those problems introduced when shifts in measurement conditions are confounded with the effect of X, including such crudities as having a different observer at O_1 and O_2, or using a different interviewer or coder. Where the use of different interviewers, observers, or experimenters is unavoidable, but where they are used in large numbers, a sampling equivalence of interviewers is required, with the relevant N being the N of interviewers, not interviewees, except as refined through cluster sampling considerations (18).

A possible fifth extraneous factor deserves mention. This is statistical *regression*. When, in Design 2, the group under investigation has been selected for its extremity on O_1, O_1-O_2 shifts toward the mean will occur which are due to random imperfections of the measuring instrument or random instability within the population, as reflected in the test-retest reliability. In general, regression operates like maturation in that the effects increase systematically with the O_1-O_2 time interval. McNemar (22) has demonstrated the profound mistakes in interpretation which failure to control this factor can introduce in remedial research.

The Static Group Comparison

The third pre-experimental design is the Static Group Comparison.

$$X \quad O_1$$
$$\text{-------} \quad \text{3. The Static Group Comparison}$$
$$O_2$$

In this design, there is a comparison of a group which has experienced X with a group which has not, for the purpose of establishing the effect of X. In contrast with Design 6, there is in this design no means of certifying that the groups were equivalent at some prior time. (The absence of sampling equivalence of groups is symbolized by the row of dashes.) This design has its most typical occurrence in the social sciences, and both its prevalence and its weakness have been well indicated by Stouffer (32). It will be recognized as one form of the correlational study. It is introduced here to complete the list of confounding factors. If the Os differ, this difference could have come about through biased *selection* or recruitment of the persons making up the groups; i.e., they might have differed anyway without the effect of X. Frequently, exposure to X (e.g., some mass communication) has been voluntary and the two groups have an inevitable systematic difference on the factors determining the choice involved, a difference which no amount of matching can remove.

A second variable confounded with the effect of X in this design can be called experimental *mortality*. Even if the groups were equivalent at some prior time, O_1 and O_2 may differ now not because individual members have changed, but because a biased subset of members have dropped out. This is a typical problem in making inferences from comparisons of the attitudes of college freshmen and college seniors, for example.

TRUE EXPERIMENTAL DESIGNS

The Pretest-Posttest Control Group Design

One or another of the above considerations led psychologists between 1900 and 1925 (2, 30) to expand Design 2 by the addition of a control group, resulting in Design 4.

$$O_1 \quad X \quad O_2 \qquad \text{4. Pretest-Posttest Control Group Design}$$
$$O_3 \qquad\quad O_4$$

Because this design so neatly controls for the main effects of history, maturation, testing, instrument decay, regression, selection, and mortality, these separate sources of variance are not usually made explicit. It seems well to state briefly the relationship of the design to each of these confounding factors, with particular attention to the application of the design in social settings.

If the differences between O_1 and O_2 were due to intervening historical events, then they should also show up in the O_3–O_4 comparison. Note, however, several complications in achieving this control. If respondents are run in groups, and if there is only one experimental session and one control session, then there is no control over the unique internal histories of the groups. The O_1–O_2 difference, even if not appearing in O_3–O_4, may be due to a chance distracting factor appearing in one or the other group. Such a design, while controlling for the shared history or event series, still confounds X with the unique session history. Second, the design implies a simultaneity of O_1 with O_3 and O_2 with O_4 which is usually impossible. If one were to try to achieve simultaneity by using two experimenters, one working with the experimental respondents, the other with the controls, this would confound experimenter differences with X (introducing one type of instrument decay). These considerations make it usually imperative that, for a true experiment, the experimental and control groups be tested and exposed individually or in small subgroups, and that sessions of both types be temporally and spatially intermixed.

As to the other factors: if maturation or testing contributed an O_1–O_2 difference, this should appear equally in the O_3–O_4 comparison, and these variables are thus controlled for their main effects. To make sure the design controls for instrument decay, the same individual or small-session approximation to simultaneity needed for history is required. The occasional practice of running the experimental group and control group at different times is thus ruled out on this ground as well as that of history. Otherwise the observers may have become more experienced, more hurried, more careless, the maze more redolent with irrelevant cues, the lever-tension and friction diminished, etc. Only when groups are effectively simultaneous do these factors affect experimental and control groups alike. Where more than one experimenter or observer is used, counterbalancing experimenter, time, and group is recommended. The balanced Latin square is frequently useful for this purpose (4).

While regression is controlled in the design as a whole, frequently secondary analyses of effects are made for extreme pretest scorers in the experimental group. To provide a control for effects of regression, a parallel analysis of extremes should also be made for the control group.

Selection is of course handled by the sampling equivalence ensured through the randomization employed in assigning persons to groups, perhaps supplemented by, but not supplanted by, matching procedures. Where the experimental and control groups do not have this sort of equivalence, one has a compromise design rather than a true experiment. Furthermore, the O_1-O_3 comparison provides a check on possible sampling differences.

The design also makes possible the examination of experimental mortality, which becomes a real problem for experiments extended over weeks or months. If the experimental and control groups do not differ in the number of lost cases nor in their pretest scores, the experiment can be judged internally valid on this point, although mortality reduces the generalization of effects to the original population from which the groups were selected.

For these reasons, the Pretest-Posttest Control Group Design has been the ideal in the social sciences for some thirty years. Recently, however, a serious and avoidable imperfection in it has been noted, perhaps first by Schanck and Goodman (29). Solomon (30) has expressed the point as an *interaction* effect of testing. In the terminology of analysis of variance, the effects of history, maturation, and testing, as described so far, are all *main* effects, manifesting themselves in mean differences independently of the presence of other variables. They are effects that could be added on to other effects, including the effect of the experimental variable. In contrast, interaction effects represent a joint effect, specific to the concomitance of two or more conditions, and may occur even when no main effects are present. Applied to the testing variable, the interaction effect might involve not a shift due soley or directly to the measurement process, but rather a sensitization of respondents to the experimental variable so that when X was preceded by O there would be a change, whereas both X and O would be without effect if occurring alone. In terms of the two types of validity, Design 4 is internally valid, offering an adequate basis for generalization to other sampling-equivalent *pretested* groups. But it has a serious and systematic weakness in representativeness in that it offers, strictly speaking, no basis for generalization to the *unpretested* population. And it is usually the *unpretested* larger universe from which these samples were taken to which one wants to generalize.

A concrete example will help make this clearer. In the NORC study of a United Nations information campaign (31), two equivalent samples, of a thousand each, were drawn from the city's population. One of these samples was interviewed, following which the city of Cincinnati was subjected to an intensive publicity campaign using all the mass media of communication. This included special features in the newspapers and on the radio, bus cards, public lectures, etc. At the end of two months, the second sample of 1,000 was interviewed and the results compared with the first 1,000. There were no differences between the two groups except that the second group was somewhat more pessimistic about the likelihood of Russia's cooperating for world peace, a result which was attributed to history rather than to the publicity campaign. The second sample was no better informed about the United Nations nor had it noticed in particular the publicity campaign which had been going on. In connection with a program of research on panels and the reinterview problem, Paul Lazarsfeld and the Bureau of Applied Social Research arranged to have the initial sample reinterviewed at the same time as the second sample was interviewed, after the publicity campaign. This reinterviewed group showed significant attitude changes, a high degree of awareness of the campaign and important increases in information. The inference in this case is unmistakably that the initial interview had sensitized the persons interviewed to the topic of the United Nations, had raised in them a focus of awareness which made the subsequent publicity campaign effective for them but for them only. This study and other studies clearly document the possibility of interaction effects which seriously limit our capacity to generalize from the pretested experimental group to the unpretested general population. Hovland (15) reports a general finding which is of the opposite nature but is, nonetheless, an indication of an interactive effect. In his Army studies the initial pretest served to reduce the effects of the experimental variable, presumably by creating a commitment to a given position. Crespi's (9) findings support this expectation. Solomon (30) reports two studies with school children in which a spelling pretest reduced the effects of a training period. But whatever the direction of the effect, this flaw in Pretest-Posttest Control Design is serious for the purposes of the social scientist.

The Solomon Four-Group Design

It is Solomon's (30) suggestion to control this problem by adding to the traditional two-group experiment two unpretested groups as indicated in Design 5.

$$
\begin{array}{lll}
O_1 & X & O^2 \\
O_3 & & O_4 \\
& X & O_5 \\
& & O_6
\end{array}
$$
5. Solomon Four-Group Design

This Solomon Four-Group Design enables one both to control and measure both the main and interaction effects of testing and the main effects of a composite of maturation and history. It has become the new ideal design for social scientists. A word needs to be said about the appropriate statistical analysis. In Design 4, an efficient single test embodying the four measurements is achieved through computing for each individual a pretest-posttest difference score which is then used for comparing by t test the experimental and control groups. Extension of this mode of analysis to the Solomon Four-Group Design introduces an inelegant awkwardness to the otherwise elegant procedure. It involves assuming as a pretest score for the unpretested groups the mean value of the pretest from the first two groups. This restricts the effective degrees of freedom, violates assumptions of independence, and leaves one without a legitimate base for testing the significance of main effects and interaction. An alternative analysis is available which avoids the assumed pretest scores. Note that the four posttests form a simple two-by-two analysis of variance design:

	No X	X
Pretested	O_4	O_2
Unpretested	O_6	O_5

The column means represent the main effect of X, the row means the main effect of pretesting, and the interaction term the interaction of pretesting and X. (By use of a t test the combined main effects of maturation and history can be tested through comparing O_6 with O_1 and O_3.)

The Posttest-Only Control Group Design

While the statistical procedures of analysis of variance introduced by Fisher (10) are dominant in psychology and the other social sciences today, it is little noted in our discussions of experimental arrangements that Fisher's typical agricultural experiment involves no pretest: equivalent plots of ground receive different experimental treatments and the subsequent yields are measured.[4] Applied to a social experiment as in testing the influence of a motion picture upon attitudes,

---

[4] This is not to imply that the pretest is totally absent from Fisher's designs. He suggests the use of previous year's yields, etc., in covariance analysis. He notes, however, "with annual agricultural crops, knowledge of yields of the experimental area in a previous year under uniform treatment has not been found sufficiently to increase the precision to warrant the adoption of such uniformity trials as a preliminary to projected experiments" (10, p. 176).

two randomly assigned audiences would be selected, one exposed to the movie, and the attitudes of each measured subsequently for the first time.

$$A \quad X \quad O_1$$
$$A \qquad O_2$$

6. Posttest-Only Control Group Design

In this design the symbol A had been added, to indicate that at a specific time prior to X the groups were made equivalent by a random sampling *assignment*. A is the point of selection, the point of allocation of individuals to groups. It is the existence of this process that distinguishes Design 6 from Design 3, the Static Group Comparison. Design 6 is not a static cross-sectional comparison, but instead truly involves control and observation extended in time. The sampling procedures employed assure us that at time A the groups were equal, even if not measured. A provides a point of prior equality just as does the pretest. A point A is, of course, involved in all true experiments, and should perhaps be indicated in Designs 4 and 5. It is essential that A be regarded as a specific point in time, for groups change as a function of time since A, through experimental mortality. Thus in a public opinion survey situation employing probability sampling from lists of residents, the longer the time since A, the more the sample underrepresents the transient segments of society, the newer dwelling units, etc. When experimental groups are being drawn from a self-selected extreme population, such as applicants for psychotherapy, time since A introduces maturation (spontaneous remission) and regression factors. In Design 6 these effects would be confounded with the effect of X if the As as well as the Os were not contemporaneous for experimental and control groups.

Like Design 4, this design controls for the effects of maturation and history through the practical simultaneity of both the As and the Os. In superiority over Design 4, no main or interaction effects of pretesting are involved. It is this feature that recommends it in particular. While it controls for the main and interaction effects of pretesting as well as does Design 5, the Solomon Four-Group Design, it does not measure these effects, nor the main effect of history-maturation. It can be noted that Design 6 can be considered as the two unpretested "control" groups from the Solomon Design, and that Solomon's two traditional pretested groups have in this sense the sole purpose of measuring the effects of pretesting and history-maturation, a purpose irrelevant to the main aim of studying the effect of X (25). However, under normal conditions of not quite perfect sampling control, the four-group design provides in addition greater assurance against mistakenly attributing to X effects which are not due it, inasmuch as the effect of X is documented in three different fashions (O_1 vs. O_2, O_2 vs. O_4, and O_5 vs. O_6). But, short of the four-group design, Design 6 is often to be preferred to Design 4, and is a fully valid experimental design.

Design 6 has indeed been used in the social sciences, perhaps first of all in the classic experiment by Gosnell, *Getting Out the Vote* (11). Schanck and Goodman (29), Hovland (15) and others (1, 12, 23, 24, 27) have also employed it. But, in spite of its manifest advantages of simplicity and control, it is far from being a popular design in social research and indeed is usually relegated to an inferior position in discussions of experimental designs if mentioned at all (e.g., 15, 16, 32). Why is this the case?

In the first place, it is often confused with Design 3. Even where Ss have been carefully assigned to experimental and control groups, one is apt to have an uneasiness about the design because one "doesn't know what the subjects were like before." This objection must be rejected, as our standard tests of significance are designed precisely to evaluate the likelihood of differences occurring by chance in such sample selection. It is true, however, that this design is particularly vulnerable to selection bias and where random assignment is not possible it remains suspect. Where naturally aggregated units, such as classes, are employed intact, these should be used in large numbers and assigned at random to the experimental and control conditions; cluster sampling statistics (18) should be used to determine the error term. If but one or two intact classrooms are available for each experimental treatment, Design 4 should certainly be used in preference.

A second objection to Design 6, in comparison with Design 4, is that it often has less precision. The difference scores of Design 4 are less variable than the posttest scores of Design 6 if there is a pretest-posttest correlation above .50 (15, p. 323), and hence for test-retest correlations above that level a smaller mean difference would be statistically significant for Design 4 than for Design 6, for a constant number of cases. This advantage to Design 4 may often be more than dissipated by the costs and loss in experimental efficiency resulting from the requirement of two testing sessions, over and above the considerations of representativeness.

Design 4 has a particular advantage over Design 6 if experimental mortality is high. In Design 4, one can examine the pretest scores of lost cases in both experimental and control groups and check on their comparability. In the absence of this in Design 6, the possibility is opened for a mean difference resulting from differential mortality rather than from individual change, if there is a substantial loss of cases.

A final objection comes from those who wish to study the relationship of pretest attitudes to kind and amount of change. This is a valid objection, and where this is the interest, Design 4 or 5 should be used, with parallel analysis of experimental and control groups. Another common type of individual difference study involves classifying persons in terms of amount of change and finding associated characteristics such as sex, age, education, etc. While unavailable in this form in Design 6, essentially the same correlation can be obtained by subdividing both experimental and control groups in terms of the associated characteristics, and examining the experimental-control difference for such subtypes.

For Design 6, the Posttest-Only Control Group Design, there is a class of social settings in which it is optimally feasible, settings which should be more used than they now are. Whenever the social contact represented by *X* is made to single individuals or to small groups, and where the response to that stimulus can be identified in terms of individuals or types of *X*, Design 6 can be applied. Direct mail and door-to-door contacts represent such settings. The alternation of several appeals from door-to-door in a fund-raising campaign can be organized as a true experiment without increasing the cost of the solicitation. Experimental variation of persuasive materials in a direct-mail sales campaign can provide a better experimental laboratory for the study of mass communication and persuasion than is available in any university. The well-established, if little-used, split-run technique in comparing alternative magazine ads is a true experiment of this type, usually limited to coupon returns rather than sales because of the problem of identifying response with stimulus type (20). The split-ballot technique (7) long used in public opinion polls to compare different question wordings or question sequences provides an excellent example which can obviously be extended to other topics (e.g., 12). By and large these laboratories have not yet been used to study social science theories, but they are directly relevant to hypotheses about social persuasion.

Multiple X Designs

In presenting the above designs, *X* has been opposed to No-*X*, as is traditional in discussions of experimental design in psychology. But while this may be a legitimate description of the stimulus-isolated physical science laboratory, it can only be a convenient shorthand in the social sciences, for any No-X period will not be empty of potentially change-inducing stimuli. The experience of the control group might better be categorized as another type of X, a control experience, an X_c instead of No-X. It is also typical of advance in science that we are soon no longer interested in the qualitative fact of effort or no-effect, but want to specify degree of effect for varying degrees of X. These considerations lead into designs in which multiple groups are used, each with a different X_1, X_2, X_3, X_n, or in multiple factorial design, as X_{1a}, X_{1b}, X_{2a}, X_{2b}, etc. Applied to Designs 4 and 6, this introduces one additional group for each additional X. Applied to 5, The Solomon Four-Group Design, two additional groups (one pretested, one not, both receiving X_n) would be added for each variant on X.

In many experiments, X_1, X_2, X_3, and X_n are all given to the same group, differing groups receiving the Xs in different orders. Where the problem under study centers around the effects of order or combination, such counterbalanced multiple X arrangements are, of course, essential. Studies of transfer in learning are a case in point (34). But where one wishes to generalize to the effect of each X as occurring in isolation, such designs are not recommended because of the sizable interactions among Xs, as repeatedly demonstrated in learning studies under such labels as proactive inhibition and learning sets. The use of counterbalanced sets of multiple Xs to achieve experimental equation, where natural groups not randomly assembled have to be used, will be discussed in a subsequent paper on compromise designs.

Testing for Effects Extended in Time

The researches of Hovland and his associates (14, 15) have indicated repeatedly that the longer range effects of persuasive Xs may be qualitatively as well as quantitatively different from immediate effects. These results emphasize the importance of designing experiments to measure the effect of X at extended periods of time. As the misleading early research on reminiscence and on the consolidation of the memory trace indicate (36), repeated measurement of the same persons cannot be trusted to do this if a reactive measurement process is involved. Thus, for Designs 4 and 6, two separate groups must be added for each posttest period. The additional control group cannot be omitted, or the effects of intervening history, maturation, instrument decay, regression, and mortality are confounded with the delayed effects of X. To follow fully the logic of Design 5, four additional groups are required for each posttest period.

True Experiments in Which O Is Not under E's Control

It seems well to call the attention of the social scientist to one class of true experiments which are possible without the full experimental control over both the "when" and "to whom" of both X and O. As far as this analysis has been able to go, no such true experiments are possible without the ability to control X, to withhold it from carefully randomly selected respondents while presenting it to others. But control over O does not seem so indispensable. Consider the following design.

$$A \quad X \quad O_1$$
$$A \qquad\ \ O_2$$

6. Posttest Only Design, where O cannot be withheld from any respondent

$$(O)$$
$$(O)$$
$$(O)$$

The parenthetical Os are inserted to indicate that the studied groups, experimental and control, have been selected from a larger universe all of which will get O anyway. An election provides such an O, and using "whether voted" rather than "how voted," this was Gosell's design (11). Equated groups were selected at time A, and the experimental group subjected to persuasive material designed to get out the vote. Using precincts rather than persons as the basic sampling unit, similar studies can be made on the content of the voting (6). Essential to this design is the ability to create specified randomly equated groups, the ability to expose one of these groups to X while withholding it (or providing X_2) from the other group, and the ability to identify the performance of each individual or unit in the subsequent O. Since such measures are natural parts of the environment to which one wishes to generalize, they are not reactive, and Design 4, the Pretest-Posttest Control Group Design, is feasible if O has a predictable periodicity to it. With the precinct as a unit, this was the design of Hartmann's classic study of emotional vs. rational appeals in a public election (13). Note that 5, the Solomon Four-Group Design, is not available, as it requires the ability to withhold O experimentally, as well as X.

FURTHER PROBLEMS OF REPRESENTATIVENESS

The interaction effect of testing, affecting the external validity or representativeness of the experiment, was treated extensively in the previous section, inasmuch as it was involved in the comparison of alternative designs. The present section deals with the effects upon representativeness of other variables which, while equally serious, can apply to any of the experimental designs.

The Interaction Effects of Selection

Even though the true experiments control selection and mortality for internal validity purposes, these factors have, in addition, an important bearing on representativeness. There is always the possibility that the obtained effects are specific to the experimental population and do not hold true for the populations to which one wants to generalize. Defining the universe of reference in advance and selecting the experimental and control groups from this at random would guarantee representativeness if it were ever achieved in practice. But inevitably not all those so designated are actually eligible for selection by any contact procedure. Our best survey sampling techniques, for example, can designate for potential contact only those available through residences. And, even of those so designated, up to 19 per cent are not contactable for an interview in their own homes even with five callbacks (37). It seems legitimate to assume that the more effort and time required of the respondent, the larger the loss through nonavailability and noncooperation. If one were to try to assemble experimental groups away from their own homes it seems reasonable to estimate a 50 per cent selection loss. If, still trying to extrapolate to the general public, one further limits oneself to docile preassembled groups, as in schools, military units, studio audiences, etc., the proportion of the universe systematically excluded through the sampling process must approach 90 per cent or more. Many of the selection factors involved are indubitably highly systematic. Under these extreme selection losses, it seems reasonable to suspect that the experimental groups might show reactions not characteristic of the general population. This point seems worth stressing lest we unwarrantedly assume that the selection loss for experiments is comparable to that found for survey interviews in the home at the respondent's convenience. Furthermore, it seems plausible that the greater the cooperation required, the more the respondent has to deviate from the normal course of daily events, the greater will be the possibility of nonrepresentative reactions. By and large, Design 6 might be expected to require less cooperation than Design 4 or 5, especially in the natural individual contact setting. The interactive effects of experimental mortality are of similar nature. Note that, on these grounds, the longer the experiment is extended in time the more respondents are lost and the less representative are the groups of the original universe.

Reactive Arrangements

In any of the experimental designs, the respondents can become aware that they are participating in an experiment, and this awareness can have an interactive effect, in creating reactions to X which would not occur had X been encountered without this "I'm a guinea pig" attitude. Lazarsfeld (19), Kerr (17), and Rosenthal and Frank (28), all have provided valuable discussions of this problem. Such effects limit generalizations to respondents having this awareness, and preclude generalization to the population encountering X with non-experimental attitudes. The direction of the effect may be one of negativism, such as an unwillingness to admit to any persuasion or change. This would be comparable to the absence of any immediate effect from discredited communicators, as found by Hovland (14). The result is probably more often a cooperative responsiveness, in which the respondent accepts the experimenter's expectations and provides pseudoconfirmation. Particularly is this positive response likely when the respondents are self-selected seekers after the cure that X may offer. The Hawthorne studies (21), illustrate such sympathetic changes due to awareness of experimentation rather than to the specific nature of X. In some settings it is possible to disguise the experimental purpose by providing plausible façades in which X appears as an incidental part of the background (e.g., 26, 27, 29). We can also make more extensive use of experiments taking place in the intact social situation, in which the respondent is not aware of the experimentation at all.

The discussion of the effects of selection on representativeness has argued against employing intact natural preassembled groups, but the issue of conspicuousness of arrangements argues for such use. The machinery of breaking up natural groups such as departments, squads, and classrooms into randomly assigned experimental and control groups is a source of reaction which can often be avoided by the use of preassembled groups, particularly in educational settings. Of course, as has been indicated, this requires the use of large numbers of such groups under both experimental and control conditions.

The problem of reactive arrangements is distributed over all features of the experiment which can draw the attention of the respondent to the fact of experimentation and its purposes. The conspicuous or reactive pretest is particularly vulnerable, inasmuch as it signals the topics and purposes of the experimenter. For communications of obviously persuasive aim, the experimenter's topical intent is signaled by the X itself, if the communication does not seem a part of the natural environment. Even for the posttest-only groups, the occurrence of the posttest may create a reactive effect. The respondent may say to himself, "Aha, now I see why we got that movie." This consideration justifies the practice of disguising the connection between O and X even for Design 6, as through having different experimental personnel involved, using different façades, separating the settings and times, and embedding the X-relevant content of O among a disguising variety of other topics.[5]

Generalizing to Other Xs

After the internal validity of an experiment has been established, after a dependable effect of X upon O has been found, the next step is to establish the limits and relevant dimensions of generalization not only in terms of populations and settings but also in terms of categories and aspects of X. The actual X in any one experiment is a specific combination of stimuli, all confounded for interpretative purposes, and only some relevant to the experimenter's intent and theory. Subsequent experimentation should be designed to purify X, to discover that aspect of the original conglomerate X which is responsible for the effect. As Brunswik (3) has emphasized, the representative sampling of Xs is as relevant a problem in linking experiment to theory as is the sampling of respondents. To define a category of Xs along some dimension, and then to sample Xs for experimental purposes from the full range of stimuli meeting the specification while other aspects of each specific stimulus complex are varied, serves to untie or unconfound the defined dimension from specific others, lending assurance of theoretical relevance.

In a sense, the placebo problem can be understood in these terms. The experiment without the placebo has clearly demonstrated that some aspect of the total X stimulus complex has had an effect; the placebo experiment serves to break up the complex X into the suggestive connotation of pill-taking and the specific pharmacological properties of the drug—separating two aspects of the X previously confounded.

---

[5] For purposes of completeness, the interaction of X with history and maturation should be mentioned. Both affect the generalizability of results. The interaction effect of history represents the possible specificity of results to a given historical moment, a possibility which increases as problems are more societal, less biological. The interaction of maturation and X would be represented in the specificity of effects to certain maturational levels, fatigue states, etc.

Subsequent studies may discover with similar logic which chemical fragment of the complex natural herb is most essential. Still more clearly, the sham operation illustrates the process of X purification, ruling out general effects of surgical shock so that the specific effects of loss of glandular or neural tissue may be isolated. As these parallels suggest, once recurrent unwanted aspects of complex Xs have been discovered for a given field, control groups especially designed to eliminate these effects can be regularly employed.

Generalizing to Other Os

In parallel form, the scientist in practice uses a complex measurement procedure which needs to be refined in subsequent experimentation. Again, this is best done by employing multiple Os all having in common the theoretically relevant attribute but varying widely in their irrelevant specificities. For Os this process can be introduced into the initial experiment by employing multiple measures. A major practical reason for not doing so is that it is so frequently a frustrating experience, lending hesitancy, indecision, and a feeling of failure to studies that would have been interpreted with confidence had but a single response measure been employed.

Transition Experiments

The two previous paragraphs have argued against the *exact* replication of experimental apparatus and measurement procedures on the grounds that this continues the confounding of theory-relevant aspects of X and O with specific artifacts of unknown influence. On the other hand, the confusion in our literature generated by the heterogeneity of results from studies all on what is nominally the "same" problem but varying in implementation, is leading some to call for exact replication of initial procedures in subsequent research on a topic. Certainly no science can emerge without dependably repeatable experiments. A suggested resolution is the *transition experiment*, in which the need for varying the theory-independent aspects of X and O is met in the form of a multiple X, multiple O design, one segment of which is an "exact" replication of the original experiment, exact at least in those major features which are normally reported in experimental writings.

Internal vs. External Validity

If one is in a situation where either internal validity or representativeness must be sacrificed, which should it be? The answer is clear. Internal validity is the prior and indispensable consideration. The optimal design is, of course, one having both internal and external validity. Insofar as such settings are available, they should be exploited, without embarrassment from the apparent opportunistic warping of the content of studies by the availability of laboratory techniques. In this sense, a science is as opportunistic as a bacteria culture and grows only where growth is possible. One basic necessity for such growth is the machinery for selecting among alternative hypotheses, no matter how limited those hypotheses may have to be.

SUMMARY

In analyzing the extraneous variables which experimental designs for social settings seek to control, seven categories have been distinguished: history, maturation, testing, instrument decay, regression, selection, and mortality. In general, the simple or main effects of these variables jeopardize the internal validity of the experiment and are adequately controlled in standard experimental designs. The interactive effects of these variables and of experimental arrangements affect the external validity or generalizability of experimental results. Standard experimental designs vary in their susceptibility to these interactive effects. Stress is also placed upon the differences among measuring instruments and arrangements in the extent to which they create unwanted interactions. The value for social science purposes of the Posttest-Only Control Group Design is emphasized.

References

1. Annis, A. D., & Meier, N. C. The induction of opinion through suggestion by means of planted content. *J. soc. Psychol.*, 1934, 5, 65-81.

2. Boring, E. G. The nature and history of experimental control. *Amer. J. Psychol.*, 1954, 67, 573-589.

3. Brunswik, E. *Perception and the representative design of psychological experiments.* Berkeley: Univer. of California Press, 1956.

4. Bugelski, B. R. A note on Grant's discussion of the Latin square principle in the design and analysis of psychological experiments. *Psychol. Bull.*, 1949, 46, 49-50.

5. Campbell, D. T. The indirect assessment of social attitudes. *Psychol. Bull.*, 1950, 47, 15-38.

6. Campbell, D. T. On the possibility of experimenting with the "Bandwagon" effect. *Int. J. Opin. Attitude Res.*, 1951, 5, 251-260.

7. Cantril, H. *Gauging public opinion*. Princeton: Princeton Univer. Press, 1944.

8. Collier, R. M. The effect of propaganda upon attitude following a critical examination of the propaganda itself. *J. soc. Psychol.*, 1944, 20, 3-17.

9. Crespi, L. P. The interview effect in polling. *Publ. Opin. Quart.*, 1948, 12, 99-111.

10. Fisher, R. A. *The design of experiments*. Edinburgh: Oliver & Boyd, 1935.

11. Gosnell, H. F. *Getting out the vote: an experiment in the stimulation of voting*. Chicago: Univer. of Chicago Press, 1927.

12. Greenberg, A. Matched samples. *J. Marketing*, 1953-54, 18, 241-245.

13. Hartmann, G. W. A field experiment on the comparative effectiveness of "emotional" and "rational" political leaflets in determining election results. *J. abnorm. soc. Psychol.*, 1936, 31, 99-114.

14. Hovland, C. E., Janis, I. L., & Kelley, H. H. *Communication and persuasion*. New Haven: Yale Univer. Press, 1953.

15. Hovland, C. I., Lumsdaine, A. A., & Sheffield, F. D. *Experiments on mass communication*. Princeton: Princeton Univer. Press, 1949.

16. Jahoda, M., Deutsch, M., & Cook, S. W. *Research methods in social relations*. New York: Dryden Press, 1951.

17. Kerr, W. A. Experiments on the effect of music on factory production. *Appl. Psychol. Monogr.*, 1945, No. 5.

18. Kish, L. Selection of the sample. In L. Festinger and D. Katz (Eds.), *Research methods in the behavioral sciences*. New York: Dryden Press, 1953, 175-239.

19. Lazarsfeld, P. F. Training guide on the controlled experiment in social research. Dittoed. Columbia Univer., Bureau of Applied Social Research, 1948.

20. Lucas, D. B., & Britt, S. H. *Advertising psychology and research*. New York: McGraw-Hill Book Co., 1950.

21. Mayo, E. *The human problems of an industrial civilization*. New York: The Macmillan Co., 1933.

22. McNemar, Q. A critical examination of the University of Iowa studies of environmental influences upon the IQ. *Psychol. Bull.*, 1940, 37, 63-92.

23. Menefee, S. C. An experimental study of strike propaganda. *Soc. Forces*, 1938, 16, 574-582.

24. Parrish, J. A., & Campbell, D. T. Measuring propaganda effects with direct and indirect attitude tests. *J. abnorm. soc. Psychol.*, 1953, 48, 3-9.

25. Payne, S. L. The ideal model for controlled experiments. *Publ. Opin. Quart.*, 1951, 15, 557-562.

26. Postman, L., & Bruner, J. S. Perception under stress. *Psychol. Rev.*, 1948, 55, 314-322.

27. Rankin, R. E., & Campbell, D. T. Galvanic skin response to Negro and white experimenters. *J. abnorm. soc. Psychol.*, 1955, 51, 30-33.

28. Rosenthal, D., & Frank, J. O. Psychotherapy and the placebo effect. *Psychol. Bull.*, 1956, 53, 294-302.

29. Schanck, R. L., & Goodman, C. Reactions to propaganda on both sides of a controversial issue. *Publ. Opin. Quart.*, 1939, 3, 107-112.

30. Solomon, R. W. An extension of control group design. *Psychol. Bull.*, 1949, 46, 137-150.

31. Star, S. A., & Hughes, H. M. Report on an educational campaign: the Cincinnati plan for the United Nations. *Amer. J. Sociol.*, 1949-50, 55, 389.

32. Stouffer, S. A. Some observations on study design. *Amer. J. Sociol.*, 1949-50, 55, 355-361.

33. Stouffer, S. A. Measurement in sociology. *Amer. sociol. Rev.*, 1953, 18, 591-597.

34. Underwood, B. J. *Experimental psychology.* Appleton-Century-Crofts, 1949.

35. Underwood, B. J. Interference and forgetting. *Psychol. Rev.*, 1957, 64, 49-60.

36. Underwood, B. J. *Psychological research.* New York: Appleton-Century-Crofts, 1957.

37. Williams, R. Probability sampling in the field: a case history. *Publ. Opin. Quart.*, 1950, 14, 316-330.

Julian C. Stanley

*Quasi-Experimentation**

This article by Stanley expands on a type of experimentation only touched upon briefly by Campbell in the preceding article. The value of this article lies in the clarity with which Stanley indicates that quasi-experimentation is not pseudo-experimentation, and that quasi-experimentation can prove very valuable when true experimentation is not possible. For a more definitive discussion of the various types of quasi-experimentation, the reader is referred to the reference below.

Julian C. Stanley, "Quasi-Experimentation," *School Review*, 73:197-205, 1965. Reprinted with permission.

In less than eight years the phrase "quasi-experimental design" has moved from the *Psychological Bulletin*[1] via Gage's *Handbook*[2] into educational research to become a serious contender with tired old "action research" for the less rigorous aspects of educational investigations. Will quasi-experimentation become another educational fad, misunderstood and misused for a while before being dropped in favor of some new false panacea? Is much of the quasi-experimentation being stirred up by the Campbell-Stanley *Handbook* chapter, despite its warnings, in fact pseudo-experimentation that would be treated better

---

* A paper read at the annual convention of the American Educational Research Association in Chicago, February 11, 1965. Gene V. Glass provided helpful comments about an earlier draft.

[1] Donald T. Campbell, "Factors Relevant to the Validity of Experiments in Social Settings," *Psychological Bulletin*, LIV (1957), 297-312.

[2] Donald T. Campbell and Julian C. Stanley, "Experimental and Quasi-experimental Designs for Research on Teaching," in *Handbook of Research on Teaching*, ed. N. L. Gage (Chicago: Rand McNally, 1963), pp. 171-246 (esp. pp. 204-7).

in a frankly associational framework? Some recent talk about finding ready-made quasi-experiments in extant collections of data makes me fearful. Let us, therefore, consider certain aspects of "quasi-" versus "true" experimentation and precautions that need to be observed.

A genuine comparative experiment requires that the experimenter manipulate two or more experimental conditions by assigning them at random—either simply or restrictedly—to the experimental units (or, what is the same, he assigns the experimental units at random to the experimental conditions). Randomization guarantees that, before the experiment begins, the means of the various conditions for *any* variable will differ only randomly. As R. A. Fisher[3] emphasized long ago, such randomization forms the basis for tests of statistical significance.

If the experimenter cannot or does not assign his experimental units at random to his experimental treatments, he performs something other than a "true" experiment. He may, for example, compare the incomes of a random sample of physicians, a random sample of lawyers, and a random sample of engineers by doing an analysis of variance. Because he did not assign occupations at random to persons, he conducts a status study, rather than an experiment. Occupational classification is undoubtedly confounded with a considerable number of characteristics of the persons, such as intelligence, age, sex, and years of education.

Using the analysis of variance or *t*-test does not change a status study into an experiment; the design of an investigation, rather than the analysis, distinguishes experiments from non-experiments.

QUASI-EXPERIMENTS

Intermediate between the frankly associational study and the experiment is a wide area called by Campbell[4] quasi-experimentation. The quasi-experimenter plans carefully, but he does not have full manipulative control of his experimental units. "The research person can introduce something like experimental design into his scheduling of data-collection procedures (e.g., the *when* and *to whom* of measurement), even though he lacks the full control over the scheduling of experimental stimuli (the *when* and *to whom* of exposure and the

---

[3] Ronald A. Fisher, *Statistical Methods for Research Workers* (Edinburgh: Oliver & Boyd, 1925).

[4] *Op. cit.*, and his "Quasi-experimental Design" in *International Encyclopedia of the Social Sciences*, ed. David L. Sills (1968), 5:259.

ability to randomize exposures) which makes a true experiment possible."[5]

In Gage's *Handbook*, Campbell and Stanley[6] offer a number of quasi-experimental designs that are deliberately "patched up" to guard against restricted generalizability of results and certain sources of bias in the estimation of treatment effects. I shall not attempt to treat them again here. Instead, I shall discuss briefly four experimental situations that illuminate certain important points.

First, recall the attempts a decade or so ago to raise the IQ's of mentally retarded children by administering glutamic acid to them. It took a series of supposedly true experiments to disconfirm initial clinical impressions that this chemical increased IQ to some extent because the early testers knew which children had been administered glutamic acid and which had not.[7] Individual mental tests permit enough wish-fulfilment to make the treated children seem, on the average, superior. Even true experimentation calls for much methodological sophistication and care in order to rule out plausible alternative hypotheses.[8] We do well to study the medical-research literature on placebos and double-blind procedures and also to recognize the many special pitfalls that characterize educational research.

QUASI-EXPERIMENTATION IN THE NINETEENTH CENTURY

Now let me hark back to the oldest quasi-experiment I know of, which was conducted with commendable sophistication on a large scale before coefficients of correlation, *t*-tests, and tables of random numbers were known to the investigator performing it. A Philadelphia physician-turned-educational-researcher, Dr. Joseph M. Rice, began his researches concerning spelling in February of 1895 and continued them for sixteen months. His results appeared in the April and June 1897 issues of *Forum*.[9]

Rice wished to ascertain whether teaching spelling a long while each day was more effective than teaching it only a few minutes and whether "mechanical" methods of teaching produced better spellers

---

[5] Campbell and Stanley, *op. cit.*, p. 204.

[6] *Ibid.*

[7] Alexander W. Astin and Sherman Ross, "Glutamic Acid and Human Intelligence," *Psychological Bulletin*, LVII (1960), 429-34.

[8] Campbell and Stanley, *op. cit.*

[9] Joseph M. Rice, "The Futility of the Spelling Grind: I and II," *Forum*, XXIII (1897), 163-72, 409-19.

than did "progressive" methods. In an educational researcher's utopia he might have been able to stratify a large population of classes on such classification variables as geographical location, size of city, size of school, type of school (e.g., public or private), socioeconomic level of community, and school grade and then to draw a stratified random sample of classes to which the experimental conditions would have been assigned at random. He might, for example, have used six experimental conditions, say 15, 30, and 45 minutes per day of spelling instruction combined with either of two methods of instruction.

Like most of us today, Rice had no such control of spelling curricula; so, instead of manipulating the variables himself, he merely observed carefully the associations of the variables as manipulated by "nature" (i.e., by various school systems and teachers) with the results of three spelling tests that he devised. (In 1918 Ayres called Rice "the real inventor of the comparative test.")[10] The extent and scope of his investigation are awesome even in this day of mass research. He secured test results in twenty-one cities on 13,000 children under his own direction and on 16,000 more by mail.

Although Rice almost certainly did not think in terms of experiments versus quasi-experiments, he soon became aware of experimental pitfalls and of plausible alternative hypotheses counter to the over-all trend of his data. Some quotations from his articles, based on extensive tables, make this clear.

> I decided to undertake a special tour for the purpose of obtaining more definite information from the teachers who had taken part in the test [by mail]. During this tour, which extended over a period of two months, more than two hundred teachers were visited. Long before I had reached the end of my journey my fondest hopes had fled; for I had learned from many sources that the unusually favorable results in certain class-rooms did not represent the natural conditions, but were due to the peculiar manner in which the examinations had been conducted.[11] [Some teachers had enunciated too plainly and strongly the difficult portions of certain words the pupils were to spell.]
>
> Just as it is impossible by the results to distinguish the mechanical from the progressive schools, so it is impossible to distinguish the

---

[10] Leonard P. Ayers, "History and Present Status of Educational Measurements," in *Seventeenth Yearbook of the National Society for the Study of Education*, Part II (Chicago: University of Chicago Press, 1918), p. 11.

[11] Rice, *op. cit.*, p. 165.

schools attended by the children of cultured parents from those representing the foreign laboring element. . . . So far as spelling is concerned, the influence of environment appears to be insignificant.[12] [But Rice seems to have overlooked differential dropouts from grade 4 to grade 8 as a plausible alternative explanation.]

As in most localities, the general results were nearly equal. . . . It is clear that the remedy does not lie in a change of method, nor in an increase of time.[13]

Eight years before Binet published his first crude scale for measuring intelligence, Rice wrote, "The younger children in a class are frequently the brighter and more mature, having overtaken the older pupils by reason of these characteristics. Moreover, . . . the best spellers are to be found, as a rule, among the brightest pupils . . . , which indicates the influence of intellect on spelling."[14] He does not tell us how he arrived at his four categories of intellect, however; presumably, they were based on teacher judgments, which probably were not uninfluenced by a child's spelling ability.

The picture is complicated by three further statements: "The influence of nationality on spelling is nil. . . . The influence of heredity on spelling must also be put down as immaterial. . . . Home environment exerts, apparently, as little influence on spelling as the other factors that I have discussed."[15] Probably dropping out of school was closely related to socioeconomic status in 1895, even in grades 4-8, so, in the light of present knowledge, we might wish to investigate differential dropout as an alternative hypothesis, even through spelling ability may be correlated only very moderately with other intellectual abilities.

Rice concludes his second article by asserting that "the results obtained by forty or fifty minutes' daily instruction were not better than those obtained where not more than ten or fifteen minutes had been devoted to the subject."[16] He appears convinced by his subanalyses that there was no compensatory mechanism at work whereby the potentially poorest spellers in his study had the most instruction; the potentially average spellers, less; and the potentially best spellers, least. True experimentation would have ruled out this possibility by randomization.

---

[12] *Ibid.*, p. 171.
[13] *Ibid.*, p. 172.
[14] *Ibid.*, p. 409.
[15] *Ibid.*, p. 411.
[16] *Ibid.*, p. 412.

LINKING SMOKING TO LUNG CANCER

In recent years we have heard through the press of one large-scale experiment that tested a vaccine for poliomyelitis against a placebo, and of a sequential quasi-experiment that finally established, to the satisfaction of most but not all thoughtful people, high probability for a causal linkage between cigarette smoking and lung cancer (i.e., if you smoke cigarettes, you increase substantially the likelihood that you will develop lung cancer). The latter started with the observation that a considerably larger number of the victims of lung cancer were smokers than were non-smokers.

Immediately, plausible hypotheses alternative to smoking suggested themselves, especially to heavy smokers. Might not lung cancer be due to air pollution, rather than smoking, and might not more of the smokers than non-smokers come from urban areas where the air is polluted by industrial smog? If so, then there would be a confounding of smoking and air pollution. Diligent researchers hastened to compare lung-cancer rates for urban residents, smokers versus non-smokers, with those for rural residents, smokers versus non-smokers. Smoking still seemed to be a potent causative agent.

What about the sex of the lung-cancer patients, someone asked? Women smoke less than men, so if a smaller percentage of women have lung cancer, who is to say whether the causative agent is smoking or maleness? Researchers then observed lung-cancer rates among women who smoked heavily versus women who smoked little or none, and similarly for men. Smoking continued to seem implicated.

Many other alternative hypotheses were advanced and tested: age, base rates, tempo of living, alcohol consumption, etc. In the numerous subclassifications, the cigarette-smokers continued to have considerably greater incidence of lung cancer than did the non-smokers. Gradually, the alternative hypotheses proposed became more involved and complex, and, because of the scientific principle of parsimonious explanation, less plausible to researchers. *Associational analysis never can establish a causal linkage in the way that a carefully controlled true experiment can,* but in many scientific areas, particularly biology and astronomy, it has advanced our knowledge greatly. Even matching of smokers with non-smokers on a large number of possibly relevant background variables and comparing lung-cancer rates with other disease rates leaves us in doubt as to the generality of the findings, because one has to discard most of the subjects as being unmatchable.

We have to *assume* that results for the matched subjects hold for the discarded ones.[17]

Pehaps we should think of the many lung-cancer studies, including the true experiments with animals such as mice, as constituting a single quasi-experiment. This points up the usual futility of one-shot quasi-experiments. Even Rice, in 1895-96, had to conduct his quasi-experiment in two stages and reanalyze his data several ways. It is extremely unlikely that a researcher will find, already collected by someone else, just the material he needs in order to study, for example, the influence of class size on educational achievement. He may begin with such data, but in order to convince other researchers that a causal link probably does (or does not) exist, he will almost surely have to collect and analyze additional data. Actually, there are two somewhat distinct points here: a single study involving a naturally occurring variable is usually not enough, and data collected by others for other purposes seldom suffice.

RETROSPECTIVE QUASI-EXPERIMENTS

A special class of quasi-experiment that presents unusual difficulties of execution and intepretation is the retrospective type. This is well illustrated by Templin's comparison of manuscript with cursive handwriting.[18] She secured samples of the handwriting of adults who as children had been taught one way or the other. Her basic problem was that manuscript- versus cursive-handwriting instruction was probably by no means essentially randomly assigned to the schools from which these children came. Differential community characteristics probably determined to an appreciable extent which method was used. Also those community characteristics probably were not related to her ability to locate the former students many years later.

In order to establish a causal link between method of handwriting instruction and legibility of handwriting of adults by retrospective quasi-experimentation, one would have to expend enormous effort to reject a considerable number of plausible alternative hypotheses. Very likely, some of these could not be tested at all, because the required data were never gathered or have been lost.

---

[17] See *Smoking and Health* (Public Health Service Publication No. 1103) (Washington, D.C.: Government Printing Office, 1964).

[18] Elaine M. Templin, "The Legibility of Adult Manuscript, Cursive, or Manuscript-cursive Handwriting Styles," in *New Horizons for Research in Handwriting*, ed. Virgil E. Herrick (Madison: University of Wisconsin Press, 1963), pp. 185-206.

Indicative of the primitive state of educational research is the fact that, so far as I can ascertain, there has never been a true experiment comparing the effects of manuscript with cursive handwriting, although all over the country one or the other or a combination of them is used regularly. Our schools "experiment" with children, in the sense that they regularly use procedures of unknown validity, but as yet true experimentation in educational contexts is rather rare. Perhaps, like certain audio-visual propagandists, we should proclaim that one true experiment with moderate power is worth dozens of status studies or quasi-experiments. Actually, of course, this is no either-or proposition. We need all kinds of research, provided (as Bridgman once said) the researcher "is doing his damndest with his mind, no holds barred."

CONCLUSION

For finding causal connections of the if-then sort, however, true experiments reign supreme, being the basis for (but not guaranteeing) "strong inference."[19] Quasi-experiments of the patched-up variety cleverly devised by Campbell are promising alternatives *if* their requirements and limitations are well recognized.[20] Trailing behind these, but still useful when other methods fail, is the quasi-experiment conducted by "nature," with independent variables such as amount of spelling instruction, smoking, class size, or handwriting method deeply entwined with confounding and interacting variables. Lowest on this list is the retrospective quasi-experiment.

Teasing causation from the snarl of naturally occurring relationships is a demanding undertaking. Quasi-experimentation is no simple pastime for the classroom teacher. It is no magic sequel to "action" research.

---

[19] John R. Platt, "Strong Inference," *Science*, CXLVI (1964), 347-52.

[20] "Factors Relevant to the Validity of Experiments in Social Settings," *op. cit.*; "Quasi-experimental Design," *op. cit.*; Campbell and Stanley, *op. cit.*; Gene V. Glass, "Evaluating Testing, Maturation, and Treatment Effects in a Pretest-Posttest Quasi-experimental Design," *American Educational Research Journal*, II (1965), 83-88.

C. J. Burke

Additive Scales
and Statistics

Basic courses in measurement always get around to a consideration of types of scales and the statistics that are appropriate to each type. Further, students are taught that such statistics as the mean, standard deviation, and the *t* test should only be applied when the data are at least at the level of an interval scale. This fact tends to cause some consternation since much data gathered in educational research are of doubtful interval scale level. In the present article, Burke argues that, at least to some extent, we can deal statistically with the numbers we collect without being overly concerned with drawing direct inferences to manipulating their referents. This argument should offer some justification to the educational researcher who has been dealing with numbers in this way.

C. J. Burke, "Additive Scales and Statistics," *Psychological Review*, 60:73-5, 1953. Reprinted with permission.

Psychological measurements do not possess the simple properties of the scales obtained for those basic dimensions of physics which have been designated as "fundamental magnitudes." The implications of this statement for quantitative psychology have been extensively studied and discussed with varying evaluations and recommendations. Frequently the recommendations have been such as to alter statistical practices, had they been followed.

Certain writers, notably Boring (2) and Stevens (6), have maintained that such statistical concepts as the sample mean and standard deviation presuppose, at the very least, a scale of equivalent units of some kind, thus casting doubt on the theoretical validity of extensive reliance on the *t* test, analysis of variance, and other statistical techniques widely used with psychological data. The resulting distrust of such widely used procedures has prompted Comrey (4) to seek their justification outside the strict limits of the traditional logic of measurement.

It is the purpose of the present paper to analyze this issue and to show that the use of the sample mean and standard deviation does no violence upon the data, whatever the properties of the measurement scale. Thus, the use of the usual statistical tests is limited only by the well-known statistical restrictions.

The argument to be given can be conducted from the axioms of probability and the axiomatic basis of measurement, but such detailed treatment would be merely pretentious, since the results which are necessary to establish the basic point are familiar to almost all psychologists.

THE NATURE OF MEASUREMENT SCALES

(The term "object" as used below should not be restricted to its usual meaning of "physical object"; rather it is to be interpreted with sufficient breadth to give the statements throughout this section meaning for psychological as well as physical measurement provided that the axioms can be satisfied.)

Objects which can be ordered on the basis of a pair of (physical, psychological, or other) relations are said to define a "dimension." For such objects there are two relations, objectual equality and objectual less-than-ness and the objects and relations satisfy the axioms of order reproduced by Comrey (4). Each object can be tagged with a number so that the numbers will satisfy a corresponding set of axioms. Thus there is a correspondence between the two systems:

(A) [Objects, objectual equality, objectual less-than-ness.]

(B) [Numbers, numerical equality, numerical less-than-ness.]

For some objects and relations, a further step is possible. An operation for combining the objects, "objectual addition," can be found such that the system:

(C) [Objects, objectual equality, objectual less-than-ness, objectual addition]

satisfies four additional axioms of combination (Comery [4]). When this is the case the objects can be tagged with numbers so that the system:

(D) [Numbers, numerical equality, numerical less-than-ness, numerical addition]

satisfies four corresponding additional axioms of combination. Thus, in this case, there is a correspondence between (C) and (D).

When the systems (C) and (D) exist and correspond, we say that the objects define an "extensive dimension" and the numbers an "additive scale." In this case, of course, the systems (A) and (B) also exist and correspond.

When the systems (A) and (B) exist and correspond, but the systems (C) and (D) do not, we say that the objects define an "intensive dimension" and the numbers a "rank-order scale."

These matters are discussed in great detail by Campbell (3) and, more adequately for psychologists, by Bergmann and Spence (1). Pertinent information is presented in papers by Comrey (4) and Gulliksen (5). For our purposes, it is important to note only that the classification of a scale as additive depends upon the presence or absence of a certain correspondence, expressed in sets of axioms, between the numbers of the scale and the objects to which they refer— with, of course, appropriate ordering relations and combinative operations for each.

THE NATURE OF STATISTICS

Statistical methods serve two major functions for psychologists.

a. They are used to summarize the salient features of individual sets of data.

b. They are used to test for differences between different experimental groups.

We shall discuss the second function in some detail, restricting our discussion to the simple case in which two groups are compared. In the typical psychological experiment the operations performed by the experimenter yield two or more sets of numbers. (In fact, unless the data exist in numerical form, means and standard deviations cannot be computed and the data are irrelevant for the present discussion.) It is obvious that two experimental groups will be judged alike or different in a given respect according as the collections of numbers classifying them in this respect are judged to be alike or different. It should be emphasized that we are here comparing the two sets of numbers *as numbers* and nothing else about them matters until after the statistical test has been made. The application of statistical techniques reflects merely our recognition of the unreliabilty of the small sets of numbers we have obtained and our unwillingness to perform the experiment again and again to determine whether the direction of the difference between our groups is reliable. We conceptualize a larger set of numbers, the statistical population, from which the sets of numbers we have obtained are two small samples, and inquire into the likelihood of two samples as disparate as we have observed arising from the given population. In answering this question, we often use the sample means and standard deviations as indices of important aspects of our collections of numbers. No interpretation other than this indicial one is intended. Means and standard deviations are used because they can always be computed, since numbers can always be added, subtracted, multiplied, and divided, and because means and standard deviations, conceived of merely as the results of operations with numbers, behave in certain lawful statistical ways.

In summary, the statistical technique begins and ends with the numbers and with statements about them. The psychological interpretation given to the experiment does take cognizance of the origin of the numbers but this is irrelevant for the statistical test as such.

Obviously, the same argument applies directly to the first function of statistics as well. The statement "The mean of these scores is 121" conveys in general the same kind of information as the statement "The median of these scores is 122."

The objection that a well-established unit is necessary before the mean and standard deviation can be computed since their value is altered by a change in the absolute value of the scores (Comrey [4]) loses cogency when one notices that the mean and median will be affected in precisely the same way by adding a given number to each number in the sample and that the standard deviation and the interquartile range will be changed in the same way by multiplying each number in the sample by a given number.

AN EXAMPLE

To establish the point in another way, we consider an example of a statistical test based on an additive measure. Suppose that we are presented with two sticks, A and B, of apparently equal lengths, fixed on opposite sides of a room, and asked which is longer. We measure them and obtain a larger number for A. The two numbers, however, are nearly the same and we decide to repeat the measurement "just to make sure." On this occasion, we obtain a larger value for B. We proceed until we have 100 measurements on each stick and wish to answer the question without taking further measurements.

There are two collections of 100 numbers each, one for stick A and one for stick B. We test the hypothesis that they differ only through the unreliability of the measurements. A moment's reflection will show that we are not at all concerned with the additive nature of the scale for length. In adding the 100 numbers to obtain a mean for the measurements on stick A, we treat them as numbers and as nothing else. We make no interpretations whatever about adding 100 sticks together—there are only two sticks. Moreover, our interpretation by means of the *t* test is unaffected by the choice of length units we have made, provided that the units are the same for the two sticks.

It is seen that the comparison of the sets of measurements on the two sticks differs in no essential way from the comparison of two sets of IQ's.

SUMMARY AND CONCLUSIONS

We have noted that: (*a*) The properties of a scale of measurement involve correspondences between sets of axioms about objects and numbers, with appropriate relations and operations. (*b*) Statistical methods begin and end with numbers.

From (*a*) and (*b*), we have deduced that the properties of a set of numbers as a measurement scale should have no effect upon the choice of statistical techniques for representing and interpreting the numbers.

References

1. Bergmann, G., & Spence, K. W. Logic of psychophysical measurement. *Psychol. Rev.*, 1944, 51, 1-24.

2. Boring, E. G. The logic of the normal law of error in mental measurement. *Amer. J. Psychol.*, 1920, 31, 1-33.

3. Campbell, N. R. *Physics, the elements*. London: Cambridge Univer. Press, 1920.

4. Comrey, A. L. An operational approach to some problems in psychological measurement. *Psychol. Rev.*, 1950, 57, 217-228.

5. Gulliksen, H. Paired comparisons and the logic of measurement. *Psychol. Rev.*, 1946, 53, 199-213.

6. Stevens, S. S. On the theory of scales of measurement. *Science*, 1946, 103, 677-680.

Jum Nunnally

The Place of
Statistics in Psychology

When looking at the journals, the reader is frequently impressed by the elegance of the statistical treatment of the data obtained. Upon closer examination, the statistical treatment begins to appear as the only elegant part of the research, and the reader is driven to the conclusion that—in spite of the fancy statistics—the old GIGO (garbage in, garbage out) rule still holds. In this article, Nunnally argues against some of the most common statistical models for use in psychology and offers some alternatives. If Nunnally's criticisms apply to psychological research, then they most certainly apply to educational research.

J. Nunnally, "The Place of Statistics in Psychology," *Educational and Psychological Measurement*, 20:641-50, 1960. Reprinted with permission.

Most psychologists probably will agree that the emphasis on statistical methods in psychology is a healthy sign. Although we sometimes substitute statistical elegance for good ideas and overembellish small studies with elaborate analyses, we are probably on a firmer basis than we were in the prestatistical days. However, it will be argued that there are some serious misemphases in our use of statistical methods, which are retarding the growth of psychology.

The purpose of this article is to criticize the use of statistical "hypothesis-testing" models and some related concepts. It will be argued that the hypothesis-testing models have little to do with the actual testing of hypotheses and that the use of the models has encouraged some unhealthy attitudes toward research. Some alternative approaches will be suggested.

Few, if any, of the criticisms which will be made were originated by the author, and, taken separately, each is probably a well-smitten "straw man." However, it is hoped that when the criticisms are brought together they will argue persuasively for a change in viewpoint about statistical logic in psychology.

WHAT IS WRONG

Most will agree that science is mainly concerned with finding functional relations. A particular functional relationship may be studied either because it is interesting in its own right or because it helps clarify a theory. The functional relations most often sought in psychology are correlations between psychological variables, and differences in central tendency in differently treated groups of subjects. Saying it in a simpler manner, psychological results are usually reported as correlation coefficients (or some extension thereof, such as factor analysis) and differences between means (or some elaboration, such as a complex analysis of variance treatment).

Hypothesis Testing

After an experiment is completed, and the correlations or differences between means have been obtained, the results must be interpreted. The experimenter is aware of sampling error and realizes that if the experiment is run on different groups of subjects the obtained relations will probably not be the same. How then should he take into account the chance element in the obtained relationship? In order to interpret the results, the experimenter would, as most of us have, rely on the statistical models for hypothesis testing. It will be argued that the hypothesis-testing models are inappropriate for nearly all psychological studies.

Statistical hypothesis testing is a decision theory: you have one or more alternative courses of action, and the theory leads to the choice of one or several of these over the others. Although the theory is very useful in some practical circumstances (such as in "quality control"), it is misnamed. It has very little to do with hypothesis testing in the way that hypotheses are tested in the work-a-day world of scientific activity.

The most misused and misconceived hypothesis-testing model employed in psychology is referred to as the "null-hypothesis" model. Stating it crudely, one null hypothesis would be that two treatments do not produce different effects in the long run. Using the obtained means and sample estimates of "population" variances, probability statements can be made about the acceptance or rejection of the null hypothesis. Similar null hypotheses are applied to correlations, complex experimental designs, factor-analytic results, and most all experimental results.

Although from a mathematical point of view the null-hypothesis models are internally neat, they share a crippling flaw: in the real world the null hypothesis is almost never true, and it is usually nonsensical to perform an experiment with the *sole* aim of rejecting the null hypothesis. This is a personal point of view, and it cannot be proved directly. However, it is supported both by common sense and by practical experience. The common-sense argument is that different psychological treatments will almost always (in the long run) produce differences in mean effects, even though the differences may be very small. Also, just as nature abhors a vacuum, it probably abhors zero correlations between variables.

Experience shows that when large numbers of subjects are used in studies, nearly all comparisons of means are "significantly" different and all correlations are "significantly" different from zero. The author once had occasion to use 700 subjects in a study of public opinion. After a factor analysis of the results, the factors were correlated with individual-difference variables such as amount of education, age, income, sex, and others. In looking at the results I was happy to find so many "significant" correlations (under the null-hypothesis model)—indeed, nearly all correlations were significant, including ones that made little sense. Of course, with an N of 700 correlations as large as .08 are "beyond the .05 level." Many of the "significant" correlations were of no theoretical or practical importance.

The point of view taken here is that if the null hypothesis is not rejected, it usually is because the N is too small. If enough data is gathered, the hypothesis will generally be rejected. If rejection of the null hypothesis were the real intention in psychological experiments, there usually would be no need to gather data.

The arguments above apply most straightforwardly to "two-tail tests," which are used in most experiments. A somewhat better argument can be made for using the null hypothesis in the one-tail test. However, even in that case, if rejection of the null hypothesis is not obtained for the specified direction, the hypothesis can be reversed and rejection will usually occur.

Perhaps my intuitions are wrong—perhaps there are many cases in which different treatments produce the same effects and many cases in which correlations are exactly zero. Even so, the emphasis on the null-hypothesis models is unfortunate. As is well recognized, the mere rejection of a null-hypothesis provides only meager information. For example, to say that a correlation is "significantly" different from zero provides almost no information about the relationship. Some would argue that finding "significance" is only the first step, but how many psychologists ever go beyond this first step?

Psychologists are usually not interested in finding tiny relationships. However, once this is admitted, it forces either a modification or an abandonment of the null-hypothesis model.

An alternative to the null hypothesis is the "fixed-increment" hypothesis. In this model, the experimenter must state in advance how much of a difference is an important difference. The model could be used, for example, to test the differential effect of two methods of teaching psychology, in which an achievement test is used to measure the amount of learning. Suppose that the regular method of instruction obtains a mean achievement test score of 45. In the alternative method of instruction, laboratory sessions are used in addition to lectures. The experimenter states that he will consider the alternative method of instruction better if, in the long run, it produces a mean achievement test score which is at least ten points greater than the regular method of instruction. Suppose that the alternative method actually produces a mean achievement test score of 65. The probability can then be determined as to whether the range of scores from 55 upwards covers the "true" value (the parameter).

The difficulty with the "fixed-increment" hypothesis-testing model is that there are very few experiments in which the increment can be stated in advance. In the example above, if the desired statistical confidence could not be found for a ten point increment, the experimenter would probably try a nine point increment, then an eight point increment, and so on. Then the experimenter is no longer operating with a hypothesis-testing model. He has switched to a *confidence-interval* model, which will be discussed later in the article.

The Small N Fallacy

Closely related to the null hypothesis is the notion that only enough subjects need be used in psychological experiments to obtain "significant" results. This often encourages experimenters to be content with very imprecise estimates of effects. In those situations where the dispersions of responses are small, only a small number of subjects is required. However, such situations are seldom encountered in psychology. The question, "When is the N large enough?" will be discussed later in the article.

Even if the object in experimental studies were to test the null hypothesis, the statistical test is often compromised by the small N. The tests depend on assumptions like homogeneity of variance, and the small N study is not sufficient to say how well the assumptions hold. The small N experiment, coupled with the null hypothesis, is usually an illogical effort to leap beyond the confines of limited data to document lawful relations in human behavior.

The Sampling Fallacy

In psychological experiments we speak of the group of subjects as a "sample" and use statistical sampling theory to assess the results. Of course, we are seldom interested only in the particular group of subjects, and it is reasonable to question the generality of the results in wider collections of people. However, we should not take the sampling notion too seriously, because in many studies no sampling is done. In many studies we are content to use any humans available. College freshmen are preferred, but in a pinch we will use our wives, secretaries, janitors, and anyone else who will participate. We should then be a bit cautious in applying a statistical sampling theory, which holds only when individuals are randomly or systematically drawn from a defined population.

The Crucial Experiment

Related to the misconceptions above are some misconceptions about crucial experiments. Before the points are argued, a distinction should be made between crucial designs and crucial sets of data. A crucial design is an agreed-on experimental procedure for testing a theoretical statement. Even if the design is accepted as crucial, a particular set of data obtained with the design may not be accepted as crucial.

Although crucial designs have played important parts in some areas of science, few of them are, as yet, available in psychology. In psychology it is more often the case that experimenters propose different designs for testing the same theoretical statement. Experimental designs that apparently differ in small ways often produce different relationships. However, this is not a serious bother. Antithetical results should lead to more comprehensive theory.

A more serious concern is whether particular sets of experimental data can be regarded as crucial. Even when different psychologists employ the same design they often obtain different relationships. Such inconsistencies are often explained by "sampling error," but this is not a complete explanation. Even when the N's are large, it is sometimes reported that Jones finds a positive correlation, Smith a negative correlation, and Brown a nil correlation. The results of psychological studies are sometimes particular to the experimenter and the time and place of the experiment. This is why most psychologists would place more faith in the results of two studies, each with 50 subjects, performed by different investigators in different places, than in the results obtained by one investigator for 100 subjects. Then we must be concerned not only with the sampling of people but with the sampling of experimental environments as well. The need to "sample" experimental environments is much greater in some types of studies than in others. For example, the need probably would be greater in group dynamic studies than in studies of depth perception.

WHAT SHOULD BE DONE

Estimation

Hypotheses are really tested by a process of *estimation* rather than with statistical hypothesis-testing models. That is, the experimenter wants to determine what the mean differences are, how large the correlation is, what form the curve takes, and what kinds of factors occur in test scores. If, in the long run, substantial differences are found between effects or if substantial correlations are found, the experimenter can then speak of the theoretical and practical implications.

To illustrate our dependence on estimation, analysis of variance should be considered primarily an estimation device. The variances and ratios of variances obtained from the analysis are unbiased estimates of different effects and their interactions. The proper questions to ask are, "How large are the separate variances?" and "How much of the total variance is explained by particular classifications?" Only as a minor question should we ask whether or not the separate sources of variance are such as to reject the null hypothesis. Of course, if the results fail to reject the null hypothesis, they should not be interpreted further; but if the hypothesis is rejected, this should be considered only the beginning of the analysis.

Once it is realized that the basis for testing psychological hypotheses is that of estimation, other issues are clarified. For example, the Gordian-knot can be cut on the controversial issue of "proving" the null hypothesis. If, in the long run, it is found that the means of two differently treated groups differ inconsequentially, there is nothing wrong with believing the results as they stand.

Confidence Intervals

It is not always necessary to use a large N, and there are ways of telling when enough data has been gathered to have faith in statistical estimates. Most of the statistics which are used (means, variances, correlations, and others) have known distributions, and, from these, confidence intervals can be derived for particular estimates. For example, if the estimate of a correlation is .50, a confidence interval can be set for the inclusion of the "true" value. It might be found in this way that the probability is .99 that the "true" value[1] is at least as high as .30. This would simply supply a great deal more information than to reject the null hypothesis only.

The statistical hypothesis-testing models differ in a subtle, but important, way from the confidence methods. The former make decisions for the experimenter on an all-or-none basis. The latter tell the experimenter how much faith he can place in his estimates, and they indicate how much the N needs to be increased to raise the precison of estimates by particular amounts.

The null-hypothesis model occurs as a special case of the confidence models. If, for example, in a correlational study the confidence interval covers zero, then, in effect, the null hypothesis is not rejected. When this occurs it usually means that not enough data has been gathered to answer the questions at issue.

Discriminatory Power

In conjunction with making estimates and using confidence methods with those estimates, methods are needed for demonstrating the strength of relationships. In correlational studies, this need is served by the correlations themselves. In measuring differences in central tendency for differently treated groups, no strength-of-relationship measure is generally used.

One measure that is sometimes used is obtained by converting mean differences for two groups into a point-biserial correlation. This is

---

[1] Technically, it would be more correct to say that the probability is .99 that the range from .30 to 1.00 covers the parameter.

easily done by giving the members of one group a "group score" of 1 and the members of the other group a "group score" of 2 (any other two numbers would serve the purpose). The dichotomous "group scores" are then correlated with the dependent variable. When the N is large, it is an eye-opener to learn what small correlations correspond to "highly significant" differences.

There is a general strength-of-relationship measure that can be applied to all comparisons of mean differences. The statistic is Epsilon, which was derived by Kelley (1935) and extended by Peters and Van Voorhis (1940). The latter showed how Epsilon applies to analysis of variance methods and recommended its use in general. Their advice was not followed, and the suggestion here is that we reconsider Epsilon.

Epsilon is an unbiased estimate of the correlation ratio, Eta. It is unbiased because "degrees of freedom" are employed in the variance estimates. To show how Epsilon is applied, consider the one-classification analysis of variance results shown in Table 1.

Table 1
HYPOTHETICAL RESULTS ILLUSTRATING
THE USE OF EPSILON

Source	Sums of squares	df	Variance Est.
Experimental treatments (between column means)	510	4	127.50
Within columns	490	119	4.12
Total	1000	123	8.13

$$(\text{Epsilon})^2 = 1 - \frac{\text{Within var.}}{\text{Total var.}}$$

$$= 1 - \frac{4.12}{8.13}$$

$$= .49$$

$$\text{Epsilon} = .70$$

Epsilon is obtained by dividing the error variance (in the example in Table 1, the within columns variance) by the total variance, subtracting that from one, and taking the square-root of the result. The one classification in Table 1 explains 49 per cent of the total variance, which shows that the classification has high discriminatory power. Of course, in this case, the null hypothesis would have been rejected, but that is not nearly as important as it is to show that the classification produces strong differences.

Whereas Epsilon was applied in Table 1 to the simplest analysis of variance design, it applies equally well to complex designs. Each classification produces an Epsilon, which shows directly the discriminatory power of each (See Peters and Van Voorhis, 1940).

Epsilon is simply a general measure of correlation. If levels within a classification are ordered on a quantitative scale and regressions are linear, Epsilon reduces to the familiar r.

A Point of View

Statisticians are not to blame for the misconceptions in psychology about the use of statistical methods. They have warned us about the use of the hypothesis-testing models and the related concepts. In particular they have criticized the null-hypothesis model and have recommended alternative procedures similar to those recommended here (See Savage, 1957; Tukey, 1954; and Yates, 1951).

People are complicated, and it is hard to find principles of human behavior. Consequently, psychological research is often difficult and frustrating, and the frustration can lead to a "flight into statistics." With some, this takes the form of a preoccupation with statistics to the point of divorcement from the headaches of empirical study. With others, the hypothesis-testing models provide a quick and easy way of finding "significant differences" and an attendant sense of satisfaction.

The emphasis that has been placed on the null hypothesis and its companion concepts is probably due in part to the professional milieu of psychologists. The "reprint race" in our universities induces us to publish hastily-done, small studies and to be content with inexact estimates of relationships.

There is a definite place for small N studies in psychology. A chain of small studies, each elaborating and modifying the hypotheses and procedures, can eventually lead to a good understanding of a domain of behavior. However, if such small studies are taken out of context and considered (or published) separately, they usually are of little value, even if null hypotheses are successfully rejected.

Psychology had a proud beginning, and it would be a pity to see it settle for the meager efforts which are encouraged by the use of the hypothesis-testing models. The original purpose was to find lawful relations in human behavior. We should not feel proud when we see the psychologist smile and say "the correlation is significant beyond the .01 level." Perhaps that is the most that he can say, but he has no reason to smile.

References

Kelley, T. L. "An Unbiased Correlation Ratio Measure." *Proceedings of the National Academy of Science*, Washington, XXI (1935), 554-559.

Peters, C. C. and Van Voorhis, W. R. *Statistical Procedures and Their Mathematical Bases*. New York: McGraw-Hill, 1940.

Savage, R. J. "Nonparametric Statistics." *Journal of the American Statistical Association*, LII (1957), 332-333.

Tukey, J. W. "Unsolved Problems of Experimental Statistics." *Journal of the American Statistical Association*, XLIX (1954), 710.

Yates, F. "The Influence of *Statistical Methods for Research Workers* on the Development of the Science of Statistics." *Journal of the American Statistical Association*, XLVI (1951), 32-33.

Robert E. Chandler

The Statistical Concepts of Confidence and Significance

The concepts of confidence and significance are too frequently confused. It is not uncommon to hear such statements as, "We are using the 5 per cent level of confidence," or, as one of the editors heard, "The results were significant at the 1 per cent level of confidence." After reading Chandler's article, it is hoped that such horrifying statements will be stricken from the tongues of all researchers.

R. Chandler, "The Statistical Concepts of Confidence and Significance," *Psychological Review*, 54:429-30, 1957. Reprinted with permission.

Recently there have been at least three different book reviewers who have commented on the confusion that currently exists in the psychological literature regarding the statistical concepts of confidence and significance (2, 7, 9). Although this confusion can be partially explained as a semantic problem, it behooves the psychologist to examine these two concepts rather closely and to adopt pristine terminology for the benefit of beginning students and individuals of other disciplines that draw rather heavily upon the psychological literature.

CONFIDENCE AND CONFIDENCE COEFFICIENTS

Confidence, a concept customarily reserved for discussions of interval estimation, is the faith which one is willing to place in a statement that an interval established by a sampling process actually contains or bounds a parameter of interest. One generally expresses this faith statistically by affixing to each interval a confidence coefficient, or confidence probability, which can be written as $1 - \epsilon$, where $\epsilon = p/100$, for $0 \leq p \leq 100$, and p is usually taken to be a very small number (1, 3, 6, 8). For example, if $p = 5$ the confidence coefficient would be .95, and one would refer to the interval with which this coefficient is associated as the 95% confidence interval.

The confidence coefficient is frequently interpreted in the following manner: If one were to draw samples of size K from a population of N elements (K naturally being $< N$) and from each sample establish a 95% confidence interval on some specified parameter of the population, then in the long run about 95% of the totality of these intervals would actually contain the parameter of interest, and approximately 100 ϵ%, or 5%, of them would not (3). This interpretation is correct, but of course assumes $\binom{N}{K}$ to be a rather large number.[1]

SIGNIFICANCE AND SIGNIFICANCE LEVELS

Significance, as contrasted to confidence, is given to the testing of hypotheses. Here one makes a statement, i.e., states an hypothesis, which will hereafter in this discussion be represented as H, that may be either true or false and then takes action on this H by accepting or rejecting it. Clearly, any one of the following actions is a likely outcome as a result of testing an H: (a) rejection of a false H; (b) acceptance of a true H; (c) rejection of a true H; or (d) acceptance of a false H. It is quite evident that actions (a) and (b) are desirable, while (c) and (d) carry the connotation of committing an error—c being the familiar Type I error or an error of the first kind, while d is called a Type II error or an error of the second kind (4, 8).

When one tests an H, the probability that he will take action c is defined as the significance level, which we will represent as α (8). Although α is generally of the same order of magnitude as ϵ, α and ϵ differ in the amount of information which they convey, for while ϵ completely tells all there is to know about "being wrong" in interval estimation, α only gives information about a very particular type of error, i.e. the action described by c. To emphasize the contrast made here between α and ϵ, one merely needs to examine the other type of error that can be made in the test of an H.

---

[1] The notation $\binom{N}{K}$ is used here as a combinational symbol to indicate the number of ways that K objects can be selected from N.

For this purpose, let β represent the probability that action d is taken, i.e. a Type II error is committed; then, by definition, $1 - \beta$ is known as the power of the statistical test or the probability that action a will occur (4, 8). Although texts in psychological statistics do not seem to place a great deal of emphasis upon the power of a test, power is the basic concept responsible for one's employing statistical tests as a basis for taking action on an H. If this were not so, to test an H at the 5% level of significance, one could simply draw from a box of 100 beads—95 white and 5 red—a bead at random and adopt the convention that he would reject the H whenever a red bead appeared. With such a test, one can readily see that not only α but also $1 - \beta$ always equals .05, or $\beta = .95$. It is this large value of β that precludes one's employing the bead-box test. For an excellent discussion of β and its relation to the alternative H against which one might be testing, the reader is referred to Dixon and Massey (4, pp. 244-261).

SUMMARY AND DISCUSSION

The admixing of the concepts of confidence and significance has become so prevalent in the psychological literature that one typically reads statements, in the reports of psychological research, indicating that certain experimental results were significant at, say, the 5% "level of confidence."

It may be that this confusion arises from the fact that one can utilize a confidence interval as a significance test (e.g., see 5, p. 241), and in doing so may hastily, but incorrectly, conclude that there is no difference between the two concepts.

Inasmuch as explicit terminology is needed to convey the probabilities of committing statistical errors in the respective areas of interval estimation and testing of hypotheses, the concept of confidence should never be associated with the statistical test of an H regardless of the nature of the test being employed.

References

1. Anderson, R. L., & Bancroft, T. A. *Statistical theory in research.* New York: McGraw-Hill Book Co., 1952.

2. Chandler, R. E. A review of Guilford's *Fundamental statistics in psychology and education.* (*3rd ed.*) *Personnel Psychol.*, 1957, 10, 272-273.

3. Cramér, H. *Mathematical methods of statistics.* Princeton: University Press, 1951.

4. Dixon, W. J., & Massey, F. J., Jr. *Introduction to statistical analysis.* (2nd ed.) New York: McGraw-Hill Book Co., 1957.

5. Edwards, A. L. *Statistical methods for the behavioral sciences.* New York: Holt, Rinehart and Winston, Inc., 1954.

6. Hoel, P. G. *Introduction to mathematical statistics.* (2nd ed.) New York: John Wiley & Sons, Inc., 1954.

7. Milton, T. E. A review of Edwards' *Statistical methods for the behavioral sciences. J. Amer. statist. Ass.*, 1956, 51, 382.

8. Mood, A. M. *Introduction to the theory of statistics.* New York: McGraw-Hill Book Co., 1950.

9. Walker, H. M. A review of Adams' *Basic statistical concepts. Educ. psychol. Measmt*, 1956, 16, 554-557.

Joseph Weitz

Criteria for Criteria

In experimental research, changes in the dependent variable (the criterion variable) are used to evaluate the effectiveness of the independent variable. The choice of dependent variable may, however, considerably affect how the independent variable appears to function. In judging the effectiveness of a teaching method, for example, whether the dependent variable is student achievement, student attitude, or teacher attitude might make considerable difference in the findings. Further, whether the measurement was taken immediately after the treatment or after a lapse of time might also make quite a difference. In this article, Weitz discusses various aspects of the criterion variable and points out how different choices can radically change the probable evaluation of the effectiveness of the independent variable.

J. Weitz, "Criteria for Criteria," *American Psychologist*, 16:228-31, 1961. Reprinted with permission.

When one selects a criterion to evaluate the effectiveness of some independent variable, the choice is frequently made on one of several bases. Forgetting reliability for the moment, these might be summarized under the rubrics of relevance, expedience, or precedence.

In the industrial area, for example, where studies of selection or training are under consideration, we try to use criterional measures which management feels are relevant to the situation, such as termination-survival, production, etc.

In learning studies we frequently use criteria which historically have been used by other investigators: number of trials necessary to a certain level of performance, latency of response, number of errors, etc.

In many instances we use criteria which are expedient. In these cases, certain behavioral measures are found readily available (or more available than those we would prefer to have), so we use them.

313

Since the criterion is a representation of the dependent variable, does the choice of the criterion have any effect on the results (or lack of them) attributed to the independent variable? If, for example, we are evaluating the effectiveness of two simulators as training devices, would our conclusions concerning the utility of these simulators vary depending upon whether we chose as our criterion: the length of time required on each simulator to reach some level of performance on the actual instrument itself, the number of errors on the actual device after N trials on each simulator, the speed with which a certain level of performance on the actual device can be reached, or the performance of individuals on the actual device 6 months after simulator training? All of these criteria can perhaps be thought of as "reasonable" yet our conclusions concerning the value of the simulator might vary, depending upon which one was chosen. If we are to evaluate our conclusions, do we not need to understand the effect of choosing a particular criterion?

I believe that certain dimensions of criteria should be studied. Given enough time and data, it should be possible to determine the effect of using criteria having certain characteristics as well as the relationships of these characteristics with those of independent variables.

Some of the criterional dimensions which might be studied are:

Time: When do you decide to take a measurement? If, for example, you are working in the field of training and are trying to determine whether training Procedure A is superior to Procedure B, when do you measure the effects of these two procedures: immediately following the training, during the training, 6 months later, or when? Far different results may occur depending on when the measurement is taken. And if this is so, conclusions reached may have to be modified depending on the time at which the measure is taken. This can also be true in areas other than training. When should we attempt to take measures of attitude change, effect of therapy, extinction of a response, etc.?

Type: What performance measure do you select and why that particular measure? If we consider a training study again, we might use as a criterion such variables as accidents, attitudinal measures, output measures, or a host of others. Or in learning we might use the number of errors, latency of response, or any of a variety of measures commonly used. Again, how dependent are our conclusions on the type of criterion we have selected? Usually our choice here is determined either by history or precedent but in some cases expediency and availability are the criteria for choosing the criteria.

Level: What level of the performance measure chosen is considered success or failure? Why that particular level? We frequently find reports which say an animal has "learned" if he responds correctly in 19 out of 20 successive trials. What is sacred about this figure? Why not 2 out of 3 or 50 out of 51? More important, what effect does the chosen level of performance have on the conclusions we reach? In selection testing, for example, we might say our criterion of success is producing 250 "grumbles" per hour or we might use as our criterion, producing at or above the average number of "grumbles" produced in one hour by a certain group of "grumble" makers. Does it matter in evaluating the test?

By studying the effect of these dimensions, and probably others, across a variety of areas, it should be possible to obtain some lawful generalizations. The sort of generalizations to which I am referring might be such things as these:

1. The shorter the time period between the introduction of the independent variable and the measurement of the dependent variable (criterion), the greater/less the likelihood of showing that the independent variable is effective.

2. The more clearly the criterion measure used resembles what might be thought of as "ultimate" criteria, the greater/less the likelihood of showing the independent variable is effective.

3. The easier the task to be performed, the more/less difficult the level of the criterion must be in order to show that the independent variable is effective.

These are some types of general hypotheses and are meant only to be illustrative. Actually the entire function relating these variables should be studied. The best guess is that the function describing any of these relationships may well be curvilinear.

Let us now examine some data to see how we would approach this problem. In studying these data we shall interest ourselves in two variables: the type of criterion selected and the level of the criterion.

The study to be discussed was performed by Cramer and Cofer (1960)[1] and was reported, in part, at the 1960 APA meeting. The purpose of the investigation was to determine the role of verbal associations in mediating transfer of learning from one list of paired associates to another.

---

[1] The author wishes to express his appreciation to Phebe Cramer and Charles Cofer for providing him with their original data.

The procedure was first to learn a set of paired associates composed of zero-association value nonsense syllables and words, then another list composed of the same nonsense syllables and other words. In the second learning half of the words (experimental) had forward association value (Kent-Rosanoff) of 30% and backward association of 0%. The other half of the words in the second learning were control words of equal Thorndike-Lorge frequency with the experimental words but nonassociated. There were eight words in all, four experimental and four control.

Various paradigms were used so that the original learning consisted of nonsense syllable-word, or word-nonsense syllable. In certain of the paradigms, forward association was possible and in others backward associations were possible. Examples of some of these paradigms are as follows:

Original Learning	New Learning	
GEX-Justice	GEX-Peace	(experimental word, forward association)
GEX-Peace	GEX-Justice	(experimental word, backward association)
Peace-GEX	Justice-GEX	(experimental word-nonsense syllable)
WUB-Tobacco	WUB-Butter	(nonsense syllable-control words)

Eighteen trials were given in the original learning, followed by a one-minute rest period. The new list learning then began and continued for eight trials.

The measure of the effectiveness of meditation on the new list learning used by Cramer and Cofer was the number of correct responses to the first members of the experimental and control pairs in the test runs on Trials 1 and 2 of the second list learning. They report that the remaining six trials showed few differences of a significant nature.

They found facilitation of second list learning as measured by the average difference in number of correct responses between experimental and controls words on Trials 1 and 2.

According to the findings of Cramer and Cofer, facilitation of second list learning occurred in all paradigms whether the direction of the association was forward or backward.

What occurs if we now examine the data, using different criteria? It will be recalled that the criterion for evaluation used by Cramer and Cofer was the difference between the number of correct responses for the control words and the experimental words on both Trials 1 and 2 of the new list learning. Now let us take a different criterion of success: the number of trials to reach a certain percentage of correct response. That is, the number of trials required to reach 50%, 75%, 100% correct on any one trial, and a fourth criterion of 100% correct on two successive trials. Notice here we are not only using a slightly different type of criterion, but also various levels of this criterion.

For Paradigm A the experimental words are of the forward association type:

Original learning: GEX–Justice

New learning: GEX–Peace

In Paradigm B the experimental words are of the reverse association type:

Original learning: GEX–Peace

New Learning: GEX–Justice

Paradigm C consists of forward associations, but in this manner:

Original learning: Justice–GEX

New learning: Peace–GEX

Paradigm D is similar to C, but with the reverse associations:

Original learning: Peace–GEX

New learning: Justice–GEX

Now our analysis consists of determining the number of trials needed to reach each of the criteria for the control words and experimental words. If there is a mediational effect with both forward and backward association, will the experimental words, as opposed to the control words, show fewer trials required to meet the various criteria?

Figure 1 shows the average difference between the control and experimental words in the number of trials required to reach criterion.

It can be seen from these curves that for Paradigm B we find a relatively large difference between the control and experimental words if we chose as our criterion 75% correct.

For Paradigms A and C we reach a relative maximum difference at the 100% criterion and for Paradigm D we find that 100% twice in succession gives us the maximal effect.

Notice that if we used certain criteria as opposed to others, we would come to quite different conclusions. For example, using 100% correct on two successive trials for Paradigm A, we would have concluded that there was no mediational effect. But for other criteria (100% correct on one trial) there is a significant difference between the control and experimental words.

In examining the paradigms we find differences in ease of learning. The order of difficulty turns out to be D easiest, C next, A next, and B hardest. This fits, in part, with other studies which indicate that S_1–R_1 then S_1–R_2 type of learning is more difficult than S_1–R_1 then S_2–R_1 type of learning. That is, learning two different responses to the same stimulus is more difficult than learning the same response to two different stimuli.

Let us look at Paradigms D and B. B is more difficult to learn than D. Before the data were analyzed (honestly!) the hypothesis was made that the more difficult the task, the easier the criterion should be

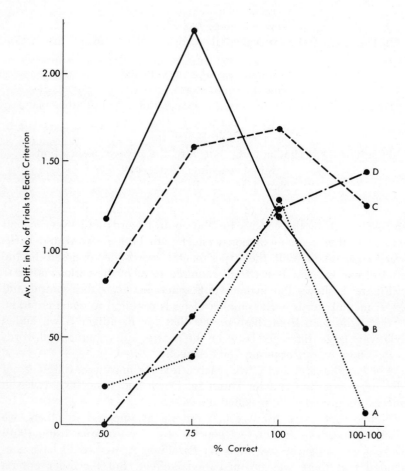

Figure 1.   *Average difference between control and experimental words in trials to reach criteria*

in order to show an effect of the independent variable; conversely, the easier the task, the more difficult the criterion should be in order to show an effect. In examining these data we see that this is precisely what we find. For Paradigm B a criterion of 75% is most sensitive in showing an effect and for Paradigm D, two successive trials of 100% shows the maximal effect. This same finding has been substantiated on data from other similar learning studies performed by Cramer and Cofer. That is, a more difficult criterion showed maximal effects for easier tasks and easier criteria showed maximal effects when difficult tasks were involved.

The importance of this finding is that, depending upon the criterion chosen, we might radically change the conclusions reached in this type of investigation.

The foregoing discussion is presented only to show the type of analysis which I believe should be made across a variety of experimental areas. It would be helpful, of course, if studies were carried out so that data could be observed for longer time periods (or more trials). This would enable one to evaluate not only the importance of criterion level, but also the effect of time at which measurements are taken. Time may be an especially important variable when attempting to obtain criteria for selection tests or in such areas as evaluating the effectiveness of certain kinds of therapy.

This approach raises the question of how frequently do we say a given procedure was ineffective in producing the hypothesized result because the criterion was of such a nature that it was "inappropriate?" For example, Crawford and Vanderplas (1959) find little evidence for mediation in a learning study not too dissimilar from Cramer and Cofer. If you examine the criteria used in these two investigations you find them quite different. At what conclusions should we then arrive? Is there or is there not mediation in paired associate learning? If the criterion chosen determines the conclusions of a study, is this not an important parameter in and of itself?

An example of an instance where the criterion might be an important parameter is in the work reported by Bitterman (1960). He was interested in a "comparative psychology of learning" and in his article he describes a number of interesting studies on a variety of animals. The investigator was apparently not as much concerned with whether fish, for example, learn faster or better than rats, but whether they learn differently. In other words, how does learning theory, built in large part from observations of the rat, fit the findings obtained from other species? This is an interesting approach. Where differences between species occur, say, in the acquisition or extinction of a habit, can the neurological organization of the animal give new insights into learning theory, and can we get greater understanding from this approach concerning brain functions?

In a series of ingenious experiments the author showed differences among species in such behavior as acquisition of habits, reversal learning, and extinction. Care was taken to manipulate such variables as motivational states, and an attempt was made to take into account various sensory differences. The one thing which disturbed me was the fact that frequently the criterion used, let us say for extinction, was the same for a fish as for a rat. Now if differences in extinction to a certain criterion *do* occur, can we say our theoretical framework must be altered, or is it possible that a criterion of performance like behaving in a particular way on 17 out of 20 trials is a different level of difficulty for a rat and a fish? If the level of difficulty is different, then can we conclude necessarily that the functions obtained are in fact dissimilar? Perhaps criterional measures should be one of the parameters in investigations of this sort.

The criterion, if properly understood, could give us further insights into the effect of the independent variable, and perhaps even help identify some of the intervening variables.

Once we know something of the nature of criterional variables and their effects on the outcomes and results attributed to the independent variable and after discovering some of the "laws" of criteria, we should be able to make clearer statements of our hypothesis. For example, should we ever set up an hypothesis stating something like: "Anxiety leads to a decrement in performance?" If we know something about criteria, we should be able to clarify our hypothesis, allowing us to state something of the nature of the performance we expect to be affected.

In substance, then, the measure of the dependent variable (the criteria) should give us more insight into the operation of the independent variable if we know the rules governing the operation of criterional measures.

Being able to make "cleaner" hypotheses, perhaps in the future we will be able to restate our anxiety hypothesis to read something like: "Anxiety leads to a decrement of A, B, C types of performance but not x, y, z kinds of performance." With this type of analysis of criteria, we should be able to determine not only the effect of anxiety on performance but also more about the nature of the relationship and in fact more about the nature of anxiety.

If we knew more about the functioning of criterional variables, we should be able to predict which criteria are relevant for assessing effects of independent variables and with this knowledge, be able to state more concerning the operation of the independent and the intervening variables.

References

Bitterman, M. E. Toward a comparative psychology of learning. *Amer. Psychologist*, 1960, 15, 704-712.

Cramer, P., & Cofer, C. N. The role of forward and reverse association in transfer of training. *Amer. Psychologist*, 1960, 15, 463. (Abstract)

Crawford, J. L., & Vanderplas, J. M. An experiment on the mediation of transfer in paired-associate learning. *J. Psychol.*, 1959, 47, 87-98.

Francis G. Cornell

Misuse of Statistics

It has been said that "figures don't lie, but liars can figure." Frequently, the worth of a particular research is evaluated by the statistics given, and these statistics can often be misleading. The numbers may be correct, but they may have been obtained in such a way as to make their interpretation meaningless for the point under discussion. In this article, Cornell points out some of the more frequent errors in the use of statistics.

Francis G. Cornell, "Misuse of Statistics," *Nations Schools* 58:58-60, September, 1956. Reprinted, with permission, from the *Nation's Schools*, September, 1956. Copyright, 1956, The Modern Hospital Publishing Co., Inc., Chicago. All rights reserved.

I like to think of statistics in three categories. First, there are figures —totals, averages of various sorts, measures of relationships such as correlation coefficients, and innumerable types of indices which describe some aspect of a phenomenon regarding schools and education. Second, there are the intricate theoretical and mechanical operations involved in advanced applications of statistical method. Finally, there is the gamut of fairly rudimentary ideas about the use of statistics in everyday decisions about school problems that are indispensable to good straight thinking.

THREE CONCEPTS OF STATISTICS

The first category has to do with how to compute a mean or a correlation coefficient or how to design a chart to portray some feature of schools or school populations. Most of this requires mathematical skill available to anyone with a ninth grade education and is now taught to everyone exposed to formal training in education. In large-scale operations most of this type of computing is now accomplished by means of mechanical and electronic devices.

Some of the second aspect, the theory, is available in courses in educational statistics, but statistical theory has been developing rapidly since World War II, and there is now enough content in mathematical statistics that several universities are offering doctorates in statistics. Fortunately, communication of statistical ideas is improving, and more and more of the advances in theory are filtering down to the practitioner.[1] This is an encouraging development, since the more our applications of statistics are derived from soundest mathematical thinking the more useful are the results.

It is not reasonable to expect educational leaders to become statisticians. All will have a course or two in statistics as a part of formal training. This will permit a knowledge of the commonest and most useful "figures" to compute in educational work and some of the theory of statistics which will help in planning effective studies and interpreting their results. But no matter how sophisticated the educator becomes technically in the subject of statistics, his decisions are useless if he is unable to work with the ideas which guide the intelligent use of statistics. Few practical applications of statistical method are complex. Usually misuse of statistics results from violations of some of the simplest rules of everyday thinking.

LOGIC, COMMON SENSE, AND STATISTICS

No statistical gadget automatically solves the problem. No single statistical index or coefficient has significance out of the context of the common sense or logic involved in the fact getting objective—whether it be purely the description of status or the testing of a hypothesis derived from highly systematized theoretical formulations. Statistical methods have been used in education as if they possessed some mystical quality of order and perfection. Statistical methods are often used in a mechanical manner as if they yielded absolute conclusions or laws

---

[1] A theory grounded, nonmathematical text is Francis G. Cornell's *Essentials of Educational Statistics*, New York, John Wiley & Sons, Inc., 1956. Contained in it are references to other sources which are of direct usefulness to the teacher or administrator.

of natural order. The method becomes the criterion. The researcher or the practitioner is lulled into this position by the comfort to him of thus being relieved of the onerous task of thinking. The I.Q., the normal curve, the correlation coefficient, factor analysis, and a long list of statistical technics are mechanically and blindly applied in this manner.

I shall not attempt to document the thoughtlessness which often is engendered by the paraphernalia of such methods. My point is simply this: More intelligence than the simple numerical manipulations of statistics is required for intelligent action and decision. In fact, an unintelligent use of statistical method can lead to some absurd conclusions.

Sometimes quantitative facts are purposely manipulated by unscrupulous persons bent on deliberately leading, through advertisements or other propaganda media, to conclusions favoring only one side of an argument. Yet, as often, these errors may be the errors of the person on the receiving end of the communication channel—the person responsible as an administrator or as a teacher for interpreting facts and, on the basis of them, taking necessary action. Or it may be the researcher who is off guard because he lacks experience with statistical methods or simply lacks good common sense and logic.

It is thus with considerable good sense that Darrell Huff has written a book called *How to Lie with Statistics.*[2] Frequently the statistical and logical slips that actually occur in daily life are more subtle than the more obvious and humorous examples which dramatize the principles violated. One such example is that of the observer who noted that persons who imbibed sufficient quantities of whiskey and water become intoxicated as did those who consumed sufficient quantities of gin and water. Applying the oversimplified canon of John Stuart Mill, expressed in "The Method of Agreement," the unwary observer concluded that since the common element in each circumstance was water, it was the water which produced the intoxication. Only an extreme naïveté concerning biochemistry would prevent one from seeing the "hidden cause" in this illustration. Similarly, only a few adults would be so ignorant of the basic verities of life that they would conclude men have more children than women from statistics showing that there are 1.8 children in families of Princeton graduates, but only 1.4 children in families of Vassar graduates.

---

[2] Huff, Darrell: *How to Lie with Statistics*, New York, W. W. Norton and Co., 1954.

At little chance of oversimplification, I list some of the more elementary principles of which one must be aware in understanding processes of school systems.

ERRORS OF MEASUREMENT: COMPUTATION AND DEFINITION

A considerable amount of misinformation leading to incorrect conclusions in dealing with numerical data is classifiable as measurement error. It has to do with the genesis of a particular figure, a score, an average, a correlation on the basis of which a person is making a judgment.

Let us suppose, for instance, that a fourth grade teacher has an average grade score of 3.2 for the arithmetic achievement of her pupils. How much does she know about the figure itself? Where did it come from? How was it collected? How was it administered? Who scored the tests? Was the scoring checked and verified to avoid clerical errors? How were results calculated? What kind of an average was computed? How reliable is the test? How were the functions of arithmetic achievement defined in selecting items for the test? How was it standardized? How were norms established? These and similar questions imply many types of errors of measurement itself.

Some of the more important pitfalls in this category are as follows:

1. *Errors in Computation.* Unless systematic means are employed in handling quantitative data to eliminate pure computational slips, a decimal point will be left out; an unverified, unchecked sum will produce an incorrect average; an overlooked negative sign will produce an error, or other accidents in processing data will occur in such a way as to yield false figures.

2. *Incorrect Yardstick.* To avoid this pitfall, we should be careful not to make judgments regarding "reasoning" ability on the basis of tests which measure chiefly "memory." Expenditure analyses showing "economies" and "savings" may invalidly be cited as evidences of the effectiveness of a school administration. The number of bacteria destroyed by a new drug in a test tube may have little to do with whether that drug destroys certain types of bacteria and prevents dental caries when it is used in a dentifrice or a mouthwash. The statistically literate person uses the proper yardstick and is critical of the kind of measurements that are used by others. He would not measure change in atmospheric pressure with a thermometer as an instrument.

3. False Accuracy. By an excessive use of figures, the overzealous novice with statistics or the purveyor of misinformation may lead his audience to an exaggerated idea of the precision and accuracy of the data. For instance, during a time of great fluctuation in school construction costs, a survey of proposed county or state building plans based on estimates would surely show that millions of dollars were to be spent. Owing to the great multiplicity of variables involved in estimating what should be spent, how much ought to be spent, how much could be spent, and what needs to be spent on school building construction in each of the districts involved, it would be difficult to justify reporting a total of $212,432,564.98. Undoubtedly the total should be reported as approximately $212 million.

In handling test data and other school statistics, it is usually good practice to carry a sufficient number of decimals on work sheets to guarantee proper accuracy in computations. An average on an achievement test may actually be computed on a calculator as 23.568. As a result to be communicated to others, however, such precision is *false accuracy*. Such tests usually involve errors of measurement such that an individual pupil's score of 24 may be useful only as indicating a region on a scale, for instance, some place between 20 and 30. As a general rule, results should be reported with no more accuracy than can be justified on the basis of the accuracy of the original data.

4. Unknown Measurement Error. As I have suggested, errors of measurement are often ignored. This consideration constantly confronts the worker in education. The building survey I referred to, based on a blanket question in a questionnaire sent to a number of local school districts, "How much expenditure would be required to replace obsolete buildings and allow for increased enrollment?" would involve an unknown measurement error. Each individual respondent would either guess or use a set of criteria or a system of estimation quite unlikely to be used by all the others. Such a survey would be a compounding of many types of errors. Often this may be avoided by depending upon objective data—relationships of pupils to square feet of floor area and age of buildings, for instance—which can be counted accurately.

5. The Uncommon Denominator. A common misuse of statistics results from fallacious employment of percentages and ratios. It is now common knowledge in our most literate educational circles that the percentage marking system is obsolete. Yet this is an anachronism which has been slow to disappear from school operations largely because of the difficulty of eliminating misconceptions of "per cent." A

GRAPHIC OPTICAL ILLUSION—CHART 1

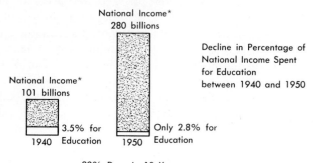

National Income*
280 billions

National Income*
101 billions

Decline in Percentage of
National Income Spent
for Education
between 1940 and 1950

3.5% for
1940   Education

Only 2.8% for
1950   Education

20% Drop in 10 Years

*Gross National Product

You're right—youngsters can't
wait! Besides, we're way
behind already. We'll have
to work hard to catch up . . .

This chart illustrates the difficulty
of representing quantities visually.
A little computation will show that
the black part of the 1940 bar
should be smaller than the black
part of the 1950 bar.

student in a school still using this system of marking and grading receives 89 per cent in algebra and 74 per cent in American history. Is his achievement better in algebra than it is in American history? Studies have shown such marks are the product of innumerable errors of judgment, including the whims and prejudices of the teacher. The common denominator, "the percentage of what," is variable and elusive. Is 100 per cent complete mastery? Is it perfection? Or, as in some cases, does it represent all the items in a test?

Expenditures for schools are often expressed in terms of enrollment, average daily attendance, or some measure of number of pupils. For instance, suppose that last year District A spent an average of $465 per pupil and suppose the expenditure per pupil for District B was $235. Whether or not District A has a relatively greater financial resource with which to provide a rich and adequate educational program depends largely upon whether or not the denominator, number of pupils, is a common one. In one case is it all pupils enrolled, while in the other case average daily attendance? And even if the denominator, by definition, is the same, were they computed in the same way? Then suppose further that the facts are as follows:

District	Total Expenditure	Number of Pupils	Number of Classrooms
A	$11,625	25	2
B	$58,750	250	8

Also, let us assume further that District A is in a sparsely popu-lated rural area where a small school and low enrollment are essential owing to conditions beyond the control of the school board in this area. You may observe now that District A has financial resources

GRAPHIC OPTICAL ILLUSION—CHART 2

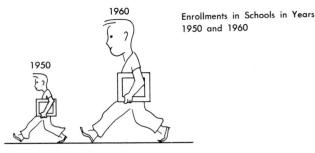

1960

1950

Enrollments in Schools in Years 1950 and 1960

By 1960 there will be 8,000,000 more children in our schools

. . . and more children going to school every year—

Another instance of a chart giving an exaggerated impression to the incautious eye. Is the 8 million enrollment increase shown on the chart exaggerated?

amounting to $5812 per classroom, but that District B has $7344 per classroom. By this method of reckoning, we see that it is possible that District B really is able to employ better trained and more experienced teachers and to have more instructional materials available in each classroom. So the expenditure per pupil in these two districts is not comparable. The denominator, number of pupils, does not show costs of low pupil-teacher ratios.

6. *The Optical Illusion.* There are many ways of graphic presentation that may give exaggerated impressions to the incautious eye.

Two charts are illustrated. Chart 1 deals with the decline in percentage of national income spent for education between 1940 and 1950. A little computation will show that the black part of the 1940 bar should be smaller than the black part of the 1950 bar. Chart 2 presumably represents school enrollment in 1950 and 1960. How many times greater is the 1960 enrollment than the 1950 enrollment? An interesting experiment is to ask friends or colleagues to estimate it by simply looking at the chart. Here are the data on which the chart was based: 1950 enrollment was 29 million; 1960 enrollment is estimated to be 37 million. This means a ratio of about 5 to 4, or about a one-fourth increase in enrollment. Is the 8 million increase exaggerated by the chart?

chapter 4

Educational Research: Findings and Conclusions

As a research effort proceeds, the time comes when the concerns of Chapter 3 are complete; the data are generated, and a statistic has been calculated. To most researchers this point is very exhilarating. The time is at hand when, to some degree, knowledge has been attained about a heretofore unknown. Despite its inherent satisfaction, this point of closure is also a point of error for many a researcher, error which precludes closure. Some err at this point by concluding only their findings. Others err by concluding far, far beyond the bounds of their findings. The focus of this chapter is the delineation of these two types of error. The readings should develop more subtle understandings of the pitfalls encountered in reaching conclusions when research findings are in hand.

Before treating the two extremes of error, it seems useful to make explicit the meanings of the terms "findings" and "conclusion." A distinction between the two can be made readily apparent by referring again to the plausible logic inference pattern described in Chapter 1. The reasoning pattern was:

Major Premise: If the hypothesis (H) is a true statement; then specified consequents (C) will be observed.

Minor Premise 1: To observe C without H being true is hardly credible due to controls for rival hypotheses of a . . . , b . . . , c . . . , and so on.

Minor Premise 2: C was or was not observed.

Conclusion: H is very much more credible, or no conclusion.

In this format Minor Premise 2 is the finding—a distinctly different component of the research process than the conclusion. The finding deals with the observations made by the researcher on the anticipated consequents. Findings are typically statistical statements about the real or chance nature of the observations. Conclusions on the other hand are verbal statements about the truth of the hypothesis being investigated. Another way of discussing this differentiation is the statistical hypothesis–scientific hypothesis discussion advanced in the first reading in this chapter.

The distinction between findings and conclusions is sometimes clarified for the researcher-to-be or the research consumer by identifying the subsidiary logical argument inherent in the overall plausible logic pattern outlined above. This second logical argument is employed to make the Minor Premise 2 statement. Did the researcher or did he not observe C, the consequent?

As was indicated in Chapter 3 differences in mean scores are not always a real difference. Thus, to make Minor Premise 2 researchers employ inferential statistics. In the process they are engaging in a logical argument of the probability of the observation. Whenever inferential statistics are employed, a disjunctive premise—two mutually exclusive statements—is involved. The researcher is stating either H_0, there is no difference, or H_1, there is a difference. Statistically we are able to examine only H_0 and our examination, or statistical analysis, allows us to either reject or fail to reject it. In effect we have established a balance which might be diagramed as

$$H_0 \hspace{4cm} H_1$$

If we can remove H_0 from the left side (reject it) we can accept H_1. Thus if our analysis results in statistical significance, we reject H_0 and accept H_1, there is a difference. If, however, we fail to reach significance, we fail to reject H_0 and the balance remains. In such a case we do not know if we have or have not *found* a real difference.

From this discussion it should be clear that research findings are items observed. Conclusions, on the other hand, are statements about the truth value of a hypothesis. How true is the assertion that program A is better than program B, that gifted children are socially more adaptive than average children, or whatever the hypothesis might be?

The distinction between findings and conclusions helps set the stage for the discussion of the two extremes of error made as researchers bring their projects to a close. As indicated earlier some conclude findings; that is, a study is set up to test a hypothesis; consequents are observed which indicate that the hypothesis is a true statement; elaborate controls are employed; data are generated; and a significant statistic is obtained through the analysis. Now the researcher concludes that the differences in the scores were real. That is not a conclusion! He saw that. It is a finding. He did not start out to determine whether two sets of scores have real or chance differences in them. Rather he set out to make a statement about the truth of a hypothesis. The scores observed were merely indicants from which to infer the truth of the hypothesis. Therefore, findings are the analyzed observations and conclusions are inferences about the truth of the hypotheses. When a researcher concludes only that he saw X or Y, he focuses on *that* observation and fails to speak to any general utility of his work.

Overgeneralizing is as much an error as concluding findings. Typically, overgeneralization occurs in one of two forms. In some cases a nonsignificant finding is made, but the researcher reports reasons, not based on evidence generated in the study, that make him believe the hypothesis is true. Consider, for example, a study in which the experimenter has a considerable emotional investment in a trial method, yet his observation fails to produce significant results. In conclusion, Biased Experimenter says, "Although the statistical analysis of these data failed to reach significance at the .05 level, the analysis could have been significant had we settled for a .25 level. It is also believed that the experimental group of teachers held an adverse negative attitude toward their principals. One of them once said that she doubted her principal's wisdom in selecting her class for this experimental program. On the basis of these feelings and the obviously more logical way of teaching _____, the experimental method has to be accepted as the more effective of the two."

The other form of overgeneralization seems a worse error than the one described above. In this case the researcher finds significantly better scores on the part of students using method A. But he does not conclude that a hypothesis asserting that method A is better than method B is true. No, he concludes that you should buy stock in insurance companies which restrict enrollment to teachers. This, he argues, is so because alert drivers have fewer accidents; teachers with fewer discipline problems are more alert; children who are happier are less of a discipline problem; and children who learn more are happier. Further discussion of this type of error seems patently unnecessary. But articles with just such outlandish logical leaps find their way into print.

The articles by Cornell, Rose, Page, and Fattu discuss the problem of research conclusions. These discussions include cautions about what can be concluded and how far conclusions can be extended.

The final article introduces a new thought, negative results. What happens when we fail to reject the null hypothesis? Have we wasted time? In this respect the editors are reminded of a statement attributed to Thomas A. Edison. After a long day of watching one filament material after another burn through, one of Edison's young assistants moaned that they had failed again. Edison said, "No, we have not failed. We now know one more material which will not work." Wolf indicates that since things can be learned from negative results we ought not to discard them so readily.

Robert C. Bolles

The Difference Between Statistical Hypotheses and Scientific Hypotheses

In the previous chapter, the article by Nunnally pointed out some of the difficulties of using statistics in behavioral research. The present article by Bolles furthers this warning in a slightly different way. The point is made that there is a difference between saying that two sets of data are different and saying that this difference supports your original hypothesis. At this point, it might be well to look back to Chapter 1 to the articles by Masson and Raths and review the relationship between the hypothesis and deduced consequences and the role of the logical argument.

Robert C. Bolles "The Difference Between Statistical Hypotheses and Scientific Hypotheses," *Psychological Reports*, 11:639-45, 1962. Reprinted with permission.

When a professional statistician runs a statistical test he is usually concerned only with the mathematical properties of certain sets of numbers, but when a scientist runs a statistical test he is usually trying to understand some natural phenomenon. The hypotheses the statistician tests exist in a world of black and white, where the alternatives are clear, simple, and few in number, whereas the scientist works in a vast gray area in which the alternative hypotheses are often confusing, complex, and limited in number only by the scientist's ingenuity.

The present paper is concerned with just one feature of this distinction, namely, that when a statistician rejects the null hypothesis at a certain level of confidence, say .05, he may then be fairly well assured ($p = .95$) that the alternative statistical hypothesis is correct. However, when a scientist runs the same test, using the same numbers, rejecting the same null hypothesis, he cannot in general conclude with $p = .95$ that his scientific hypothesis is correct.

In assessing the probability of his hypothesis he is also obliged to consider the probability that the *statistical model* he assumed for purposes of the test is really applicable. The statistician can say "*if* the distribution is normal," or "*if* we assume the parent population is distributed exponentially." These if's cost the statistician nothing, but they can prove to be quite a burden on the poor *E* whose numbers represent controlled observations not just symbols written on paper.

The scientist also has the burden of judging whether his hypothesis has a greater probability of being correct than other hypotheses that could also explain his data. The statistician is confronted with just two hypotheses, and the decision which he makes is only between these two. Suppose he has two samples and is concerned with whether the two means differ. The observed difference can be attributed either to random variation (the null hypothesis) or to the alternative hypothesis that the samples have been drawn from two populations with different means. Ordinarily these two alternatives exhaust the statistician's universe. The scientist, on the other hand, being ultimately concerned with the nature of natural phenomena, has only started his work when he rejects the null hypothesis. An example may help to illustrate these two points.

Consider the following situation. Two groups of rats are tested for water consumption after one, the experimental group, has been subjected to a particular treatment. Suppose the collected data should appear as shown in Table 1.[1]

Table 1

NUMBER OF ANIMALS IN EACH GROUP DRINKING
A GIVEN AMOUNT OF WATER

N	0 cc.	1 cc.	2 cc.	3 cc.	4 cc.	. . .	12 cc.
Control Ss	15	3	2	0	0	. . .	0
Experimental Ss	12	3	0	0	4	. . .	1

After the data are collected, *E* can pretend he is a statistician for a while and say to himself, "Let's assume the populations are normal and try a *t* test." The *t* statistic is encouragingly large but not large enough (which is just as well because of the difficulty that would arise in attempting to justify the assumption of normality). Several trans-

---

[1] The problem, the data, and the claim of significance are those of Siegel and Siegel (1949); what follows is my construction.

formations of the data are tried, but they don't help. Our E recognizes that he needs another statistical model. Perhaps a non-parametric test would work, one which is not sensitive to the great skewness of the data, and one which makes no assumption about the underlying distribution. A Mann-Whitney test is discouraging. A chi-square test (tried even though the expected frequencies in the important cells at the tails of the distribution are really too small) does not even approach a significant value.

By this time E, weary of being an amateur statistician, consults a professional one who tells him that, *if* we can assume the populations have exponential distributions, then we can use Festinger's test (1943). This works ($F = 4.83$). In due time E publishes a report in which a highly significant ($p < .01$) increase in water consumption is attributed to the experimental treatment.

Inspection of the table, however, should lead to some skepticism. If our E has actually discovered anything about nature, he has found that (1) most animals under these test conditions don't drink more than 2 cc., and (2) his experimental treatment may make a *few* animals drink a good deal more than normal, 4 cc. or more.

It is necessary to digress a moment in order to notice that throughout this whole scientific episode our E's behavior has been above reproach. Even when he was acting like a statistician he wasn't *just* hunting for a test that would work; he was also searching for a test and a model, that would fit his particular problem. The *t* test will not work, not just because it is inappropriate from a statistical point of view, but also because it tests the wrong thing. The *t* test tests whether the means are different. The Mann-Whitney test, for another example, is appropriate in the statistical sense, but it too is primarily sensitive to differences in means, and so is likely to pick up only the first phenomenon our E has discovered (that most Ss drink very little) and not the second (that some Ss respond to treatment). E should use a test which is sensitive to his special problem such as the Kolmogorov-Smirnov test which is highly sensitive to differences in the *shapes* of distributions, or a test specifically for the difference in *skewness* between the two distributions.[2]

Enough statistical digression. The point about which our E, as a scientist, should be concerned is the discrepancy between the high level of statistical significance obtained ($p < .01$) and the lingering doubts he must have whether there may be some explanation for his data other

---

[2] Or he may replicate the study to get a larger *n* so that other tests will have more power. This is probably the best approach, especially if he varies the experimental conditions in order to find out how to get better control over the rare event.

than the experimental treatment (subjective $p = ?$). There are two very good but often ignored reasons for the discrepancy, as I suggested above. One source of doubt is that the probability of correctness of the scientist's hypothesis depends not only upon the probability of rejecting the null hypothesis, but also upon the probability that the statistical model is appropriate. Now, with the non-parametric tests there is little problem here, and in fact, that is their great virtue.[3]

Our E with the thirsty rats wisely eschewed the t test, and he probably would have even if it had yielded significance, not because it was "wrong," but because it would not have given him any assurance that his scientific hypothesis had been confirmed. But what, we may ask, is the probability that the populations which his two groups represent are actually distributed exponentially? I must say they don't look exponential. The samples are much too small to give us any assurance that the model might be appropriate. Let us be generous and say that the model has a .50 chance of being applicable. What becomes of E's claimed high significance level?

Poor E has a more serious matter to worry about, a more vexing source of doubt. His whole case hinges on the performance of one animal, the one that drank 12 cc. The remaining 39 Ss don't give him a thing, with any test. Now suppose that the true state of affairs is this: The experimental treatment really has no appreciable effect upon water consumption. But let us suppose, however, that there occurs, every once in a while, a bubble in the animal's home cage drinking tube, which prevents normal drinking. If this were the case, and if bubbles occur, say, 2½% of the time, then about 50% of the time a bubble S will appear in the experimental group, so E will get just the results he got about 50% of the time.[4] Moreover, if he continues to use the Festinger test, we can expect him half the time to get highly significant differences in support of his hypothesis, whatever his hypothesis may be!

The problem here, basically, is that statistical rejection of the null hypothesis tells the scientist only what he was already quite sure of

---

[3] The power of the Mann-Whitney, for example, is usually cited as approaching .95 that of the t test, in those conditions where the latter is appropriate. Considering that there is usually at least a .05 chance that any given set of data does not come from a normal population, the Mann-Whitney emerges as perhaps the more powerful test for testing scientific (as against statistical) hypotheses. Moreover, its loss of statistical power with small samples may be more than offset by the scientist's gain in assurance that the underlying model is appropriate.

[4] The other half of the time the experiment will be disastrous for E's hypothesis, however. He had better just do the study once; that way he has at least a .50 chance of getting high significance in the favorable direction, and no more than a .50 chance of discovering that the real world is full of bubbles.

—the animals are not behaving randomly. The fact the null hypothesis can be rejected with a p of .99 does not give E an assurance of .99 that his particular hypothesis is true, but only that *some* alternative to the null hypothesis is true. He may not like the bubble hypothesis because it is *ad hoc*. But that is quite irrelevant. What is crucial is that the bubble hypothesis, or some other hypothesis, may be more probable than his own. The final confidence he can have in his scientific hypothesis is not dependent upon statistical significance levels; it is ultimately determined by his ability to reject alternatives.

Consider another illustration. Suppose we are interested in whether a certain stimulus will have reinforcing power for a certain group of 20 animals. After pretraining on a straightaway, we run them 15 trials in a T-maze which has the stimulus in question on one side and not on the other. We collect our data and graph them in the hope of seeing a typical learning curve. But what we find is Fig. 1. All is not lost, though, apparently, because it is still possible to conclude from the data that the stimulus *did* have a reinforcing effect, and that the associated p value is less than .002![5]

The first thing to look for is whether there is a rising trend in the points of Fig. 1. It turns out that the best fit line *does* rise, but that an F test for the significance of the trend shows it to be less than would be expected on the basis of the day-to-day variation. To find a significant difference anywhere here, we have to ignore the data of Fig. 1 and turn our attention to the number of responses made by each S to the "reinforced" side, during its 15 trials. The 20 such scores have a mean of 8.8 which proves to be highly significantly different from the expected value of 7.5 ($p = .002$). (The learning curve, correspondingly, runs along at about 59% instead of 50%.) What this significance test tells us is that the animals probably weren't running randomly.[6] But it is a long way from that to the inference that learning has occurred because of the special stimulus.

One hypothesis with a high *a priori* probability is that most of the animals gave scores that lay quite close to 7.5 but that one or two animals, with strong unlearned position habits, continued going to the side to which they had gone on the first trial. The probability that in the sampling process, just those one or two animals with strong

---

[5] The problem, the data, and the conclusions are D'Amato's (1955). Note that performance on the first trial was at 50%. This was pre-arranged by putting the reinforcer on both sides for half the Ss and on neither side for the other half.

[6] No one who has ever run animals would seriously consider that they might run randomly. What the null hypothesis implies in empirical terms is that the different animals were doing different things at different times so that the total set of *scores* looks as if it were random.

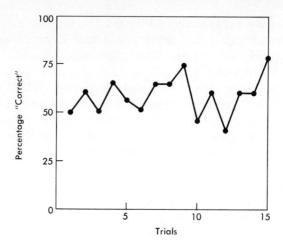

Figure 1. *The performance of rats alleged to have learned to go to one side of a T-maze*

position habits should be placed under the same condition, and under the particular condition that the "reinforcer" was on their preferred side, is fairly small, but still a great deal larger than the reported significance level. This hypothesis can be ruled out, however, but by certain features of the data and not on grounds of its *a priori* probability. We can deduce from the small SD (1.47) that few of the animals could have had position habits of appreciable strength. In fact, we can deduce (with a little effort) from the size of the SD that no more than one S could have had extreme position habit, and that even this was not actually the case, since one S could not have moved the mean from 7.5 to 8.8. Hence, we must conclude that the distribution represents a tightly bunched set of scores, whose mean is indeed significantly larger than 7.5.

But this suggests another hypothesis, which does account for the data, and which also has a high *a priori* probability. The hypothesis is simply that most animals have slight position habits. According to this hypothesis, any particular animal could be expected to go to one side 8 or 9 or 10 times out of 15. (We have already noted the high significance level indicating how consistent this is.) The setting of the performance level at 50% on the first trial is a red herring; it does not set the expected percentage correct at 50%—that would be true in any case before it was known which was the preferred side for a given animal. Now that the data are in, we can see (according to this hypothesis) that the preferred side happened to be predominantly on the same side for which S was "reinforced." To assess the probability that a significantly high proportion of the animals had the "reinforcement" on their preferred side (which would be good evidence that the reinforcement was effective), we must go back to the data of Fig. 1. Performance over the last 14 trials was at 59%, while the performance on Trial 1 was 50%. The question is whether E's performance on Trial 1, when he was selecting the side to put the critical stimulus, is significantly different from the 59% baseline for the animal's performance?[7] The answer is that it is well within the trial by trial variation. There was that much or more variation from the mean on 6 of the trials.

So, what it comes down to is that the animals did show slight but consistent preferences for one side or the other; the p figure of .002 shows this. The important question is whether these slight and consistent preferences are due to a slight but consistent effect of the experimental treatment, or whether they would have occurred without the treatment and E was just a little unlucky in trying to counterbalance them. Which is the more probable?

The point of this message is not that it is futile to do experiments (although it might be wise to be cautious of some of the statistician's favorite designs). Rather, the emphasis should be upon the distinction between why scientists run statistical tests and why statisticians do it. The former run tests for the same reason they run experiments, in the attempt to understand natural physical phenomena. The latter do it in the attempt to understand mathematical phenomena. The scientist gains his understanding through the rejection or confirmation of scientific hypotheses, but this depends upon much more than merely rejecting or failing to reject the null hypothesis. It depends partly upon the confirmation from other investigators (e.g., Amsel & Maltzman, 1950; Wike & Casey, 1954), particularly as the experimental conditions are varied (e.g., Siegel & Brantley, 1951; Amsel & Cole, 1953). Confirmation of scientific hypotheses also depends in part upon whether they can be incorporated into a larger theoretical framework (e.g., Hull, 1943). Final confirmation of scientific hypotheses and the larger theories they support depends upon whether they can stand the test of time.

These processes have to move slowly. As Bakan (1953) has observed, the development of a scientific idea is gradual, like learning itself; its probability of being correct increases gradually from one experimental

---

[7] Or put another way, what is the probability that 20 animals, all with slight position habits, will distribute themselves on one particular trial so that the group will depart 9 percentage points from its mean value.

verification to the next, as response probability increases from one trial to the next. The effect of any single experimental verification is not to confirm a scientific hypothesis but only to make its *a posteriori* probability a little higher than its *a priori* probability. Our present day over-reliance upon statistical hypothesis testing is apt to obscure this feature of the scientific enterprise. We have almost come to believe that an assertion about the nature of the empirical world can be validated (at least with a probability level such as .95 or .99) in one stroke if the data demonstrate statistical significance. Is it any wonder then that our use of statistical hypothesis testing is rapidly passing from routine or ritual?

SUMMARY

One of the chief differences between the hypotheses of the statistician and those of the scientist is that, when the statistician has rejected the null hypothesis, his job is virtually finished. The scientist, however, has only just begun his task. He must also be able to show that the statistical model underlying the test is applicable to his empirical situation because whatever significance level he obtained for the test, his confidence in his scientific hypothesis must be reduced below that by any lack of confidence in the model. Furthermore, confidence in his scientific hypothesis is reduced by the plausibility of alternative hypotheses. Hence the scientist's ultimate confidence in his hypothesis may be far lower than the significance level he can report.

References

Amsel, A., & Cole, K. F. Generalization of fear motivated interference with water intake. *J. exp. Psychol.*, 1953, 46, 243-247.

Amsel, A., & Maltzman, I. The effect upon generalized drive strength of emotionality as inferred from the level of consummatory response. *J. exp. Psychol.*, 1950, 40, 563-569,

Bakan, D. Learning and the principle of inverse probability. *Psychol. Rev.*, 1953, 60, 360-370.

D'Amato, M. R. Transfer of secondary reinforcement across the hunger and thirst drives. *J. exp. Psychol.*, 1955, 49, 352-356.

Festinger, L. An exact test of significance for means of samples drawn from populations with an exponential frequency distribution. *Psychometrika*, 1943, 8, 153-160.

Hull, C. L. *Principles of behavior*. New York: Appleton-Century, 1943.

Siegel, P. S. & Brantley, J. J. The relationship of emotionality to the consummatory response of eating. *J. exp. Psychol.*, 1951, 42, 304-306.

Siegel, P. S., & Siegel, H. S. The effect of emotionality on the water intake of the rat. *J. comp. physiol. Psychol.*, 1949, 42, 12-16.

Wike, E. L. & Casey, A. The secondary reinforcing value of food for thirsty animals. *J. comp. physiol. Psychol.*, 1954, 47, 240-243.

Francis G. Cornell

Jumping to Conclusions

After we have gathered our data and analyzed them, is our task done? The obvious answer is no, we must now interpet the data so that we can decide what action, if any, to take. The previous article by Bolles pointed out the significant difference between the statistical hypothesis and the scientific hypothesis. This article by Cornell warns of some of the dangers of too loosely interpreting the data that is obtained. This article is a companion to the one by Cornell in Chapter 3, and it might be well to review that one before reading this one.

Francis G. Cornell, "Jumping to Conclusions," *Nation's Schools*, 58:77-9, October, 1956. Reprinted, with permission, from the *Nation's Schools*, October 1956. Copyright 1956, The Modern Hospital Publishing Co., Inc., Chicago. All rights reserved.

In a preceding article I illustrated some of the more obvious ways in which people make "errors of fact." It is convenient to think of another category of logical booby traps which must be avoided by both producers and consumers of statistics. These we put under the heading of "errors of interpretation." Previously I discussed critical questions about the meanings of data; now we look at problems of drawing conclusions from the data.

One of the first mistakes that can be made in the interpretation of data is to fail to take into account all of the questions I have already discussed regarding the validation of the data themselves. So, in a sense, my system of classification is only a matter of emphasis, for, in actual statistical thinking, the interpretations, meanings and conclusions can be derived only in conjunction with the kind of dependability we can place upon our basic information. After all, our interest in statistics is a functional one—an interest in statistics as a tool, as an instrument of thinking, as an instrument of inquiry. Therefore, we view with considerable lack of interest educational facts collected for the sake of facts or because somebody started collecting such facts

years ago. An interesting speculation has to do with the amount of
time and energy wasted in schools and school systems in assembling
facts of dubious functional value. Our first type of error of interpretation will therefore have to do with facts.

1. *Irrelevant Data.* There seems to be an infinite variety of ways
in which people can cite, from an authoritative source, information
which seemingly proves a point but which, in reality, has little to do
with it. Of course, different kinds of invalid measurement discussed
earlier, such as the "incorrect yardstick," or failure to establish the
comparability of data, yield the "so what" statistics.

The most convincing argument used with legislative bodies and
school boards about problems of school building planning, financing
schools, school organization, the curriculum, and teaching personnel
problems is one based on a survey showing *average practice* throughout
the United States, or in similar types of districts and the like. Such
information on what other schools do may be important to a local
school board. However, most frequently these data are used as a
norm or as a means of setting a *standard.* Anyone who is familiar
with the pitiful inadequacies of thousands of classrooms will view
with skepticism the use of average practice as a criterion of what
ought to be. Surveys showing *what is* are very useful in giving us
"actuarial" information. It is logical, however, that decisions about
individual school systems should be based upon designing and
planning for the purposes and needs of the people in the individual
community—not the mythical average community.

There is a danger of making the statistics that happen to be available the criterion without first establishing the philosophy of the school,
stating the objectives, formulating the goals, and only then seeking
the data which are relevant to the purposes set forth. The same thing
is true in working with pupils or students in a classroom. If the objectives are pupil growth, improvements in social habits, attitudes and
ability in reasoning and critical thinking, achievement should be
measured as early as possible in these terms and not by the most
available test or score, particularly if this should be data on memory
or simple recall.

In viewing schools and school systems, we must guard against the
misuse of "actuarial" information for "clinical" purposes. A test norm
is a sort of average. There may be enough demonstrated correlation
between a test of academic aptitude and school achievement to yield
"achievement expectancies" on various levels, but individual schools
with their unique school populations and their own sets of educational
objectives are the exceptions that prove the rule.

2. *The Glittering Generality.* Statistics are often misused in simple syllogisms. Many persons are "categorical thinkers" and otherwise violate rules of logic in a way that results in jumping to conclusions. You no doubt know many persons of this type. Persons with certain features, persons of certain body types, persons of a certain race, religion, nationality or social class—such persons who have appeared to be aggressive, or dull, or impulsive, or who have possessed some other behavioral characteristic—often become the prototype by which other individuals who may be classed likewise are judged.

Many prejudices are formed by false generalization on restricted observations. Pupils are often discriminated against in marking and promotion because of this error. It also may influence the way in which administrators and school boards select teachers. This type of error in interpretation yields invalid guides or standards for the operation of schools, arbitrary standards which actually may impede progress of schools—standards bearing upon what to teach, how to teach, where to build a building, how to build the building, how to assign pupils, and so forth.

The difficulty in generalizing from a single set of observations is one of the reasons the science of statistical method is worth a block of time in the curriculums of our teacher training institutions. Considerable progress has been made in the development of statistical methods which help a person guard against this pitfall in planning investigations and in making use of statistical conclusions.

Many of the errors in this category are treated by the statistician under the heading "sampling" or "statistical inference." One type of blunder is to generalize from an *inadequate* sample. A palliative which was effective for one person during one instance of distress has been assumed to be a cure. That is to say, a generalization has been made on the basis of only a single observation.

Then there are frequent instances of the *sample that is not a fair sample.* There are important conditions which the statistician would demand for a group of individuals to be a fair "sample" of a population. Very often the subjects for a study are chosen, as a matter of convenience, from the nearest elementary school or a class the investigator happens to be teaching. Such a choice is probably not fairly representative of the larger population which is the real object of study, and the investigator is logically restricted to conclusions regarding the sample itself, no generalization whatever being justified.

Results of a questionnaire distributed to all high schools in the state of New Jersey, but of which only 35 per cent were returned, would produce information upon which the researcher could generalize only

with serious uncertainty. The 35 per cent of high schools is a group
selected on unknown bases. They represent a "chunk" and not a fair
sample. If the objective of an opinion poll is to learn the attitudes of
the adult population in a community toward some educational question, interviews with only those attending P.T.A. meetings would not
provide a fair sample of the adult population of the community.

3. *False Cause and Elusive Factors.* One of the commonest types of
erroneous statistical conclusion is to suppose a cause and effect relationship between two variables observed to be related. The mere
co-variation of measures does not guarantee functional interdependence
of the variables. When one is dealing with the relation of two or more
measures, the "facts" *do not* speak for themselves. The possibility of
a genuine functional interdependence between the variables must
meet the test of reasonableness. We may find, for instance, that, as sales
of tobacco have increased, teachers' salaries have increased. Except
in a tobacco growing area, increases in teachers' salaries are hardly
caused by increases in sales of tobacco. What is missing in the picture
is a whole complex of other factors which are common to both variables.
There is no direct functional relationship between the two, but both
are consequences of the development of the economic activity of the
country. This in turn makes possible larger national income to support
both education and expenditure and changes in the desires and wants
in our culture, permitting the increases in school attendance and holding power of our schools as well as increases in the consumption of
cigarets and tobacco.

The real cause must be found, and hidden factors must be accounted
for. An educational researcher could set up an experiment comparing
some new method of teaching arithmetic in "experimental" classes with
so-called "control" classes in which arithmetic is taught in the usual
manner. If the experiment is not designed in such a way as to take
into account many factors which may affect the results, the researcher
may falsely attribute to the *new method* the superior gains in achievement which he finds in his study. The superior achievement of the
experimental group may be the result of the greater enthusiasm and
higher motivation of the experimental teachers or, as often happens,
the selection of *exceptionally able* teachers for the tryout of new
materials or methods. Then, too, the classrooms in which the experiment is taking place may be those in which there is a greater emphasis
on, more time for, and more practice on arithmetic.

4. *Hidden Values.* In arriving at conclusions from figures or statistics, individuals are purposely or unwittingly prejudiced by their
own value systems. Frequently, the overzealous and careless researcher

is inclined to color his interpretations by his own hopes, beliefs and expectations.

A *New York Times* report on a test given to college students on American and world geography gave the percentages of college students answering the several questions correctly. Fewer than half knew the population of the United States, that Nevada was the smallest state in population, that the Coulee Dam was in Washington, or that when it is noon in New York it is 5 p.m. in London. The chances are good that one whose philosophy of education leans toward the academic and classical would consider these results as evidence that our educational system is sagging. On the other hand, the "experience" curriculum advocate or the supporter of other theories of education would consider the same facts as irrelevant. The latter would point to many objectives in education, important in his opinion, other than memorization of simple fact. So we see that the way people interpret data is often a product of predilections, feelings, attitudes, beliefs or stereotypes.

Some of the classical fallacies in reasoning that produce biased conclusions from evidence may be recognized from the study of logic. These are:

Argumentum ad hominem. Attacking the person who submits a proposition rather than attacking the proposition.

Argumentum ad populum. A direct appeal to popular prejudices or "the gallery."

Argumentum ad misericordiam. A play on emotions through an appeal to pity and popular sympathy.

Argumentum ad verecundiam. Appealing to authority or justifying and validating an idea by quoting an authoritative person or group.

An important device of the propagandist is an appeal to prejudices, fears, hates, idealism, love, religion or patriotism or to the sense of justice, pride, hope or courage. He makes this appeal by the use of invective and "name calling" or by denouncing persons, causes or ideas with emotionally charged words, or by establishing a psychological connection between what he is presenting and something esteemed by his audience.

Highly difficult research technics are important today. However, it probably is unnecessary for a great number of persons directly concerned with the development of educational programs to attain high levels of proficiency in complex methods of scientific inquiry. On the other hand, it is not expecting too much for large numbers of persons engaged either in research or in programs of action to be familiar at least with the sense of the foregoing ideas.

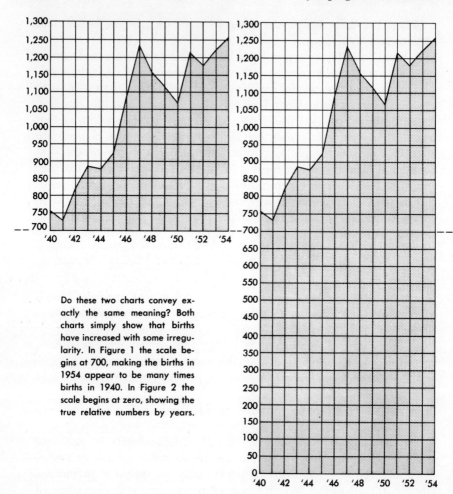

Do these two charts convey exactly the same meaning? Both charts simply show that births have increased with some irregularity. In Figure 1 the scale begins at 700, making the births in 1954 appear to be many times births in 1940. In Figure 2 the scale begins at zero, showing the true relative numbers by years.

Figure 1.   *Number of children born to residents of City X, 1940-54*

Figure 2.   *Number of children born to residents of City X, 1940-54*

If both technicians and practitioners think along the lines of the logic of the scientific method, groups consisting of professional persons and laymen working together in problem solving situations can be more effective. They will know enough about the ways of *improperly* supplying evidence. Effective decisions can be made as to when an expert may be needed to assist in technical research problems. Minimum essentials of critical thinking applied to the data of school programs and school systems should move the decision making processes of school organizations forward toward more purposeful goals more efficiently reached.

Arnold M. Rose

Generalizations in the Social Sciences [1]

This article could probably have been included in Chapter 3, since it does deal with some problems of design. It was included in this chapter, however, because it seemed to the editors that the significant aspect had to do with the results of research. Since—as Rose points out—it is impossible to draw samples representative of everyone, to whom can we generalize our results? This question is particularly pertinent in education where much research is done on a relatively small sample in a single school system. Although Rose is not aiming his criticisms at education, they equally well apply.

Arnold M. Rose, "Generalizations in the Social Sciences," *American Journal of Sociology*, 59:49-55, 1953. Reprinted with permisison.

Some social scientists confuse the conditions necessary for generalization, which might be called "generalizability," with the generalization itself. For example, they may believe that, by dealing with the "forms" or "processes" of human behavior rather than with the "content," one achieves generalizations regardless of the representativeness of the data used; or that by "abstracting to a higher conceptual level" one achieves generalizations regardless of the representativeness of the data.

When social scientists seek generalizations about all human beings, rather than, say, about members of a specific culture or a specific organization, their sample is invariably nonrepresentative. No one has yet studied a representative sample of persons or behavior from all cultures at all periods. The nearest approximations are those of an-

---

[1] This paper was prepared as a report to the Laboratory for Research in Social Relations, at the University of Minnesota, which is supported jointly by the university and the Carnegie Corporation of New York. None of the other members of the Laboratory should be held responsible for these views.

thropologists who make cross-cultural surveys,[2] but even they neglect historical and subcultural variations. Most other social scientists, while they specify the limited universe which their sample represents, imply that their findings apply beyond that universe without indicating why this should be true.[3] Consequently, there is a growing science by analogy. The conclusion of many an excellent study based on a limited sample is couched in the form of a universal generalization, and there are otherwise well-conceived studies of "industrial productivity" or "psychological warfare" conducted on volunteer student subjects in a classroom. While it is desirable to eliminate "extraneous" variables in laboratory experiments, it is questionable whether it is legitimate to generalize about industrial productivity where there is no motive to produce, or to generalize about psychological warfare when there is no war. The trouble is not that the laboratory experiment is a method not applicable to the study of human behavior but that a conclusion about the relation between an independent and a dependent variable under one set of circumstances cannot be applied, as it stands, to the relation between the same two variables under other circumstances.[4] It is still an unverified assumption that "cohesiveness" (to take one concept frequently generalized) in one situation, or induced by one means, is the same as cohesiveness in another situation, induced by another means—as some of the followers of Moreno seem to imply. This procedure reifies the concept.

---

[2] For example, G. P. Murdock, Social Structure (New York: Macmillan Co., 1949). Most of the findings in cross-cultural surveys are correlations considerably below unity. The universals claimed by Murdock are not in the form of associations among cultural variables but in the form of institutions alleged to be discovered in all cultures without exception. The work of the cross-cultural anthropologists is challenging and promising, but it is doubtful if they have achieved more than superficial and tentative generalizations.

[3] Except those who seek generalizations only about particular nations, subgroups, or institutions. The public opinion pollers, for example, almost invariably specify the limited universe which their sample is intended to represent and are not concerned with anything outside it.

[4] An illustration of the dangers of engaging in science by analogy is provided in the engaging study by Muzafer Sherif (reported in a preliminary way in Rohrer and Sherif [eds.], Social Psychology at the Crossroads [New York: Harper & Row, Publishers, 1951], pp. 388-424). Sherif experimentally creates hostility between two artificially separated groups of boys and shows how the hostility was induced by separation and rivalry in sports and other camp activities. While the experiment is ingenious and fascinating, one questions whether the conclusion about separation and rivalry has any relevance—as Sherif seems to believe—for the study of relations between Negroes and whites in the United States. For one thing, an essential factor in Negro-white relations is a syndrome of culturally determined attitudes known as "racism," which is not present in the relations between two groups of white Protestant boys at camp.

What rationale can be used to justify the procedure of generalizing beyond the universe of which the cases studied are deemed a representative sample?

One rationale can be built around homogeneity. If there is no variation in the persons or behavior to be studied, then any sample— no matter how drawn—is representative. Most natural scientists operate on this basis, and they almost never disturb themselves about selecting a random or stratified sample before describing its characteristics or experimenting with it. A gram of pure magnesium is representative of all magnesium, and a healthy liver is representative of all healthy livers. The chemist has a concept of purity in a substance, and the biologist has a concept of a healthy and properly functioning organ or organism. While purity and homogeneity are certainly not identical concepts, they may be said to have the same methodological function in regard to the matter considered here. When observations or experiments are essayed, the scientist makes a considerable effort to secure pure or healthy specimens, but beyond that he has no need to select a random or a stratified sample. The social scientist is in the same position when he is dealing with behavior that is unmodifiable, or practically unmodifiable, among men—so that one individual is, for the purpose at hand, like any other. We do not yet know all the categories of unmodifiable behavior, but research will add to the list. In general, we can probably say that behavior which is determined almost completely by heredity and behavior which is determined by universal experiences are practically unmodifiable. These may include the reflexes, the learning process, the psychiatric mechanisms, perhaps many of the processes of socialization and of crowd behavior. Much further research—including that of anthropologists and historians—is needed to determine what behavior is unmodifiable. Once found, it can then be studied almost regardless of how the sample is chosen, making sure only that one has not included in the sample a defective or pathological specimen. If the bias in sampling is not related to the variables studied, then a lack of representativeness in the sample has no limiting influence on the generalizability of the conclusion. The difficulty is that we do not know the specific biases in a nonrepresentative sample much less their relationship to the variables under study.

Many social scientists—particularly political scientists, institutional economists, and certain categories of sociologists—deliberately limit their studies to our own culture. Their findings are in the nature of cultural or institutional generalizations. Most historians and many anthropologists do purely descriptive studies in which the issue of generalization is not raised. It is largely the social psychologists, sociologists, and social anthropologists dealing with variable human behavior who have to seek a rationale for generalizing from nonrepresentative samples. The problem of variation confronts them not only in the sense that they do not know whether their findings would hold under different cultural conditions but also in that not *all* their own cases conform to the generalization true for *most* of their cases. Their generalizations usually take the following form: "When condition *A* was established, and *C, D, E, . . . , N* eliminated, *B* followed in 80 *per cent* of the cases; *or,* in a group in which *A* was induced, as compared to a group in which *A'* was induced and extraneous variables randomized, a *greater degree* of *B* was manifested." Such conclusions are never completely satisfactory, as there is variation in the dependent variable not explained by the variation in the independent variable, even though extraneous variables have been held constant or randomized. Such a variation may represent differences in subcultures or in individual experience, although it may also be due simply to errors of measurement.[5] The physical and biological sciences find some variations in their conclusions, but these are tiny in comparison to those found in social science, and repeated replications show they are distributed normally. The variations in the conclusions of natural science may therefore be attributed to errors of measurement. These are the so-called "chance errors." The large size and often irregular character of variations in

---

[5] At least two quite diverse metaphysical positions are held by contemporary social scientists regarding the nature of social laws. One is that all human behavior is determined by a finite number of causes, which—if known in their entirety, as universal laws—would allow for the prediction of every person's behavior under all circumstances. The other position is that human behavior is determined by the laws of probability, so that at best we can make actuarial predictions that will ultimately have high, although not perfect, accuracy when applied to specified categories of people but that will always be lacking a good deal when applied to any single individual. The differences between the two positions can be best illustrated by examining the forms which they hold generalizations should take:
  I. Holding constant *C, D, E, . . . , N,* when situation *A* develops, then *B* will follow.
  II. Holding constant *C, D, E, . . . N,* when situation *A* develops, then *B* will follow 80 per cent of the time (80 is, of course, an arbitrary figure).
I hold to the former position, which I believe to be the metaphysical position taken by natural scientists from Galileo through Einstein, with the discoveries of Bohr and Heisenberg representing no intrinsic exceptions but rather a technical inability to achieve as much knowledge about the movement of individual particles as is desired. I emphasize adherence to the first position because the statements in the text may *appear* to be predicated on the second position. An illustration of the second position is offered in the following quotation: "Social science . . . must be subject to the same criteria as any other branch of science. Its end product is predictions which can be expressed in the general form given *a, b, c, etc.,* the odds are *p* to 1 that *t* will occur" (Elbridge Sibley, *The Recruitment, Selection, and Training of Social Scientists* ["Social Science Research Council Bulletins," No. 58 (1948)]).

social science conclusions suggest, on the other hand, failure to control important variables.

Since American culture contains numerous subcultures, we would expect not only heterogeneity in the reactions in any one sample but also different results from different studies of the same variables. Unfortunately, there have not been replicative studies in most areas of the social sciences.[6] The term "replication" has been used with at least two meanings. In one use it is a repetition of a study of a given problem with research procedures and measuring devices as similar to the original as possible but with a different sample. In another sense, replication means any effort to test the conclusion of a previous study, using any scientifically proper research procedure and measuring devices with the new cases. In this paper, concerned as it is with the stability of the conclusion (or generalization) rather than with the re-use of procedures and techniques, the term "replication" is used in the latter sense. Thus we are interested in all studies that state the observed relationship between what are purported to be the same set of variables, regardless of methods or measures used. On a few subjects there have been not only replicative studies but also sytematic summaries of them. The bibliography at the end of this article lists all the replicative studies in sociology and social psychology which the author could find in the published literature.

The annotated list reveals that there is little consistency in the conclusions of the studies reported. The differences might be due to one or more of several circumstances: (1) the cultural variations in the composition of different samples; (2) different indices or measures of the major variables; (3) different personalities or approaches of the experimenters or other data collectors; (4) different social conditions under which the data were collected; (5) different factors measured under the same name. If we are to know which of these is responsible for the variation in findings, it is necessary to control the last four much more carefully. If the variation in the persons studied is important, it is much too complicated to control readily.

With these observations in mind, we can specify at least some of the conditions necessary for securing more consistent replications in the social sciences.

1. While an isolated hypothesis can be scientifically proved or disproved, it would be more efficient if the proposition for which verifica-

---

[6] Donald Young has pointed out the lack of replicative studies. See his "Limiting Factors in the Development of the Social Sciences," in *Research Frontiers in Human Relations, Proceedings of the American Philosophical Society,* XCII (November 12, 1948), 330.

tion is sought were a logical part of a general theory. (However, many of the better-executed studies in sociology have completely ignored any sort of theory.) A theory may be defined as an integrated body of definitions, assumptions, and general propositions covering a given subject matter from which a comprehensive and consistent set of specific and testable hypotheses can be deduced logically. The hypotheses must take the form: "If A, then B, holding constant C,D,E, . . . ," or some equivalent, and thus permit of causal explanation and prediction.

A *good* theory is one with (*a*) definitions, assumptions, and general propositions consistent, in so far as possible, with previous research findings and with careful, although perhaps not systematic, observations; (*b*) a "minimum" number of definitions, assumptions, and general propositions; (*c*) deduced hypotheses in readily testable form; and, (*d*) crucially, verification of its deduced hypotheses by proper scientific methods.

Certain values of theory which have led investigators in the older disciplines to use it extensively should lead social scientists to reach generalizations that are capable of being replicated. In the first place, theory guides the formation of hypotheses and trains investigators to look for facts which may ordinarily not be readily apparent. In the second place, it allows the conclusions of older studies to gain support from new research and to provide some of the data of new research. Furthermore, it provides a guide for the selection of research problems among the infinitely large number of possible hypotheses. Finally, it permits research to proceed systematically and allows conclusions to be brief and readily communicable.

There are dangers in the use of theory in science. For one thing, it channelizes research along certain lines. If the theory ultimately proves to be wrong, many years of work are wasted and new ideas have not had a fair chance for expression. Then, too, certain assumptions and definitions are inevitable in theory; but they may limit observation. Without a theory we might have alternative definitions and assumptions within the same piece of research. Moreover, the concepts that are necessary in theory tend to be reified. To reify concepts may be a general human characteristic which the use of theoretical definitions seems to stimulate. There is also the danger that before a theory can be completely verified (which is practically never), its specific conclusions may be applied to areas outside their scope. Studies of the maze learning of rats have been used to guide the development of children, and conclusions about neurotic behavior among adults had been suggested as a chief guide for the understanding of politics. There is the danger that rival theories of human behavior, such as are inevitable in a democratic and pluralistic society, encourage distortion of simple facts. Scientists frequently agree on statements of fact but seriously disagree on their significance or explanation on a theoretical level. Sometimes even the immediate causes of the facts are the subject of agreement, but the more basic ones suggested by theory are not.

2. The second proposal for achieving more consistent replications is that propositions be started in terms capable of being generalized. If the categories or variables of a proposition are specifically spatial or temporal, obviously the proposition cannot be generalized. Any body of data can be stated in terms of generalized or localized categories. For example, a number of facts about a sample of persons can be classified according to residence, to socio-economic class, to life-satisfaction. If residence is the variable, the data can never be used to verify propositions other than those referring to the specific locations. If socio-economic class is the variable, the data can be used to verify propositions that refer to the culture or subculture in which that class structure exists. But if life-satisfaction is the variable, the data can be used to verify universal propositions, since presumably all men evaluate their lives in terms of satisfaction. However, simply choosing categories that are capable of being generalized does not in itself generalize the proposition when verified. The verified proposition still has no validity beyond the universe from which the sample is drawn: hence the need for replications.

It is obviously impossible to secure a representative sample of all men, from all cultures at all times. Most propositions will never claim validity beyond the given culture, usually our own. Since this is so, propositions stated in terms of categories frankly limited to our culture should be nearly as useful in research as propositions whose variables are universal. They may have as much predictive value. Possibly a happy compromise between a universal generalization, desirable but unattainable, and a frankly culturally limited generalization is a proposition stated in universal terms and then restated with the variables specified for the culture to be studied. The restated proposition, when verified for the culture studied, is highly amenable, of course, to reconversion into its universal form when other studies in other cultures or in different social situations later justify the universal form. In the specific study, the historical premise, "in our culture," serves to hold constant numerous variables that could not otherwise feasibly be held constant in a strict experimental design.[7]

---

[7] An example of its use in sociology is my paper, "The Adequacy of Women's Expectations for Adult Roles," *Social Forces*, XXX (October, 1951), 69-77.

3. Even within our culture it is so difficult to secure a representative sample for research on most variables that it would be well to have some device that could be employed to obviate the need of it. The purpose in securing representative samples for verifying general propositions is not the same as the purpose in securing representative samples for a survey or a public opinion poll. The latter explores the distribution of certain attributes in the population. The former simply inquires whether the proposition will hold good for data in the entire *range* of the distribution. It is usually easier to estimate roughly where various points on a distribution are than to secure a representative sample of a large, complex, and widely distributed population. Replication should be at various points, especially the extremes, of the distribution of the population. The distribution differs somewhat for each independent variable, since it should cover the range of possible interpretations of, or reactions to, the independent variable.

It is often difficult to replicate a study on divergent populations with the same observer or experimenter, the same index or measure of the independent variable, and the same conditions of observation or experimentation. Making these things as simple as possible will, of course, aid in approximating them over and over again during replications. But a certain amount of variation is almost inevitable, and it will prevent exact replication. The terms of the proposition must be broad enough to cover the variation.

Replications, to be useful in the way that they have proved useful in the natural sciences, must be undertaken systematically. If one replication secures results consistent with the original finding, further replications should vary slightly the conditions of the original study. If one replication fails to secure results consistent with the original finding, further replications should approximate even more closely the conditions of the original study. The scientific function of replications, in addition to verification, is to set the limits under which the generalization is valid.

4. Just as an infinite number of discrete hypotheses can be advanced about social behavior, so can an indefinitely large number of different frameworks of assumptions and definitions. Rather than proceeding at random, it is preferable to develop some criteria for setting up a framework of definitions and assumptions. The criteria should also be used in selecting an isolated hypothesis, since a tremendous amount of time can be wasted in testing, disproving, and discarding hypotheses. Possible guides for setting criteria are given below.

(a) Definitions, assumptions, and variables in hypotheses which have proved valuable in previous research should be given special attention before being created *de novo*. The result will then contribute to a cumulative product, and it should have a better chance of verification and successful replication.

(*b*) Definitions, assumptions, and variables should bear relation to observations by the investigator, or to meanings perceived by the subjects, or at least to what psychiatrists claim are unconscious meanings. Some research has been set up with definitions, assumptions, and variables from the imagination of the investigators which can hardly be expected to be relevant, manipulable, and productive of verifiable hypotheses. We need not, of course, go all the way back to the old-line behaviorists and insist that all variables (stimuli and responses) be materially observable; but some relation to perceived reality, conscious or unconscious, is desirable. A person told to feel cohesive with strangers in a group may manifest more cohesiveness when observed or tested than a person not told to feel cohesive, but it is questionable whether this cohesiveness operates in the same way as cohesiveness developed through years of personal contact. This may meet one of the criticisms and weaknesses of the laboratory experiment in the social sciences—namely, that it is "unrealistic."[8] It may not be necessary for the laboratory situation to be realistic, but it probably is necessary for the *variables* to be realistic. Of course, the test of a variable is not its apparent realism but whether or not it has a consistent effect. Of all the myriad of variables which a strong imagination can dream up, only those are likely to have an effect which bear some relation to social or psychological reality, conscious or unconscious. In the future, more powerful tools and better-trained observers may be able to perceive more that is realistic than social scientists can today.

(*c*) One of the best ways of choosing, among a large number of possible hypotheses, the one or few most likely to be verified is to have an initial period of informal and unsystematic, but thoughtful and critical, observation, using whatever relevant descriptive studies and general information may be available. This is especially important in the early stages of any science, before frameworks of assumptions, definitions, and tested propositions are known to be workable and

---

[8] G. E. Swanson anticipates many of the usual objections to the use of the laboratory experiment in studying social behavior by showing that the criteria for validity in the latter are the same as the criteria for validity in field studies. But he falls into the error of assuming that generalizability is generalization: for example, in making a suggestion for the study of cultural factors in the laboratory, he says: "Suppose that we move from the particulars to a higher level of generalization." This may, of course, simply be unfortunate wording. See his "Some Problems of Laboratory Experiments with Small Populations," *American Sociological Review*, XVI (June, 1951), 349-58, esp. pp. 355-56.

fruitful. Too frequently in research today an arbitrary or fortuitous guess of a social scientist whose experience is necessarily limited is called a hypothesis. This is a wasteful procedure, even if the experimental design for the ensuing study is rigorous.

Finally, perhaps none of our proposals for the improvement of research design will lead to generalizations that will stand up under systematic replication. Our techniques of acquiring data may not be delicate and precise enough to isolate the basic elements of human behavior and social organization. In that case, we must refine techniques before we can achieve any reliable and valid generalizations.

Bibliography of Replicated Studies

A. SUMMARIES OF REPLICATIONS

1. Karl F. Schuessler and Donald R. Cressey. "Personality Characteristics of Criminals," *American Journal of Sociology*, LV (March, 1950), 476-84. Survey of studies correlating personality traits and criminality. Conclusions not consistent.

2. Arnold M. Rose. *Studies in the Reduction of Prejudice*, chap. i. Chicago: American Council on Race Relations, 1947; 2d ed., 1948. Survey of experimental studies on reducing intergroup prejudice. Conclusions not consistent. *On the same material*: Robin M. Williams, Jr. *The Reduction of Intergroup Tension*. New York: Social Science Research Council, 1947. Conclusions not consistent.

3. Robert R. Sears. *Survey of Studies of Psychoanalytic Concepts*. ("Social Science Research Council," No. 51.) New York, 1943. Conclusions not consistent.

4. Dorothy S. Thomas. *Research Memorandum on Migration Differentials*. ("Social Science Research Council Bulletins," No. 43.) New York, 1943. Survey of studies on selective factors in migration. Conclusions not consistent.

5. Ralph M. Stogdill. "Personal Factors Associated with Leadership," *Journal of Psychology*, XXV (January, 1948), 35-71. Survey of studies of physical and personality traits of leaders. Conclusions not consistent.

6. Raymond B. Cattell. "The Cultural Functions of Social Stratification. II. Regarding Individual and Group Dynamics," *Journal of Social Psychology*, XXI (February, 1945), 25-55. Summary of studies of the effects of social stratification on the acquired characteristics of individuals; includes studies on class mean differences in intelligence and character

traits, such as honesty, aggression, and maladjustment. Items pulled out of studies and interpreted to be consistent.

7. Allen Edwards. "The Retention of Affective Experiences—a Criticism and Restatement of the Problem," *Psychological Review*, XLIX (January, 1942), 43-53. Summary of studies dealing with the Freudian theory that unpleasant experiences and events are repressed. Conclusions not consistent.

8. Jerome D. Frank. "Recent Studies of the Level of Aspiration," *Psychological Bulletin*, XXXVIII (April, 1941), 218-26. Summary of studies on level of aspiration. Frank is not concerned with a specific hypothesis but cites several studies on each of several determinants of levels, such as knowledge of group performance or personality traits. Consistent findings on some things but not on others.

9. W. A. Kerr. "Correlates of Politico-economic Liberalism-Conservatism," *Journal of Social Psychology*, XX (August, 1944), 61-77. Summary of studies on a series of factors which are supposedly related to liberalism-conservatism, such as parental attitudes, religion, etc. Consistent findings on some things but not on others.

10. Milton Metfessel and Constance Lovell. "Recent Literature on Individual Correlates of Crime," *Psychological Bulletin*, XXXIX (March, 1942), 133-64. Summary of factors associated with criminality in various studies and of factors associated with different types of crime. Conclusions not consistent.

11. Alexander Mintz. "A Re-examination of Correlations between Lynchings and Economic Indices," *Journal of Abnormal and Social Psychology*, XLI (April, 1946), 154-60. Considers studies by Hovland and Sears, Raper, and Thomas which correlate lynching with economic variables, criticizing the statistical method. The three studies had the same general conclusions.

12. Llewellyn Queener. "The Development of Internationalist Attitudes. III. The Literature and a Point of View," *Journal of Social Psychology*, XXX (August, 1949), 105-26. Summary of studies of prestige as a determinant of international attitudes. Also concerned with "negative prestige." Conclusions interpreted into a consistent framework.

13. H. M. Richardson. "Studies of Mental Resemblance between Husbands and Wives and between Friends," *Psychological Bulletin*, XXXVI (February, 1939), 104-20. Summary of studies on selective mating where selection is based on physical resemblances and/or similarities in intelligence, attitudes, and personality traits. Some consistency in findings for intelligence, interests, and attitudes but not for personality traits.

14. Julian B. Rotter. "Level of Aspiration as a Method of Studying Personality," *Psychological Review*, XLIX (September, 1942), 463-74. Summary of studies on the effect of success and failure on explicitly set goals. Concerned with the consistency of an individual's response and with whether or not there is a relationship between the responses and personality traits. Conclusions not consistent.

15. Anselm L. Strauss. "The Literature on Panic," *Journal of Abnormal and Social Psychology*, XXXIX (July, 1944), 317-28. Summary of descriptive features and causes of panic as cited by various authors. Not complete studies. Some consistency in descriptions, although less agreement on causes.

16. William W. Wattenberg. "Delinquency and Only Children: Study of a Category," *Journal of Abnormal and Social Psychology*, XLIV (July, 1949), 356-66. Studies of the relationship between delinquency and being an only child: whether, being only children, they become spoiled; or whether, being exempted from the effects of sibling rivalry, they have an advantage over other children. Conclusions not consistent.

B. REPLICATIVE STUDIES IN WHICH COMPARISON WITH ORIGINAL STUDY
IS MADE BY AUTHOR OF REPLICATION

1. Walter Firey. *Land Use in Central Boston*, pp. 76-86. Cambridge: Harvard University Press, 1947. Replicative of E. W. Burgess, in R. E. Park and E. W. Burgess (eds.), *The City* (Chicago: University of Chicago Press, 1925), and of Maurice R. Davie, "The Pattern of Urban Growth," in *Studies in the Science of Society* (New Haven: Yale University Press, 1937), pp. 142-61. See also Lloyd Rodwin, "The Theory of Residential Growth and Structure," *Appraisal Journal*, XVIII (July, 1950), 295-317. Studies of "typical" patterns of modern city growth. Conclusions not consistent.

2. Eleanor C. Isbell. "Internal Migration in Sweden and Intervening Opportunities," *American Sociological Review*, IX (December, 1944), 627-39. Replicative of Samuel A. Stouffer, "Intervening Opportunities: A Theory Relating Mobility and Distance,"*American Sociological Review*, V (December, 1940), 845-67, and of Margaret L. Bright and Dorothy S. Thomas, "Interstate Migration and Intervening Opportunities," *American Sociological Review*, VI (December, 1941), 773-83. Studies of "intervening opportunities" as a determinant of distance in migration. Conclusions consistent.

3. Paul Wallin. "Cultural Contradictions and Sex Roles: A Repeat Study," *American Sociological Review*, XV (April, 1950), 288-93. Replicative of Mirra Komarovsky, "Cultural Contradictions and Sex Roles," *American*

Journal of Sociology, LII (November, 1946), 184-89. Conclusions consistent.

4. Paul H. Landis. "Personality Differences of Girls from Farm, Town, and City," *Rural Sociology*, XIV (March, 1949), 10-20. Replicative of A. R. Mangus, "Personality Adjustments of Rural and Urban Children," *American Sociological Review*, XIII (October, 1948), 566-75. Studies of relative "adjustment" among rural and urban children. Conclusions not consistent.

5. G. S. Klein, H. J. Schlesinger, and D. E. Meister. "The Effect of Experimental Values on Perception: An Experimental Critique," *Psychological Review*, LVIII (March, 1951), 96-112. Replicative of J. S. Bruner and L. Postman, "Symbolic Value as an Organizing Factor in Perception," *Journal of Social Psychology*, XXVII (May, 1948), 203-8, and of L. F. Carter and K. Schooler, "Value, Need and Other Factors in Perception," *Psychological Review*, LVI (July, 1949), 200-207. Conclusions not consistent.

6. J. F. Rosenblith. "A Replication of 'Some Roots of Prejudice,'" *Journal of Abnormal and Social Psychology*, XLIV (October, 1949), 470-89. Replicative of G. W. Allport and B. Kramer, "Some Roots of Prejudice," *Journal of Psychology*, XXII (July, 1946), 9-39. Conclusions consistent except in two minor respects.

7. Bradley Reynolds. "A Repetition of the Blodgett Experiment on 'Latent Learning,'" *Journal of Experimental Psychology*, XXXV (December, 1945), 504-16. Replicative of H. C. Blodgett, "The Effect of the Introduction of Reward upon the Maze Performances of Rats," *University of California Publications in Psychology*, XXXI (1928), 114-34. Conclusions partially consistent.

8. F. Stuart Chapin and Sheldon Stryker. "Confirmation of Results of an Ex Post Facto Experimental Design by Replication," *American Sociological Review*, XV (October, 1950), 670-72. Replicative of F. Stuart Chapin, Clarence A. Johanson, and Arthur L. Johnson, "Rental Rates and Crowding in Dwelling Units in Manhattan," *American Sociological Review*, XV (February, 1950), 95-97. Conclusions not consistent.

9. Georg Karlsson. *Adaptability and Communication in Marriage: A Swedish Predictive Study of Marital Satisfaction.* (Uppsala, Sweden: Almquist & Wiksells Boktryckeri Aktiebolag, 1951. Replicative of Harvey J. Locke, *Predicting Adjustment in Marriage: A Comparison of a Divorced and a Happily Married Group* (New York: Henry Holt & Co., 1951). For a direct comparison see Harvey J. Locke and Georg Karlsson, "Marital Adjustment and Prediction in Sweden and the United States," *American*

Sociological Review, XVII (February, 1952), 10-17. Most conclusions consistent.

10. Gerhart H. Saenger. "Social Status and Political Behavior," *American Journal of Sociology*, LI (September, 1945), 103-13. Replicative of P. F. Lazarsfeld, B. Berelson, and H. Gaudet, *The People's Choice* (New York: Duell, Sloan & Pearce, 1944). Replicates only in parts, but these parts are consistent. Also consistent with one conclusion in the 1944 study is a finding by Alice S. Kitt and David B. Gleicher, "Determinants of Voting Behavior," *Public Opinion Quarterly*, XIV (Fall, 1950), 393-412.

11. T. W. Adorno, E. Frenkel-Brunswik, D. J. Levinson, and R. N. Sanford, *The Authoritarian Personality* (New York: Harper & Row, Publishers, 1950); B. Bettelheim and M. Janowitz, *Dynamics of Prejudice* (New York: Harper & Row, Publishers, 1950); N. W. Ackerman and M. Jahoda, *Anti-Semitism and Emotional Disorder* (New York: Harper & Row, Publishers, 1950). Replicative of E. L. Hartley, *Problems in Prejudice* (New York: King's Crown Press, 1946). Results generally, but vaguely, consistent.

12. Virgil R. Carlson and Richard S. Lazarus. "A Repetition of Williams' Experiment on Stress and Associated Rorschach Factors," *American Psychologist*, VII (July, 1952), 317. Replicative of Meyer Williams, "An Experimental Study of Intellectual Control under Stress and Associated Rorschach Factors," *Journal of Consulting Psychology*, XI (January-February, 1947), 21-29. Conclusions not consistent.

13. L. Festinger, S. Schachter, and K. Back, *Social Pressures in Informal Groups* (New York: Harper & Row, Publishers, 1950), and T. Caplow and R. Forman, "Neighborhood Interaction," *American Sociological Review*, XV (June, 1950), 357-66. Independent studies, both arriving at the conclusion that, in a homogeneous neighborhood, the frequency of association with different neighbors is a direct function of the proximity of the neighbor's front and back doors to one's own.

14. S. Schachter, N. Ellertson, D. Gregory, and D. McBride. "An Experimental Study of Cohesiveness and Productivity," *Human Relations*, LV, No. 3 (1951), 229-38. Replicative of Kurt Back, "The Exertion of Influence through Social Communication," *Journal of Abnormal and Social Psychology*, XLVI (1951), 9-23. The two articles show that the more cohesive a group the more influence it is able to exert on its individual members. Other laboratory experiments on this hypothesis have been conducted at the universities of Michigan, Texas, and Uppsala but are not yet published. Field studies verifying the same hypothesis are L. Festinger, S. Schachter, and K. Back, *op. cit.*, and A. Rose, S. Schachter, and H. Zetterberg, "Social Responsibility as Affected by Group Standards and Cohesiveness" (unpublished). All four studies support the hypothesis, but there are minor variations in results.

C. REPLICATED STUDIES OF ATTITUDE DIFFERENTIALS

In studying a given attitude in various segments of the population, differ-ent investigators report differentials on certain background factors. Attitudes on race have frequently been studied, and the present author has summarized all empirical studies on this subject up to 1947.[9] The following is a brief summary, from this source, of the differentials reported in the scientific literature on race attitudes.

1. In seven studies, it is reported that northern white college students are more favorable to Negroes than are southern white college students. In four studies, it is reported that there is no significant difference, in atti-tudes toward Negroes, between northern and southern and southern students or (in one study) that northern students are more anti-Negro than southern students.

2. In five studies, it is reported that girls or women have more liberal race attitudes than do males. In two studies, it is reported that males are more liberal than females. In two studies, significant sex differences are found, but they vary by type of attitude. In four studies, no significant differences in race attitudes were found between the sexes.

3. In three studies, students with higher I.Q.'s were found to be more favorable toward minority groups than the less intelligent students. In three other studies, no significant relationship was found between I.Q. and race attitudes.

4. Three studies report that rural or small town students have more liberal race attitudes than do urban students. Two studies report that urban students have more liberal race attitudes than do rural students. Two studies report no differences between urban and rural students.

D. REPLICATIVE STUDIES, IN A SINGLE REPORT, BASED ON DIFFERENT
SAMPLES OR ON SAME SAMPLE AT DIFFERENT TIMES

1. Samuel A. Stouffer *et al. The American Soldier.* 4 vols. (Princeton: Princeton University Press, 1949-50). Conclusions consistent on some subjects but not on others.

2. Clifford Kirkpatrick and John Cotton. "Physical Attractiveness, Age, and Marital Adjustment," *American Sociological Review,* XVI (February, 1951), 81-86. Conclusions not consistent.

3. Louis Guttman. "Mathematical and Tabulation Techniques," in Paul Horst *et al., The Prediction of Personal Adjustment* (New York: Social

---

[9] Arnold M. Rose, *Studies in Reduction of Prejudice* (2d ed.; Chicago: American Council on Race Relations, 1948), chap. iii.

Science Research Council, 1941), pp. 360-62. A prediction of personal adjustment gave a coefficient of multiple correlation of +.73. The second one—using the same measures on a different sample—was +.04. Author attributes this to sampling error of insufficient cases and too many variables.

4. Arnold M. Rose. "Rumor in the Stock Market," *Public Opinion Quarterly*, XV (Fall, 1951), 461-86. Conclusions consistent.

Ellis Batten Page

Educational Research: Replicable or Generalizable?

A very real dilemma is faced by every researcher who attempts to conduct an experiment in education. Since he toils in an area of applied research the educational researcher has two masters, replicability and generalizability. Page defines them adroitly, making clear the nature of their competition and discussing some of the many trade-off decisions that must be faced.

Ellis B. Page, "Educational Research: Replicable or Generalizable?" *Phi Delta Kappan,* 39:302-4, March, 1958. Reprinted with permission.

Not long ago a teacher working on his doctorate in education became involved in a serious research problem. It is in education a particularly common problem, about which researchers and even some "experts," apparently blind to its real meaning, make rather dangerous blunders. It is the often difficult choice between the *experimentally replicable* study or the *educationally generalizable* one: between a study which is easy to duplicate in method *and result,* or one which has relevance to what actually occurs in a school. It is, as education attempts to become more scientific, an increasingly crucial question.

Ernest, the high school teacher, was trying to investigate certain effects of praise and blame on the learner. As an educator, he was interested in the classroom conditions; but, as a trained researcher, he was interested also in a tightly controlled experimental design. He had at his disposal only 150 students in five classes. He wanted to teach them a task, then "praise" them or "blame" them, and study certain effects of the praise or blame.

For certain well-known considerations, it was desirable that Ernest's students be *independent, i.e.,* that no student should behave the way he did because of the treatment *someone else* received.[1] In some cases we can assume independence even when students are treated as members of the same class—e.g., when, among other things, there is no chance of inter-student communication. But often this assumption may not correctly be made (even though many experimenters make it, invalidating their conclusions). Ernest, aware of the danger, reluctantly decided that he must run his subjects one-by-one. He would call them one at a time into a laboratory situation, ask that they keep everything secret from the others, praise them or blame them in isolation, and measure the results. He would run all subjects personally, after school, in their usual classroom; in these ways their relationships would be usual. But they would not be in the usual group setting, nor in the usual course of study, nor would the usual grade-motivations apply; and countless other conditions would differ from the normal school routine. In other words, Ernest found that *in order to isolate classroom processes he had to erect conditions different from those of the classroom, and in doing so alter the very processes he wished to measure.* The problem is related to the physicist's familiar poser: that the observation itself changes the phenomena one wishes to observe. In education this problem often requires some sacrifice of either replicability or generalizability. The purpose of this paper is to emphasize the dilemma, and to suggest which is the more important alternative.

Replicability should be plain enough. As used here (sometimes the term is used quite differently), it means that if other people repeat the experiment using the same procedures, they will achieve the same results. If Ernest found under his experimental conditions that praise and blame affected his students a certain way, he would expect others who repeated the conditions to discover the same effects. If they could not, those effects would be a kind of phenomenological freak, something unique and unstable, meaning either that the world was not as orderly as supposed, or that the treatment Ernest *thought* caused the difference—praise versus blame—was not the true cause at all. If he could not assume such replicability, what would be the point of publishing his results?

Generalizability should be equally plain. As used here, it refers to an *educational* generalizability, the ability to assume that the experi-

---

[1] Since this article is not the place for statistical rationale, the reader is referred to A. L. Edwards, *Experimental Design in Psychological Research* (New York: Holt, Rinehart and Winston, 1950), 446 pp., E. F. Lindquist, *Design and Analysis of Experiments in Psychology and Education* (Boston: Houghton Mifflin, 1953), 393 pp., or to any other standard text of experimental design. Particular attention should be given those sections dealing with controls, randomization, interactions, and the assumptions underlying tests of significance.

mental results will occur in (other) *school* occasions, when those teaching will be professional teachers and those learning will be young human learners, *i.e.*, in what we normally consider the educative process, involving subject matter, former conditions of failure and success, school bells, blackboards, and all the rest of it. If Ernest found that praise and blame affected his students a certain way, he would expect *somewhat* the same results with slightly different words of praise, different learning tasks, timing, different students and teachers. Otherwise, why should he publish or, for that matter, even experiment? For, as some reflection will show, if we in education cannot assume generalizability from event to event, we could not learn by others' experiences, or even by our own.

If an experiment is to contribute anything substantial, both of the attributes, replicability and educational generalizability, are plainly necessary. Actually, they will support each other, in ideal circumstances. Suppose Ernest, for instance, had unlimited sampling power. He would then have no dilemma; he would secure classes in hundreds of schools throughout America, run hundreds of different experiments concerning praise and blame, under the supervision of a large number of teachers, all of whom would be sophisticated, obedient, impartial (and, of course, randomly selected!). Such conditions, if they were not actually self-contradictory, would yield results which would be, in our sense of the terms, both replicable *and* generalizable. But even if such experimentation were realizable, its cost would be prohibitive.

In present circumstances, Ernest, having to choose between conditions which will foster one ideal or the other, must be very careful where he goes for advice. A certain number of educational researchers, though statistically and psychologically experienced, are committed to the rock-solid replicability of the laboratory. And such a one—call him Dr. Labs—might advise Ernest thus:

> Now wait, your problem is already too loose. Take them one-by-one, all right, because then they're independent. But you don't want it in the same classroom. Your students will have special feelings about your classroom that other students wouldn't have about theirs. And special feelings about you. What's more, *your* "Good" and "Poor" will not be the same as another teacher's. Someone else may come along, try your experiment, and get different results. And you can't get what would really be best, a random sample of teachers. So forget using a real teacher. Eliminate that source of error. Use a machine instead, one that will always be the same, and will blink green and red.

The specific advice will of course differ from one Dr. Labs to another, but the burden will always be the same: forget education and worry about your *experiment*. If Ernest does so he may well end with another study in "learning," suspended in air, pure, shiny, educationally empty. For by now, it is hoped, the folly of such advice is plain. If "one source of error" is eliminated by the substitution of machine for man, replicability would, it is true, benefit; but generalizability would suffer an incalculable loss. For to be educationally generalizable, conditions must be generalizable to the "educative process," that process usually concerned not with green and red lights, but with a human "Good," "Poor," or other verbalizations spoken or written by a teacher for his own pupils, often in the presence of other pupils, and so on. *That is what the term "generalizable" means.* And such transfer of result can only be assumed because some similarity of conditions exists between experiment and classroom.

Suppose we visualize such similarity as a scale running from A to Z. We are interested, let us say, solely in the effect that "Good" will have on an average class when spoken by an average teacher. Like all averages that are guessed from sampling, this teacher is an elusive shadow whom we can never observe. He is all we care about; our experimental conclusions will be valid only if they are true about *him*. Yet the most we can do is guess about him. Let us say that when this shadow says "Good" to students in an average class, the effect may be represented on our scale by the letter A. There are now at least four different ways that we can guess what A might be like:

(1) The best way is plainly to take a *truly random sample* of teachers, and study the experimental effects of the way *they* say "Good." These effects will range, say, between A and G or I. As we increase the number of our sample, we will have an increasingly sharp idea of the nature of A. With a large random sample we may reach conclusions which will be both replicable and generalizable. Yet in many experiments a truly random sample of teachers is probably impossible. The unwilling, uncooperative, preoccupied, far away, will be necessarily excluded from the population, and so will others.

(2) When these elements are excluded, we have a *biased sample* of teachers; and it is usually impossible to say exactly how this bias will influence the experimental effects. We still know that, regardless of where A falls, our sample is averaging somewhere between A and I. But we no longer have a sure method of estimating where A lies. Now our guesses about our average teacher are truly guesses, without much empirical justification. Replicability will be sure only when any later experimentation biases the sampling in the *same way*.

(3) Once admitting the difficulties of achieving a fair sample, a third possibility is to use a *single teacher* as the giver of praise and blame;

and this is probably the most common "solution." A single experimenter, such as Ernest running his own students, is much like a biased sample; yet even the shaky guesses derivable from a biased sample become less defensible. Ernest achieves results. Are they close to A, or are they closer to H? Now replicability is sure only if the same experimenter is used again—or, of course, someone else who has whatever unknown qualities have produced the result. As Dr. Labs feared, when the experiment is attempted by someone else, he may achieve different results; then Ernest's own conclusions will have uncertain, unreliable meanings.

(4) A fourth alternative is the use of some *machine*, or analogous animal experiment, which eliminates the vexing influence of human differences. Provided that a machine's construction were specified in enough detail, its effects would be faithfully replicable. Objectively considered, however—and that is the only way we have of considering it—the machine's position on the scale of similarity would be out beyond P, or R. It may reassure Dr. Labs to know that the green light's effect at some unguessable position P or R is absolutely replicable at that point. To some a "fact" of this kind is comforting; but to be so comforted is to surrender our goal, which is the study of A. It is facts about A, the average teacher, that we are interested in, and not facts about machines P and R (or even a random sample of machines, whatever that would mean). It must be stressed that this objection to the mechanistic experimentation of the laboratory is reasoned, not from the usual humanistic ideals, but from one of the home-grown experimental ideals—sensible research design. Furthermore, this objection applies not only to machine and animal models, but to human experimentation as well, when the tasks and surrounding conditions move too far from A: from the school conditions under investigation.

We are then in something of a paradox. Although a considerable degree of replicability seems necessary if an experiment is to represent a statable truth, generalizability appears to be far more fundamental, *i.e.*, the similarity of conditions to those actual educative conditions in which children commonly learn. The results will often be "looser"; but they will nevertheless be closer to A—and will therefore have more relevance to A—than will many tightly reproducible laboratory studies. For it must be maintained that, *when "A" is considered to represent the true average experimental effect, nearness to A is the only criterion of an experiment's usefulness.*

If this is the moral, it is a disturbing one for Dr. Labs and his predilection for absolute laboratory controls. But it is a reassuring one for the individual teacher busily studying his students. As Professor William Briscoe said (in a letter to the author): "It seems to me that when we allow ourselves to get very far away from people, from understanding them, appreciating them, and loving them at all ages, we are out of the field of education." His words appear to be not only a humanitarian, cautionary maxim for the administrator, but solid, statistical sense for the educational researcher as well.

Nicholas Fattu

Prediction:
From Oracle to Automation

In the broadest sense all research has at its base prediction. The researcher wants to say, "If I do this, then that will happen," or, "If these conditions obtain, then we may expect to find those kinds of reactions." In one sense then the value of a piece of research may be determined by the degree of accurateness of its prediction. In this article Fattu discusses prediction theory and how various prediction schemes work. If education is to move forward, then it must move away from the most popular and successful of all prediction techniques—hindsight prediction.

Nicholas A. Fattu, "Prediction: From Oracle to Automation," *Phi Delta Kappan*, 39: 409-12, 1958. Reprinted with permission.

Outside of womankind, few topics have intrigued and tormented mankind more than the problem of predicting the future. As predictions become more accurate, decisions and their associated consequents become less subject to uncertainty and insecurity. Decision, to be sure, is more than prediction. It is a form of information processing. Data flows in and a recommended course of action comes out. The mechanism has at least three basic components: a prediction system that deals with alternative futures, a value system that handles conflicting purposes, and a criterion that integrates the other two and chooses an appropriate course of action. The present discussion is restricted to the prediction component of the decision process.

Prediction in education traditionally implies linear correlation and regression. We shall try to examine some alternative procedures.

Bross (2) indicates that the only foolproof, 100 per cent correct method of prediction is *hindsight prediction*. Prediction of an event that has occurred is popular and widespread. Fortune tellers, certain politicians, newspaper columnists, and commentators use it with excellent results. All that is needed is skillful use of ambiguous, or even contradictory, remarks and an ability to forget selectivity.

Virtually all legitimate prediction schemes find their basis in a study of the past. The first step toward prediction is the search for characteristics that are stable or invariant. Several levels of such persistence can be distinguished.

The simplest prediction is that based on *proximity*. Thus if it is raining today, one would predict it will rain tomorrow. In weather forecasting this sort of prediction is often hard to beat. The meteorologist, using data from numerous weather stations combined with his involved air-mass computations, makes forecasts that are only about ten per cent more frequently correct than the man who uses proximity prediction. As Bross indicates, "this is not because modern methods are bad, but because persistence methods are good." In weather forecasts they give correct prediction about three-fourths of the time, so that there is little room for improvement.

Proximity prediction works well in a comparatively stable or slowly changing situation. It is useful in predicting life expectancy rates, but of little use in the stock market where the premium is placed on predicting the changes. All the information that is needed for proximity prediction is the happening of the event immediately before the prediction.

A second forecasting scheme is *trend prediction*. This method assumes that change is constant. If the stock market rises exactly one point each day, trend prediction assumes that the rise of one point per day continues. Trend prediction often gives a good prediction in the immediately adjacent time interval, but it usually yields ridiculous long range forecasts. Thus in student population forecasts over adjacent time intervals, trend prediction often yields satisfying accurate predictions. Extrapolation far beyond this boundary gives silly forecasts. Curve fitting methods, particularly linear curves, are useful here. The method is dependable only as long as the trend remains constant. Even gradual changes extrapolated far enough can yield serious error.

Cyclic prediction, which assumes that cycles are constant, has been effectively used in long range predictions of the occurrence of sun spots, lemming and locust plagues, and tide predictions. Early success stirred hopes that here was the key to seeing the future. This method uses more data than proximity and trend predictions. In fact, the standard alibi for failure is that the records do not go back far enough. Non-linear curve fitting methods, harmonic, and Fourier functions have provided useful methods.

The favorite method for prediction in education is *associative prediction*, which assumes a stable relationship between events. On a low level of discrimination this relationship may be expressed as a "cause," or an antecedent, *i.e.*, "low intelligence" causes "low school grades." When we stick to the simple meaning of the word *cause* little harm is done. An antecedent that precedes an event will be identified. The temptation to expand, however, is great. An antecedent may not be obvious. Of the many events we might study, only a few will have any discernible relationship with the events we may wish to forecast. Unless a great deal of care and judgment is exercised in the search for the antecedent, the whole process degenerates into nonsense. Fortune tellers use associative prediction, their antecedents being the fall of cards or the configuration of tea leaves. So far, they have failed to show that the antecedents used are relevant to the events being predicted.

Most common and most widely used of the relevant associative procedures are linear (single and multiple) regressions. These traditional methods are effective only insofar as the linear function selected represents linear relationships actually present in the data. In the case of several variables, traditional computations are often tedious and frustrating. Computational simplification by a variety of linear procedures, Dwyer (8), and by use of electronic data processing equipment, Wrigley (29), has made the task more tractable.

However, the method has several limitations. It imposes a single functional relation and summation of weighted variables. If the function and the summation happen to be appropriate, the method provides accurate predictions. When the situation is not so determinate, as when the relationships are not simply linear and additive, it may be still possible to apply an appropriate alternative procedure.

Forecasting efficiency, error of estimate, coefficient of determination, etc., do not recognize that the value of a measure may vary with the particular decision for which it was to be used. In admitting students to medical school, for example, an error of prediction regarding a superior person does no harm. So long as it is desirable to admit both X and Y, it does not matter if the equation overestimates X's grades and underestimates Y's. Only errors which cross the borderline, so that a man is admitted who should not be, and vice versa, impair the value of the prediction. The problem has been dealt with by Ferguson, Guttman, Loevinger, and others. Cronbach (5) appraises these efforts.

Horst (15) suggested alternative procedures designed to overcome some limitations of the traditional approach. Thus the traditional method considers various measures against a single criterion, *i.e.*, predicting college grade point average from entrance test scores and high-school record. In contrast, Horst describes a procedure for differential prediction that should prove helpful to students and college counselors. Instead of predicting a single overall grade point average, the method provides for prediction of performance in a variety of curricula. The same data (test battery) is differentially weighted for each prediction. This method still suffers from rigidity of the single function for each prediction.

Several investigators attempt to surmount the obstacle of the rigidity of relationship assumption in *associative prediction* by a *pattern prediction* procedure. Fricke (11) and Ellson (10) suggest an empirical con-figurational method. Fricke uses a coded test profile to predict academic achievement, based on the assumption that students with the same pattern get the same grades. In a multiple regression equation, each variable has a constant beta weight. For an individual, the contribution of a particular score is not affected by the magnitude and relation of other scores. Fricke suggests that actually what might be called a dynamic suppressor variable relationship may be operating in the coded profile prediction method. Perhaps in order for a particular predictor to be able to exert its influence on the criterion, specific amounts of other predictors must be present. The method is very simple and very tedious because of the large number of profiles possible. Ellson's (10) conditional probabilities are essentially comparable to Fricke's means.

Other pattern methods that are used for prediction and for study of item responses are described by McQuitty (21), Osgood, and Cron-bach. Helmstadter (13) describes an empirical comparison of fifteen of these empirical methods for estimating profile similarity. The method is useful where precise statements of functional relationships are absent and the approximate statements obtainable by statistical techniques are often inadequate because of the nonlinearity of the data or non-quantitative character of the observations by which the data were obtained. Profile methods are said to yield more accurate predictions than the traditional multiple regression procedures. They are, how-ever, largely empirical procedures based on incomplete mathematical models and are subject to the limitations of strictly empirical pro-cedures.

The classification aspects of prediction have been explored by means of discriminant analysis as described by Tatsuoka and Tiedeman (26). In 1936 Fisher considered the problem of getting a linear combination of variables which would, better than any other linear combination, discriminate between two chosen groups.

In educational research, investigators often face the problem of classifying individuals into two or more mutually exclusive groups.

With these, we first ascertain whether or not there is a stable difference in the observations among the groups. For those data in which a significant group difference exists, attention then turns to *distances* separating pairs of the groups, directions in which groups differ, and *assignment* to one of the groups of an unclassified individual known to belong to one of the groups. Significance, distance, direction, and assignment are the issues of discriminant analysis.

The sixth and final prediction method is *analog prediction*. Analog prediction sets up a correspondence between a model and a set of events. The model is usually simpler and more manipulable than the events. Reasoning by analogy is acceptable only when the analogy is relevant. Properly used, analogy can be a powerful tool for prediction. This is especially true if a mathematical model can be constructed. By mathematical arguments, the performance of the model can be predicted. If the model represents the significant variables of the real event, these events can then be forecast by analogy.

Use of scale model airplanes in a wind tunnel to predict certain performance characteristics of full-sized aircraft is possible because the significant performance variables are associated with shape and contour rather than size. The use of experimental animals to standardize a drug destined for eventual human use is also an example.

Associative prediction, of course, has a statistical model as a base. From the standpoint of a valid predictive model for educational decisions, this statistical model has only limited utility. The traditional theory views a test as a measuring instrument intended to assign accurate numerical scores to some characteristic of the individual. It emphasizes precision of measurement and estimation. When determining the breaking strength of steel beams, one can't argue that one error is more serious than another of equal magnitude, hence measurement theory is appropriate.

In practical testing, a quantitative estimate is not the sole object. Often a choice among several alternatives having different payoff functions must be made. Testing here is valuable only insofar as it helps assign the examinee to the proper category, as in the case of discriminant analysis. However, discriminant analysis is still tied to measurement theory. When a physical measuring instrument is used to control an industrial process, decision theory is a more satisfactory model than measurement theory.

In his recent book, *Psychological Tests and Personnel Decisions*, Cronbach (6) explores the possible relevance of game and decision theory to decisions involving educational prediction, and suggests that it provides a more satisfactory model than the traditional measurement model. A major contribution of the approach through decision theory is that it points toward a variety of needed empirical studies. Thus many current personnel procedures are based on assumptions regarding the interaction of the characteristics of the individual and the nature of the treatment to which he is assigned, but these implicit, widely-held assumptions have been scarcely tested, if at all. Similarly, it is held that tests used for placement require different validation from those in general use. Cronbach convincingly indicates that the conceptual tools of decision theory make the tester aware of problems which hitherto have been minimized or overlooked. Restatement of testing problems in these terms should assist test users in understanding what assumptions they are making and how adequate their procedures are. For a more comprehensive treatment of game theory, see Churchman, Ackoff, and Arnoff (3). Similar methods have been effectively used by Votaw and Dailey (27) and Votaw and Leiman (28) in handling the personnel assignment problem for the Air Force.

As more and more automation is introduced into data processing, new ways of thinking about prediction problems will have to be developed. Bross (2) indicates that "people must have the very latest electronic gadget, but they cling tenaciously to ideas and methods of thinking that were obsolete" long ago. To prevent valid application of this accusation, educational decision makers during the next decade will be studying and using the concepts of operations research and decision theory.

Bibliography

1. Birnbaum, A., *Efficient Design and Use of Tests of Mental Ability for Various Decision-making Problems*. Randolph Air Force Base, Texas: School of Aviation Medicine, January, 1957.

2. Bross, I. D. J., *Design for Decision*. New York: The Macmillan Co., 1953.

3. Churchman, C. W., Ackoff, R. L., and Arnoff, E. L., *Introduction to Operations Research*. New York: John Wiley and Sons, Inc., 1957.

4. Cronbach, L. J., *A Consideration of Information Theory and Utility Theory as Tools for Psychometric Problems*. Urbana: College of Education, University of Illinois, 1953.

5. Cronbach, L. J., "The Counselor's Problems from the Perspective of Communication Theory," in *New Perspectives in Counseling*, V. H. Hewer, editor. Minneapolis: University of Minnesota Press, 1955.

6. Cronbach, L. J. and Gleser, G. C., *Psychological Tests and Personnel Decisions*. Urbana: University of Illinois Press, 1957.

7. Dwyer, P. S., *Selection and Linear Combinations of Tests in Relation to Multiple Criteria and Differential Classifications.* Personnel Research Board, Research Note 7, Department of the Army, 1953.

8. Dwyer, P. S., *Linear Computation.* New York: John Wiley and Sons, Inc., 1951.

9. Edwards, W., "The Theory of Decision Making," *Psychological Bulletin,* 51:380-418, 1954.

10. Ellson, D. G., "A Method for Technological Prediction," pp. 31-50 in *Information Theory in Psychology: Problems and Methods,* H. Quastler, editor. Glencoe, Illinois: Free Press, 1955.

11. Fricke, B. G., "A Coded Profile Method for Predicting Achievement," *Educational and Psychological Measurement,* 17:98-104, 1957.

12. Girshick, M. A., "An Elementary Survey of Statistical Decision Theory," *Review of Educational Research,* 24:448-466, 1954.

13. Helmstadter, G. C., "An Empirical Comparison of Methods for Estimating Profile Similarity," *Educational and Psychological Measurement,* 17:71-82, 1957.

14. Horst, P. A., "Determination of Optimal Test Length to Maximize the Multiple Correlation," *Psychometrika,* 14:79-88, 1949.

15. Horst, P. A., "A Technique for the Development of a Differential Prediction Battery," *Psychological Monograph,* 68, No. 9 (Whole No. 380), 1954.

16. Horst, P. A., "Optimal Test Length for Maximum Differential Prediction," *Psychometrika,* 21:51-67, 1956.

17. Horst, P. A., "Pattern Analysis and Configural Scoring," *Journal of Clinical Psychology,* 10:3-11, 1954.

18. Horst, P. A., and MacEwan, C., "Optimal Test Length for Maximum Absolute Prediction," *Psychometrika,* 21:111-125, 1956.

19. Long, W. F., and Burr, I. W., "Development of a Method for Increasing the Utility of Multiple Correlations by Considering Both Testing Time and Test Validity," *Psychometrika,* 14:137-161, 1949.

20. Luce, R. D., and Raiffa, H., *Games and Decisions: Introduction and Critical Survey.* New York: John Wiley and Sons, Inc., 1958.

21. McQuitty, L. L., "Isolating Predictor Patterns Associated with Major Criterion Patterns," *Educational and Psychological Measurement,* 17: 3-42, 1957.

22. Maxwell, A. E., "Contour Analysis," *Educational and Psychological Measurement,* 17:347-360, 1957.

23. Meehl, P. E., "Configural Scoring," *Journal of Consulting Psychology,* 14:165-171, 1950.

24. Meehl, P. E., *Clinical vs. Statistical Prediction.* Minneapolis: University of Minnesota Press, 1954.

25. Sarbin, T. R., "A Contribution to the Study of Actuarial and Individual Methods of Prediction," *American Journal of Sociology,* 48:593-602, 1942.

26. Tatsuoka, M. M. and Tiedeman, D. V., "Discriminant Analysis," *Review of Educational Research,* 24:402-420, 1954.

27. Votaw, D. F., Jr. and Dailey, J. T., "Assignment of Personnel to Jobs," Human Resources Research Center, *Research Bulletin 52-24,* 1952.

28. Votaw, D. F., Jr. and Leiman, J. M., "An Approximation Method of Solving the Personnel Assignment Problem," *Technical Memorandum PL-TM-56-14,* Personal Laboratory, AFPTRC, July, 1956.

29. Wrigley, C., "Data Processing: Automation in Calculation," *Review of Educational Research,* 27:528-543, 1957.

Irvin S. Wolf

Perspectives in Psychology: Negative Findings

As one reads the professional journals, he is struck by the fact that the majority of researches reported are successful; that is, the major hypothesis was supported, or at least the null hypothesis was rejected. From this observation the naive reader may assume that all research is successful; the more sophisticated reader knows that, generally, only successful research gets published. In this article, Wolf makes a plea for the publication of negative results, pointing out the obvious (apparently) advantages of knowing what does not seem to be true as well as knowing what appears to be true. If only positive results were published, would Platt's call for strong inference technique stand a chance?

I. S. Wolf, "Perspectives in Psychology: Negative Findings." *Psychological Record*, 11: 91-5, 1961. Reprinted with permission.

The logic associated with testing the null hypothesis is deceptively appealing. Every beginning class in statistics seems to be intrigued and persuaded by the example of being able to disprove, but not to prove, that all crows are black. The impossibility of proving the proposition is presented as the timeless problem of induction—when may we be confident our observations are sufficiently extensive and accurate to escape tentativeness, to exclude the possibility of the negative case?

The compelling arguments for following this interpretive device are accompanied by problems neglected by slaves to its use. Involved are situations both where the null hypothesis is rejected and where it is accepted. In the former we are sometimes too ready to conclude with finality that the obtained difference is true, and dependent upon the chosen experimental variable. Overlooked are admonitions regarding limitations of statistical tools, which, no matter how elaborate, cannot be expected to correct for problems of control or observation. Perhaps

383

it is the present aura of unguarded respect for quantification and all that is mathematical that leads to careless use of statistical procedures in our descriptive, investigative, and interpretive enterprise. Rejection of the null hypothesis occurs only at a particular level of confidence and requires assumptions of representativeness of sample and absence of constant errors built into the design or measurements. Interpretations based on rejection of the null hypothesis also must remain tentative. To make significance at the .05 level *the* criterion of acceptability as a legitimate conclusion gives a statistical rule the status of final arbiter over the admissability of scientific evidence. We need to be.on guard against this species of absolutism, overconfidence in reaching truth by a single route, statistical or otherwise. Publishing patterns at least suggest such overconfidence exists. Rejecting the null hypothesis seems almost an end in itself. Perhaps there is a basis for the charge that in some of our journals there is little more than psychological "trivia" dignified by impressive exercises in experimental or statistical design. The worthwhileness of method alone cannot determine the worthwhileness of the result.

THE PROBLEM

Among the present trends one which should cause concern is that of minimal attention to negative findings; few studies are reported where the null hypothesis was not rejected. An editor of this journal once warned that accepting a particular manuscript might lead to our becoming "typed" for publishing negative findings. That these should be available and are not has been emphasized (Goldfried and Waters, 1959; Wolins, 1959; Sterling, 1959).[1] The latter reviewed a single volume of each of four psychological journals and found that of the 362 papers none was a replication of a previously published paper. Tests of significance were employed in 294. Only eight of these reported failure to reject the null hypothesis when attention was focused on the study's major issue. Sterling observed further that this situation could result either from editorial or author decision or both.

---

[1] Each year there appear articles admonishing us with regard to uses and abuses of statistical tools. During the present manuscript's maturation in the file, several papers commenting on its topic have been discovered in recently appearing journals (Goldfried & Walters, 1959; Sterling, 1959; Wolins, 1959; McNemar, 1960; Rozeboom, 1960). It is not without some embarrassment that we have proceeded to publish these notes, but the fact that some of the points are not completely unshared perhaps attests to our sanity . . . and then nearly all those discussing the issues have at some point stressed the importance of "replications".

USES OF NEGATIVE FINDINGS

Negative findings should be considered for communication to colleagues; such pieces of research with some theoretical or practical import, competently studied and interpreted, should be accepted in the literature. Despite apparent reluctance to report negative findings, their recognition may prove profitable in various ways: by directing attention to relationships which do *not* exist; by refining our knowledge of the factors which lead to conflicting positive and negative findings in studies with similar conceptual parentage; in drawing attention to repeated "near misses" (e.g., at the .10 level); in demonstrating the possibility of having rejected the null hypothesis in a previous study when it should have been accepted, etc.

Prevailing attitudes disparaging negative findings may lead a discouraged investigator prematurely into other areas. The least that can be gained from publication, if attainable, is that other workers may be directed to avoid treading the same inconclusive steps.

Comparison of similar studies with positive and negative findings may lead to more refined delimitations of significant variables.

Even a neutral reviewer of the literature may be handicapped where he has no basis for choice between two studies with differing theoretical orientations, each reporting positive findings perhaps with equal significance levels. The problem of choice probably could be resolved were he aware of negative findings in the replications of one. In time, of course, we might expect a preponderance of positive findings to be reported for the other. Prior to that, wasteful theoretical and experimental decisions would be unavoidable.

Convinced of the significance of a particular negative finding one may seek, through a replication of the experiment or through collecting of other instances from the literature, to "confirm" the absence of relationship. While greater confidence may inhere in building conceptually upon rejection of the null hypothesis, there is no logical basis for concluding that "no differences" or "no correlations" are non-existent in nature. Tests of hypotheses which are of sufficient theoretical or practical significance to lead to repeated observations by the same or different students but which always end in failure to reject the null hypothesis, begin to approximate "proof" that differences cannot be obtained under these conditions. Perhaps the dog is *not* capable of color vision but a more tentative statement would be that color discrimination has not been demonstrated. The caution of the latter form has much in its favor despite the fact that we usually communicate the former. That the proper technique for demonstrating color vision in the dog has not been utilized must be considered a possibility; comparable caution in interpreting the positive findings of color vision in other species is also wise (e.g., the possibility of inadequate control of brightness or some other variable not now recognized). We need constant vigilance with *both* positive and negative findings.

A decision in proposition building by the serious scientist will be based on preceding studies, nearly identical, and related; yet the acceptability of evidence tends to be time-bound. Studies are evaluated as discrete, scientific episodes. The theory is supported (or not) on the basis of our success or failure in rejecting the null hypothesis—in *this* group of manipulations. Which is more acceptable—several instances of significance at the .10 level for repeated tests of one hypothesis or one "success" at the .05 level for another? While the former many times fails to reach consideration in our theory building, the latter achieves acceptance and even if in error resists correction simply because negative findings in future tests are not reported.

It is not inconceivable that a completely autistic theory, appealing perhaps because of its bizarreness (or the professional status of its author), would be tested a sufficient number of times so that results involving a Type I error would occur. Even though statistical significance was achieved on a chance basis, or because of some constant error (which statistics cannot be expected to correct), the studies carefully executed and reported may now become a part of the literature. The students of the investigator, particularly if he is a distinguished one, and their students now perform replications of the original experiment or deduce related research projects. Again out of the mass of studies some will produce positive findings and they too will find their way into the literature. Those failing to achieve statistically significant differences, or even those with results in the opposite direction (when the one-tailed test was pre-selected), will probably be rejected by the student himself and the experiment will be redesigned (doctoral committees as well as editors are reputed to prefer positive findings). With final "success" in achieving positive results the preliminary studies become known as "pilot" work; although the dissertation summarizes the whole investigative effort, the positive findings have a central position in the limited space available in our journals. Today it is not considered proper to shift one's statistical stance during the course of an investigation (e.g., changing from a one-tailed to two-tailed test). Perhaps with equal fervor we should insist upon presentation of negative findings for a study which, prior to its execution, was agreed to be a fair replication. Positive findings become established by being accepted and printed, but the set of attitudes discriminating against negative findings tends to protect a Type I error.

We could pursue the hypothetical history of a theory one step further. Still another student may now get his MA for counting the references to the author of the original papers. Although misgivings are expressed regarding the interpretations because of rumored failures to find consistent support, the theory will be glorified for its heuristic contributions!

CAUTIONS

It should be made clear that, although the foregoing was offered as an indictment of present neglect of negative findings, all such results do not have equal status. Significance of the hypothesis being investigated, care in the execution of the study, consistency (and inconsistency) with results obtained in similar studies—all help to determine the evaluation of a particular negative finding. Not the least of the factors is how great was the "miss" (at the .06 or .40 level).[2] We must remain sensitive to our constructional procedures. Negative findings too, in a study with inadequate methodology or conceptualization, can be misleading. (How much has been attributed to instinct or constitutional factors because of the inability to demonstrate learning!).

SUMMARY

Some of the dangers of translating rules for testing the null hypothesis into absolutistic criteria for the acceptability of scientific evidence have been discussed. Rules so used take the place of events and other determiners of investigation molding the course of psychology. An attitude of tentativeness still needs to be maintained with positive findings. Replications are to be encouraged. Negative findings provide information and need a more favorable audience among psychologists—

---

[2] Eysenck (1960) points to the essentially "subjective" nature of the verbal descriptions, significant and non-significant, used in dichotomizing the continuous series of p values around arbitrary points of .05 or .01. He recommends abandoning this translation procedure (involving other terms like "almost significant" or "significant at the 10% level") and the implication of successful or unsuccessful research. Presenting the p values themselves would permit a reader to make an interpretation in terms of evaluations of this and related studies and of other factors. Also, see Sterling (1960) pg. 30.

388 Perspectives in Psychology: Negative Findings

if only for the reason that prejudices against their publication (by both editors and investigators) tend to perpetuate a false conclusion based upon rejection of the null hypothesis when it should have been accepted. Judicious consideration and communication of negative findings seem necessary for the development of our science.

References

Eysenck, H. J. The concept of statistical significance and the controversy about one-tailed tests. *Psychol. Rev.*, 1960, 67, 269-271.

Goldfried, M. R. & Walters, G. C. Needed: publication of negative results. *Amer. Psychologist*, 1959, 14, 598.

McNemar, Q. At random: sense and nonsense. *Amer. Psychologist*, 1960, 15, 295-300.

Rozeboom, W. W. The fallacy of the null-hypothesis significance test. *Psychol. Bull.*, 1960, 57, 416-428.

Sterling, T. D. Publication decisions and their possible effects on inferences drawn from tests of significance—or vice versa. *J. of Amer. Statist. Ass.*, 1959, 54, 30-34.

Wolins, L. Needed: publication of negative results. *Amer. Psychologist*, 1959, 14, 598.

Marvin R. Goldfried and Gary C. Walters

Needed: Publication of Negative Results

This short item needs little comment save reference to the logical inference pattern discussion in Chapter 1.

Marvin R. Goldfried and Gary C. Walters, "Needed: Publication of Negative Results," *American Psychologist*, 14:598, 1959. Reprinted with permission.

The usual first step in an experimental study is a search of the literature for previous work relevant to the proposed research. Certainly no problem exists if the researcher finds the work has been done. Unfortunately, the only studies that are likely to appear in any journal are those which come up with "publishable results" (i.e., results that are statistically significant). If an experiment yields "negative results" (i.e., results which fail to confirm the tested hypothesis), the findings are usually relegated to the experimenter's filing cabinet and are likely to remain there. This approach can hardly be thought of as extending scientific communication.

It is suggested that the value of negative results has been underestimated. Negative findings can add to our knowledge by indicating unfruitful aspects of a given problem, thereby eliminating wasted research time and energy. In building up the empirical foundation of a science, it is important to know not only what *does* exist, but what does *not* exist as well.

A way of coping with this problem would be to have a place to publish these findings. This could be done by establishing a *Journal of Negative Results*. Considering the cost and limited space of present-day publications, such a journal could follow the format of the *Psychological Abstracts*; investigators could obtain detailed descriptions of the studies from the authors. Investigators would then be able to make more adequate surveys of the work done in their areas. One risk might be the inclusion of studies whose findings were due to methodological inadequacies; but in this area where communication is practically nil, errors of commission are more desirable than errors of omission.

chapter 5

Educational Research: Theory Development and Applicability

The practicality of theories has long been debated. Educators have aligned themselves at four positions on this matter. Some feel that theories are of little value in the day-to-day conduct of schooling and say so loud and clear. To them only practical matters matter. A second group says that theories are valuable, but in the performance of their duties no evidence of this can be deduced. A third group has a strong belief that theories must have practical application, and that practice must have a theoretical basis. Unfortunately this group (and the Editors include themselves) have been ineffective at communicating this belief. Finally some educators believe that theory is an end unto itself. To them anything that appears practical is of minimal importance.

The assumption behind this chapter, and indeed the entire book and the research process itself, is that theory and practice are or should be mutually reinforcing aspects of a professional endeavor. Through theory the professional should be able to make logical predictions about the efficacy of a practice. Through the assessment of the effects of a practice, theory can be modified and extended, or both.

At least two difficulties can be isolated which mediate against the acceptance of theory as an integral aspect of the educator's behavior. Too often statements posed as a theory are not a theory at all. At best such conglomerate statements fail to help the individual understand or make predictions about his profession. At worst such conglomerates lead people in the wrong directions. In either case these nontheories confirm an established distrust of the value of theory.

The second difficulty is a problem of abstraction. Communication about the nature of theory seems to require a level of abstraction in discourse that is rejected by the practical man. Thus, when we try to help people learn to discriminate between theory and nontheory, we employ terms such as "system," "assumptions," "correlaries," "postulates," and "hypotheses." Since all of these terms have little impact and perhaps less meaning to the practical man, he not only tunes them out, but he marks another tally on the ledger for the uselessness of theory.

But theory development is and must be the continued end which justifies the process of research. The date at which we will know everything is a long way off. Until that time our work fails to qualify as a profession if we do not have, and continue to expand, a systematically generated body of knowledge *which affects the nature of practice.* As indicated in the Platt article in Chapter 1, the areas which seemingly make the most rapid advancements are characterized by: (1) a structuring of what is currently known and assumed into a system; (2) the use of that system to derive tentative explanations (hypotheses) for the still unknown areas; (3) the empirical test of those hypotheses; and (4) alteration or extension of the structure based upon those empirical findings. Such a process is theory development. Its name is research. And its end is improved practice.

In the readings for this chapter the Editors have tried first to select a stage setting. The article by Lee considers the nature of theory, and is presented as that stage setter. Beyond this, two articles have been chosen that speak to the utility of theories. Although dated 15 years ago, Gordon's plea for better theories is pertinent today. This fact is a direct commentary on the progress of education over a period of dramatic change in the dollar support for educational research. Through Kerlinger's article, we return to the question of practicality. This time, however, the focus is on the degree to which practicality constrains research.

The next two articles take a different but related track. The spiral of current knowledge, theory specification, hypothesis testing, and theory strengthening is not as clear and clean as it sounds. Almost universally, research projects contain methodological inadequacies, inadequacies that cannot be predicted by foresight alone. Thus it is rare that we can totally accept conclusions from a completed study. The articles by Stinnett and Fox guide the reader in evaluative strategies. Stinnett's focus is on statistical analysis, while Fox proposes a global evaluation. The perceptive reader will note that the evaluation proposed by Fox contains style aspects and an assessment of the researcher himself.

The Editors believe that the basic format of *Educational Research: Selected Readings* provides a strategy for evaluating research, a strategy which has four elements: (1) problem delineation; (2) logical inference pattern; (3) data generation techniques; and (4) data analysis techniques. If the research evaluator determines the degree to which these four elements are carried out in a study, he has two valuable gains: first he can make a well-based quality statement about the soundness of conclusions stated; and second, *he has identified points and procedures which can be improved in a subsequent study.* This latter gain, the contribution a study makes to our knowledge of methods of studying a problem, is all too often overlooked. It should not be. Two things can be learned from a completed research project: information about the problem, and information about studying the problem.

After the strength of the conclusions of a completed research is established, one final task remains. The research process is, as asserted earlier, a component in our expanding knowledge system. If we are to systematically expand, we must concentrate on the implications of research findings and conclusions for theory. Both Van Dalen and Kerlinger stress this point. We use theory to propose hypothetical explanations for unknowns. We use research to test the adequacy or truth value of our hypothesis. Finally we should incorporate our conclusions in our theory to reduce what is unknown and to develop stronger theory from which to evolve more piercing hypotheses.

Harold N. Lee

Theoretic Knowledge
and Hypothesis [1]

In the opening article of this final chapter, we are presenting a discussion of
the nature of theoretic knowledge. It seemed appropriate to discuss the nature
of theory before the role of theory in research was considered. As later articles
are read, it might be well to refer back to this one in order to keep a perspective of what is referred to as theory.

Harold N. Lee, "Theoretic Knowledge and Hypothesis," Psychology Review, 57:31-7,
1950. Reprinted with permission.

There is one problem in which all psychologists and all philosophers
are interested—the problem of knowledge. If they are not, they ought
to be. It is true that sometimes one meets either a scientist or a
philosopher who thinks and says that he is not interested in the problem. I have had a philosopher say to me, "I am interested in metaphys-
ics not epistemology. First we must find out what reality *is.* Knowledge
is just a part of it." Similarly, I have had a scientist say to me, "Why
raise problems about knowledge? I look and see. The facts speak for
themselves." This scientist was not a psychologist, and I hope that
psychologists are not so naive either about seeing, or about how lo-
quacious facts are.

It is sometimes said that too much emphasis on the criticism of
method is a sign of decadence in any field of study. Perhaps it is;
but on the other hand, too little interest may be a sign of naiveté. The
person who takes methodology or the problem of knowledge for
granted is at the mercy of various unconscious prejudices and assumptions. These unrecognized and therefore uncriticized assumptions

---

[1] Read as the presidential address at the Forty-first Annual Meeting of the
Southern Society for Philosophy and Psychology, April 15, 1949.

will continually creep in to vitiate his findings, and to set him at sword's points with those of his colleagues who have acquired different assumptions.

I have nothing against assumptions as long as they are not unrecognized and uncriticized. In fact, I am going to start from an assumption which I am explicitly calling to your attention. I shall present it to you here uncriticized, but that is because of the limitations of time and of your endurance. I have criticized it elsewhere. The assumption is that the most reliable way to gain generalized knowledge about the world around us—how it is constructed and what is in it—is by the use of the scientific method.

Note that I say *generalized* knowledge. That means theoretic knowledge. And note also that the theoretic knowledge with which my assumption is concerned is the knowledge of the world of experience. The application of the scientific method in the way indicated gives rise to the empirical sciences, or, if you wish, the natural sciences.

I suppose that all of you will agree with me in my basic assumption; and certainly the large majority will agree also that psychology is one of the empirical sciences. Thus the method of gaining reliable generalized knowledge in psychology is by the use of the scientific method. Most of you are acquainted with the role of hypotheses in natural science. All natural laws are, in the last analysis, generalizations of great scope, and these generalizations are hypothetical in nature.

Science does deal with facts, but only as raw material. Facts are useful in so far as they yield laws, theories, hypotheses. They do not speak for themselves. No fact ever told an investigator what law it embodied. The investigator has to dig the generalization out of the accumulated mass of facts.

The interrelationship between fact and theory itself constitutes a problem. The ascertainment of fact is itself not independent of theory. Facts are not what is ultimately and irreducibly given in experience. Facts are what we are aware of in perceptual experience—but that is a different matter. It was long ago pointed out by psychology that concrete perception always includes a reference to past experience. Perception of fact is an interpretation of what is immediately and irreducibly given in the activity of the senses and in imagery in terms of past experiences and future possibilities of action. Facts, in other words, always include a conceptual element. Facts mean something, both in reference to past experience and to future action, and meaning is conceptual.

We may call whatever is ultimately and irreducibly given in experience, perceptual intuition, *i.e.*, that of which we are immediately aware in perception. It is true that in concrete experience we are aware of facts, and that the intuited elements are analyzed from the concrete facts; but this is because we are all more or less adult human beings with inescapable references to past experience and future possibilities of action. We cannot free ourselves from the past and the future except by the processes of analysis and abstraction.

The colors, shapes, and sounds in our experience are intuited, but these intuitions are never the whole of concrete adult experience. The concrete object of our perception is a tree or a telephone pole or juke box. These are perceptions of fact, and facts are always interpretations of intuited content in terms of concepts. "Tree," "telephone pole," "juke box": these words name concepts. I remind you, however, that I am not here making inexpert and speculative pronouncements about genetic psychology. I am engaged in epistemological analysis.

These considerations, however, are taking us afield. My subject is not the nature of fact but the nature of the theory. It is true that fact is not independent of theory, but neither is it the same as theory. Theory is general. Facts are particular. That means that a fact has a special locus in space and time, and each separate fact has a different locus. Theory is not tied down to a special locus. Theory is general. This means that it applies to many facts in many different loci of space and time. Facts may be perceived. Theories, on the other hand, are conceptual.

I realize that the word "theory" is not always used in the way in which I am defining it. A newspaper editorial, in condemning a view contrary to its own, will sometimes say, "That is only theory; it won't work." Such uses of the word "theory" are not very precise. I do not know exactly what the editorial writer means. The expression is probably his way of saying that, in his opinion, his opponent's views are hot air, empty and distasteful to all right-thinking persons.[2]

In this paper I shall use the words "theory" and "theoretic" to refer to knowledge that is general in nature. General principles are theoretic, and a body of interrelated general principles is an elaborated theory.

We are now ready for the major thesis of this paper. It is as follows: all theoretic knowledge is hypothetical.

---

[2] As Sir Arthur Eddington remarks: " 'Right-thinking person' is, of course, a modest way of referring to oneself" (1, p. 2).

As soon as I make this statement, the status of mathematical and logical principles may occur to you. These are indisputably theoretic, and they are usually regarded as certain. Their certainty, however, is only *relative to their premises*. If the postulates of a mathematical or a logical system are true or correct, then the theorems are certain. The foregoing statement is certain, but note that it is hypothetical.

These statements, however, do not represent the kind of theoretic knowledge nor the kind of hypothesis into which I want to inquire. The certainty here arises because the mathematical and logical principles are not about anything. They may be *applicable* to experience, but they are not *about* experience. Mathematical and logical principles are certain *a priori*, and that is because they are analytical and do not carry with them any statement of their applicability.

When I say that all theoretic knowledge is hypothetical, what I want to call to your specific attention is theoretic knowledge about the world we live in, generalizations about empirical matters, statements whose meaning lies in their application to experience.

The type of hypothesis to which I am referring is the explanatory hypothesis of natural science. Such a hypothesis, when it fully and explicitly performs its explanatory function, is stated in the form of a proposition in formal logic—the "if-then" proposition, where the "if" clause is called the antecedent and the "then" clause the consequent.

It is customary for writers on science to distinguish between a scientific hypothesis and a scientific law. I shall nevertheless maintain that formally there is no essential difference. If we wish, we can refuse to call any principle a law unless it is wide in scope and has received a high degree of verification. It may nevertheless remain true that the knowledge which this law expresses is hypothetical. I think that the day is past when scientists can say with Karl Pearson:

> Scientific law is valid for all normal human beings, and is *unchangeable* so long as their perceptive faculties remain at their present stage of development" (5, p. 104).[3]

I hope that the day is past when scientists are *disposed* to say this, especially when they place emphasis on the word "unchangeable."

The terms "law," "theory," "hypothesis" can all be used in a narrower or a broader sense. In the narrower usage the distinction between them depends on a difference in the degree to which they are based on

---

[3] Italics mine. Pearson emphasizes that scientific law is relative to human beings, but he used the word "hypothesis" only for a "working hypothesis." In his terminology a generalization is a hypothesis when it has not been or is being "put to the test of experience." It is a law when it has passed the test. See p. 120.

evidence and have been confirmed by evidence. Thus we can call a generalization based on little evidence and with little confirmation a guess or speculation; with more we call it a hypothesis; with still more, a theory; and with most evidence and confirmation, we call it a law. There is nothing very precise about this contrast of terms. The usage is mostly traditional. We still talk about the law of gravitation, but about the theory of relativity.

What I am proposing is that in the broader, more functional use of the terms, all generalizations are theoretic and theory is hypothetical. I am not talking merely about the use of words. I am talking about the nature of theoretic knowledge, no matter what it may be called: whether it is categorical and yields certainty or whether it is always hypothetical and yields only probability.

Let us return to the laws of science. These are inductive; that is, a generalization is stated on the ground of experience with particulars. Of course these laws are usually stated categorically, but this is merely a linguistic convenience. The knowledge that they convey may not be categorical. The kind of knowledge that they do convey can be found in a consideration of their genesis and the relation they have to the particulars. Generalizations do not just grow on particulars and wait for us to come along and pick them off.

The important point is that generalizations are always intended to be explanatory of the particulars. We say that if such and such a generalization holds, then this and that particular will follow. To take a concrete example: "If all policemen have big feet, then it is not surprising that Willie, the pride of the finest, wears number 12 shoes."

It would be better to cite more important generalizations. In 1919 the Royal Astronomical Society sent expeditions to Brazil and to West Africa where a total eclipse of the sun was predicted to take place. The expeditions were to observe especially the positions of stars close to the sun, because if the general theory of relativity holds, then the apparent position of stars close to the sun should be displaced outward approximately 1.7 seconds of an arc. No one had ever noticed this phenomenon, but now when it was looked for, the phenomenon did make its appearance. The stars were observed to be displaced approximately the amount predicted, subject to inaccuracy of observation and measurement (2, pp. 152-155). In 1922, with instruments of greater precision, the displacement was further verified (3, p. 17). These were crucial observations in establishing the general theory of relativity.

Note that I have been careful to retain the hypothetical form of the statement of the principle. "If the systematic body of generalizations making up the theory of relativity holds, then certain events will take place." Thus on the ground of accepting the general theory, the events, when they do take place, are explained. When the events have never been observed before their prediction, the explanatory power of the hypothesis is spectacularly revealed upon their observation. Cases in point are the first observation of the planet Neptune and the case I have already described, the displacement of stars close to the sun. Nevertheless, the principle is the same when the hypothesis explains something previously observed, such as the advance of the perihelion of Mercury (2, p. 150; or 3, p. 22) or the occurrence of an ordinary eclipse of the sun or moon.

When I say that scientific hypotheses explain particular occurrences, I am not using the word "explain" in a metaphysical sense. That is, the hypothesis is not the "reason why" the particular event takes place. Perhaps the assumption that the event takes place because it is commanded to do so by the generalization gave rise to the term "natural law" (6, p. 245). No scientist today, however, would hold this view, and the term "law" is understood to be derived from a metaphor. Scientific explanation of particulars means that the occurrences of many different kinds of particulars can be related to each other in an intelligible manner by means of generalizations under which all can be subsumed.

A scientific hypothesis or theory is a generalization of wide scope which expresses the correlations of many particular events. It can be assumed to be true only to the degree to which it accomplishes this task. It is not known *a priori*; it is not given in any immediate knowledge. We say it is elicited from the particulars themselves.

This process can be described briefly as follows. Particular experiences are perceived. As soon as we start thinking about them—in fact, perhaps in the very act of perception itself—they are subjected to analysis, that is, they are broken up by thought into parts. If any part or any collocation of parts is regarded by itself or without reference to other parts, the process of abstraction has taken place. Abstraction means thinking of something outside of the concrete context where we find it. Generalization consists in noting that we can abstract the same characteristics or conditions from more than one particular instance. Thus a generalization applies to or covers several particular instances.

Such in brief is the genesis of a scientific hypothesis, theory, or law. Let me summarize as far as I have gone. A scientific theory says, "If generalization G is true, then particulars a, b, c . . . follow." The latter are subsumed under the generalization and thus explained by it.

If we accept the generalization, the particulars of experience are rendered intelligible. This is the only way of rendering the particulars of experience intelligible—relating them to each other by means of generalizations under which they can be subsumed. Thus the general theory of relativity explains the displacement of stars near the sun and the progression of the perihelion of Mercury. Newtonian mechanics and gravitation do not explain these phenomena. This means that they cannot be subsumed as special cases under the generalizations of the Newtonian theory.

Now to go on: I am proposing that all inductive knowledge, whether it is to be found in the body of natural science or in philosophy or elsewhere, is of this same nature. We have no other way of making valid generalizations from experience than by analysis and abstraction from our perceptions. There is no other way of rendering anything in experience intelligible but by relating it to other things through the generalizations thus obtained. By pure reasoning you can arrive at valid conclusions, but you cannot show that these conclusions apply to anything in experience. Thus all empirical theory (and by that I mean all theory about anything except itself) is made up of generalizations, the validity and the truth of which lie in their explanatory power and effectiveness. All empirical theoretic knowledge is hypothetical and finds its justification in its verification.

Now let us go back again to the verification of scientific hypotheses and consider them from a strictly logical point of view. The form is: if generalization G is true, then particulars a, b, c, . . . will happen. Suppose that we observe a, b, and c. Does that prove G in any strict sense of the word "proof"? The answer is simply *no*. The general theory of relativity predicts that stars near the sun will be seen to be displaced outward 1.7 seconds of an arc. They are so seen. That does not prove the theory or even contribute to its proof. The theory predicts that the perihelion of Mercury will advance approximately 43 seconds of an arc per century more than predicted by the Newtonian theory. It is seen to advance at this slightly more rapid rate. Does that prove the theory? Again, of course, the answer is *no*, not in the strict sense of the word "proof."

To suppose that a hypothesis is proved by the truth of the consequences is to perform the simple fallacy of affirmation of the consequent. This is *always* a fallacy. Not all the consequences in the world can prove the hypothesis. The observation of consequences does contribute toward the verification of hypotheses, but verification is not proof. The observation of consequences is usually held to increase the probability of the truth of the generalization, though there is a dispute between adherents of different theories of probability as to how this can be.

What does it mean then to talk about the "truth" of a hypothesis? A scientific hypothesis is justified to the degree it is verified. Its verification lies in its explanatory power, and explanation means the degree to which different particulars of experience can be interrelated and thus be shown to be intelligible by means of subsuming them under suitable generalizations. Theoretic truth then is defined in terms of rendering experience intelligible.

I suggest that this is the full meaning of empirical theoretic truth. Perhaps practical truth and perceptual truth are different matters and differently to be explained. That question is not at issue now. I am giving a theory of theoretic truth, and when I say that my theory of truth is true, I aim to be consistent. I mean that it is a hypothesis which, so far as I can see, has great explanatory power.

I do not see how psychologists or philosophers can claim to be exempt from the consequences of this hypothesis. Mathematicians and logicians are exempt, for their theories are not about empirical matters. Both psychologists and philosophers, however, claim most of the time to be talking about something in experience. In so far as they are concerned with experience, they are not exempt. Their theories are hypotheses that are justified only by their explanatory power.

At the present time there is a good deal of feuding between different schools of psychological thought. It is taken for granted that philosophers are always feuding. I think that this is not only regrettable, but if there is anything in the thesis of this paper, it is theoretically unjustified and perhaps even a little absurd. No one has any theoretic truth that is more than hypothesis. It does not seem probable from an examination of how hypotheses are formed that any one hypothesis can be established so firmly as to render all alternatives impossible.

Feuding among philosophers and psychologists—and especially the intellectual intolerance upon which it is based—is theoretically unjustified. This is not meant, however, to discourage lively controversy. When a new hypothesis is proposed it should be attacked and defended with vigor. Only in this way can it be thoroughly tested. Today we are apt to judge that Priestley's attack on the new combustion theory of Lavoisier was not well taken. Perhaps Priestley held to the phlogiston theory too long and against too much evidence; but perhaps his attacks on the combustion theory helped to establish it by forcing its defenders to subject it to thorough testing.

On the other hand it is good that new hypotheses should not be accepted until all conceivable attempts to overthrow them have been made. It is also good that the supporters of a new hypothesis should hold on to it and push it, so that it will not get lost in the shuffle, or even worse than that, get squelched by authority.

There should be no such thing as scientific authority, although unfortunately there is. In the 1880's C. A. McMunn made a contribution to the understanding of the way in which the transfer of oxygen from hemoglobin to the tissues takes place. After a little controversy, he was put down by the bio-chemist Hoppe-Seyler, who twenty years earlier had made the very important discovery of the role of hemoglobin in carrying oxygen from the lungs to the tissues. Hoppe-Seyler printed a note alongside McMunn's last paper saying that he considered further discussion superfluous. McMunn apparently subsided; at any rate discussion was dropped, and it was not discovered that he was correct and Hoppe-Seyler incorrect until forty years later, in the 1920's (4, p. 170). It might have saved forty years if McMunn had been a little more tenacious of his hypothesis.

All philosophers and all psychologists are engaged in the same kind of task in so far as they are all trying to understand something. Understanding is achieved by the formulation of generalizations and the construction of theory. Theoretic knowledge is hypothetical, and is true in so far as the hypothesis does what it is set up to do. There is no justification whatever for one person to assume that his theories are absolutely true and those of his opponents are so false that only a stubborn ass could continue to hold them. *All* hypotheses must be tested in every conceivable way. Let the opponents suggest and work up tests. Unless they have something constructive of this kind to say, let them keep silent and spend their energies not in quarreling but in developing their own hypothesis and welcoming the suggestions of tests made by their opponents. If the hypothesis will not stand the test, it is no good anyhow. A hypothesis cannot be established by refusing to test it, but only by testing it in every conceivable way.

We shall all get further toward our goal of understanding if we cooperate. The intellectual enterprise is a common and co-operative endeavor, and its furtherance should not be hindered by personal bickerings and unfriendliness that are utterly incompatible with its nature. The view that all theoretic knowledge is hypothetical gives no basis for dogmatism in either philosophy or science. The dogmatist is one who is absolutely certain of his knowledge.

If we are not to be dogmatists, then are we, *ipso facto*, skeptics? The thesis of this paper gives *no* comfort to skeptics either. The skeptic denies the possibility of theoretic knowledge. I do not deny it. On the other hand, I assert that we have it. We have a great deal of it. Furthermore, all understanding (in the literal epistemological sense of the word "understanding") is in terms of theoretical knowledge. And there are many things about this world that we do understand. The view that theoretic knowledge is hypothetical does not conjure away this understanding.

References

1. Eddington, A. *The philosophy of physical science.* New York: The Macmillan Co., 1939.

2. Einstein, A. *Relativity, the special and general theory.* New York: Holt, Rinehart and Winston, 1920.

3. Frank, P. *Relativity and its astronomical implications.* Cambridge, Mass., 1943.

4. Mees, C. E. K., & Baker, J. R. *The path of science.* New York: John Wiley & Sons, Inc., 1946.

5. Pearson, K. *The grammar of science.* London: A. & C. Black, 1892.

6. Zilsel, E. The genesis of the concept of physical law. *Phil. Rev.,* 1942, 51, 245-279.

Garford Gordon

Better Theories
Needed in Research

The relationship of research and theory is a circular one. Research may grow out of already-existing theory. Such research tests the validity of the theory and causes modification as necessary. Research may be used to *develop* theory, which leads to research to *test* the theory, which brings us around the full circle. In any case, theory is indispensable to research. In the present article, Gordon takes educational researchers to task for their more or less unscientific attitude toward theory in education. He maintains that better theories are needed, and that education will not progress until such theories are developed.

Garford Gordon, "Better Theories Needed in Research," *Phi Delta Kappan*, 34:219-21, 1953. Reprinted with permission.

Science has always been plagued by the human desire to find easy solutions. The trouble with such solutions has usually been that they do not work. Unfortunately, much effort goes into would-be universal theories which are supposed to solve all problems arising from man's experience with the mysterious universe of which he is a part. The originators of such theories become emotionally attached to their ideas and find it impossible to face the fact that nature does not conform to the requirements of their so-called laws. Instead of recognizing that science is an attempt to describe the nature of the universe, they try to make the nature of the universe fit the description they have so laboriously invented. Thus have arisen the fallacious explain-all theories which have so bedeviled the intellectual development of mankind. Fortunately, the improvement of observational techniques and the widespread application of the results of scientific inquiry to everyday living, have made it very difficult to explain away physical phenomena which do not fit into preconceived systems of natural science. Unhappily, the data and

405

techniques of the social sciences do not demonstrate quite so emphatically the weaknesses of fallacious theories in their fields. The science of education is one of the chief sufferers from this situation.

It is unfortunate that the prestige of individuals is so often at stake when educational theories are discussed. No man can be indifferent to the fate of his system of ideas when its acceptance will make him an authority in the field and its rejection will make him a nonentity. The tendency of educators at all levels to attribute to the opinions of experts a validity equal to or greater than that of objective experience, is unquestionably the greatest single deterrent to the development of a science of education. It is not only that the expert himself is thereby given an almost fatally ardent motive for patching up his theories until they can "explain" anything that may be observed; but the natural human tendency to identify oneself with leaders, causes the rank and file to accept unverifiable explain-all theories as worthy aids to educational research.

THE CURSE OF EXPLAIN-ALL THEORIES

Explain-all theories are unquestionably the curse of modern educational research. It is impossible to test them, for any fact that fails to fit them can be ascribed to some unexplained influence that is after all in harmony with the theory. When this sort of thing is applied to life in general and called astrology or numerology, we very rightly scoff at the naïve attempts of the apologists to explain away the facts of life that fail to match with their pet system. However, when the IQ failed to predict scholastic success on as accurate a basis as was claimed, educators unhesitatingly looked around for excuses. For instance, if a student did better than his IQ predicted, they "knew" that the test had not been properly given and that his "real" IQ was higher than the obtained one. On the basis of evidence alone, it would have been more correct to say that the IQ is not a significant measure of intellectual capacity. This point of view has now been adopted by many educators, but it is still rejected by many others—though none can give a compelling, logical reason for rejecting the evidence of experience in favor of the requirements of a theory. Actually, no such reason exists and, in fact, any theory requiring the explaining-away of evidence obtained by experience is for this very reason disqualified as a scientific instrument.

This article is not concerned with the value of the IQ as an educational measurement, for it may well be that suitable modifications of the theory can make it a valid scientific concept, and many such modifications are now being considered. But, did you find yourself automatically objecting to the last paragraph? Or have you transferred your allegiance to an achievement quotient, or to an expectancy age, or to some other logical equivalent of the IQ? Or are you convinced that some one change in teaching techniques or administrative practices will solve all or most of our educational problems? If you can truthfully answer "No" to the preceding questions, ask yourself how many of your colleagues could do likewise. All who cannot do so illustrate the point being made here.

RANGE OF MEASUREMENTS LIMITED

What is wrong with using IQ's or national norms or other numerical measures? Nothing, if you keep in mind exactly what they mean. However, all mathematical measures presuppose certain very definite conditions. The results of most experience do not meet these conditions. Therefore, scientists do not as a rule try to deal with all experience, but only with such limited aspects as will permit the presupposition to be made that the necessary conditions for the mathematical treatment of the data obtained, are fulfilled. When most educational measures are treated in this manner, they turn out to be limited to a much smaller range of applications than their creators usually claim for them.

The remedy for many of the troubles of educational science is the abandonment of unjustifiable assumptions as to the applicability of the laws of probability to educational measures, and the coordinated collection of sufficient data in specific fields of educational research to enable the mathematical forms most appropriate to these fields to be determined. This is an expensive remedy. It will require that most accepted laws and rules of education and educational psychology be recognized as purely rule of thumb approximations, a remedy very expensive emotionally for many of us. It will also require the carrying on of coordinated research on a scale far in excess of that now in existence. This will be expensive in time, energy, and money.

COOPERATIVE RESEARCH NEEDED

In fact, the whole thing will be so expensive, that it may well appear that this article merely says that education is not a science and cannot become one. This is not true. The basic conditions for scientific investigation can be met by education; and, when they are met, the science of education can be placed on as firm a footing as the sciences of chemistry or physics. The raw materials of education are schools and classes and children, not crystals and molecules and atoms. No physical scientist can proceed scientifically with just one molecule or atom; neither can an educator proceed scientifically with just one class or student. One physical scientist can deal with millions of atoms and molecules; but it will take the whole profession of education to deal with an adequate number of schools and classes. It is this need for large-scale cooperative research that distinguishes the science of education most sharply from the other physical and biological sciences.

At present, anyone's opinion on educational matters is as good as the next. The only thing that commands common acceptance is personal reputation or common prejudice. That used to be true in the physical sciences, also. The present difference in status between these sciences and the science of education is not due to chronology nor to differences in subject matter. There are more atoms in a spoonful of water than students in all the schools on earth, and no two of those atoms are exactly alike; and the Stanford-Binet formulation of the IQ is older than any of the present theories of atomic structure. No, the difference is due to the fact that the physical scientists do not claim more than their observations warrant (regardless of what their so-called interpreters may do), whereas too many educators have claimed too much for their inventions.

THE REQUIREMENTS OF SCIENTIFIC THEORY

Perhaps, however, the chief trouble is that most persons engaged in the scientific study of education do not know the requirements that a scientific theory must meet. Theories serve a definite purpose in the structure of science, and this imposes certain restrictions on them. They are assumed descriptions of the way in which the elements of the universe are related; but, since they are tools required by science in its efforts to describe the universe, the assumptions underlying them cannot be chosen with complete arbitrariness. In particular, the assumptions on which any theory is based must not contradict the basic assumptions of science nor deny the aspects of science that justify its existence.

Furthermore, to be of any use to science, theories must either be based on fewer arbitrary assumptions than previous theories describing the same conditions, or else must result in a markedly simpler description of the universe. Also, to be of scientific worth, theories must be capable of verification by means at hand. That is, they must be a means of describing the universe as it is or can be observed. In other words, a theory must be able to fulfill its purpose as a guide to observation.

THEORY—THE TOOL OF DISCOVERY

On the other hand, to have scientific worth, theories must not deny the existence of observations that have been made or are being made. Theories that declare everything not provided for in their systems to be "unreal," or "merely subjective," or the like, are improper theories.

The most important requirement that scientific theories must meet is that they be capable of serving as tools for discovering more about the universe. No theories that attempt to explain everything can meet this requirement. Such theories provide in advance for a description of all possible events; and, therefore, must assume all possible explanations in their premises. This means that the results of these theories are all contained in their assumptions so that there is no provision for observation to act in revising them. In other words, they are not capable of verification. Examples of this type of theory are those which declare that all is due to the stars, or neurones, or environment, and so forth. In fact, any theory that describes all of any class of phenomena as being caused by a certain other phenomenon is invalid, for it can always be assumed that the relation exists but that observation has not been extensive enough or accurate enough to detect it. This type of theory carries its own built-in verification and serves to describe itself and not the external universe.

There are several other requirements that must be met by scientific theories. If, in addition, theories are to serve as a basis for mathematical treatment of observational data, still other criteria must be met. But no matter how well a theory meets the requirements for a good scientific theory and avoids the causes of invalidity, it can never be proven to be perfect. This is because the description of the universe that is furnished by a theory is in terms of the assumptions of the theory. Ignorance of this basic limitation of all theories would seem to be the reason for some of the most serious weaknesses found in present work in educational science.

SOUND THEORIES NEEDED

It is possible to make educational theories that meet all the requirements for good scientific theories; and some sound ones are needed. They need not be—in fact, they cannot be—perfect; but they must be capable of fulfilling their role in the structure of educational science. The creation of such theories is the responsibility of informed leadership in educational research. There is now some such leadership; but the need for widespread cooperative research cannot be met by a few persons only. It is to be hoped that every leader in education will study the nature of science and become an informed leader in the promotion of scientifically valid educational research.

T. M. Stinnett

Check That
Statistic

A further warning about the misuse of data from research—Stinnett points out some ways in which obtained data has been badly misinterpreted through incomplete understanding of the statistic that was presented. It is incumbent upon the educational researcher to present his data in such a manner that his results cannot be used to misinform or deceive.

T. M. Stinnett, "Check That Statistic," *Educational Record*, 38:83-90, 1957. Reprinted with permission.

Was it Josh Billings who said: " 'Twasn't my ignorance that done me in; 'twas the things I knowed that wasn't so"?

This quip seems peculiarly applicable to the current ferment over alleged weaknesses in education and the popular pastime of manipulating data in support of individual conclusions. Everybody is getting into the act; and a statistic may be found, and is being found, to support a variety of viewpoints. It might be said that we are rapidly developing a body of folklore about education.

While this article will deal with the careless manner in which educational statistics often have been kicked around, there are complaints from other fields. For example, Herblock, the *Washington Post and Times Herald* famed cartoonist, in his latest book *Here and Now* devotes a chapter (cartoons and text) to "Tell Me Not in Mournful Numbers." He takes dead aim at the manipulation of figures by government officials. Some case examples which he describes: The Hoover Commission reported that the Navy had stocked enough canned hamburger to last 60 years. Herblock says the present Navy strength of 886,000 men could consume this stockpile in two meals. Another statistic, glibly repeated by one official after another during the early days of the Eisenhower administration, asserted that since inauguration day government employees were getting to work 27 minutes earlier in the morning. An enterprising reporter checked with the highway departments of the District of Columbia, Virginia, and Maryland, which reported no perceptible change in the flow of traffic. The officials who had made the statement, when asked for their authority, simply quoted the previous person who had made it. And there was the famous numbers game of a senator in 1950: "I hold in my hand a list of 205" (or 81 or 57) "people employed by the State Department who are Communists." Nobody has ever found out which number, if any, was correct. This writer does not vouch for the accuracy of the statistics cited above. They are mentioned merely to illustrate a problem which is becoming increasingly important to those of us in education.

How carefully did you check that statistic you used in your last speech? Did you pick it up from a speech you heard or read, or from a magazine article, and then repeat it as the gospel truth? Did you go back to the source and get it straight, in unadulterated form? More important, did you accept it at face value or did you dig into all of its ramifications and limitations and get a perspective of its real meaning?

The personal pronoun used in the preceding paragraph might well be changed to the first person singular, not out of modesty as much as out of a sense of guilt. Indeed, the knowledge of incautious and sometimes injudicious use of data has impelled this writer to believe that the hazards of such practices ought to be emphasized.

This is no laughing matter. There are recent examples of widely quoted, generally accepted statistics on educational problems which have been used to support a conclusion proven, upon closer scrutiny, to be unwarranted. There is reason to believe that many of these loosely used statistics are causing great harm.

Perhaps the matter was not so serious in the days when educators lived in a world largely inhabited by themselves. They could mumble their statistics and nobody's mind was confused, except possibly another educator's. Moreover, educators for the most part have learned to be wary of categorical interpretations of data. But we are now rapidly moving well into a period in which the public is taking an increasingly active role in the study and determination of educational affairs. And the average layman reads as he runs, especially in matters outside his own field of vocational interest. He tends, quite naturally, to dote on the showy, shocking statistic.

Thus one false statistic, or one statistic isolated from other relevant data, or one misinterpreted statistic can cause irreparable damage by creating distorted images in the public mind. How many millions of dollars have been extracted from an unwitting public by "scare statistics" designed to stampede people into correcting some presumed weakness in our schools is, of course, unknown. But it is an interesting speculation.

Let us examine some recent examples of statistics which seem to have been loosely used and consider the devilment they may cause.

Take as Exhibit A the statement that fewer than half of our public high schools are offering physics and chemistry. The immediate inference of the public from such a statement is that more than half of our high schools have grown insensitive to the needs of our technological society and are not concerned with providing instruction in those two basic sciences. Another immediate image that arises in the public's mind as a result of the statement is that half or more than half of our high school students do not have the opportunity, even if they wanted to do so, to pursue courses in physics and chemistry. Here is the wording of the statement:

> If this were not sad enough, more than half (53 per cent) of our high schools do not teach physics at all. In half our schools students simply have no access to this subject which is so important to an understanding of the technological world in which they will spend their lives. Half of our high schools do not teach chemistry either.
>
> Two generations ago, in 1890, one in every five high school students studied physics. Today it is only one out of every 22. More than half of all students back in those days studied algebra; now it is less than one-fourth. The study of chemistry has fallen off 30 per cent. These are the statistics of the United States in the era of technology.[1]

This statement was made in a public address by a high governmental official, none less than the chairman of the United States Atomic Energy Commission, whose connection with nuclear research was of such a sensitive nature that it inevitably caused great concern on the part of the public regarding the adequacy of our high schools and their offerings, both in terms of our expanding technological needs and in terms of our security requirements. In addition, this statement had all the ingredients calculated to set editorial writers, slick magazine editors, and radio and television commentators drooling.

Was this statement true? If not, how did the speaker arrive at such interpretations or misinterpretations?

---

[1] Lewis L. Strauss, "Freedom's Need for the Trained Man," in *The Growing Shortage of Scientists and Engineers:* Proceedings of the Sixth Thomas Alva Edison Foundation Institute, November 21-22, 1955 (New York: New York University Press, 1956), p. 19.

The statement about the number of high schools offering physics and chemistry, to the best of our knowledge, was not true; and the figures quoted on enrollments are seriously misleading. Yet the misinterpretation arose in quite a normal way. There is no doubt that the statement was sincere, and the full text reflects an honest intent to help improve the situation alleged to exist in our high schools. One cannot be precisely sure of it, since no source of information for this statement was cited by the speaker, but the evidence seems to point to the probability that Mr. Strauss, or his speech writer, came across a study, published by the United States Office of Education in 1950, of the offerings of American high schools for the first term of the school year 1947-48.[2] In a table[3] there is the assertion that only 47.8 percent of the high schools sampled offered physics and 49.4 percent offered chemistry. There it was in black type, apparently a definitive and unequivocal statement. This was bound to mean that about 53 percent of our high schools did not offer physics and about 50 percent did not offer chemistry. But did it mean this?

Was this the exact meaning of the table? Not at all; this is a good example of "things are not what they seem," especially statistics. Let us examine the text which accompanied the table. The text says:

> More schools offer the regular science courses and more pupils enroll in them than was reported by the schools for this study. This is due to the fact that some schools make a practice of alternating science courses in successive years. Alternating courses commonly involves ninth-grade general science and biology, and chemistry and physics. *Data concerning the extent to which alternating of science courses is practiced in public high schools were not obtained in this study.*[4]

The random sample of high schools contained in this study numbered 715 out of about 24,000 high schools in operation in 1947-48, or 3.09 percent of the total number of high schools. Thus, it is clear from the author's explanation that the figures included in the table did not include those high schools which alternate the two sciences—physics and chemistry—in the sense that those schools offering chemistry in the fall term of 1947-48 would report no offering in physics and those offering physics would report no offering in chemistry.

---

[2] Phillips G. Johnson, *The Teaching of Science in Public High Schools, Inquiry into Offerings, Enrollments, and Selected Teaching Conditions,* 1947-48 (Washington: Government Printing Office, 1950).

[3] *Ibid*, Table 4, p. 5.

[4] *Ibid*, p. 4.

While the precise figure on the number of high schools which alternate the sciences may not be known, since that is a practical and common procedure in small high schools, some idea of the extent of erroneous interpretation of the data in the table referred to above is indicated by the fact that about two-thirds of the 24,000 high schools in 1947-48 had enrollments of 300 or less.

It is well known that small high schools, because of limited enrollment and teaching staff, alternate certain subjects. For example, in the field of science they will offer general science one year and biology the next so that all high school students in the first two years will be able to study both subjects, but only one in any given year. They also alternate physics and chemistry in the junior and senior years in the same manner.

At the time this statement was made, many educators were concerned about the distorted picture it presented and made efforts to have it corrected. But, like most statements that attract popular interest, overtaking it was impossible. Thousands of editorials, news stories, and speeches have picked up this statement and drummed it into the minds of the American people. And the erroneous and misleading parts of the statement continue to march across the printed pages, into speeches, and into the scripts of commentators, despite the fact that a new study by the Office of Education shows how far afield this statement was. The Office of Education released in June 1956 a sampling study by Kenneth Brown[5] which found that only 23 percent of our high schools did not offer physics or chemistry, and these were predominantly small high schools which enrolled only about 6 percent of our high school students. Moreover, Brown's study found that instead of the alleged one in twenty-two high school students taking physics, that about one in five were pursuing the subject, and "the number of pupils in chemistry has not declined 30 percent during the past 60 years—it has increased more than twentyfold. Two-thirds of the high school pupils take algebra, instead of onefourth."[6]

The differing reports on science enrollments point up another statistical booby trap which Brown's study describes. His calculations, as he is careful to explain, are based upon the percentages of the appropriate grade enrollments which are pursuing a given sub-

---

[5] Kenneth E. Brown, *Offerings and Enrollments in Science and Mathematics in Public High Schools*, U. S. Department of Health, Education, and Welfare, Office of Education, Bulletin No. 118 (Washington: Government Printing Office, 1956).

[6] *Ibid*, p. 2.

ject, while the study from which Mr. Strauss apparently took his data was based upon the percentages of the total high school enrollments. For example, one may say that only 25 percent of all high school students in a given year are taking algebra and this might be accurate. At the same time, it could be said that 66 percent of all ninth-grade students are enrolled in algebra in the same year. Both statements might be accurate, but which of the two provides the correct interpretation?

Or, consider the case of the Educational Testing Service report to the Carnegie Corporation which had financed a study by ETS of the teaching of mathematics in elementary and secondary schools.[7] ETS came up with the report which said, "Although all states require education courses, one-third of the states will certificate high school teachers of mathematics without any college preparation in math." This was a case of a statistic not meaning what it seemed to.

Apparently ETS somewhere found the statement that one-third of the states issue general or blanket high school certificates for teaching in the academic fields and came to the conclusion that this meant that there were no requirements in those states for teaching mathematics. The fact is that 18 states do issue such a certificate, or did at the time the ETS study was made (the number is now 17), but all have prescriptions either in certification requirements or in accrediting requirements, which the employing school official is expected to enforce on teachers he employs to teach math in the high schools. In other words, not a single state is without requirements of college preparation in math for high school math teachers. Again, this statement was picked up and widely circulated by the slick magazines, by newspapers, and repeated by public speakers, calling attention to the horrible situation in which our educational authorities are unconcerned about whether teachers of mathematics know any math or not.[8]

To judge this statement fairly, it should be said that no comprehensive, conclusive data are available on the number or proportion of teachers with teaching assignments outside their fields of competence. It would seem logical to assume—because of the long-sustained and critical shortage of teachers, if for no other reason—that there are thousands of such teachers. But this is quite a different matter

---

[7] *Mathematics Education* (Princeton, N.J.: Educational Testing Service, 1956).

[8] For a detailed repudiation of this statement gone astray, see "Math and Science Again" (Editorial Comments), *Journal of Teacher Education*, September 1956, pp. 194, 267-73.

from viewing the situation as one of neglect or indifference by the state certificating agencies.

Now, let us take one of those glamorous catchall statements that again causes the educational writers, editors, and speakers to jump apprehensively through verbal hoops. The statement asserts "that to supply our need for elementary and secondary school teachers in the next decade will require one-half or more of all of our college graduates. And of course this is impossible." To our best knowledge, this statement was first made by an official of one of the wealthy foundations. It was published in the Fund for the Advancement of Education's excellent booklet *Teachers for Tomorrow* and, based on the assumptions set forth in the text, a good case is made for its soundness. This statement has been widely publicized and has been repeated in thousands of speeches. It goes on and on like the poetic brook. At first this statistic seems unassailable. But is it? Let us examine it for a moment.

Currently the schools are consuming anywhere from 150,000 to 175,000, maybe more, new teachers each year, whereas college graduating classes were down to 285,000 in 1955 and to an estimated 325,000 in 1956. These data alone would support the statement. But let's dig in a little. If it could be assumed that all teachers who take jobs each fall must come from the previous college graduating class, the statement would be conservative. Actually, however, thousands of college graduates from former years who had prepared for teaching but who went on to graduate schools, or went into the armed services, or into industry, or even into marriage return each fall to teaching. In what numbers these people enter teaching each year is not known. We do know that some states are recruiting as high as one-half of their new teachers each fall from these sources. Moreover, if all states now required, or should require in the near future, college graduation as a prerequisite to certification and teaching, the statement would be more nearly valid. The fact is, or was at the time the statement was made, that some twenty-one states and territories still are certificating beginning elementary teachers below the degree level. But, of course, these teachers cannot be counted in the estimate as having to come from the college graduating class.

This is an easy, catchy statement which promptly brings editorial writers and other news outlets to a posture of attention. It may be argued that it is a useful statement in that it serves to point up an admittedly acute situation. But it is easy to overdo statements designed to arouse the public. One of the probable results of the statement is to impel some school boards and some segments of the public to accept the thesis that the teaching load must be increased radically, with compensations in the form of untrained teacher aides and mechanical assistance, thus cutting down the number of qualified teachers needed and the number of classrooms which have to be built. And fuel was added to this fire by an additional statement from the same source that, "We already have enough teachers, if they were properly used."

In connection with the above statement, let us consider a by-product, a statistic gone astray. A magazine article painted in glowing terms the miraculous benefits of the Bay City, Michigan, experiment in using teacher aides. Carefully documented timetables showing how teachers spent their time before and after aides were used were included. These tables were presented to illustrate how teachers were relieved of "nonprofessional" duties and were able to give more individual instruction to children. The article delivered the extraordinary statistic that teachers, after teacher aides were employed, spent 80 percent more time in personal counseling for students.[9] This was phenomenal; it was staggering in its implications, until someone dug down into the data and found that the increased time amounted to four minutes per day.[10]

Let us turn now to another statistic, one for which my commission[11] is responsible because it was released in one of its publications. Moreover, this writer must plead guilty to using this without adequate qualification. It is to be found in the report of the 1955 teacher supply and demand study.[12] This statistic was that only 128 high school physics teachers were prepared in that year, the implication being that this was the total supply to fill all the teaching jobs in that field in the ensuing year, including new positions resulting from increased enrollments and to replace those who quit each year. Again this statistic has been quoted and requoted, printed and reprinted, kicked around in such a way as to lead many people to believe that teaching physics in the high schools is practically extinct. When one examines critically the precise meaning of this bare statistic, however, he finds a lot of qualifications and extenuating circumstances. First, only those

---

[9] Arthur D. Morse, "Bay City Beats the Teaching Shortage," *Colliers*, November 11, 1955, pp. 37-41.

[10] From an unpublished committee report of the Michigan State Department of Public Instruction, as quoted in *Journal of Teacher Education*, June 1956, p. 148.

[11] National Commission on Teacher Education and Professional Standards, National Education Association.

[12] National Education Association, Research Division, "The 1955 Teacher Supply and Demand Report," *Journal of Teacher Education*, March 1955, pp. 23-71.

persons whose major field of concentration is physics and who at the same time took professional preparation for teaching are included in the 128 figure. All those who have completed a second major or a minor in physics or completed sufficient semester hours to be certificated to teach physics in their respective states are not included. Also not included in the 128 are those who completed a comprehensive major in the field of science and who are therefore eligible for certification to teach all the science subjects in high schools—this is a typical pattern in most states. A subsequent report,[13] made when the total of new physics teachers reported had grown to 189, sought to be more definitive about the total supply of physics teachers and other science fields by stating:

> Students graduating with preparation in the comprehensive field of science are listed in "General Science" (1788 in 1955 and 2121 in 1956). Doubtless many of these graduates have completed full majors in biology or chemistry or physics, but each is counted only once. Thus, a physics major who also has the required preparation in both biology and chemistry to teach general science is listed in the latter field only.

Doubtless this explanatory statement should have been included in the earlier annual reports on teacher supply; to have done so would perhaps have been to forestall misinterpretation of the data. Moreover, the teachers prepared in many fields, through special programs for college graduates of earlier years, are not reported in the annual national study.

Nobody knows precisely how many people qualified to meet the certification requirements to teach physics in our high schools complete preparation each year. The same would be true of chemistry or of biology. But the figure of 128 is still being used to scare children at night as well as to leave the great American public gnawing at its fingernails over the threat of losing our superiority in atomic and technological weapons to Russia, and over the threat to our industrial progress.

Let us jump now momentarily to the field of teacher certification. One instance of misinterpretation of data regarding this phase of education has been cited. My friends in the academic departments of colleges and universities persistently confront me with the fact that about half of our states do not specify completion of any prescribed

---

[13] National Education Association, Research Division, "The 1956 Teacher Supply and Demand Report," *Journal of Teacher Education*, March 1956, p. 39.

number of hours in general education as a prerequisite to certification. Immediately, the conclusion is drawn that the certification authorities in these states are not concerned with having broadly educated teachers, that they are concerned only with persons who have had the specified number of hours in professional education. The facts are that certification authorities have long since discovered that this matter can best be left to the institutions and that no teacher education institution worthy of the name will graduate a teacher without a solid, basic core of general education. This is another case of a statistic that does not mean what it appears to.

Or, consider the case of a distinguished layman who has become excited about the inability of liberal arts graduates of his university to secure state certificates to teach in the high schools of his state. He has concluded, after finding out that high school teachers in his home state must present a prescribed number of hours in education, that graduates of his university would be compelled to go to the state teachers colleges and spend a year or two working on "dull, duplicated, watered-down education courses." The facts are that a graduate of his university can obtain in his own university the hours required for full certification. Moreover, this graduate could probably begin teaching immediately in that state on an emergency certificate and would be permitted to work off the hours in his own university during the summer.

To be evenhanded in this matter of using and interpreting statistics—to illustrate that it is not a matter of deliberate or willful misuse, but rather a matter of checking original sources and careful interpretation—another statistic which has led to some erroneous conclusions may be cited from the commission's annual teacher supply and demand study. Since 1954 this annual study has reported a shocking proportion of those completing requirements for teaching each year who do not in fact take teaching jobs in the fall following their graduation.

In the 1956 study, for example, data from 26 states, covering 77 percent of the eligible elementary school teachers and 72.3 percent of the eligible high school teachers in the class of 1955, reflected that only about 80 percent of the elementary school teachers and about 63 percent of the high school teachers, and 71 percent of all teachers completing preparation in 1955 actually took teaching jobs in the fall of 1956. On the face of it, this is generally interpreted to mean that fully one-fifth of those who have prepared for elementary teaching and nearly two-fifths of those who have prepared for high school teaching do not become teachers, that they turn thumbs down on teaching as a career, go into some other occupation, wasting, in some measure, years of college study.

Is this conclusion justified? No. All one can be certain about is that, beyond question, those proportions did not accept teaching jobs in the fall following their graduation. An analysis of what they did the year following their graduation will give some indication of the fallacy of assuming that they are irrevocably lost to teaching. Fully one-third of those who did not take teaching jobs went into military service or graduate schools. Only one-sixth of this group were known to have taken jobs in nonteaching fields. There are no data on the numbers of these deflectors in a given year who do enter teaching in subsequent years. It may reasonably be assumed to be rather large, perhaps equaling the deflectors in the current year. But the usual interpretation is that the deflectors, about one-third of the total supply each year, are forever lost to teaching. Obviously this is another statistic requiring fuller analysis.

The above lists only a few of the recent, more glaring misinterpretations of statistics which have been carefully, scientifically derived and, almost without exception, carefully interpreted by their creators. After all, when a researcher painstakingly sets forth the assumptions on which data are derived and interpreted, even though the conclusions and interpretations differ widely from those of another researcher using different assumptions, each may be valid.

The danger arises from the loose use of statistics without stating the assumptions or the qualifications which are indicated.

And now for a solid clincher to the case this paper attempts to make. After this manuscript was in the hands of the editor, the writer's attention was called to a passage which unwittingly misrepresented the statistics in a statement which was being severely criticized for this very sin. The passage was reworded correctly—we hope.

Check that statistic!

James Harold Fox

Criteria of
Good Research

The value of a particular piece of research is not so much that it fits the reader's already preconceived prejudices, but rather that it meets certain criteria that indicate that the results may be depended upon. In this article, Fox proposes seven admittedly rather subjective criteria which may be applied to evaluate the results of a given research project.

James H. Fox, "Criteria of Good Research," *Phi Delta Kappan*, 39:284-6, 1958. Reprinted with permission.

Research is one of the means by which we seek to discover the truth. It is based upon the tacit assumption that the world is a cosmos whose happenings have causes and are controlled by forces and relationships that can be expressed as laws and principles. Discovery of these controls of nature provides us with a hunting license to search for ways of controlling our environment.

Unfortunately, the research methods available to us are far from perfect. Mankind, in the slow evolution toward civilization, has to date found only three basic approaches to the discovery of truth—authority, logic, and controlled observation. Until about 300 years ago, efforts to discover the truth largely depended upon recourse to authority and logic. Since that time researchers have placed increasing emphasis upon controlled observation supported by the logic of mathematics.

Many of the natural phenomena that we would like to study do not yield readily, however, to any combination of the three known research methods. For some aspects of the truth there are no earthly authorities, only inadequate kinds of mathematical logic, and no known means of controlled observation. True, the extension and refinement of research methods are steadily enlarging the scope of research. However, the closer we come to discovery of a part of the truth, the greater the scope of the unknown seems to become.

Because of these limitations, research rarely reveals to us the whole truth about anything. Discovery of what seems to be the truth concerning the nature of some part of the process of learning often turns out later to be only a crude approximation of the truth. Discovery of a new teaching technique that seems at first to have universal application usually turns out later to have only restricted use. It seems wiser, therefore, to view research findings as a means of approximating the truth instead of revealing the ultimate truth.

How closely the results of a particular piece of research approximate the truth depends upon its quality. Since research efforts vary widely in quality, the question of how much confidence can be placed justifiably in the findings of a particular research is one of considerable importance. The main purpose of this article is to suggest a few common-sense criteria that may assist practical schoolmen to distinguish between research that merits a good deal of confidence and research whose findings should only be accepted with reservations.

1. *The purpose of the research, or the problem involved, should be clearly defined and sharply delineated in terms as unambiguous as possible.*

The statement of the research problem should include analysis into its simplest elements, its scope and limitations, and precise specifications of the meanings of all words significant to the research. Failure of the researcher to do this adequately may raise legitimate doubts in the minds of readers as to whether the researcher has sufficient understanding of the problem to make a sound attack upon it.

2. *The research procedures used should be described in sufficient detail to permit another researcher to repeat the research.*

Excepting when secrecy is imposed in the national interest, research reports should reveal with candor the sources of data and the means by which they were obtained. Omission of significant procedural details makes it difficult or impossible to estimate the validity and reliability of the data and justifiably weakens the confidence of the reader in the research.

3. *The procedural design of the research should be carefully planned to yield results that are as objective as possible.*

When a sampling of a population is involved, the report should include evidence concerning the degree of representativeness of the sample. A questionnaire ought not to be used when more reliable evidence is available from documentary sources or by direct observation. Bibliographic searches should be as thorough and complete as possible. Experiments should have satisfactory controls. Direct observations should be recorded in writing as soon as possible after the event. Efforts should be made to minimize the influence of personal bias in selecting and recording data.

4. *The researcher should report, with complete frankness, flaws in the procedural design and estimate their effect upon the findings.*

There are very few perfect research designs. Some of the imperfections may have little effect upon the validity and reliability of the data; others may invalidate them entirely. A competent researcher should be sensitive to the effects of imperfect design and his experience in analyzing the data should give him a basis for estimating their influence.

5. *Analysis of the data should be sufficiently adequate to reveal its significance; and the methods of analysis used should be appropriate.*

The extent to which this criterion is met is frequently a good measure of the competence of the researcher. Twenty years of experience in guiding the research of graduate students leads the writer to conclude that adequate analysis of the data is the most difficult phase of research for the novice.

The validity and reliability of data should be checked carefully. The data should be classified in ways that assist the researcher to reach pertinent conclusions. When statistical methods are used, the probability of error should be estimated and the criteria of statistical significance applied.

6. *Conclusions should be confined to those justified by the data of the research and limited to those for which the data provides an adequate basis.*

Researchers are often tempted to broaden the bases of inductions by including personal experiences not subject to the controls under which the research data were gathered. This tends to decrease the objectivity of the research and weaken confidence in the findings.

Equally undesirable is the all-too-frequent practice of drawing conclusions from study of a limited population and applying them universally. Good researchers specify the conditions under which their conclusions seem to be valid. Failure to do so justifiably weakens confidence in the research.

7. *Greater confidence in the research is warranted if the researcher is experienced, has a good reputation in research, and is a person of integrity.*

Were it possible for the reader of a research report to obtain sufficient information about the researcher, this criterion perhaps would be one of the best bases for judging the degree of confidence a piece of research warrants. For this reason, the research report should be accompanied by more information about the qualifications of the researcher than is the usual practice.

Some evidence pertinent to estimates of the competence and integrity of the researcher may be found in the report itself. Language that is restrained, clear, and precise; assertions that are carefully drawn and hedged with appropriate reservations; and an apparent effort to achieve maximum objectivity tend to leave a favorable impression of the researcher. On the other hand, generalizations that outrun the evidence upon which they are based, exaggerations, and unnecessary verbiage tend to leave an unfavorable impression.

Of course, the seven criteria listed above are not the only earmarks of research worthy of confidence. A relatively complete list would be much more extensive. However, it is hoped that the brief list will be of some assistance in helping readers of research reports to assess their worth.

Obviously, such assessments must be largely subjective, since the criteria are couched in relative terms. The writer is unaware of any present means of categorically classifying the worth of research objectively. If, however, the criteria help to make readers more constructively critical of reported findings of research, they will have served their purpose.

Fred N. Kerlinger

Practicality and Educational Research

The task of the classroom teacher is to see that the children in her charge receive an education; the task of the local school administrator is to see that the teacher's task is possible; and the task of the educational researcher is to try to discover the best way for the teacher and administrator to perform their tasks. On the surface these considerations seem to be practical. However, Kerlinger maintains that consideration of practicality has unnecessarily shackled the educational researcher. Practice does not arise in a vacuum; it must either grow out of value judgments or out of theory. As long as educational research is aimed at the practical, value judgements may play a larger part than theory.

Fred Kerlinger, "Practicality in Educational Research," *School Review*, 67:281-91, 1959. Reprinted with permission.

It was Lord Beaconsfield, I think, who defined the practical man as one who practices the errors of his forefathers. Many educators, even in universities, pride themselves on being practical men. Their concern, they say, is with the practical problems of practical teachers in practical schools—teachers who deal with the practical problems of practical children of practical parents. This concern requires that educators be practical men who can help schools and teachers solve their practical problems. What are the implications of this concern, or over-concern, for educational research and for the training of graduate students of education?

Most educational research has sprung from the desire to solve practical educational problems. Do certain children have difficulty with reading? Then study these children. Examine whatever special characteristics they may have, and try various methods of teaching. One of them may help. Do children learn better when they are taught with group-centered methods or with teacher-centered methods? Compare classes taught with the two "methods," and find out.

Problems like these could be multiplied indefinitely. They all emphasize practicality. They all seek to improve the educational situation in some way, usually in a methodological way. The sentiment behind such thinking is commendable. Better education is envisioned, and educational reform is proposed to help achieve what is envisioned.

But ordinarily commendable sentiments of themselves do not solve problems. And problems are not always solved by a direct problem-solving approach. Indeed, many problems in education may not even be the problems they are thought to be. Which method best promotes the reading of first-graders? This problem, for example, is not really a problem of method. It is a basic scientific problem, the solution of which might better be speeded not by concern with phenotypic and superficial aspects of the problem but by concern with fundamental psychological problems. Two such fundamental questions may be: What are the basic factors in the reading act? What is the relation between teachers' perceptions of their role, the methods they use, and children's achievement?

I could go on listing educational questions that need answers badly, but these should be enough to illustrate the point that overconcern with practicality blinds us to the real problems we face. The problem in this example is basically not that of the differential effects of various teaching methods on children's reading. This problem is only a small and relatively unimportant part of a larger problem that must be solved, a larger scientific problem that is both theoretical and practical: the problem of asking the right questions, hypothesizing the right (or the wrong) answers, and studying aspects of the problem scientifically.

It is quite likely that there is no educational theory. We may have here part of the reason why educators have rarely preoccupied themselves with theory in the scientific sense. It is likely that educational theories are really sociological or psychological theories, especially the latter. Curriculum research, for example, is a field of inquiry that seems purely educational. But on reflection, it becomes apparent that much or most of this field is psychological. It is generally agreed that curriculum may be defined as all the experiences used by the school to achieve educational objectives (1). The key word in this definition is *experience*. Unless we are dealing solely with status investigations —whose purpose is simple determination of what exists, of what is being done—curriculum research implies the relation of children's experiences to other variables, such as teaching methods and organization of subject matter. Almost all the variables that could be mentioned are related in some fashion to the learning and growth of children, and learning and growth are largely psychological problems. Measurement of the variables involved is also a psychological problem. So are most of the variables in which educators are interested—intelligence, aptitude, motivation, achievement.

If this reasoning is correct, then educational theory is really a mixture of psychological and sociological theory, with a dash of what might be called philosophic theory. Generally speaking, educators are not trained in sociological and psychological theory. Consequently, even when they want to deal with their problems theoretically, they are in the peculiar situation of not having any educational theory, as such, to deal with. At any rate, theory as theory is ordinarily not studied by graduate students of education, though theory is recognized as part of the preparation of graduate students of psychology, sociology, economics, and political science. The concern of graduate students of education, as I said earlier, is primarily with "practical" problems of education, particularly the practical problems of schools, administrators, and teachers. They study, for example, the administration of American schools, the merits of various experiences in language arts, the improvement of instruction, the relation of school to community, among other subjects, the main emphasis of which is practical.

An important qualification is necessary here. While most of the curriculum of the graduate student of education emphasizes the practical, discussion of the subjects studied is heavily "theoretical" in the common-sense use of the term, though not in its scientific sense. Theory in science usually means a body of theorems, postulates, and concepts that present a systematic view of a subject, especially by specifying relations among the variables of the area covered by the theory. This definition of *theory* is quite unlike the common-sense definition of the term, a definition that seems to mean almost anything but practical. If someone is talking, say, about the relative virtues of two curricula in the elementary school, he could be said to be talking "theoretically," since, under the circumstances, it might be impossible to put one of the curricula into effect. This qualification has another aspect: while most graduate study in education is basically practical and non-theoretical (in the scientific sense), it is heavily laden with values, a fact that is often unrecognized. But let us get back to our problem.

Is the effect of this practical emphasis good or bad? As the major emphasis of the educator in the university, practicality is narrowing, crippling, blinding, and generally bad. Even in the teachers college, concern with practicality alone is bad enough, but when practicality becomes the overriding concern of the university educator, in schools of education or in any other schools of the university, then it is antithetical to the objectives of the university (2). I have in mind over-riding concern with all programs that have practical ends—whether they are extension programs, adult-education programs, or programs in school-community relations, human relations, or intergroup rela-tions. I am not saying that these programs of themselves are bad; I am saying that overriding concern with them is bad, that lack of concern with theory in the scientific sense is bad. Why?

No matter what we do, what we say, what we teach, theory is im-plied. A colleague may say to me, "The core curriculum is better than the traditional curriculum." He is making a value judgment on the basis, usually, of very little, and perhaps highly suspect, evidence—from the scientific point of view. Of course he has a right to his opin-ion. And he may have evidence for his statement in his own experi-ence, or he may have other evidence that is "good." But he should real-ize, especially if he is an educational leader, that he is making a value judgment and not stating a fact. He is implying a theory, a theory that could be tested for its validity. To make very clear what is meant, let's elaborate on the core curriculum.

Suppose I say to my colleague, "Why do you think that core is bet-ter?" "It helps children learn better," he tells me. "Why?" I ask him. "It's an integrated experience and integrated experiences help chil-dren learn better." "What do you mean by 'learn better' and 'inte-grated experience'?" I go on in this fashion—as long as he lets me—until I can get some elements of a theoretical structure. My colleague may say to me, "I'm not, and cannot be, concerned with all the theo-retical implications of the core program. I'm a practical educator who has to get the job done." True, but only partly true.

He is a university man, and, by definition, a university man is dedi-cated to the pursuit and transmission of knowledge. And the pursuit of knowledge has generally been defined—at least in psychology, so-ciology, and education—as the scientific pursuit of knowledge. Thus, he should perforce be concerned with the theoretical, since without theory little scientific investigation is possible. Yet if I have persuaded my colleague to recognize that the problem of the core program is basically a theoretical problem and not a practical problem, we have gone a long way. We can then plan a research program to get answers to our question, answers that will be more than opinion.

One of the most insidious effects of a basically practical emphasis in education is to convert education into a religion with a more or less elaborate dogma. Unfortunately, religions are not always recognized as religions and thus escape the safeguards and scrutiny built around religions to protect religious as well as other freedoms. No one would think of saying—out loud at least and especially to graduate students:

"Catholicism is better than Protestantism" or "Christianity makes better citizens of children than other religions do." But many educators do not hesitate to say: "The core curriculum is better than the traditional curriculum." "Group-centered teaching methods are better than teacher-centered methods." "Children learn better in a friendly atmosphere." "Children grow as wholes." Again, what does all this have to do with science and education?

Aside from the conversion of education into religious dogma, the practical view of educational research, I believe, has six or seven interdependent deleterious consequences, all of which center on the first consequence. This first consequence has already been discussed: concern with practicality of research unduly constricts research objectives and, in so doing, conceals the real scientific problems that lie beneath the surface of the superficial practical problems. As a further example, we may cite studies designed to test the effectiveness of various audio-visual methods, when the scientific problem is actually one of basic motivation and learning processes. Audio-visual methods may serve only to supply variety in teaching, and variety usually leads to enhancement of motivation. Overconcern with methods, then, would tend to shut off research on the more basic and important problems of motivation in education.

The second consequence is very close to the first. Concern with practicality and with practical results in educational research—and indeed, in industrial and military research—acts as a very strong social pressure on the staffs of university schools of education and public school systems. Practicality becomes a social norm, a rule of proper educational research behavior, that tends to force the scientist away from the really significant scientific problems of education. It is difficult for any individual to buck a strong tide of this kind, and the scientist is no exception. He may buck the tide, but in doing so he may lose the approval and support of his institution and his colleagues. Science is, at least in part, a social process. Scientists need to work and talk with their colleagues. In how many schools of education can a scientist discuss, say, the relationship between reinforcement schedules and school achievement? General ignorance of science and the scientific mode of thinking operate to strengthen the social norm for practicality. One must get results that "count." Curiosity, the playing with data and relationships, the pursuit of interesting if elusive and "impractical" problems—all these become expensive luxuries that cannot be afforded.

The third consequence is that educational research seems to have a generally unscientific bias. The essence of science is, of course, prediction and control (not in the narrow sense, however), but science is also concerned with understanding—understanding of the complex relationships among variables, understanding of universal laws. Science is a constant preoccupation with, and curiosity about, underlying causes, even though the scientist may eschew the use of the word *cause*. The practical criterion, however, demands short-term results to improve school practices, even though commitments may be made to long-term research projects. Such a criterion leads away from rather than toward science and new discoveries.

Again, take research in reading. Practicality has evidently operated powerfully in this field. As a consequence, few if any fundamental problems have been solved. Most research, while important in the sense that any reliable knowledge is important, is superficial and peripheral. Factor analysis, one of the powerful tools in the psychological and scientific armamentarium, has been used only rarely. Thus, the basic factors behind reading accomplishment, as far as scientific empirical evidence is concerned, still remain obscure.

A fourth consequence of the concern with practicality is indirect. Many practical investigations, even though they may not lead us very far scientifically, give the educational worker a spurious sense of adequacy. The idea is often expressed: "We have enough research. Let's do something about implementing it." Many teachers feel that a great deal of research has been carried on and that much is known about education. We should be less preoccupied with research and more preoccupied with putting the findings of research into practical effect, they insist. The argument has truth, of course, as many arguments do; but it is spurious. It assumes that scientific research has endpoints where one can stop, if only temporarily. However, let's put aside this line of thought and concentrate on our main point. Practical research can make enormous efforts without getting very far, since many basic discoveries are made only accidentally (3). Again, research can create a spurious feeling of adequacy. A great deal is done, and it seems to be enough, even though scientifically little has been accomplished.

The spurious feeling of adequacy that arises when a great deal of practical research is under way leads us to another consequence: the channeling of many talented workers into practical efforts like action research. Advocates of action research believe, and perhaps rightly, that much research evidence gathers dust on shelves in universities and schools. What is needed is research that has greater assurance of being implemented by practitioners in the field. The rise and popularity of action research owes much to the emphasis on the practical, but, like all other short-term practical objectives, this one can and does lead to a negation of science in education. Fundamental research is impeded to the extent that workers in educational research concentrate on action research. It is not that action research, as such, is necessarily poor research; it is simply that action research can distract and delude research workers and practitioners. It can be scientific, naturally. But the chances of its being so are slim when it is aimed almost exclusively at practical results and their implementation (4).

A sixth consequence of practicality is that funds from sources outside the university are devoted largely to practical research projects. One large, powerful foundation that channels substantial sums into education and educational research gives preference to projects that seem to lead to fewer teachers for more students—in sum, to the efficient handling of large classes by fewer teachers. Money, of course, is at the root of this emphasis. Many see educational television as a way of helping to solve the problem, in higher education, of too few professors for too many students. Research projects that show promise of finding evidence that educational television is as good as or better than the traditional classroom stand a good chance of getting funds. On the other hand, I suspect that it might be difficult to obtain funds for a proposal for a basic study of the more general consequences of educational television. Most, perhaps all, educational television research projects that have been publicized in the last two or three years have had the narrow aim of showing that the educational results of teaching by television are satisfactory. The possibility that educational television might have a deleterious effect on students and their learning or on academic freedom is hardly considered. For example, is it possible that the widespread use of educational television could lead to a pervasive restriction of academic freedom with a consequent insidious effect on the learning of college students, not to mention the possibly devastating consequences on the attitudes and learning of students in public schools? Questions like these are ignored. But my point is still the same: when practicality rules, funds and efforts are aimed at practical research and not at fundamental scientific research (5).

Last but certainly not least in the list of consequences of practicality is the general lack of competence and confidence on the part of graduate students of education to handle important theoretical issues and complex research designs and projects. I am not insisting that practicality is the cause, but it is one of the causes. Practicality is often used by students of education as a rationalization for not being bothered with theory and with the comparatively difficult and often abstruse technical matters with which graduate students in psychology, say, have to cope. Too often, one hears the plaint, "What does all this theory, measurement, and statistics have to do with me and my work? All I want is to learn how to be a better administrator (teacher, counselor). My needs are practical. Theory is meaningless to me." Needless to say, such students have a distorted notion of theory and science, and, worse, they get little or no opportunity to learn theoretical and scientific thinking, since the prevailing social and educational norms are the practical ones under discussion. With such an attitude it is difficult for the student to become competent in scientific research and in the disciplines necessary to scientific research. While practicality and scientific objectives may not be exactly incompatible, they certainly seem not to have been congenial colleagues.

I have been negative. But I would like to end on a positive note. It is evident, to me at least, that research in education is changing and changing for the better. Quite slowly but nonetheless plainly, the emphasis is shifting in some institutions from exclusive concern with practical ends to more preoccupation with fundamental approaches to educational problems. To raise the level of graduate education, more students of education are being required to study research design—and not just research methods—measurement, statistics, and even mathematics (6). Research studies of considerable theoretical importance are being published (7). The studies are also showing increasing sophistication in statistics and measurement. They are still strongly dominated by practicality, but there are signs of cracks in the structure. In fifteen years, we shall probably not recognize educational research. It will be preoccupied with problems of scientific significance as well as problems of practical importance. The disciplines and tools necessary for the scientific testing of theory will be accepted as part of the learning experience and equipment of all or nearly all graduate students of education.

Notes

1. William H. Bristow and O. I. Frederick, "Curriculum Development," in Walter S. Monroe (ed.), *Encyclopedia of Educational Research* (New York: The Macmillan Co., 1950), pp. 307-14.
2. For a discussion of the objectives of the university closely related to this argument, see Fred N. Kerlinger, "The Functions of the University Professor of Education," *School and Society*, LXXXV (February 2, 1957), 35-37.

3. I am not saying that practical research never has value. On the contrary, significant scientific hypotheses and discoveries are sometimes turned up in the course of research oriented toward the solution of practical problems. I am saying that major concern with practical ends impedes the advance of scientific discoveries and growth in education. Another important point is the effect of sole concern with consequences. To be concerned with consequences, as such, is not bad, naturally. But not to be concerned with theory that relates consequences to antecedent variables in a systematic manner is undesirable.

4. On several occasions, students have told me, when I have suggested that they study statistics and measurement to prepare their theses competently, that they were more interested in practical results and planned to do action research, where such knowledge and skills are not so necessary. My response has usually been that proper field research of any kind generally requires as much or perhaps even more knowledge and skill than laboratory research.

5. The channeling of funds only into practical projects is not inevitable. Witness the fact that large sums are being granted for basic research in psychology. See, for example, issues of the *American Psychologist* for 1957 and 1958. My point is that educators think that channeling of funds for practical research is good. Thus educators reinforce the tendency of foundations to allocate funds for practical projects.

6. The preoccupation of graduate schools of education with research "methods" is another example of the powerful and narrowing influence of practicality. Do you want to do research on something? The first step is to find a "method," the "right method." The emphasis is not on the problem but on the method. And, by implication, the emphasis is on practical results, since methods are means to ends and thus means for getting practical results. The conception of methods as tools dictated by, and subservient to, research problems is de-emphasized and even ignored.

7. A good example is the recent volume of the Harvard school-executive studies: Neal Gross, Ward S. Mason, and Alexander McEachern, *Explorations in Role Analysis* (New York: John Wiley & Sons, Inc., 1958). One other example: David G. Ryans, "The Investigations of Teacher Characteristics," *Educational Record*, XXXIV (1953), 370-96.

D. B. Van Dalen

The Relationship of Fact
and Theory in Research

The author argues that facts and theories are intimately related; that one does not really make a contribution without the other. It is, therefore, the responsibility of the educational researcher to relate his findings (facts) to already existing theories or to use these findings to develop new theories.

D. B. Van Dalen, "Relationship of Fact and Theory in Research," *Educational Administration and Supervision*, 45:271-4, 1959. Reprinted with permission.

The average man thinks the scientist deals with facts and the philosopher is concerned with theorizing. To the layman, facts and theories are diametrical opposites. He thinks facts are definite, real, concrete and their meaning is self-evident. Theories, in his opinion, are mere speculations that cannot become facts until sufficient proof is found to support them.

The scientist knows that isolated, random facts can contribute little to the advancement of knowledge. Consequently, he does not rely solely on induction—observing facts, but also engages in deduction—theorizing about facts. Realizing that facts do not speak for themselves, he tries to see relationships between facts or some way of ordering them in a meaningful way. The scientist holds that theories and facts are reciprocally interdependent. That is, theories are not mere speculations, for they are built upon facts; and when facts are gathered, ordered, and seen in relationship, they constitute a theory. Theories provide natural and logical explanations for facts.

Because theorizing plays a much greater rôle in research than most people realize, the following paragraphs will explore some of the ways it contributes to the advancement of knowledge.

THEORY DEFINES THE RELEVANCY OF FACTS

To do research, men must determine what kind of phenomena they should study. Scientists cannot collect facts about everything. They must narrow the area of their interest. For example, investigators may study the game of baseball in the sociological framework of play, or in the physical framework of stress and velocity, or in the economic framework of supply and demand. By constructing a specific theoretical framework for their investigations, scientists determine what kind of facts are relevant to each study. Facts do not identify themselves as relevant, only a theory can do that.

THEORY DEVELOPS SYSTEMS OF CLASSIFICATION AND A STRUCTURE OF CONCEPTS

Every science develops a structural foundation to facilitate research. Scientists in each field construct theoretical frameworks for classifying their facts. Geologists develop systems for classifying rocks, and botanists develop systems for classifying plant life. Research workers in each field also develop certain terms or concepts which serve as short hand symbols that represent major processes or objects in a given subject matter. These concepts make it easier for scientists to communicate their findings. These specialized scientific vocabularies often are unintelligible to the layman, but the concepts or short hand symbols convey considerable compact information to the scientist. If a scientist did not develop theoretical structures, he would be seriously handicapped in his work and unable to advance knowledge.

THEORY SUMMARIZES FACTS

Theorization is used to summarize the fundamental knowledge within a given field. These summaries range from relatively simple generalizations to exceedingly complex theoretical relationships. A summarization may merely describe the observations man makes of a given phenomena. For example, in a study concerning the practice of granting varsity letters, an investigator may summarize his observations in a set of descriptions. On a somewhat higher level of summarization, an investigator may construct generalizations about the relationships between phenomena. For example, he may summarize the relationship between varsity letters, honor rolls, certificates of achievement, and honor societies by generalizing that these phenomena are means of motivating pupils or means of giving recognition for high attainment. Theorizing on a still higher level may lead to an attempt to integrate some of the major empirical generalizations made by scientists into a more comprehensive theoretical framework. Einstein endeavored to do this in his theory of relativity.

THEORY PREDICTS FACTS

A generalization about data made by the theorizing process enables the investigator to predict the existence of unobserved instances conforming to the generalization. For instance, educational psychologists have made the following generalizations: When children learn a baseball-throwing skill much improvement occurs during the initial learning stages. Thus, educational psychologists can predict that a child learning any similar skill will experience an initial achievement spurt. Correspondingly, they can predict that where children have practiced these skills, the pattern of improvement made will conform to the theory. Theory, therefore, can predict where no data is presently available. Theory directs the attention of research workers to particular phenomena. It tells him what facts he should be able to observe. Thus, theory is a powerful beacon that scientists can use to extend knowledge.

THEORY POINTS OUT NEED FOR FURTHER RESEARCH

Since theories generalize about known facts and predict facts, they also indicate areas where knowledge is deficient. Theories, particularly in the social sciences, may lack supporting evidence in one or more aspects. Such theories need further supporting evidence to provide the maturity and vitality essential for their proper functioning. Because theories suggest where evidence is lacking, they are an excellent source to turn to when in search of research problems.

In pushing back the frontiers of knowledge, scientists are very dependent upon the process of theorization, but they cannot construct or confirm any theory without the aid of facts. Theories and facts interact constantly. One depends upon the other. They are inextricably interwoven.

FACTS STIMULATE THEORIZATION

The history of science is replete with instances of simple observations of facts that have led to well-known advances in human knowledge. For instance, when Archimedes observed water overflowing while he was taking a bath, he grasped the principle of displacement. When Newton saw an apple fall, he developed the principle of gravitation. When Watt watched steam escape from a teakettle, he visualized the principle of steam power. Thus facts can stimulate the theorizing process. Of course, everyone is not capable of leaping from a fact to a theory; many men made the same observations as Newton, Watt and Archimedes without being intellectually stimulated. Facts can only initiate theorization when an alert, disciplined, and imaginative mind observes them and mentally constructs a possible explanation for them.

FACTS TEST THEORIES

Facts determine whether a theory can be confirmed or should be rejected or reformulated. After constructing a theory about some aspects of learning, an educator may find many facts that conform to his theory. These facts tend to strengthen the theory. However, the educator may find facts that do not confirm the story. These facts indicate a need for either rejecting the theory or reformulating it to fit the new facts. It is upon facts that theories eventually must adjust.

FACTS CLARIFY THEORIES

Theories are refined and clarified as knowledge accumulates. For example, theories in the new social sciences are apt to be elusive and ill-defined. But further observation and experimentation may reveal facts that not only agree with the theory, but also state in detail and with precision what the theory states in a general way. Thus, facts help in clarifying and redefining theory.

In summary, there is a constant and intricate relationship between fact and theory. Facts without theory or theory without facts lack significance. Facts take their significance from the theories which define, classify, summarize, and predict them. Theories possess significance when they are built upon, clarified, and tested by facts. Thus, the growth of science is dependent upon the accumulation of pertinent facts and the formulation of new or broader theories.

Fred N. Kerlinger

The Mythology of
Educational Research:
The Methods Approach

This article was chosen to end the chapter on theoretic considerations, because it appeared to pull together many of the things that the previous articles on the role of research had been trying to say. Research that does not grow out of theory or that does not lead to new theory is barren. Education has been guiltier of ignoring theory than almost any other field, and the result is a bewildering array of data (frequently contradictory) that usually leads nowhere. Further, this article seems to be a fitting one upon which to end this book of readings, because it states clearly what the editors believe to be the major problem in educational research today.

Fred N. Kerlinger, "The Mythology of Educational Research: The Methods Approach," *School and Society*, 88:149-51, 1960. Reprinted with permission.

The mythology of educational research is a body of legends and beliefs purporting to be the rationale, purpose, and methods of educational research. It has an essentially mystical character which seems to be rooted in the past. To question the mythology amounts to heresy.

The foundations of the mythology are: a general ignorance among educators of science and scientific research; an overwhelming preoccupation with practicality; and a negative and sometimes anti-intellectual attitude toward science and research. Educational research often has been criticized for its triviality, superficiality, and scientific naivete. It has been said that these deficiencies are due to education being a young discipline, to the lack of imagination of educational researchers, to lack of theoretical development, and to general lack

441

of sufficient attention to the canons of science.[1] These points have truth. But more important, perhaps, are the mythology and the knowledge, training, attitudes, and values of people doing, supporting (or not supporting), and consuming educational research—the educators themselves.

The mythology of educational research includes a number of interesting individual myths: methods, statistics, measurement, practicality,[2] "educational research is special and different," action research, etc. The concern of the present essay is the methods myth, one of the more influential of the myths in distorting the research thinking of educators and students of education.

The methods myth seems to be very prevalent in the research thinking of American educators. The teaching of educational research in university schools of education, for example, seems to concentrate largely on "methods of research." Indeed, what is perhaps the most-used text in educational research courses is entitled "Methods of Research."[3] The methods approach is rather narrowly pragmatic. If you want to investigate an educational problem, you must do some research on it. In order to do the research, you need a method. So find a method, the "right" method. Concomitantly, the way to train students in research is to teach them "methods of research."

An example may help to clarify the point being made. Perhaps the most naive form the methods approach takes is the idea that if you want information on an educational subject, then use the "survey" and/or mail questionnaire. It is difficult to tell which of these is the more hackneyed and misused. Both are usually done poorly. This is *not* to say that the school survey has no useful function. It is an important part of the educational enterprise. But to confuse a school survey—which is basically clerical work of a higher order—with a scientific study of the relations among certain variables is another matter. For example, we might do a survey to determine the success of a new system of school consolidation. This is perfectly legitimate and necessary. But to call such an investigation research, much less scientific research, is misleading. Such a study can be scientific. Needless to say, however, the great difficulties in the way of scientifically

---

[1] *Cf.*, B. O. Smith, in W. S. Monroe, editor, "Encyclopedia of Educational Research" (New York: The Macmillan Co., 1950), pp. 1145-1152.

[2] The practicality myth has been discussed elsewhere. See the writer's article, "Practicality and Educational Research," *School Review*, 67:281-291, Autumn, 1959. Other myths will be discussed in future articles.

[3] C. V. Good and D. E. Scates, *Methods of Research* (New York: Appleton-Century-Crofts, 1954).

studying anything as complex as a drastic change in educational administrative practice and its effects on educational outcomes are hardly appreciated.

A basic aspect of the methods approach is the general idea that gathering data constitutes research. This is closely related to the notion that science is fundamentally concerned with gathering, classifying, and storing facts. It is a confusion of the taxonomic function of science with science itself. In addition, it is a static view of science and research which emphasizes fact-gathering and which reinforces the methods approach, since it leads to a search for the best "methods" for gathering facts.

Part of the scientific research activity unquestionably consists of gathering and classifying facts. But a more advanced and fruitful notion of research is a dynamic one which conceives it as an ongoing scientific activity in which hypothetical and theoretical propositions are tested systematically, not necessarily and primarily to yield knowledge (although this is, of course, important), but to help refine and formulate theories and to yield further hypotheses for further testing. Few educators seem to have this conception of research. The notion which seems to be held is that the purpose of research is to increase knowledge so that education, particularly school practices, can be somehow improved. This is not necessarily a wrong notion; it is, rather, an incomplete and too narrow one. What it succeeds in doing is to choke off higher-level, theoretically oriented investigations in education.[4] It also distracts attention from the most important part of scientific activity—theory-building and testing—and focuses attention on a less important part of science—so-called methods of research. Thus, education becomes saddled with a methods orientation, and the attention of students of education tends to be distracted from research problems and the theories behind them.

The argument on the other side of the question seems to be that education is not ready for theories, that many more facts are needed, and that the facts gathered must be pertinent to the solution of practical educational problems. But no area of investigation is ever "ready"

---

[4] An interesting example of this tendency is the explanatory material for research proposals put out by the U.S. Office of Education, Department of Health, Education, and Welfare, in connection with Public Law 531 on cooperative research projects. Under the heading, "Criteria for the Evaluation of Proposals for Research Under P. L. 531," 13 criteria are given, not one of which says anything directly about basic research or theory in educational research. The first of these is significant: "1. The proposed research, survey, or demonstration is concerned with the development of new knowledge directly applicable to the educational process or with new applications of existing knowledge to the problems in education."

for theory; facts by themselves are meaningless; and facts gathered only for practical ends tend to throttle scientific activity. Cohen put it nicely:

> . . . There is, however, no genuine progress in scientific insight through . . . accumulating empirical facts without hypotheses or anticipation of nature. Without some guiding idea we do not know what facts to gather. Without something to prove, we cannot determine what is relevant and what is irrelevant.[5]

Education needs both data and fact-gathering *and* the systematic testing of theoretical and hypothetical propositions in a rigorous fashion. But an emphasis on methods leads persuasively to a stereotype of educational research as mere data-gathering, since methods are devised to gather data. This mode of thinking makes it difficult, if not impossible, for the educational scientist to work in a theoretical framework.[6] The scientific purposes of theory, prediction, and control are lost with such a viewpoint, and it is probably just these features of science which are the most fruitful stimulants of scientific curiosity and scientific research.

What implications does the methods myth have for educational research? Because of space limitations, only two of these will be discussed. Perhaps most obvious is the effect on graduate curricula. Evidently few schools of education require systematic and thorough study of research design, statistics and statistical inference, and measurement. Courses offered in these fields tend to be practical and "consumer-oriented." They are designed supposedly to help students understand ("consume") rather than to do. When a course in research is offered, it tends to stress the various so-called methods "appropriate to educational research"—the normative-survey, the causal comparative method, the case study, the correlation method, and so on.[7] Little or no stress is put on design of research springing from the adequate

---

[5] M. R. Cohen, "A Preface to Logic" (New York: Meridian Books, 1956), p. 148.

[6] It is interesting and distressing to note that the large foundations interested in educational problems are channeling huge sums of money into research with rather narrowly conceived practical ends. Unfortunately, little of this support seems to go to theoretically oriented investigations. Apparently one must show that the results of one's research will help make a better educational world, especially according to the foundation's definition of a better educational world.

[7] Good and Scates, *op. cit.* Significantly, the earlier edition of this work carried a whole chapter called "The Classification of Research Methods" in which attempts to categorize educational research were summarized. This chapter is one of the best pieces of evidence of the tendency I am discussing—the tendency to think directly and basically in methods terms. See C. V. Good, A. S. Barr, and D. E. Scates. "The Methodology of Educational Research" (New York: Appleton-Century-Crofts, 1936), Chap. V.

statement of a problem or problems, statistical inference and probabilistic thinking are de-emphasized, and the many recent, significant developments in social scientific and other branches of research—multivariate analysis, such as the analysis of variance and factor analysis, the mathematics of sets, matrices, and probability, and the several important developments in measurement—either are ignored or dismissed in a few words.

Judging from the products of doctoral students of education and the understanding of educators of science and scientific research, courses in educational research have been failures. They neither have trained students to do research and to use statistics and measurements, nor have they given students much understanding of these matters. It is not claimed that the methods approach is the cause of the much-bemoaned incompetence of doctoral students of education in handling thesis problems. It is, rather, a symptom of the deeper disease of educational thinking, outlined earlier as the foundations of the mythology, which can be epitomized in three words: ignorance, practicality, anti-intellectualism.

The immediate point is that doctorates are conferred upon methods-oriented doctoral students, some of whom will be the future educational leaders who have to train the next generation of students. The argument often is used that schools of education are and should be basically concerned with turning out practitioners and not "theoreticians" and researchers. But whether this should be so, while pertinent, is not the real issue. The hard fact is that the professors of the next generation are selected from the doctoral students of this generation. If the training now is no better, or even worse, than it was in the past, then we can expect nothing more than a perpetuation of the mythology with, perhaps, a few more, newer, and possibly more defensive rationalizations than have been used in the past. Along with this is the equally devastating thought that the present attitudes of doctoral students tend to become the future attitudes of educators in general. Thus, the relatively narrow methods-centered and even covert anti-intellectual attitudes of present doctoral students—due to their training, the social milieu in which they train, and the mythology—become the attitudes of most educators.

A second implication or consequence of the methods approach in educational research thinking is the cultural lag attendant upon such a conception of research. Educational research is perhaps 10-20 years behind other related fields of research. Psychological research, for instance, has well incorporated into itself the multivariate thinking of Fisher, Thurstone, and others. More important, a large proportion of psychological research is science-oriented and not methods-oriented.

The same is more or less true of sociology and sociological research. But not so in education. The school of education which insists that its doctoral students learn to understand science and to use modern scientific analytic tools seems to be rare. The emphasis, instead, is on the vague vagaries of methods which, in the last analysis, help the educational doctoral student—or, for that matter, any investigator in education—very little. On the contrary, they seem to be successful only in confusing the student. They confuse him, as hinted earlier, because they lead him to believe that research problems can be solved mainly with their aid. And, generally speaking, this is not so. The graduate student of education needs to learn, among other things, the nature of science and how the scientist thinks and works, modern multivariate approaches *and their rationale*, and modern modes of analysis of data. There are other indispensable ingredients, naturally. For instance, the student also needs to understand modern measurement conceptions, such as the recent advances in thinking on the validity problem.[8] But a good start could be made by simply dropping out of the curriculum of the graduate education school the whole methods approach as it has been preached for decades and by substituting rigorous courses in research design and scientific thinking.

Lest too negative an impression be left with the reader, it should be noted that there are visible chinks in the educational research armor. Occasional excellent studies always have been published—but they have been too occasional. In the last four years or five years, however, there has been an increasing upsurge of significant and well-designed and executed studies.[9] It probably is still true that many or most doctoral theses continue to be poor. But if the present trend toward broader theoretical and methodological thinking continues, educational research will be revolutionized. And it is the business of schools of education to hasten and not to hinder this revolution. Above all, it is the business of schools of education not to create and perpetuate mythologies, but to destroy them.

---

[8] *E.g.*, see E. E. Cureton, in E. F. Lindquist, editor, "Educational Measurement" (Washington, D.C.: American Council on Education, 1951), pp. 621-694.

[9] Four good examples of this upsurge are: N. Gross, W. S. Mason, and A. W. McEachern, "Explorations in Role Analysis: Studies of the School Superintendency Role" (New York: John Wiley & Sons, Inc., 1958); E. B. Page, "Teacher Comments and Student Performance: A Seventy-Four Classroom Experiment in School Motivation," *Journal of Educational Psychology*, 49: 173-181, Aug., 1958; D. G. Ryans, "The Investigation of Teacher Characteristics," *Educational Record*, 34: 370-396, Oct., 1953 (general report on a series of studies); I. Sarnoff, *et. al.*, "A Cross Cultural Study of Anxiety Among American and English School Children," *Journal of Educational Psychology*, 49:129-136, June, 1958.

Author Index

Subject Index